Acknowledge No Frontier

Acknowledge No Frontier

The Creation and Demise
of New Zealand's Provinces,
1853–76

André Brett

OTAGO

Published by Otago University Press
Level 1, 398 Cumberland Street
Dunedin, New Zealand
university.press@otago.ac.nz
www.otago.ac.nz/press

First published 2016
Copyright © 2016 André Brett

The moral rights of the author have been asserted.

Published with the assistance of Creative New Zealand

ISBN 978-1-927322-36-9

Editor: Anna Rogers
Design and layout: Fiona Moffat
Index: Robin Briggs
Maps: Allan J. Kynaston

Cover: Nelson in 1842. John Waring Saxton, PUBL-0011-06-2, Alexander Turnbull Library, Wellington

Printed in New Zealand by Printing.com Ltd, Wellington

Contents

The lust of a pioneer
Will acknowledge no frontier
'Six Months in a Leaky Boat', Split Enz

Dedicated to my grandmothers, Eunice Frater and Patricia Brett,
for teaching me the value and the joy of history.
I admire you more than you will ever know.

Acknowledgements

Ishare a birthday with the provincial system, 17 January, so it is perhaps fitting I have found myself studying its history. Fortunately I have managed to survive for a few years longer than the system, which perished less than four months shy of completing its 24th lap around the sun. I am a Kapiti Coast lad but my interest in New Zealand history was not piqued until I had lived about half my life in Australia, when I wrote an essay on women's suffrage in one of Robert Horvath's exceptional undergraduate courses at the University of Melbourne. I suspect nobody is more surprised by this than Robert himself.

The University of Melbourne conferred my PhD in 2014 and this book evolved from my thesis. I owe a substantial debt to my supervisors, Stuart Macintyre and Patricia Grimshaw, of whom I cannot speak highly enough. It has been both an honour and a pleasure to work with them, and their advice, insights and meticulous proofreading have been of extraordinary value – especially their continued interest well after the cessation of their supervisory obligations. I am also grateful for feedback, advice and discussions with Tom Brooking, Jo Bunce, Richard Hill, John Hirst, Andrew May, Erik Olssen, Len Richardson and Angela Woollacott.

The School of Historical and Philosophical Studies at the University of Melbourne has been very good to me. I would like to record my appreciation for travel grants – from the Faculty of Arts as well as the School – that made my research possible. I have relished my time as part of the School's vibrant community of postgraduates. I cannot possibly thank everybody individually, and apologise sincerely to those omitted, but in particular I have enjoyed the company and taken advantage of the time of Alex Burston-Chorowicz, Alexandra Dellios, Gretel Evans, Angus Ferguson, Emily Fitzgerald, Timothy Gassin, Bronwyn Lowe, Jessica Melvin, Pete Minard, Susan Reidy, Tyson Retz, Thomas Rogers, Shane Smits, Gonzalo Villanueva, Chloe Ward, Natasha Wilson and Keir Wotherspoon.

I am delighted with the support of Otago University Press. It is fitting for a book on provincialism to be associated with this venerable institution of Otago Province.

Publisher Rachel Scott has always been forthcoming and encouraging, and my editor Anna Rogers led me expertly through a process both fruitful and illuminating. The manuscript is all the better for her keen eye and insights. For assisting me with my research, I would like to extend my appreciation to the staff of the National Library of New Zealand and the Alexander Turnbull Library, Archives New Zealand, the State Library of Victoria, the Auckland City Library, and the libraries of the Universities of Melbourne, Auckland, Canterbury, Otago and Victoria University of Wellington. Thanks also go to Teresa Durham, administrator of VUW's School of History, for facilitating access to a number of MA theses at very short notice. I am grateful for permission to reproduce images from the collections of the Alexander Turnbull Library, Auckland Art Gallery, Auckland Libraries, Hocken Library, Hokitika Museum, National Portrait Gallery in London, Nelson Provincial Museum, Public Record Office Victoria, Puke Ariki and the Wairarapa Archive.

I have, of course, a number of personal debts of gratitude. I am considerably indebted to my family for their support. In particular I must thank my mother Sharon Brett, who throughout my life has had more confidence in my abilities than I have possessed. Her constant encouragement of me to follow my passion means she is probably the first person to blame for my pursuit of New Zealand history. My father, Douglas Brett, has never let me get away with saying something I cannot justify, thereby fostering the qualities essential for good scholarship. My friends have provided unfailing encouragement and diversions, especially Alison Dorman, U-Wen Low and Holly Williams. Alison was an excellent proofreader. I would also like to extend my gratitude to Charlotte Whild, who came with me for most of this journey and learnt far more than she ever cared to know about the provinces.

In his preface to *The Provincial System in New Zealand*, W.P. Morrell hoped that he would be acquitted of provincial bias in his analysis of provincialism. Although I retain my childhood affection for any sporting team that cares to represent the Wellington region, I too wish to express this hope. My family has been in New Zealand since the early 1840s. In that time we have lived in most, if not all, of the former provinces and I am descended from fine Central Otago and Wairarapa stock. I spent more time writing this book in the former Auckland Province than anywhere else in New Zealand, and I am appreciative to Fran Lawrence and Malcolm Whild for all the times they hosted me in Torbay, Waipu and Pakowai.

Finally, I must acknowledge my favourite musicians. I am incapable of writing without putting on headphones and all of my friends and colleagues know my usual excuse for missing a social engagement: 'Sorry, I'm going to a gig.' Much of my writing is planned or revised mentally in the breaks between bands at concerts. It may be abnormal to devote space to thanking bands, but in my case it is essential; nothing I do is divorced from my passion for music. It would be impossible to list every band or album that has been important to me while researching the provinces. My interest in New Zealand's culture has been fostered by the unparalleled output of Flying Nun Records, particularly The Chills and The Bats, and by Neil Finn's projects (especially Crowded House). Melbourne's live music scene has sustained me for years; in particular, it feels as if I spent half my doctoral candidature enjoying concerts by my friends in Alpine. Internationally, Alcest have changed the way I think about music, nostalgia, and the past. Every time I need inspiration or to be reminded why history matters, their discography is at hand. So too are masterful, compelling, or just plain catchy songs by bands as diverse as Agalloch, Anathema (especially their unparalleled 1998–2001 output), Caspian, God Is an Astronaut, Ladytron, Pinback, Porcupine Tree, Pure Reason Revolution, Russian Circles, The Shadows, eighties U2, The Verve and my shoegaze heroes Medicine and Ride.

This book may be an argument for the importance and interest of New Zealand's provinces, but let these prefatory remarks be an argument for the ineffable pleasures of music. Support your live music scene. In the words of the Massachusetts band The Hotelier, 'Enjoy the simple things in life because you can, like your family, friends, community and local bands.'*

---

* This lyric is from 'Our Lives Would Make a Sad, Boring Movie' on The Hotelier's 2011 album *It Never Goes Out*. After I shared a draft of this paragraph with the band, they performed the song for me at their 6 December 2015 concert at the Reverence Hotel, Footscray, a gesture for which I wish to record my sincerest gratitude.

Above: The original six provinces of 1853. Taranaki was called New Plymouth until 1858. Stewart Island was not included in any province at this stage.

Opposite: The provincial system expanded to comprise 10 provinces, although only nine existed at any one time. Hawke's Bay was created in 1858, Marlborough in 1859, Southland in 1861 (and

Auckland ●

AUCKLAND

New Plymouth ●
TARANAKI

● Napier

**HAWKE'S BAY
(1858)**

WELLINGTON

Nelson ●   ● Wellington
Blenheim (provincial capital 1865–76) ●
                            ● Picton (provincial capital 1861–65)

NELSON   **MARLBOROUGH (1859)**

Hokitika ●

WESTLAND (1868)   **CANTERBURY**

                    ● Christchurch

Rangitata River
Timaru & Gladstone Board of Works (1867)

NORTH

OTAGO

● Dunedin

0   100   200
KM

● Invercargill
**SOUTHLAND
(1861–70)**

Stewart Island (part of Southland, 1863–70; Otago, 1870–76)

reunited with Otago in 1870), and Westland was first proclaimed an autonomous county in 1868 and then a province in 1873. Picton was the original capital of Marlborough but Blenheim was de facto capital in 1860–61 and secured the status officially from 1865. Stewart Island was incorporated into the provincial system from 1863. The Timaru and Gladstone Board of Works was created in 1867 to devolve some measure of power to South Canterbury.

Author's Note

Although the use of the term 'Pākehā' for people of British or European descent during the colonial period is perhaps anachronistic, since few would have used it at the time, it allows an ease of distinction not possible with the contemporary 'British' (I use this to refer to people in Britain) or the simplistic 'white'.

Also anachronistic is my distinction between movements for separation (advocacy that part of New Zealand separate from the rest of the colony and form a new colony within the British Empire) and secession (the desire to establish part of an existing province as a new province within the existing political structure of New Zealand). Both movements were generally referred to as separation in the provincial era, but using the two terms provides a greater and beneficial degree of analytical clarity.

The terms provincialism and localism describe related but distinct phenomena. Provincialism refers to the system of provinces and a belief in its importance, significance and viability. Localism refers to the loyalty of individuals to their particular locality. In the early days of the provinces, these two were often closely related, even coterminous. By 1875 this was no longer the case; each province was subdivided by localism in multiple towns, villages and rural districts.

Introduction

New Zealand in the early twenty-first century can be rugged and windswept, but it is also vibrant and cosmopolitan, with firmly established links between all major centres. Every significant geographical barrier has been conquered and the population is dispersed across all cultivable parts of the land. Borders do not divide New Zealanders, but they possess a patchwork of firmly held provincial identities and enjoy provincial anniversaries as annual public holidays. Provincial sport evokes particularly strong emotions – especially the national preoccupation, rugby. Passions can run high when it comes to provincial *anything* in New Zealand. 'New Zealand ends at the Bombay Hills' is a common expression, implying that Auckland and everywhere else north of an otherwise nondescript range of hills are somehow unworthy of being considered part of the same country; Aucklanders twist the expression to suggest the same about everywhere to the south. These rivalries are more than a competition between New Zealand's largest city and the rest of the country. For example, South Island neighbours Canterbury and Otago share a long-standing rivalry in which being born north or south of the Waitaki River counts for everything.

Yet all these uses of the adjective 'provincial' are made bizarre by a simple glance at a map. New Zealand does not have provinces; it is a unitary state. There are no legislative bodies beneath the central government in Wellington, only local government units that have been known as regional and territorial authorities since a programme of reforms in 1989. Despite the passion shown by New Zealanders for their provincial identities, most are unaware that these once had an existence in law. New Zealand was divided into provinces, originally six and ultimately 10, though only a maximum of nine ever existed simultaneously. The provincial era, 1853–76, is an often forgotten chapter of New Zealand's history, but it was a crucial and formative one, with an enduring legacy. During these years national, regional and local identities were forged. Provincial councils shaped patterns of development, and allegiances were formed both in attachment to existing provinces and in opposition to them. The provinces were first to really grapple with many significant aspects of New Zealand history – from education to railways, charitable welfare to land regulations – and in the process shaped decades of debate and initiative.

Why were the provinces created? What factors influenced their demise? Why did New Zealand electors transfer their loyalties to central governments, and support the abolition of the provinces, yet continue to possess enduring provincial identities? More broadly, where does New Zealand fit within the larger pattern of self-government in British settler societies? How much say did settlers have in shaping their institutions?

These are the questions at the heart of this book. It argues that the energy for political innovation and structural reform came not from London but from within the young colony, and that the failure of provinces to open their hinterlands to economic development underpinned New Zealand's transition to a unitary state. *Acknowledge No Frontier* examines the flaws within the provincial system – flaws of circumstance and of performance – and how these allowed the central government to use public works as a means to gain popular support for abolition. It begins in the decade before the provinces to comprehend how and why they were originally implemented. It then explores the early years of provincialism, when the system had its greatest claim on settler loyalties, before turning to a series of issues that beset the provinces during the late 1850s and 1860s: restless hinterlands, new provinces, North Island warfare, South Island separatism, administrative bungles and financial strife. These factors contributed to the dramatic upheavals of the 1870s, allowing the central government to justify its appropriation of public works previously provided by the provinces. The development of New Zealand with railways and other works shaped the fortunes of the provincial system, and as time and space were compressed in the early decades of the modern New Zealand polity, so, too, was the role of the provinces. Within a web of provincial public works failures, the central government was able to position itself as solely capable of providing for the wants of the population.

When the formal colonisation of New Zealand began in 1840, British policies for the internal administration of settler colonies had shifted a long way in a relatively short time. A profound innovation was pioneered in British North America, the rump of colonies that remained after the American Revolution of 1776: responsible self-government, under which colonies possessed an executive accountable to a representative parliament that held authority for domestic affairs. The largest and most significant North American colonies, acquired from France in 1763, were Upper and Lower Canada (now Ontario and Quebec). Upper Canada, settled predominantly by Loyalist refugees from America and British immigrants, followed English laws and traditions; Lower Canada, with a majority French population, maintained French practices. The political systems in both granted some modest democratic rights before the 1830s, but the governor possessed an absolute veto and local oligarchies accrued considerable political authority. In both Canadas reformers, seeking greater democracy and accountability, revolted in 1837–38.

One domino effect was feared and another occurred. Britain, unwilling to surrender any colonial possession lest it inspire wider imperial disintegration, crushed the rebellions and commissioned Lord Durham to report on the unrest. His recommendations led to the merger of the two colonies in 1841 as the United Province of Canada, to assimilate French Canadians more fully into the British world while using Lower Canada's financial solvency to cure Upper Canada's financial ills. Durham also sketched an outline of responsible government to accede to numerous demands of democratic reformers while retaining the Crown's ultimate authority. His intention was to offer the minimum degree of autonomy that Canadians would accept while consenting to remain in the British Empire. Responsible government, nonetheless, was not granted immediately to United Canada, as the British feared French Canadians would dominate the legislature. In 1848 neighbouring Nova Scotia was accorded the privilege, and United Canada followed the next year. The innovation spread rapidly, driven by what Benjamin T. Jones calls 'a colonial feeling of dual nationalism', whereby colonists were loyal to their British heritage and took a civic pride in their new home. Events in the colonies, as Jones and Phillip A. Buckner have shown, had their own momentum independent of London as settlers pressed for the autonomy necessary to advance local interests. By the time New Zealand received responsible government in 1856, a mere 16 years after the country was opened to organised settlement, almost all the British 'dominoes' in North America and Australasia enjoyed the privilege.[1]

In Australia, New South Wales had evolved from its origins in 1788 as a penal colony to become an increasingly significant cog in the imperial economy, especially for its pastoral industry. Tasmania, known as Van Diemen's Land until 1856, had been detached from New South Wales in 1825 and established as a separate colony. This overcame difficulties in administering geographically separate and rapidly growing settlements in an era before the steamship or telegraph, and it set a trend. Most subsequent Australian colonies were also carved from New South Wales. Western Australia, known as the Swan River Colony when founded in 1829, was from the outset a separate colony, since Britain's initial claim to New South Wales did not encompass the western seaboard of the Australian continent. In 1836, however, the territory of New South Wales was reduced with the excision of South Australia, and during the 1840s Victoria pressed increasingly firmly for separation. It achieved success in 1851 and Queensland followed in 1859. By this time all the Australian colonies apart from Western Australia enjoyed representative and responsible government. This heightened political authority went hand in hand with access to land; power offered permanency and security in landed tenure. Land on both sides of the Tasman – its control, sale and exploitation – was central to colonial politics.[2]

New Zealand was also part of New South Wales for the brief period between February and November 1840. The push for more localised and autonomous administration in Australasia, through the creation of new, self-governing colonies, was a formative influence on New Zealand's governance and development. At the same time, back in Britain, the Chartist movement captured public interest with its demands for universal (male) suffrage, the secret ballot, electorates of equal size and similar democratic measures. These campaigns informed New Zealand settlers' expectations that their governments be accessible and responsive, as did the reality of life in a new colony where an aloof government could spell social and commercial ruin.

From the outset New Zealand had broad freedom in its internal affairs. Governors throughout the empire enjoyed considerable latitude in their administration of colonies, checked more often by local elites than by the Colonial Office in London.[3] It was in any case difficult for Britain to exercise close control, given the distances involved. This was especially the case in New Zealand, where George Grey, during his first term as governor from 1845 to 1852, shaped the colony's administrative direction more than any other figure. He and London agreed on the general principle of localised administration for New Zealand: its decentralised settlement demanded some devolution of powers, but its small size, both in area and population, made dividing it into multiple colonies impractical. Grey clashed, however, with the Colonial Office's specific provincial proposals and ultimately prevailed; the system that was inaugurated in 1853 owed much to him. Once responsible government was introduced, the Colonial Office was unwilling to intervene in any affairs it considered purely domestic. This proved particularly crucial for the fate of provincialism in 1858, when legislation allowing for new provinces was passed, and in 1875, when the campaign for abolition reached its zenith.

Pivotal to the central government's success in abolishing the provinces, though not designed to achieve it, was a bold national public works plan introduced by

Julius Vogel as he appeared in
the 1860s during his ascent to
the top of New Zealand politics.
1/2-053949-F, Alexander Turnbull Library,
Wellington

treasurer Julius Vogel in 1870. Vogel's scheme has been known by a number of names. For contemporaries it was simply *the* Public Works Policy, while some historians have dubbed it Vogelism. Other writers, including railway historians Geoffrey B. Churchman and Tony Hurst, have opted for the Great Public Works Policy, and that is the term adopted here, since it captures the spirit and scope of Vogel's ambitions. The policy was central to what James Belich calls the 'progress industry', which played a key role in New Zealand's colonisation. He defines it as an 'interacting complex of economic activities … centred on growth and development' that formed a 'motley whole … greater than the sum of its parts'.[4] In New Zealand, as elsewhere in the English-speaking world, this industry brought together a steady stream of immigrants, the provision of easy credit, the existence of speculative markets and the rapid creation of towns, farms and public works to service them.

The most visible form of the progress industry was the rapid construction of transport networks – in New Zealand's case, initially harbours and roads, then railways – but it was supported heavily by the banking sector and government activity. The progress industry enjoyed a wide network of allies, especially extractive industries such as gold and timber and the booms they engendered.[5] New Zealand then was heavily dependent on external capital, primarily from the London money market and the more developed Australian colonies. Between 1840 and 1886, wholly encompassing the provincial period, the value of New

Zealand's capital imports exceeded its export income.[6] Provincial development occurred within a context of dramatic flows of capital, goods and people from Britain and elsewhere in the British world to the empire's outermost fringe. Public works were a crucial component of this arrangement and affected every aspect of colonial life. They brought isolated settlements together, overcame geographical barriers, opened new markets, connoted progress and innovation, created financial headaches for governments and shaped electors' perceptions of their central and provincial authorities.

Historians' prolonged neglect of provincialism and abolition is astonishing. A brief flowering of unpublished postgraduate research in the mid-twentieth century analysed developments in specific provinces, but the only published treatment of provincialism as a whole dates from 1932 by William Parker Morrell, a remarkable scholar of imperial history.[7] Morrell successfully condensed a turbulent period into a coherent and readable narrative, but his analysis and conclusions provide an insufficient understanding of provincialism's demise. He belonged to a generation of scholars trained in British universities who viewed New Zealand not on its own terms but as an extension of the British Empire. In seeking to show how 'progressive' settlers transplanted British institutions to the colonies, these scholars failed to recognise that a separate set of circumstances internal to New Zealand shaped the colony's development.

Provincialism was a distinctive response to New Zealand's needs and problems, not a mere copy of overseas institutions. Multiple colonies, as in Australia, was not workable with such a comparatively small population. No other British colony received such a quasi-federal structure, and the federations formed elsewhere in the English-speaking world were created by the union of colonies rather than their subdivision. Although London participated in the conception of provincialism during the 1840s, especially through Earl Grey's contribution of 1846 (discussed in Chapter 1), the system's design owed more to the ideas of Governor George Grey and others with experience in New Zealand. Once the system was operational, it evolved as a result of local activity, took on powers not anticipated by London and disappeared in a manner that illustrates vividly the autonomy settlers possessed. The story of the provinces highlights the dangers of locating in London the driving force of all facets of imperial history.

Despite the quality of Morrell's work, it is necessary to question his approach and some of his conclusions. This is not to say that his scholarship has been completely superseded: as a historical analysis of the legal and legislative side of New Zealand

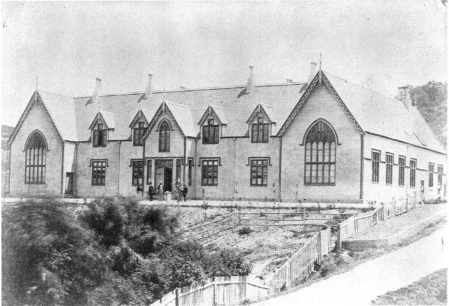

The status and significance of provincial councils are captured by their accommodation in grand civic buildings. Seen here are the council chambers of Nelson (c. 1870) (top) and Wellington (c. 1859). The Wellington building housed the General Assembly from 1865 and burned down in 1907. The Nelson building was demolished in an act of civic vandalism in 1969.

Nelson Provincial Museum Collection C1348; George Henry Swan, 1/2-003739-F, Alexander Turnbull Library, Wellington provincialism, it requires little revision. But in focusing primarily on central politics and on Otago province, and relying heavily on official records, he overlooks other major chapters of the provincial narrative. The failure of the six original provinces to develop their hinterlands led to the creation of new provinces in Hawke's Bay, Marlborough and Southland, which in turn illustrated the shortcomings of the system as a whole. Morrell views these provinces through brief asides; it is time to restore them to centrality within the narrative, so that provincialism's evolution and demise can be fully understood. Much of this book is concerned with the restlessness of hinterlands and the consequences that followed their establishment as new provinces. Provincial history was made just as much in isolated gullies and river valleys as it was in legislative chambers.

Southland in particular played a major role in bringing the system unstuck during the 1860s, when hasty investment in railways brought the province to its knees, and this highlights another major theme overlooked by Morrell and other scholars: the significance of transport. Morrell ignores most public works before 1870, even though settlers demanded little else so vociferously or consistently, and he gives a conflicting account of the Great Public Works Policy. He first suggests that it threatened provincialism's viability, but later argues that it did not make a major contribution.[8] Yet the development of land transportation networks contributed to the extension and deepening of inland settlements, and shifted New Zealand away from a purely oceanic alignment.[9] The spread of settlement pushed against Māori autonomy, and their position in provincial history also requires greater recognition. This book offers a preliminary sketch of Māori contributions, from the role they played in the rejection of the proto-provinces in 1848 to the effects of war and proposals in the 1860s for a Māori province.

Many of the sources now available were not readily accessible in Morrell's time. He relied greatly on government documents and, like most of his contemporaries, consulted a narrow selection of newspapers – seven, some for very limited runs. In recent decades, historians have gained greater awareness of the importance of the press in colonial New Zealand: the public expected newspapers to be partisan and politicians considered press advocacy essential to electoral success.[10] The rise of digitised, searchable newspaper databases has made the local character of politics in colonial New Zealand markedly more accessible. Although digital coverage is not always perfect – gaps and silences remain, even unintentionally, in online databases[11] – the broad range of consultation possible today was unthinkable in Morrell's time.

A full discussion of every aspect of provincial politics would require many volumes. It is essential to recognise that there was not initially a gulf separating adherents of provincialism and centralism. David Gordon Herron, whose scholarship is discussed in more depth in Chapter 3, revealed that there was no binary distinction in the 1850s; politicians' commitment to provincial or central causes was determined more by their success at forming government at either level than by any ideological preference.[12] Nonetheless, the labels remain useful indicators of an individual or publication's allegiances at specific moments, and from the 1860s the binary became more distinct. It has particular analytical usefulness from 1870, when those politicians threatened by the centralisation of the Great Public Works Policy kicked back with provincialist demands. Throughout the provincial period, each province, and numerous regions within most of them, had distinctive variations and experiences. Political issues such as goldfields administration and education policies were significant but did not influence abolition and have been ably discussed by other historians.[13] This book covers the major political developments – and many colourful stories – to understand the system not only from the perspective of the traditional four main centres but also from towns as different as Blenheim, Hokitika, Pirongia, Riverton, Thames and Wanganui.

Many themes played upon the viability of the provincial system, and it is impossible to understand any of them in isolation. Even before the provinces were formed in 1853, events in the 1840s conspired to define the system in a manner that would affect its long-term existence. Some historians have taken provincial abolition as predictable or inevitable.[14] This attitude is sometimes grounded in the assumption that, to be viable, provinces require either a large population or vast territory. However, other relatively small countries – in terms of area or population or both – maintain federal structures to this day: Austria, Switzerland and the Federated States of Micronesia, for example. Size is an inadequate answer anyway, since, because of its rugged topography, New Zealand contained a considerable degree of artificial distance in transport and communications well into the twentieth century.[15]

Other historians have invested more time in trying to explain the demise of the provinces, attributing responsibility to factors as diverse as warfare in the North Island in the 1860s and central forestry policy in the early 1870s. The warfare-as-centralisation argument has been particularly resilient across generations; Morrell supported it. It suggests that the New Zealand Wars enabled the central government to acquire power at the expense of the provinces, and that fallout from wartime arrangements highlighted provincial difficulties in promoting colonisation. This argument, however, which is the subject of Chapter 8, overstates several reasons: the influence of war beyond combat zones, the shortcomings of provincial administrations in military settlement policies, and the transfer of powers away from the provinces. War was significant, but it was not *the* factor in provincialism's demise – there is no inexorable link between the two, and few provincial responsibilities were threatened by the wartime expansion of the central state.[16]

Another popular explanation, which has much to recommend it, is the financial position of the provinces. Historians as diverse as Tom Brooking, Gary Hawke and Muriel Lloyd Prichard are right to suggest that, through abolition, New Zealand aimed to remove impediments to Vogel's ambitious borrowing programme and secure more favourable terms on the London money market.[17] Financial considerations, especially inequality between provinces and a perceived lack of security for provincial loans, were serious issues with which politicians grappled. The problem comes when these are taken to be inherent or inevitable determinants. Financial struggles illustrated but did not cause provincialism's problems; the symptoms should not be mistaken for the disease. Put simply, financial explanations do not go deep enough.

The role of public works looms large. Railways were the biggest public work of the day and sat at the forefront of Victorian technological progress. They did not exist in isolation. New Zealand was originally a littoral society; in the 1840s and 1850s a premium was placed on harbour works and constructing roads to link these ports with nearby towns and farms. From the 1860s telegraph wires fanned across the colony and Ron Palenski has shown how important this process was to centralisation and the development of a New Zealand identity.[18] Railways acquired an even greater prominence. The invention of the railway was revolutionary in both the old and new worlds. Economic historians, sometimes employing counter-factual analyses to determine how the British and American economies might have grown without the railway, have reached varying conclusions about the statistical significance of the railway's contribution.[19] It is a mistake, though, to consider the railway in purely economic terms and most transport historians have moved on from narrowly statistical analyses. Railways had a profound effect on the environment, society and politics. Michael Freeman describes railways as a 'cultural metaphor … deeply embedded in the evolving structures of Victorian society' and 'enmeshed in the spirit of the age'. They were, therefore, 'cast not as institutional undertakings but as social phenomena'.[20] The manner in which railways reshaped cities, changed urban patterns of growth and influenced life in Victorian Britain has been thoroughly investigated.[21] Copious literature exists on the United States experience, and the role of railways in shaping American settlement and economic patterns has been widely debated.[22] As Sarah H. Gordon emphasises, America's '[e]xchange of goods and people, ideas and cultures all took place in the context of railroad transport' until the interwar period.[23] Studies exist for settler societies such as Argentina and Canada but not New Zealand, even though themes such as Gordon's invite consideration.[24]

New Zealand was a rare settler colony founded *after* the invention of the railway. Settlers arrived with preconceived notions of rail's social, economic and cultural importance. Yet even the best historians of New Zealand transport have hurried through the provincial era with very limited analysis of how railways affected provincialism.[25] High-quality histories of Canterbury and Southland's provincial railways are now out of print and focus on the technical history of the railways rather than analysing their relationship to broader political or social developments.[26] Long overdue for elaboration is Philip Ross May's 1975 observation that '[f]rom the 1870s colonial politics often ran on railway tracks', building on a less colourful remark by Keith Sinclair in 1963.[27] Yet the significance of railways and development did not emerge from nowhere in 1870; they were also the major provincial political issues of the 1850s and 1860s. North Island warfare, administered centrally, sometimes masks that fact. This book will show that the evolution and demise of the provinces are inseparable from settler demands for and government policies regarding railways and development.

In *Vanished Kingdoms*, Norman Davies suggests five mechanisms for state failure on the basis of his European case studies: implosion, conquest, merger, liquidation and infant mortality.[28] Conquest is self-explanatory and irrelevant to provincialism's demise. Implosion too is irrelevant, since no province disappeared through sudden collapse into multiple separate parts in the style of the former USSR, though some provinces did lose restless hinterlands. One merger occurred when Southland rejoined Otago, but this was unique. None of these categories can be applied to the system as a whole. More useful are Davies' remaining two mechanisms: liquidation, the deliberate suppression of a political entity; and infant mortality, the failure of a young polity to develop fully functional internal organs or maintain an autonomous existence, ultimately succumbing to external 'vultures'. Yet does either category fit provincial abolition? From the beginning the provinces had to contend with rivals, but they started life blessed with power – both perceived and legislative – and all the necessary administrative tools. Liquidation is harder pressed to explain processes of domestic structural reform than the ruptures necessary to split an independent state into multiple parts. Europeans may have settled in New Zealand, but the conditions of colonial politics did not replicate those of Europe. Could provincial abolition represent a sixth mechanism?

Bernard Attard argues, commendably, that the colonial state functioned to raise capital for development and that internal politics could be remodelled to achieve this objective.[29] He relies, however, on acceptance of the 'gentlemanly capitalism' thesis that London financiers drove imperial expansion and colonial development.[30] New Zealand settlers demonstrated an assertive independent streak from the mid-1840s, and the final decision on abolition lay with them at the 1875–76 election, a de facto referendum on provincialism's future. An emphasis on financial borrowing simply indicates a deeper problem: the inability of the provinces to develop. It overlooks what was actually happening throughout the colony, from the halls of power in Wellington to muddy paddocks in Southland, commercial offices in Auckland and Dunedin to gold seekers on isolated and lonely rivers in Westland. What did settlers expect provincial governments to do? How did these demands create a need for borrowing and why did borrowing become more difficult? Why did the provinces struggle to colonise New Zealand or make more effective use of their borrowings? Ultimately, what were the consequences for provincialism when settler demands were not met?

These questions need to be answered with a keen and sympathetic eye to the interaction of local peculiarities with national development policies in order to understand why the provinces disappeared, to identify where this story sits within imperial history, and to determine whether the disappearance of the provinces conforms to international patterns of political demise or represents a new category. Electors were rarely concerned with abstract matters of colonial finance, and many came under the sway of booster politicians who foresaw, glimmering beyond the horizon, future riches far greater than any present debt. Allegiances were not determined by balance sheets or sophisticated political theory. Settlers needed public works and development to provide a comfortable life and to promote the success of their locality, and they were willing to give their loyalty to anybody capable of providing this development. This is the surprising and counter-intuitive story of how vociferous parochialism and self-interest brought New Zealanders together as one people.

Chapter 1

A Divided Colony

The term 'the provinces' in New Zealand ordinarily refers to the sub-national system that became active from 17 January 1853. In a country where government has usually featured only two tiers, national and local, this provincial system was the only fully functional intermediate tier that ever operated between the two. It was preceded by an earlier unsuccessful attempt at provincialism – a proto-provincial system – in the 1840s. This was outlined by the 1846 Constitution Act of the British parliament, framed without meaningful input from New Zealand and largely suspended in 1848 as a result of obvious shortcomings. Little has been written on this largely forgotten aspect of New Zealand's evolution,[1] but it is impossible to understand the formation of the 1853–76 provinces without exploring the prior framework or understanding the needs and demands of early colonial New Zealand. It was a deeply divided colony, where ideological differences were as profound as geographical cleavages. The introduction of the provinces and their early controversies make sense only when seen in the context of the previous decade. The influence of the 1840s raises an important question: Were the qualities that brought about the provinces' demise a result of the circumstances of their birth?

The colony of New Zealand began life as a dependency of the British colony of New South Wales on 6 February 1840 after the Treaty of Waitangi was signed between Britain's representatives and Māori chiefs. Domestic administration was initially centralised, with the organs of government located in one town, but the shortcomings of this approach became apparent almost as soon as the treaty's ink had dried. The 'official' settlements where the government sat and British administrators lived were located in the north of the North Island – first Russell in the Bay of Islands and then Auckland from 1841. The first New Zealand Company settlement of Wellington was near the southernmost point of the North Island, and it was soon to be followed by Nelson at the top of the South Island and New Plymouth on the North Island's west coast. The company pursued the 'systematic colonisation' of New Zealand through the theory of one of its driving

Edward Gibbon Wakefield in 1823. A few years later he formulated his theory of systematic colonisation while in Newgate Prison for abducting an heiress.

Engraving by Benjamin Holl, 1826, after a painting by Abraham Wivell. D13224, National Portrait Gallery, London

forces, Edward Gibbon Wakefield – an impetuous man of grand ideas and grander personal ambition, who alienated colleagues with worrying frequency. Wakefield deplored the existing standard of colonisation, believing Britain had granted too much free land to colonists, thereby creating an allegedly crude society defined by sharp labour shortages that were often resolved with slavery or convict labour. He proposed to dispose of land at a 'sufficient price' to provide the colonial government with funds to encourage the emigration of wage-earners from Britain, but to restrict the speed at which they could acquire their own property. This would both ensure a labour pool and provide an incentive for labourers to earn the money to achieve independence through property ownership.

In a country that was wholly undeveloped, in Pākehā eyes, and in an era before the introduction of steamships to the southern Pacific, communication between settlements was arduous and lengthy.[2] Sailing ships plied the coast at the mercy of notoriously inclement weather; because of the low demand for intersettlement travel, such voyages were infrequent. Any settlement not blessed with the organs of government was isolated, and activities requiring official approval were subject to long delays. New Zealand's inaugural governor, naval officer William Hobson, played a major role in shaping the colony's history. After conducting surveys in the region of a nebulous Melbourne in what is now the Australian state of Victoria, he visited the North Island for the first time in 1837. Upon his return to England in

Auckland as sketched from Smales Point in 1843, when it was capital of New Zealand. Shortland Street is prominent at centre right and St Paul's Church can be seen on the hill in the left background. Some significant features depicted here are now lost: Commercial Bay has been filled in (Fore Street, along its foreshore, is now Fort Street a couple of blocks inland); Point Britomart (left rear) and Smales Point have both been quarried. Edward Ashworth, 1935/1/7, Auckland Art Gallery Toi o Tāmaki

1838 he proposed a treaty with Māori, and the next year was appointed to establish a British colony in New Zealand. He arrived in the Bay of Islands on 29 January 1840 and after securing the Treaty of Waitangi was faced with the business of founding a colonial government. The first capital, Russell, was unfit for purpose, but his decision to locate the government in Auckland, near the bulk of the Māori population and distant from the New Zealand Company's influence, was controversial. It was backed by the Colonial Office, defying Wellingtonian expectations for their settlement, located at the centre of organised Pākehā colonisation.[3] A fierce rivalry consequently developed between north and south, governor and company.[4] Auckland viewed the southern settlements as ill sited, illegally founded and lacking prudence in dealings with Māori; Wellington viewed Auckland and the official administration as out of touch, draconian, settled by a lower standard of colonist and beholden to interests detrimental to the company's success. Both views were quickly taken to extremes and lacked even a façade of self-awareness, but at their core each possessed some truths about the other.

Northern and southern settlers nonetheless shared common goals. Their leading priorities were security in property via land titles and security in person via protection from interracial conflict. The difficulty was that steps taken towards achieving one made the other more problematic, and New Zealand's distance from the Colonial Office created a feeling of remoteness and a desire for more immediate and local administration. From an early stage representative self-government was seen as the most practical way to achieve both forms of security, especially in the southern settlements, where the New Zealand Company expected some form of local government to be granted forthwith. An ideological preference for representative self-government played into this viewpoint, but it was secondary to the anticipation of practical, daily benefits. This was particularly the case for colonists in company settlements, who felt increasingly insecure after what they regarded as failures by Hobson and the Colonial Office. Clashes in perception, interests and preferences, however, meant that New Zealand endured 13 years of indecision, inaction and ill-fated experimentation before receiving a functional provincial system. The geographical separation and political conditions and rivalries peculiar to the earliest years of colonisation were the justification for establishing decentralised administration, but such an atmosphere was not conducive to the formulation of a lasting provincial system.

England provided settlers with a template of how they expected local government to function. Sometimes England represented what New Zealanders did *not* want, such as parish vestries dominated by corrupt or incompetent elites. Until the early 1830s, English local government was a ramshackle affair that struggled to face the challenges of poverty, urban sprawl and population movement created by the Industrial Revolution. The system acquired greater coherence under the Poor Law Amendment Act of 1834, which ushered in the strict regimen of Victorian workhouses, and the Municipal Corporations Act of 1835, which established a uniform system of municipal boroughs in urban areas with councils elected by ratepayers. In practice, the franchise of these municipalities was not as wide as parliament anticipated – they were solidly middle class, largely inaccessible to the working classes – but they provided a model for a young colony and its new towns. Rural parishes remained by far the most common unit of local government, but they were not a significant influence on New Zealand's sub-national organisation. Their extensive and often oligarchical powers allowed officials to interfere in many spheres of daily life, an unattractive prospect for settlers seeking greater democracy and opportunity than they had enjoyed at home and for whom memories of the 1835 municipal reforms were fresh.[5]

For all the lessons derived from England, the colonial form of sub-national government was never going to be a carbon copy. Single-purpose local boards would prove popular in New Zealand for the management of harbours, roads, health and the like, which followed an English pattern of creating a dizzying array of statutory authorities for special purposes.[6] However, such authorities did not proliferate in New Zealand until the 1860s. As in other Australasian colonies, its small and scattered population made impossible a fully stocked English system of boroughs, shires, counties, parishes and boards.[7] These terms later entered the lexicon of New Zealand local government, especially after the demise of the provinces, but in the 1840s a simpler and decentralised system was necessary. It had British antecedents, but it was crafted and evolved in response to local circumstances – albeit sometimes ineffectively and without foresight.

New Zealand's adventure in provincialism began not in 1853 but, in a loose sense, on 3 May 1841. On that date the imperial act of 16 November 1840, which made New Zealand a colony separate from New South Wales, came into effect. At this time, Pākehā knew the three major islands as the Northern Island, Middle Island and Stewart's Island. (The Middle Island became known predominantly as the South Island within decades, and the passage of time also shortened the other names to the North Island and Stewart Island.) When New Zealand's separate colonial status was formalised, Hobson proclaimed new titles for the islands. From north to south, they were christened New Ulster, New Munster and New Leinster.[8] This nomenclature was merely geographic and initially held no particular significance for the devolution of administration. The names never caught on, and even in the 1840s some people did not know which was which without looking at a map.[9] They were, however, the first faint harbinger of the creation of the provincial system: under the 1846 Constitution Act, these titles would be applied not to the islands, but to the provinces within them.

Names – or the rejection of them – could help to form the identity of new settlements, but the system of government attached to those names meant much more. Wellington's first settlers established a council for local administration in March 1840. However when reports of its existence reached Hobson in May, he declared it treasonous and earned Wellington's unrelenting ire.[10] Unsurprisingly, the press in 1841 greeted Hobson's 'wholesale Hibernification' of nomenclature with all the xenophobic sarcasm of immature journalism.[11] Wellington had bigger concerns than topography and Hobson's declaration seemed to completely overlook everything of importance.

In the short term, Wellington's wish for local government went largely unfulfilled and power remained in the hands of Hobson's nominated executive. Government was administered centrally, except for the judiciary and policing, which required decentralisation.[12] Legislation and appointments were made at the prerogative of Hobson's administration, which contained just one Wellingtonian – who was dismissed for publishing derisive comments about the government. News both of his dismissal and the establishment of separate courts for the north and south reached Wellington on 24 March 1842.[13] Southern settlers, however, were granted just one court, in Wellington, even though the north received two, in Auckland and the Bay of Islands, to sit over a Pākehā population roughly half that of the south. By this time, a second New Zealand Company colony had been founded: Nelson, across Cook Strait on Tasman Bay at the top of the South Island.

Nelson settlers were, naturally, dissatisfied with this state of affairs, especially as they routinely found it difficult to communicate with Wellington. Their frustration led Willoughby Shortland, local administrator of the government between Hobson's death in September 1842 and the arrival in Auckland of the new governor Robert FitzRoy in December 1843, to sign authorisation for a legal 'District of Nelson', encompassing the South Island and Stewart Island. A criminal and civil court would sit within this district, with sessions to be held monthly from the third Tuesday of January 1843.[14] On 14 January 1843, however, just three days before this date, the editor of the *Nelson Examiner*, Charles Elliott, lamented that nothing had come of Shortland's proclamation. 'Where is our County Court …? Where is our Judge? Where are our Jury Lists? … and where, oh where, is the Government Brig? Verily and indeed this is a pretty state of things.' He wished that Nelson would at least receive clarification of what to expect from Auckland, as 'this trifling with our most important interests … and playing at government is enough to try beyond endurance the patience of a community of Jobs'.[15] The earliest seeds of provincialism were sown in a field of intersettlement discontent. Centralism did not work, and ad hoc localisation was frustrating.

Settlers wanted an active role in their administration and representation in their government. In 1840 the Colonial Office encouraged Hobson to introduce municipal government, since nothing else was 'more consonant with the English character and habits' to train colonists in the duties of representative government.[16] A municipal corporations ordinance, passed in January 1842, briefly inaugurated

Nelson in 1842 about a year after it was founded, showing the town and part of the harbour. Note the settlers in the foreground who are 'taming' the land – surveying, camping, and building a house. John Waring Saxton, PUBL-0011-06-2, Alexander Turnbull Library, Wellington

the first decentralised government in New Zealand. Elections in Wellington were fiercely contested, and settlers, unable to detach themselves from the pressure of immediate interests, indulged in unsavoury squabbles.[17] It was all for nothing. The ordinance was poorly drafted and even the New Zealand Company accepted that the Colonial Office had to disallow it.[18]

The botched attempts of Hobson and Shortland to decentralise administration were followed by Governor FitzRoy's equally ineffectual measures. FitzRoy was a highly intelligent man who had excelled in the Royal Navy and became a pioneering meteorologist, but his difficulties with local government in New Zealand reflected a wider struggle to impose authority and municipal order on a divided colony with few resources and little Colonial Office support.[19] He established a Southern Division in early 1844 and appointed as 'superintendent' Major Matthew Richmond, previously the police magistrate in Wellington and loyal to officialdom. This position was created partly because of New Zealand Company pressure, but hopes that an individual sympathetic to company goals would be appointed were not realised.[20] Richmond's title was worth little more than the paper on which it was printed: he had almost no executive or fiscal powers and none of the avenues of independent action open to his prototype in the Port Phillip District (now Victoria) of New South Wales. Settlers saw him as an agent of Auckland rather than as a local leader. The *Nelson Examiner* did not mince words describing 'that amiable but really useless functionary' and lamented the expenditure required to support

Robert FitzRoy, as well as governing New Zealand, was captain of the HMS *Beagle* on Charles Darwin's famous voyage, and is seen here in England in the early 1860s when he was a leading hydrologist and meteorologist. He coined the term 'weather forecast'.

Maull and Polyblank, x13984, National Portrait Gallery, London

officials whose offices were created without local consultation.[21] Company pressure secured FitzRoy's recall by the Colonial Office in 1845 on account of economic and military difficulties largely not of his own making. FitzRoy sought to vindicate his policies in print. Tellingly, in these thoughtful reflections on his turbulent tenure, he almost entirely overlooked the 'useless functionary' he created, making no reference to Richmond by name or to his responsibilities and actions.[22] It is surprising that he failed to justify the superintendent and rebut settler accusations of excessive bureaucratic spending – surprising, but illustrative of the position's insignificance and inadequacy.

Since Auckland could supply no acceptable remedy, the New Zealand Company looked increasingly to the Colonial Office and the British parliament. With the support of Whig and Radical MPs, Wakefield – who was yet to travel from Britain to 'his' colony – and other company representatives placed unrelenting personal and journalistic pressure upon Robert Peel's Conservative government, seeking support from its moderate members.[23] These efforts produced results. An extensive debate on representative and local government took place in the House of Commons on 17–19 June 1845.[24] Opinion was hotly divided regarding the company's colonising schemes and its legality. The House entertained a whirlwind of claims and accusations pertaining to land titles, management of waste lands and the rights and diplomatic status of the Māori population.[25] A bipartisan conclusion in favour of representative government emerged from this debate. It was no surprise that company advocates such as Charles Buller, who initiated the debate, supported self-government. More notable was Peel's concession that 'representative government will be suited for the condition of the people of that Colony'. This should, however, be granted only incrementally, beginning with municipalities and expanding as settlements grew in size and in communication with each other.[26]

Peel's acknowledgement of the need for local management and the difficulties of bringing together representatives from small, scattered settlements anticipated provincialism. After the debate, Colonial Secretary Lord Stanley wrote to George Grey, the dashing young governor appointed to replace FitzRoy. Grey, only in his early thirties, had already been governor of South Australia after impressing his superiors in England as an adventurous officer in the British army. He combined radical democratic intellectualism with autocratic personal tendencies, learnt Māori and earned considerable mana with iwi throughout the colony, possessed a talent for persuasion that could make the greatest blunder appear ingenious, and cut a complex and remarkable figure that continues to divide opinion. Grey was one of the most important figures in New Zealand provincialism. His career in shaping New Zealand's internal political structure began when Lord Stanley urged him to 'direct your attention … to the formation of local municipal bodies' with considerable powers of taxation and bylaws, possessing authority 'over a considerable district'.[27] Although the recommendation was for *municipalities*, not provinces, it is clear that these bodies were to be larger in scope than English municipalities. The company continued to pressure the Peel government, Wakefield advocating 'municipalities' with more powers than any province ever possessed. William Ewart Gladstone, who succeeded Lord Stanley as colonial secretary, never endorsed such extreme ideas but came to favour a sub-division of the colony into northern and southern provinces.

The process of conceiving the provinces was therefore well under way when Peel's ministry fell and Earl Grey – no relation of George Grey – became colonial secretary under Lord John Russell. This occurred at the same time as repeal of the increasingly unpopular Corn Laws, steep protectionist tariffs that protected British cereal producers from cheaper imports. Britain was experiencing a pronounced shift to a more diverse and pluralistic society, and a key development was the rise of free trade and the adoption of an open economy. This transformed the empire's commercial basis: the colonies were no longer dependencies bled to profit London but valuable allies and markets for British imports, exports and capital.[28] Earl Grey possessed a passionate, dogmatic belief in free trade that fuelled his enthusiastic

Henry Grey, the third Earl Grey, whose tenure as colonial secretary profoundly influenced Britain's Australasian possessions. The tea is reputedly named for his father.

Camille Silvy, Ax7430, National Portrait Gallery, London

promotion of federation in Australia, Canada and New Zealand. Federal unions necessitated a high degree of commercial liberty, fostering the free trade values so dear to Grey. His specific desire for free trade among the Australian colonies also influenced New Zealand's constitution. A federal structure promoted both stability and free trade: it would militate against the risk of New Zealand splitting into separate colonies and promote commercial openness should the North and South Islands experience divergent patterns of development. Accordingly New Zealand – like Canada and the Australian colonies – deserved self-government, but with the maintenance of paternalistic imperial ties to ensure stability, maintain the supremacy of free trade and regulate its interactions domestically, with other colonies and with Britain.[29]

The ideas developed by Lord Stanley and Gladstone evolved under Earl Grey into a constitution featuring a complex three-tier system of government. In part it represented new ideas of colonial governance espoused by Lord Durham in his famous report of 1839, which led to the creation of the United Province of Canada in 1841. Here the idea of responsible government was taking shape to resolve the tension between local self-government and imperial unity by providing freedom of internal administration while maintaining Crown authority.[30] The New Zealand constitution, however, did not facilitate union between two quite different colonies, as in Canada, but sub-divided a previously unified colony into two provinces with their own legislatures. In Canada, assimilating French Canadians into the British Empire was one goal of union.[31] On the other hand, a sub-division of New Zealand acknowledged that, unlike the South Island, the North Island, with its large Māori population, faced much larger problems of racial contact and assimilation. James Stephen, permanent under-secretary of the Colonial Office, drafted the constitution and provided a thread linking the policies of the three successive colonial secretaries.[32] Consequently, when it went before parliament, it was introduced accurately as reflecting 'the views of both the late and the present Government'.[33] The constitution's convoluted development gave it a life of its own in London. Before it reached New Zealand, it even produced offspring: the Colonial Office proposed a similar system for New South Wales, to considerable colonial objection.[34]

The 1846 Constitution Act's approval was a formality. Little else about it would be. The political structure was overly complex for such a small society, embracing various features of representative and federal government without quite achieving any of their ideals.[35] It provided local government via municipal corporations possessing powers equal to those recently reformed in England, with local councillors elected by all resident adult males – in theory this included Māori, but they were effectively excluded by a provision requiring English literacy. Above municipalities were provincial assemblies, with the colony divided into two or more provinces by governor's proclamation and representatives elected by municipal councillors. At the peak was a general assembly, its representatives drawn from provincial parliaments. In essence, the municipal corporations would be electoral colleges for the provincial councils, which in turn would perform the same function for the general assembly. This recalled the practice of unreformed English governance before the 1830s, where the franchise in some municipalities was so limited that only the members of the local governing body had a vote in selecting the town's representatives in the House of Commons.[36] Both provincial and central assemblies would also have a nominated upper house. The act itself gave away little about the administration of Māori land, the issue that would ultimately bring about its doom. These details occupied much space in Earl Grey's extensive instructions to Governor Grey that accompanied the legislation.[37]

Earl Grey justified the system of indirect elections and stocking superior legislatures with members of inferior bodies as 'prov[ing] an effectual security against the otherwise too probable conflicts between the local and the general Legislatures'.[38] He dwelt little on this topic, which would prove so controversial in New Zealand. It was his belief, informed by imperial history, that local self-government by municipal corporations was the leading priority and such bodies would provide a foundation from which central government would evolve. Here the influence of James Stephen is apparent. Stephen was convinced that municipal government and centralisation were both necessary and desirable: municipalities because of the isolation of settled districts, and centralisation to avoid proliferation of conflicting legislation on such matters as customs duties. Drawing lessons from Canada and New South Wales, he was, however, wary of unfruitful competition and rivalry between different levels of government, and sought the advantages of both centralisation and decentralisation through a labyrinthine pyramid that appealed easily to Earl Grey's faith in federalism.[39] It is hard to say what is more surprising about this form of government: its inherent complexity, or that Britain thought it any way suitable for a Pākehā population of 13,274.[40]

The 1846 constitution was influential not so much for what it did (or did not do) as for the consequences of its failure. It is a telling document that casts light on New Zealand society at the time, and its public reception brought to light the first signs that a federal-style decentralised government was not necessarily as suited to New Zealand as to other colonies. It generated heated debate in all three major settlements, especially regarding Māori and land policy. This was a journalistic watershed. The press was emerging from tumultuous and unstable beginnings, settling into the influential political role it would occupy during the provincial era, and this was the first substantial policy debate to occupy its pages. Auckland's early newspapers had been subject to government suppression, especially by the singularly pompous and tactless Shortland; all major players in Auckland's press for the next couple of decades participated in or witnessed this battle with officialdom.[41] The dismissal of Shortland by FitzRoy and then the arrival of Grey ushered in a freer press. Meanwhile, in the south, the New Zealand Company viewed the press as part of Wakefieldian colonisation, but did not succeed in controlling it because company and settler interests diverged during the 1840s.[42]

By the middle of that decade press divisions had become clear. Agitation for self-government was organised through openly partisan newspapers that functioned as de facto political representation.[43] Auckland was split between the pro-Grey *New Zealander* and the opposition's *Southern Cross*; the latter, although founded in 1843, suspended operations for 26 months before July 1847. In Wellington there was a battle between the pro-Grey *Spectator* and the hostile *Independent*, while in Nelson the *Examiner* began life with company funds but asserted a measure of independence and produced some of the colony's most erudite content. The Bay of

Islands, which had declined in significance ever since the government moved to Auckland, no longer had a newspaper, and the other major settlement of the period, New Plymouth, had none until 1852.

Details of the constitution began to reach New Zealand in February 1847, but the full text and instructions did not arrive until June. Two major themes emerged from the constitution's reception – uncertainty over the best form of government, and the need to limit Pākehā control over Māori. Settlers uniformly decried the proposed system as too convoluted, though in Wellington enthusiasm for representative government tempered concerns. Both leading publications there had initially feared that the system resurrected the spirit of rotten boroughs, such as Old Sarum and Gatton, in Britain's unreformed House of Commons before 1831.[44] In these electorates, a handful of people – seven, in the named examples – elected two members each. The *Independent* did, though, come to accept that New Zealand's complex situation required a complex solution.[45] Meanwhile the *Spectator* hedged its bets. It praised Earl Grey's 'able instructions' and, as a pro-government organ, expressed full confidence in George Grey's capacity to implement the constitution.[46] Nonetheless, it implicitly maintained a critique first aired in February that the constitution 'gives us *too much of the machinery and too little of the principle* of representative government'.[47] Nelson's *Examiner* was guarded at first, approving some principles while detecting 'some blemishes'.[48] However, in a lengthy June editorial devoted to the finer points of political science, it condemned the constitution's 'graduated system' of government as a point of 'failure' that would engender political apathy among a population unable to elect holders of higher offices.[49] It is impossible to tell whether this condemnation reflected the local mood in Nelson or proprietor Charles Elliott's personal convictions; the style tacitly indicates the latter, and Elliott viewed the press as a tool to mould public opinion.[50] Resolutions later passed by town meetings indicated popular preference for direct elections and simple, streamlined government, but whether this influenced the *Examiner* or vice versa is hard to say.

Auckland was consistently opposed. It first struggled to rouse itself from apathy: the *New Zealander* – the only newspaper active at the time – editorialised in a perfunctory manner.[51] By 12 June it had sunk into sarcastic mockery of a 'precious specimen of Whig legislation'.[52] A fortnight later a less derogatory editorial was more cutting. To justify the lack of 'jubilee shouts [or] bonfire rejoicings, to commemorate the dawn of political liberty', the editor argued that the constitution was theoretically sound but practically lacking – a document 'prepared, not for us, but for the English at home'.[53] The *New Zealander*'s staunch rival, the *Southern Cross*, was resurrected in July to advocate for the 'Senate', a loose group of businessmen and radicals hostile to the government. Its founder, William Brown, opposed Governor Grey on numerous fronts. He, like other businessmen who provided contributions, viewed the press as a valuable weapon against governors and the *Southern Cross* quickly resumed its role as a critic of the colonial administration.[54] Yet its denunciation of the constitution as 'an absurdity' in which no Aucklander 'seems to feel the slightest interest' was a surprising show of unity with the *New Zealander*.[55] Auckland's bitterly divided political landscape could unite in opposition to the constitution.

Like the southern settlements, Auckland feared the burdens of a complex system. Financial concerns cut across geographical and ideological divides; settlers wanted representation but saw no need for sprawling bureaucracy. A smaller but more representative system was the core desire, although there was no agreement or even suggestion of how this was to be achieved. The *New Zealander* conceded that the lack of long-term political stability made it hard to ascertain the ideal system for the colony: 'our requirements are not yet well enough known, even here – much less in Downing-Street'.[56] No contributor ever wrote to suggest otherwise. This was not merely a matter of competing political aspirations – it was an indication of *unclear* political aspirations grounded in vague, generalised desires. It was fairly clear what the colonists did *not* want, and what ideals they supported, but there was no clarity or specificity of purpose. This was not a promising foundation for constitutional government or provincialism.

The matter of race relations differed completely from the debate about the structure of government. Earl Grey's instructions were blunt. He fiercely denied Māori rights to the majority of New Zealand's land and enunciated a policy fundamentally opposite to the Treaty of Waitangi, arguing that Māori had surrendered all land not owned by individuals.[57] Earl Grey did not take full leave of his senses, acknowledging that a policy of claiming all lands held in common by iwi could no longer be pursued in full. Because 'particular tribes have been taught to regard [large tracts of waste land] as their own', the supposed rights of the Crown could not practically be applied to them without controversy and confrontation. Governor Grey was therefore to regard Earl Grey's arguments as 'the foundations of the policy which, as far as it is within your power, you are to pursue'.[58] Earl Grey firmly urged the governor to prohibit the sales of tribal land to any individual or organisation except the Crown. The sale to settlers of land purchased from Māori was to provide funds for systematic colonisation and public works. This issue struck at the heart of early New Zealand society, tying together the need for public funds, the desire for land and the hot emotions of interracial politics.

These instructions sparked intense debate throughout the colony, though poor communication between settlements meant it was typically conducted on narrow, very local terms. Auckland's response was a carefully disguised panic. The *New Zealander* refrained from printing Earl Grey's comments on land as they reflected 'a breach of faith' towards Māori, and it was confident George Grey would not follow such orders.[59] Instead, it hoped the constitution would be 'buried in oblivion' to avert a loss of moral influence or the lowering of Pākehā character in the eyes of Māori.[60] The *Southern Cross* contended that Earl Grey wished to deprive Māori of their birthright and that Britain would be more honest if it simply said that, as the stronger of the two peoples, it determined to seize land for itself. Although this newspaper represented speculators who sought to profit by purchasing land directly from Māori without a Crown intermediary, it bluntly and succinctly summed up the fears of Pākehā in Auckland, who were surrounded by a much larger Māori population. If the instructions were acted upon, they were 'certain to cause the destruction of the present colonists, and bring on a war of extermination of the natives'.[61] This was not simply a matter of ideological opposition, but a stark fear grounded in daily experience. Opposition to the constitution's land policy united early Auckland.

The south could not have been more different. When 'H', a *Spectator* contributor, echoed Auckland's attitudes and sparked Wellingtonian debate with his passionate disapproval of Earl Grey's instructions, he was immediately denounced by the editors of both Wellington papers and numerous contributors.[62] If even a pro-government paper such as the *Spectator* was willing to throw in its lot with the New Zealand Company and land-hungry settlers and assert that 'the successful progress' of colonisation depended on 'strict adherence' to Earl Grey's instructions, then it is not hard to ascertain the mood of early Wellington.[63] Its outlying districts, especially the Wairarapa, were vast, fertile and inhabited by few Māori – and Earl Grey's instructions meant the land was there for the taking. Although eloquent opponents of such flagrant land-grabbing existed, as represented by 'H', they were a minority.

Wellington's strictures were nonetheless mild compared with Nelson's hard-line attitude. The South Island had a small Māori population that presented little threat to Nelson's safety, and Pākehā animosity towards Māori land claims had been solidified since a confrontation in the Wairau Valley in 1843 that was sensationally labelled the 'Wairau Massacre'. Subsequent government inaction further frustrated Nelsonians.[64] Whatever misgivings the *Examiner* had regarding the structure of government were trampled underfoot by delight in the land policy, which showed no consideration for Māori. James Cook's right of discovery, the paper argued, defined New Zealand as a British possession from 1769. This meant that 'waste land' was already vested in the Crown, which should not have to buy its own land from Māori.[65] So extreme was the *Examiner* that it not only dismissed Auckland's fears, but also lambasted the *Spectator* for perceived deficiencies in its support for British possession of New Zealand. The constitution was a godsend to the colony's future prosperity, and the *Examiner* feared that any less than total commitment would see it wasted. This reflected local agitation that had festered for years, and the introduction of representative institutions would stymie obstructive governors. '[T]he Representative Assemblies, which must soon be elected, will now be able to control such questions, and we trust that we shall never see them lose sight of this the first and most important [issue] to the welfare of the colony.'[66]

In light of northern panic and the rapacious enthusiasm of southern settlers to claim Māori land, Governor Grey moved quickly to dissuade Earl Grey. In the north, a 'small fraction' of people, Pākehā, would govern the 'large majority', Māori, and 'the race which is in the majority is much the most powerful of the two … they would [not] be satisfied with, and submit to, the rule of the minority'.[67] Any attempt to appropriate vast tracts of Māori land without compensation would have dire consequences. It was little wonder that the later 1852 constitution excluded Crown and Māori lands from provincial jurisdiction.

Uncertainty about the ideal form of government showed the tenuous foundation upon which provincialism in general was established, while race relations and land excited the most public comment and obliterated the constitution. The preference for a representative central government was universal, but there was little conception of what the lower levels of government should look like. Was provincialism doomed from the start? No, this measure of disunity was not inherently fatal. Many criticisms were specific and negotiable; there was agreement on general principles. The disunity does demonstrate, however, the difficulties faced by the framers of any provincial system, who had to reconcile competing visions. The origins of abolition are discernible here; in the colony's early years, the divergent interests of its disparate settlements undermined the basis of the provincial system. Nonetheless, the 1846 constitution *could* have survived, possibly in a modified form, had it not been for Earl Grey's instructions regarding Māori land. Permitting settlers so much power over land had potentially disastrous implications, especially given southern intentions. George Grey was justified in fearing the consequences of so few Pākehā legislating to the detriment of so many Māori. But his predilection for retaining centralised power, and widespread settler desire for a more favourable constitution unencumbered by a financially burdensome bureaucracy, meant there was a distinct possibility that Māori were exploited as a convenient foil or excuse.

George Grey sent fervent representations against the constitution to London in May 1847, but a response was almost a year away.[68] This placed him in an awkward position. He did not wish to act without instructions from the Colonial Office, but there was considerable pressure for government reform and at least *some* steps towards representative institutions. Unaware that the British parliament had just passed a Suspending Act for the constitution, Grey formally defined provincial boundaries via proclamation on 10 March 1848 – less than a month before news of the suspension finally reached New Zealand.[69] The northern province, New Ulster, consisted of the North Island north of a line drawn eastwards from the mouth of the Patea River. It governed those Pākehā in the Bay of Islands, Auckland, New Plymouth and other small coastal footholds, and made a nominal claim of governing vast swathes of Māori territory. New Munster no longer referred exclusively to the South Island but also encompassed Stewart Island and the lower portion of the North Island. Like New Ulster, the claim to administer territory beyond Pākehā settlement was largely nominal. To complicate matters further, in late 1846 Earl Grey commissioned Edward John Eyre to be lieutenant-governor of New Zealand – the head of authority in whichever province was not home to the governor. As an adventurer in South Australia Eyre had made a favourable acquaintance with George Grey when the latter was governor there, but the two were poor colleagues in New Zealand and Eyre was swiftly relegated to the status of lame duck.[70]

The partial but miserably insufficient realisation of provincial institutions re-energised the campaign for representative government after the disappointment of the constitution. Agitation did not emerge overnight. After the furore of mid-1847 the new system was in fact ushered in quietly until the Suspending Act arrived in early 1848. It developed by increments – the concept of new provinces as indicated by the constitution, the commissioning of Eyre, his arrival in Wellington and Grey's proclamation of provincial boundaries that resurrected Hobson's nomenclature. News of suspension arrived via the *John Wickliffe*, the ship carrying the first Scottish colonists to the new southern settlement of Otago, and filtered up the country. The documents carried by the *John Wickliffe* were not the Suspending Act itself, but preliminary despatches to the same effect from Earl Grey to Governor Grey.[71] Suspension was valid for five years, during which time a new constitution would be

The proto-provincial system of New Ulster and New Munster as proclaimed under the 1846 Constitution Act, with main Pākehā settlements of the time. Although Stewart Island was part of New Munster Province, it was not placed in any province when the new system was proclaimed in 1853 (the Chatham Islands also technically fell within New Munster, although no administration was provided and they were never subsequently allocated a province). The names of the provinces originated in 1841 when they were used as geographical nomenclature and had a different scope to their provincial application from 1846. New Ulster in 1841 referred to the whole North Island, New Munster to the South, and New Leinster to Stewart Island.

framed for endorsement by the British parliament. In the meanwhile New Zealand would remain a Crown colony under the authority of the governor. This news brought optimism to southern settlers, especially as Earl Grey intimated that in this period the governor could introduce a limited and direct form of representative government, at least in New Munster. Both sides of southern politics celebrated the replacement of the constitution's 'cumbrous and complex machinery'.[72] The *Spectator*, keen not to appear inconsistent, emphasised that 'those who were desirous of seeing [the constitution] in operation were influenced less from the admiration of the proposed plan than by the important and valuable principle of representative institutions'.[73] Now, they hoped, constitutional matters would settle. The *Examiner's* lament that 'every despatch from Downing-street … brings us some change' would have struck a chord.[74] All the settlers asked for now were, in the *Independent's* words, 'favourable deeds' from Grey: the establishment of a representative assembly in New Munster as a 'stepping-stone' to a new constitution.[75] This mood of self-congratulation did not last, bogged in the mire of four years of wrangling.

When the news reached Auckland, the mood was far more divisive. Suspension 'absorbed the public mind, and cast all questions of a mere local nature into the shade'.[76] Predictably the *New Zealander* rejoiced that Grey's advice had been accepted, but the *Southern Cross* unleashed stinging invective against 'being deprived for five long years of our birth-right – Representative Government'.[77] It conceded that specific details warranted suspension, but subjection to irresponsible rule rankled and Grey was not forgiven for his 'studied effort to lower the relative character of the Northern Settlers in the estimation of the Home Government' in his despatches emphasising the particular instability of New Ulster.[78] A battle quickly erupted between the political communities represented by the two papers. The *New Zealander* celebrated the constitution's demise and backed a movement to thank George Grey for saving New Zealand from Earl Grey's 'monster'.[79] The *Southern Cross* shot back with denunciatory and at times juvenile editorials.[80] Auckland politics were now clearly polarised and communicated via editorial slinging matches; once unified by fears of conflict with Māori, Aucklanders were divided over particulars.

Yet they had more in common than their hyperbole suggested. Both sides wanted a more representative, simpler constitution, and local spirit was pronounced. Suspension was seen not only as an ideological political divide, but also as a geographical one; not only of officials versus opposition but also north versus south. The perception of Grey as favouring the southern settlers furthered regional rivalry that made provincialism appear desirable in 1852. Ironically, this geographical–historical divide obscured the convergence of settler goals: the unwillingness of each region to be subjected to distant rule – whether from London or a New Zealand capital – brought their constitutional objectives *together*. The provincial vision was becoming clearer.

Chapter 2
A Constitution for New Zealand

Five years. Policymakers in London, officials in New Zealand and settlers themselves had a window of opportunity within which to shape a constitution that fulfilled their goals. New Zealand was expanding rapidly. The founding of Otago in 1848 and Canterbury in 1850 added to the problem of geographically dispersed settlements, and the Pākehā population more than doubled from 13,274 in 1846 to 26,707 in 1851. The constitution was shaped by competition and hostility between northern and southern settlers, distance between settlements, the belief that each settlement possessed unique characteristics that demanded the devolution of government, and George Grey's perception of these issues. Grey became chief author of the constitution, with the Colonial Office accepting most of his proposals. He ostensibly based his work on Earl Grey's original document but departed considerably from it, and the New Zealand Company also enjoyed influence through the presence of Edward Gibbon Wakefield, William Fox and Henry Sewell in England.[1] It was no mere edit of 1846, and George Grey's ideas and Fox's federalism ensured provincialism's prominence.

Significantly at this juncture the provinces became institutions solely for Pākehā. George Grey originally sought to include Māori within the franchise, but because of public objections he confined electorates to those districts with a substantial Pākehā population, wherein Māori had to meet the same requirements to enrol.[2] This effectively disfranchised Māori, since few could read and write English or owned sufficient land under individual title. Grey was influenced by his attorney-general, William Swainson. In old age, Grey gave to a sycophantic scribe a fanciful account of composing the constitution in solitude on the slopes of Mount Ruapehu.[3] However, two decades before, during the debate over provincial abolition, he conceded that Swainson was his 'chief assistant … [who] drafted its most important clauses'.[4] Swainson's religious beliefs predisposed him to a humanitarian view of 'protecting' Māori, and his views were aired publicly on 17 November 1848. He believed that disfranchisement would *benefit* Māori in a manner that maintained, in his mind, a

George Grey, the dashing
young governor.

7-A3952, Sir George Grey Special
Collections, Auckland Libraries

noble purity. Māori not only had 'no desire' for the vote; it would do 'nothing for their real benefit and improvement' while thrusting upon them responsibilities that 'subject[ed] them to all the evils of bribery, drunkenness, perjury, and corruption'.[5] Furthermore, enfranchising Māori would create the reverse of the 1846 constitution's problem – they would allegedly enjoy unfair dominion over Pākehā. Māori were therefore excluded from the system, and as protection from exploitation Pākehā political power was restricted to passing laws for Pākehā. Provincialism became a Pākehā entity, beyond which Māori communities would ostensibly continue to exist without Pākehā interference or restriction. Māori, once invoked as key barriers to an unwanted constitution, now mostly disappeared from debate.

The constitution focused on Pākehā concerns, and most formative for provincialism was the simple reality of New Zealand's geography rather than any ideological commitment to a three-tiered system of government. Despite advances in the individual settlements, there was no worthwhile improvement in regional communication during the 1840s, and the proliferation of settlement compounded the problem. Local officials foresaw administrative difficulties but were unable to affect colonisation plans: experienced surveyor Felton Mathew condemned the 'numerous evils' of siting Otago so far from Auckland.[6] Each settlement was a world unto itself, self-reliant in most important aspects and lacking regular, efficient ties to any other. Communication, whether by land or sea, was laughably slow. As the

Nelson Examiner noted, there was 'little chance of the capital of New Zealand sinking in the esteem of the Southern settlements from any excess of intimacy' – Nelson went without contact from Auckland for over three months in 1848.[7] There were difficulties even over short distances: the voyage between Nelson and Wellington took 36 hours in ideal conditions, but prominent settler (and soon-to-be premier) William Fox endured a six-day voyage in May 1850.[8] This was a bother for central government and infuriating for far-flung colonists awaiting action or legislation. A letter to the earth's core could scarcely have had a more arduous journey.

A provincial system seemed the only option, and expansion of settlement meant more than two provinces were needed. Grey made a token effort to appease the most pressing demands by calling together, in Wellington in December 1848, a Legislative Council for New Munster. Yet his decision to nominate the council rather than hold elections impressed nobody and during its drawn-out session of 1849 the council largely dealt with minutiae.[9] The settlers' real goal was a new constitution with elected representatives. They at least got some idea of what this constitution might contain when Grey opened the Legislative Council. For the first time publicly, he outlined numerous constitutional proposals and explained the logic and ideas guiding his thought.[10] Most of these measures were accepted by the Colonial Office and represented in the 1852 constitution. The topic of provincialism was not explored in depth, but Grey indicated that he 'believed New Zealand would be divided into four Provinces, he knew it would be divided into three'.[11] Furthermore, because of the distances between the settlements, Grey felt that 'large powers should, in the first instance, be given to the separate [provincial] Councils'.[12]

He had, however, been typically cagey; he expressed his views more lucidly in private. In a despatch to Earl Grey, he outlined the rationale behind a provincial system in greater detail. Provinces – and their possession of large powers – were necessary because of 'their distance from the chief seat of Government, and the great difficulties at present experienced in communicating with the different portions of such extensive Islands'.[13] Granting the provinces excessive power could, however, result in the 'great misfortune' of New Zealand being 'split up into so many Sovereign States'. The central government would therefore be granted permission to increase the subjects on which New Zealand-wide laws were to be made. This, the governor forecast, would occur as 'the means of communication are made more perfect' and the provincial councils would take on the form of district councils with somewhat greater legislative powers.[14] This was a surprising measure of centralism for a man whose entry into elected politics in 1875 was predicated on defending

Dunedin and its harbour as viewed from Stafford Street in 1849, not long after the foundation of the Otago settlement. Charles Henry Kettle, C-010-001-a, Alexander Turnbull Library, Wellington

provincialism, but as his most eminent biographer notes, Grey's incorporation of new ideas and suggestions over the next three years strengthened his provincial tendencies.[15] Similarly, the establishment of Otago and Canterbury influenced his emphasis on provincialism, as seen in proposals he made to Earl Grey in 1851.[16] Nonetheless, Grey's foresight that improved communication would reduce or negate the need for provinces meant the system was founded on a weak basis as a temporary expedient. The means for provincialism's long-term survival were not provided, even though at their birth they were to be local centres of political association.

Settlers themselves were divided on the necessity of a provincial system. The new settlers in Otago viewed provincialism as essential; they did not see it as a temporary answer that would fade away. Frustrated with what they saw as George Grey's half-measures and unfulfilled promises, they petitioned the British parliament for redress in December 1851. They lamented the 'uncertainty of maritime communication' between Otago and the New Munster government in Wellington and the inefficient administration this spawned.[17] The subdivision of New Munster into multiple provinces was necessary. The Otago Association, which organised emigration from Scotland to Otago, feared the region's small population would be included in a larger province and suffer more distant administration. John McGlashan, the association's secretary, appealed personally to the Colonial Office, arguing that Otago should be a separate province because of its remoteness.[18] Otago's provincial advocates did not imply that this should be a temporary measure; it was a permanent solution, allowing them to manage their own affairs. After all, the resolute, strong-willed leader of the settlement, William Cargill, had been advocating local autonomy since 1846, before Dunedin was even founded.[19]

The Cook Strait settlements were more conflicted. Their brief dalliance with provincialism through New Munster's nominated Legislative Council was not encouraging. The champions of representative institutions, the *Nelson Examiner* and *Wellington Independent*, were ceaseless in their mockery. The *Examiner* initially hoped the council would be crushed but came to sarcastically enjoy it possessing 'a little rope' as even supporters forsook it.[20] Otago was also appalled; to one early settler the nominee system seemed devised 'to tone down – as it appeared to our exasperated minds – the severe and naked reality of a pure despotism, lodged in the single person of His Excellency the Governor-in-Chief'.[21] Even the *Spectator*, once the council's champion, fell conspicuously quiet.[22] The whole New Munster experiment was a disappointment. Grey kept a resentful Eyre on a very short leash, limiting the province's autonomy by limiting his funds. Eyre struggled to restrain the independent spirit of some nominees and he and Grey were incapable of working together harmoniously.[23]

Thus a prominent anti-provincial strain arose, especially in Nelson, where provincialism was seen as unnecessary, especially as its residents were not only campaigning for the capital to be moved to Cook Strait, but expected it to happen. Not long after the New Munster council sitting ended, the *Examiner* denounced provincialism as 'one of the greatest robberies ever practised on a people'.[24] Resuscitating anti-constitution arguments of 1847, it stated that provincialism was wholly inappropriate to New Zealand because of the extravagance and expense for a small population. This view maintained support. On 27 December 1850 one of the largest public meetings in Nelson's history passed 10 resolutions, the eighth of which urged centralism and intimated a rejection of provincialism. A resolution asserting that the only legitimate reason for sub-dividing New Zealand was to contain racial unrest in New Ulster passed unanimously without debate.[25] Local municipalities, not provinces, were sufficient to cater to local wants. A counter-petition with 175 signatories contested some of the meeting's resolutions, but agreed completely regarding provincialism and felt municipalities were sufficient for local affairs.

This pamphlet, printed by opponents of Fox who wished to maintain strong imperial connections, is one of the best examples of political satire of the period.

Eph-D-POLITICS-Wellington-1851-01, Alexander Turnbull Library, Wellington

Provinces were 'cumbrous, expensive, and ostentatious' and would either include districts of dissimilar interests or require a ruinously expensive multiplication of provincial organs.[26]

Although Wellington was more likely to become the colonial capital than Nelson, opinion there was more divided. A number of large public meetings endorsed a series of resolutions that were vocal on responsible government but silent on provincialism. They seemed to regard a central executive and legislature as the sole government needed above the municipal level.[27] This, however, was not a universal attitude. William Fox, elected by these meetings as Wellington's political agent in England, vociferously demanded provincialism. Fox, who arrived in Wellington in 1842, was prevented from practising his calling as a lawyer after a dispute with officialdom but became the New Zealand Company's principal agent in the colony. When the company was wound up in 1850 Fox was happy to return to England and push his constitutional views on behalf of Wellington. He viewed New Zealand's main settlements as 'six several colonies' in their 'distinct character' as well as their geographical separation. Localism demanded administrative devolution. To 'ensure effective government, they should be politically as independent of each other', not in the sense of being divided into six *actual* colonies, but as provinces bestowed with as many powers as possible, bound together in federation.[28] On this matter, the views of Fox, an ardent opponent of Grey, were harmonious with the pro-government *Spectator*, which as early as 1849 urged provinces as 'consonant to the wishes of the settlers'.[29] Those settlers in Wellington and Nelson who *did* view provincialism as unnecessary could assess the issue from a position of relative luxury. Their belief that the capital would inevitably soon move southwards nullified the tyranny of distance. Provincialism, in this sense, was a question of proximity to power.

A new constitution finally went before the British parliament in mid-1852. Unlike the negative reception given to the 1846 constitution, this one was keenly anticipated throughout New Zealand. Fragments of news arrived throughout September and October 1852, conveying drafts and parliamentary debates. In late October, the Constitution Act, passed on 30 June, arrived in the colony and spread to all the settlements during November. With each new morsel of information, no matter how shaky, newspapers became rife with speculation and opinion. In Wellington the *Spectator* proclaimed that the constitution, in draft form, reflected the will of the colonists, while the *Independent* saw fit to reluctantly accept it: 'we have no objection to accept the Bill *under protest*, and to try to turn it to the best account we can'.[30] John Robert Godley, esteemed as the founder of Canterbury, distrusted the wide franchise but commended the constitution to fellow Cantabrians as an instrument for achieving the settlement's ideals.[31] Aucklanders were far more captivated by the discovery of gold on the Coromandel Peninsula, but nonetheless waited anxiously for the final text.[32] New Plymouth, the smallest and most marginal of the original six settlements, finally acquired its own newspaper, the *Taranaki Herald*, in 1852. It quibbled, like the *Independent*, with small details, describing the draft constitution as 'excellent on first sight', but 'defective on examination'.[33]

The people of Otago, less worried with particulars and more interested in the sheer achievement of representative institutions, made the other colonists look lethargic. On 5 November 1852 news of the successful passage of the constitution through the British parliament reached Dunedin. James Barr recalled that 'every dweller in Dunedin, on receipt of this glorious news, exhibited all the signs of the most exuberant and unrestrainable joy; that every exultant male colonist, literally or figuratively, flung his hat into the air, and rushed off to wring the hand of everybody he met, and to join in every form of demonstration that the resources and enthusiasm of the moment could devise'.[34] The next day, the *Otago Witness* proclaimed the 'important intelligence' with an uncharacteristically excitable fully capitalised header in boldface type.[35] A subsequent edition recounted the festivities:

> *A crier was sent through the Town ... the large bell presented to the First Church of Otago was set a-ringing, and the colours were hoisted on the flag-staff ... [a] bonfire on the hill reflected upon the water, shedding a lurid glare over the whole town, and had a very striking effect. The report of small arms was incessant ... an impromptu fire balloon was sent up ... a salute was fired in honour of the occasion ... fun and frolic was universal; the greatest good humour prevailed the whole evening; there was not a quarrel nor an angry word; – all seemed determined to do their utmost to welcome the tidings of the glorious Constitution.[36]*

Apart from gold discoveries, which dominated New Ulster's papers much more than New Munster's, the constitution was the talking point of 1852. The *Lyttelton Times*, Canterbury's first newspaper and one of New Zealand's most erudite early publications, admirably captured the overall response: 'We believe the satisfaction expressed at the measure, has been general throughout the colony: that the faults in the new law which mar its integrity should escape our notice, was not to be expected ... [but the colonists] have been far more inclined to dwell with satisfaction upon the large measure of real self-Government which it bestows ...'[37]

After much struggle for representative institutions, many colonists, especially newspaper editors, had formed ideas of precisely what provisions the constitution should, and should not, contain. Complaints were registered on petty issues of fleeting importance, but they should not be taken as signs of hostility: they did not strike at the constitution's heart, as in 1846. The particulars were debatable but the general theme of the constitution was roundly accepted. As far as provincialism went, there was no dissent, not even in Nelson.

George Grey formally received the Constitution Act and royal instructions on or about 25 December 1852 while in Wellington. Unlike in 1847, he did not write a panicked response to the Colonial Office; Māori–Pākehā relations were less fraught than in the 1840s and the new constitution was within the colony's means. He proclaimed the constitution on 17 January 1853, effective immediately. In his despatch to Sir John Pakington, the new colonial secretary since February 1852, Grey praised 'so important a measure' as 'admirably adapted to [New Zealand's] present state and future wants'.[38] Well he might, since it reflected his authorship, even if the small number of changes made in London were a source of personal irritation.

As the constitution stipulated, Grey proclaimed the division of New Zealand into six provinces, the 'six colonies' of William Fox, three in each island.[39] 'New Munster' and 'New Ulster' disappeared into the ether of historical trivia, replaced by Auckland, Taranaki and Wellington in the North Island and Nelson, Canterbury and Otago in the south. Even before proclamation of the constitution reached the ever-enthusiastic citizens of Dunedin, representatives of the Otago Settlers' Association canvassed the city and its suburbs to ascertain the mood of electors and acquire preliminary nominations for representatives.[40]

The constitution established a bicameral parliament, with an elective House of Representatives and, contrary to Grey's more democratic draft, a Legislative Council nominated by the governor.[41] After the establishment of responsible government in 1856, it became convention that the governor accept the nominees of the ministry, although there was no formal requirement to do so. The provincial councils were unicameral, with a separately elected superintendent. Electorates at both central and provincial level were a mixture of single and multi-member constituencies. Electors could vote in all central and provincial electorates for which they satisfied modest property requirements, while superintendents were elected by the province at large on the principle of one man, one vote. Superintendents resembled a modern American president or state governor, in that they were popularly elected, did not sit in the popular assembly and had the power to assent to provincial legislation; many immodestly saw themselves as lieutenants to the colonial governor in Auckland. They also, however, shared similarities with colonial premiers: they went out of office with the dissolution of their council, generally had to choose their executive from council members and could be dismissed by the governor upon receipt of a petition signed by a majority of councillors. Superintendents were not granted executive authority constitutionally but empowering ordinances were passed to allow for such daily administration. They were the heads of provincial government, even if some executive councils – again created by provincial ordinances rather than by constitutional design – increasingly asserted provincial responsible government, seeking to make the executive responsible to the legislature. Settlers wished to maintain British parliamentary traditions, and provincial councils were often seen

John Pakington, colonial
secretary from February to
December 1852. Earl Grey
occupied the position for the
preceding six years; Pakington
was the first of 10 men to rotate
through it over the next eight.

Herbert Watkins, Ax7914, National Portrait
Gallery, London

as local miniatures of the House of Commons. It was hard, though, to apply this precedent when superintendents sat outside council, and Otago in particular had lengthy disputes over the superintendent's degree of responsibility to the council.[42]

The provinces were not autonomous entities within a federation; only the central government enjoyed sovereignty and provincial powers were somewhat limited. The degree of provincial self-government lagged behind Canada and that which five of the six Australian colonies soon enjoyed, and the provinces lacked the constitutional status those in Canada possessed under the confederation of 1867. The central parliament was empowered to 'make laws for the peace, order, and good government of New Zealand, provided that no such laws be repugnant to the law of England'.[43] Pakington, in his instructions to Grey, explained that Britain aimed to provide 'powers as extensive as it was possible to confer, consistently with the maintenance of the prerogatives of the Crown'.[44] The New Zealand parliament could legislate on any matter, including those for which provinces had already legislated. Thirteen topics, from the regulation of weights and measures to the postal service, marriage and laws specifically designed to disadvantage Māori relative to Pākehā, were excluded from provincial jurisdiction. In all other matters central legislation trumped provincial in the case of any conflict.

Apart from these exclusions, the constitution nowhere enunciated separate roles or expectations for the two levels of government. Pakington's instructions further confused the matter. He first described the provincial councils' functions as 'comparatively unimportant … [and] limited to local objects'. Unlike his predecessor, Pakington favoured municipalities rather than a federal structure and hoped the provinces would decline gradually to a municipal status.[45] He later suggested, however, that with a full machinery of provincial councils, the central parliament need not meet often and no constitutional requirements were necessary to fix the time or duration of parliamentary sessions. Were the provinces glorified municipalities whose function was to handle local matters inappropriate for a national forum? Or were they powerful bodies responsible for most aspects of government, overseen by a lean central government that met rarely and only handled issues where national consistency was desirable? The failure to clarify this issue stimulated the next 23 years of provincialists and centralists fighting to assert the force of their interpretation and interests.

Particularly significant to the function and authority of the provinces were the limits placed upon their finances. A key question underlying early colonisation was who would pay for New Zealand's economic progress. In the 1840s it was clear that neither Māori nor settlers were willing or able, and that the colony's success depended on being underwritten by the British taxpayer for some years.[46] However, once New Zealand was granted representative and then responsible government, it was expected to take on an increasingly greater share of the burden. This created a new question: What financial powers would be granted to each level of government? The 13 exclusions on provincial jurisdiction included a prohibition on provinces raising customs duties. Moreover, the revenue from sales of Crown lands went to the central government. (The provinces immediately fought for and received their land fund in the compact of 1856.) Provinces had some lucrative sources of income such as auctioneers and publicans' licences, but the only funds provided constitutionally were through clause 66. This allowed surplus central government revenue to be distributed to the provinces in proportion to their contributions to that revenue.

This left the provinces rather dependent on the central government. Soon they were provided with half of customs and land revenue (initially two-thirds of customs), originally by financial circular of George Grey in August 1853 as parliament was yet to meet, and then modified by the General Assembly in another circular of October 1854.[47] Central revenue came primarily from three sources: customs duties, land sales and any fees or charges mandated by legislation. This never included direct taxation during the provincial era, although there was no prohibition against either central or provincial governments raising tax. Settlers felt direct taxation was an evil they had left in England, which meant even many local bodies created in the 1860s raised funds through fees and tolls rather than rates.[48] In a lightly populated, widely dispersed colony, collecting direct taxes could cost as much as they raised and, especially in Māori areas not truly under Pākehā authority, they relied on a level of state coercion that did not exist. This was illustrated by Governor FitzRoy's abortive reforms of 1844 that attempted to introduce an income tax enforced by little more than idealistic faith in settler honesty.[49] Direct taxation was not introduced until after provincial abolition. A land tax was enacted in 1878, a deeply unpopular property tax followed in 1879 and a progressive income tax was an early initiative of the first Liberal government in 1891.[50] The political climate of the provincial era meant that direct taxation was rarely entertained as a serious option for provincial governments.

New Zealand's pattern of settlement in the late 1840s and political preferences of settlers in the early 1850s shaped provincialism. Provincial divisions appeared logical, but because New Zealand had not been fully settled by Pākehā they were inevitably unstable, framed to respond to problems of the late 1840s, especially with communication. Nobody sought to create a permanent intermediate tier of government that would provide good regional administration in a more unified New Zealand. Rather, the provinces were created in such a short-sighted manner that they did not take into account potential new settlements beyond the six major 'colonies' already established – new settlements that, within five years of the constitution's introduction, would become restless. Nonetheless, this did not condemn the provinces to extinction, only to protracted demands for reform or a slow process of devolution to glorified municipal councils. The condemnation to extinction would have to come from the provinces themselves.

Chapter 3
The Dawn of Provincialism

When the first central and provincial elections were held between July and December 1853, the provincial ballots aroused acute passions throughout the country – especially in Auckland, where the most virulent contests occurred – while the central ballot sometimes received a lukewarm, even indifferent response. New Zealand lays claim to a proud national electoral history that emphasises the early inclusion of women and Māori in political life, but when the 1853 election was held, almost all electors were Pākehā males and the provincial councils met before the national General Assembly. A few Māori men, mainly in Auckland, also qualified to vote, but most Māori were excluded as they held their land under common rather than individual title and therefore failed the property qualification.[1]

The provinces made good use of their primacy and stamped their authority on the political map. This was sustained in the 1850s because, for most settlers, they were the political institution closest to home, representing accessible, accountable government. In 1853, too, settlement had not yet dispersed far beyond the provincial capitals and their immediate areas: hinterland dissatisfaction with the provincial capitals developed only as settlement spread. This became a major bone of contention in the General Assembly between those who promoted central authority, and the defenders of provincial power. The 1850s, free from warfare and violent controversy, were calm compared with the previous decade and the next, and this breathing space allowed centralists and provincialists to tussle for supremacy, both individually and institutionally. So were the 1850s a heyday for the provinces, or was this a house divided against itself? Did central government manoeuvring undermine the provinces swiftly and fatally, or did provincialists unwittingly set a course for outright abolition?

The peculiarities of New Zealand's Pākehā political structure in the 1850s have been poorly studied. David Gordon Herron produced scholarship of remarkable depth and insight in the 1950s, but he published little of it before his early death on the slopes of Mont Blanc in 1960 robbed New Zealand of one of its most promising

One of Wellington's 'Three
Fs': Isaac Featherston. He
superintended Wellington from
1853 to 1871, making him the
longest-serving superintendent
of any province.

97-193/638, Wairarapa Archive

historians. His work was complemented by more narrowly focused research into Auckland's politics, but none of this has made much of a dent on broader perceptions of the period.[2] In the public consciousness, the 1850s often appear as a blank between the conflicts of the 1840s and 1860s, but they were a crucial and vibrant period in the history of provincialism.

One of Herron's observations must be borne in mind when studying the 1850s: 'centralist' and 'provincialist' were not binary distinctions. Many politicians were provincialist or centralist depending upon whether they held provincial or central offices and how successful their loose party groupings were in provincial elections. Wellington's 'Three Fs' provide a good example – Isaac Featherston, a popular community leader and doctor who was founding editor of the *Wellington Independent*; William Fitzherbert, a merchant who turned to pastoralism; and William Fox. They were unfailing ultra-provincialists, and Herron suggests, plausibly, that this was attributable to their consistent hold on Wellington's provincial power relative to their poor success nationally.[3] Yet even centralists in the 1850s did not question the survival of the provincial system – the debate concerned provincial freedoms versus central control. For instance, one of the leading centralists of the 1856 session of the General Assembly, Henry Sewell, told the House that he could not consent to reducing the provinces to the level of municipalities as 'rightly used, and under proper checks, the large powers of the Provincial Governments may be turned to valuable account'.[4] When centralism later morphed into abolitionism, some centralists of the 1850s opposed abolition.

There were no consistent party labels during the 1850s. The division of the Crown colony era between 'officialdom' and 'liberalism' broke down when the constitution was proclaimed. The lack of any formal party organisations prohibited the ready application of British political terminology to New Zealand's politicians – 'Tories' were not self-identified, but described thus by more progressive politicians. Even 'centralism' and 'provincialism' were defined and applied inconsistently; Wellington in particular perceived any control from Auckland as 'centralism'. Nor were the labels always accepted: the *Lyttelton Times* thought centralism 'repugnant to all the political instincts of Englishmen' and provincialism 'repugnant to their educated sympathies'.[5] Both terms were often used derisively, and were applied to individuals by their opponents.

Nonetheless the terminology stuck, though it was an imperfect ideological indicator. There were no party programmes, politicians were drawn almost entirely from the same upper echelon of the social and economic classes, and political differences accordingly tended to revolve around details rather than principles.[6] This is not to suggest the legislatures were harmonious. Quite the opposite was true, and Jim McAloon has shown that there was no oligarchy or unity of views among wealthy politicians.[7] Ultra-provincialists sometimes disagreed fervently on issues unrelated to provincial power. George Grey's successor as governor, Thomas Gore Browne, once pointed out that 'conflicting interests may at any moment convert an overwhelming majority into an insignificant minority', citing the specific example that 'the southern provinces would probably unite in objecting to Auckland as the seat of Government, but would differ among themselves as to which of their own provinces should obtain the preference'.[8] This was a time of confusion, when New Zealand was forming its political identities.

Voters proved to be more committed to and passionate about their own province than national government. This was evident from the moment elections took place, even though it was unknown whether provincial councils would meet before or after the first session of the General Assembly. Elections, especially the early ones, were somewhat of a luxury in provincial-era New Zealand. The trials of colonial life demanded much of settlers, many of whom had neither the time nor the inclination for politics. This was especially true of those outside townships: they had little contact with or information on candidates, they had to travel hours or even overnight to register or vote, and demanding daily work often excluded more than a passive interest in politics. Elections were often held on weekdays, a significant impediment to working-class voters. Because there was no requirement for electorates to go to the polls simultaneously, elections could drag over weeks and months. To satisfy a constitutional requirement, writs for the first elections were issued by 17 July 1853, but the various provincial and central polls sprawled from July to December.

Colonial politics were colourful and vibrant at all levels, and campaigns were vociferous. In December 1852 John Robert Godley forecast that many would 'be disgusted by the turmoil and agitation and strife inseparable from the working of a popular constitution'. Some conservative settlers certainly were disgusted, but many embraced the franchise enthusiastically in the spirit of Godley's exhortation that 'we were never meant to enjoy quiet lives … man [is intended] to work, to struggle, and to strive'.[9] Not all electioneering was honourable. The secret ballot was not introduced until the 1871 election (and not until the 1938 election in Māori seats). Votes had to be declared orally, which made bribery and intimidation easier. Many elections were marred by 'treating': alcohol-fuelled entertainment for, or bribery of, voters at public houses, funded by candidates or their supporters. Nelson's 1853 superintendency poll produced, according to one moralist, 'scenes more revolting to humanity, and more derogatory to this settlement, than the oldest settlers had before witnessed'.[10] This habit was imported from England along with others both positive and negative; elections essentially reflected English traditions, with some colonial modifications.[11]

The absence of any legal enrolment requirement meant that only sufficiently interested individuals enrolled and voted. Men aged 21 and over could enrol if they met property qualifications: freehold of £50, leasehold of £10 per annum, or a householder with an annual rent of £10 in towns or £5 in rural areas. Householders could register only for the electorate in which they lived, but freeholders and leaseholders could register for any electorate in which they held land. Political enthusiasm in the 1850s meant enrolment was high, with 70–80 per cent of the adult male population ostensibly enrolled, but lax oversight meant many rolls were grossly inflated. In Auckland, an absurd 120 per cent of adult males were registered, while in Canterbury, where scrutiny was more rigorous, the figure was only 50 per cent.[12] Neill Atkinson notes that it is hard to ascertain how many were eligible to enrol – the franchise, although generous, excluded sizeable groups such as itinerant workers and new arrivals, who did not possess property or had not owned it for the six months required by law. He estimates that about a quarter of adult males were not eligible and that a third of eligible males did not avail themselves of the right to enrol.[13] Any study of political attitudes therefore largely excludes those who, through lack of access or interest, did not participate in elections. What can be determined, however, is that those who participated in the political process saw their provincial councils as more immediate, accessible, contestable and significant than the General Assembly. Elections were determined on a first-past-the-post basis, with electors in multi-member constituencies possessing as many votes as there were vacancies. Superintendency elections were most popular, followed by provincial councils, then the assembly last.[14]

The most significant election results for provincialism were in Nelson. Provincialism may have achieved even greater popularity in other settlements, but Nelson was least favourably disposed to it before 1853, so the settlement's enthusiasm is important. New Zealand liberalism blossomed in Nelson, yet the 1853 election has been poorly studied beyond Jim McAloon's short but lucid analysis.[15] One of his predecessors, Lowther Broad, puzzled over the 'very little interest' taken in central elections, 'surprisingly little – considering the past agitation for representative institutions', compared with the vigorous political advocacy provoked by the provincial elections, especially for the superintendency.[16] Because the capital had not been moved to Cook Strait as anticipated, Nelson sought a powerful provincial government to fill the void, and provincialism was leaner and cheaper than anticipated. For months the *Examiner* was filled with political editorials, letters and electioneering championing or denouncing the three candidates: Francis Jollie, a moderate, and Edward Stafford and John Waring Saxton, both liberals. Stafford, a spirited man born into the Anglo-Irish gentry who became a runholder after migrating to New Zealand, dithered about whether to stand for superintendent or the General Assembly and caused the liberal split.[17]

Nelson's liberals experienced no small measure of disquiet before the elections, but Jollie was ultimately trounced. Stafford emerged victorious with 251 votes to Saxton's 206 and Jollie's 130 and went on to an auspicious political career. In the provincial capital, the seven-way battle for five council seats was also a 'very severe contest' conducted with 'great briskness'.[18] By contrast, its two General Assembly seats were uncontested as only two candidates stood. A similar pattern emerged in rural seats, especially Waimea. It cast 350 votes for the superintendency but less than half that number turned out for the General Assembly, even though the former proceeded routinely while confusion surrounding who was nominated for the General Assembly and who had withdrawn from contention led to a great scramble for votes on the day.[19] Despite its previous objections to provincialism, Nelson used the ballot box to express greater interest in provincial over central government.

Auckland Province had the most hotly contested provincial elections. At face value, this is surprising: since Auckland was the seat of national government, the General Assembly was not distant and inaccessible. The 1853 superintendency election, however, was an opportunity to settle numerous long-simmering political scores. The struggle between the Crown colony officials of the Constitutional Association and the liberals and radicals who were loosely grouped under the title of the Progress Party made Auckland 'the most highly-politicized community in the colony'.[20] The Progress candidate was William Brown, the founder of the *Southern Cross*; his opponent was none other than Grey's protégé Lieutenant-Colonel Robert Wynyard. The commander of the colony's armed forces, Wynyard acted as administrator of the central government for the 18 months between Grey's departure and the arrival of a new governor.

The stage could hardly have been better set for political strife. Auckland swiftly descended into a contest best described as vituperative, deceitful and corrupt. Some of the language in the *Southern Cross* expressed the inflamed passions. Wynyard's electoral committee allegedly displayed 'an extreme deficiency of judgement … they know little or nothing [of electioneering] … and have consequently heaped blunder upon blunder'.[21] Wynyard's candidacy itself, in light of his official status, was 'the greatest impropriety'.[22] Similar invective against Brown flowed from the pens of Wynyard's supporters, encouraged by the proprietors of the *New Zealander*. In the end, Wynyard was successful solely because of the vote of military veterans in the Pensioner Settlements electorate in South Auckland. Progress Party stalwarts cried corruption to no avail.[23] Having devoted their energies to winning the superintendency, the Brownites were destroyed in elections for the provincial council, suggesting they were not the experts on electioneering that they claimed to be. The battle, however, was not over as Auckland members of the General Assembly continued the bitter local squabble in national parliament for years.[24] Even at the level of the national vote, Auckland's provincial politics reigned supreme, dictating policies, candidates and attitudes.

Provincialism dawned with greater decorum in the rest of the North Island. Apart from a brief disturbance on the day of nominations, Taranaki's three-way contest for the superintendency was peaceful and the *Herald* issued a warm congratulation for 'the creditable nature in which the whole affair was conducted – creditable alike to the Province, the Candidates, and the Electors'.[25] In this small settlement of 1905 settlers, all but 30 of the 383 electors turned out to vote. The victor, a respected young settler by the name of Charles Brown, was 'drawn in triumph through the town by a troop of enthusiastic young men'.[26]

In Wellington there was no contest for the superintendency. Isaac Featherston's considerable stature as a community leader meant he faced no opposition. Some of his allies in the fight for representative institutions questioned his candidacy, believing that Grey had bought him by granting wide powers to superintendents.[27] It was little wonder, however, that Featherston was quite taken with contesting the superintendency despite persistent ill health, since he was a vehement provincialist. Henry Sewell, a prominent Canterbury settler and soon to be the the first central premier, saw him as 'bent on establishing the nearest possible approach to republican independence in the Province'.[28] At the nomination on 2 July 1853 Featherston, unchallenged, was put forth, seconded and declared elected.[29] The *Independent* provided lavish coverage of the event; the *Spectator*, formerly a critic of Featherston but acknowledging his overwhelming success, was almost mute, though the two papers quibbled over attendance at the nomination.[30] The *Independent* captured the significance of the occasion: 'the unanimity in the choice was so remarkable and so conspicuous, as we shall never again perhaps witness in any future election in New Zealand.'[31] It was not entirely correct, though – Otago had similar confidence in its sole candidate in its superintendency election of September 1853.

The superintendency came to Featherston by default, but other elections in Wellington occasioned the same heated competition seen throughout New Zealand. The recent arrival of Edward Gibbon Wakefield and his son Edward Jerningham Wakefield set the political scene alight. Featherston, notoriously hot-tempered, had little time for the Wakefields. Edward Gibbon, seeking influence, established a power base in the Hutt Valley on the basis of his land policies, which favoured the Hutt's smallholders.[32] The language of the press was not much more restrained than that in Auckland, but it was a less even contest because only the *Independent* represented a stable market. The *Spectator* was in flux, transitioning from pro-Grey roots to support of the Wakefield party.[33] Featherston-aligned candidates secured six out of the seven provincial council seats allocated to the City of Wellington in an election contested by 16 men, attracting roughly 420 voters.[34] By contrast, the two City of Wellington seats in the General Assembly were not contested after the third candidate withdrew at the last minute – despite one of the candidates having 112 vote pledges it is doubtful that the contest would have achieved the provincial election's numbers.[35] Similarly, in the Hutt Valley, at least 198 electors voted with

Edward Gibbon Wakefield in the 1850s, after his migration to New Zealand.

1/2-031744-F, Alexander Turnbull Library, Wellington

'great spirit' to elect four provincial representatives from a field of seven, but there was no contest for the two national representatives.[36] There was at least a contest for Wellington Country at both levels, and the provincial contest drew more interest.[37] One historian has suggested that after Wellington realised the capital was unlikely to be moved south in any hurry, it 'lost interest in the affairs of the colony and became ultra-provincial'.[38] This is certainly a plausible explanation for Wellington's voting pattern and general political climate; after it became the capital in 1865, Wellington's passion for provincialism waned.

Canterbury's superintendency election largely avoided the evils of treating and a bitterly hostile press. The solitary newspaper, the *Lyttelton Times*, had no rival at which to fling insults before the inaugural edition of the *Canterbury Standard* in June 1854, and conducted itself in a spirit of impartiality – a particularly commendable quality given it was then edited by James Edward FitzGerald, a candidate himself. Immediately after the demise of provincialism, one pioneer looked back fondly to Christchurch's first election: 'our elections in those days were better conducted than in the present; we had not then the pestilential element of "larrikinism" which is so rife now, and which makes many public meetings so objectionable.'[39] Even Sewell, sometimes overly critical, felt that '[e]very thing went off in good humour'.[40] Three men contested the superintendency – FitzGerald, the first Canterbury settler ashore and a gifted orator; Henry Tancred, a philosophical man whose electioneering was impaired by a speech impediment from a broken jaw; and Colonel James Campbell, a late entrant whom Sewell considered an 'old goose' who promised anything, including '[a] bit of the moon to one voter, a planet or so to another'.[41] Ultimately, 318 electors participated; FitzGerald emerged the victor with 135 votes after Campbell caused a split in Tancred's votes – Campbell secured 94, leaving the more able Tancred to finish last with 89.[42]

Unlike the provinces to its north, Canterbury did not show a clear preference for provincial elections. A handful more voters turned out for the provincial council elections than for the General Assembly, but not enough to be significant.[43] Cantabrians were consistent folk, showing little preference for one electoral body over the other and fulfilling equally their civic duty to both. By the early 1860s, however, as Herron notes, they too were seen as holding a pronounced preference for provincial elections.[44] No doubt Canterbury's flourishing provincial conditions influenced that shift.

The final province to elect a superintendent, Otago, need hardly have waited. It was clear that the small, close-knit community would elect its tenacious leader, William Cargill. He was a conservative and sometimes autocratic Scotsman of strong religious views, in whose honour Invercargill was named in what was then Otago's southernmost region. There was an opposition, fronted by Robert Williams, but they later recognised their cause was futile and abandoned it, especially after a failed attempt to include Māori, who may have favoured Williams, on the electoral roll.[45] On 6 September 1853 James Macandrew – a feisty and entrepreneurial man soon to become famous as an Otago superintendent himself – nominated Cargill, citing over 220 pledges of support. The nomination was seconded, and with no other candidates advanced, Cargill was duly elected.[46] The *Otago Witness*, with the caveat that it was Cargill's mouthpiece in the settlement after his critics at the *Otago News* had been silenced, captured the certainty of the occasion: 'It having been generally understood that there would be no contest, there were only about 80 Electors present.'[47] This was still a respectable turnout for a no-contest in a lightly populated settlement.

The only elections contested in Otago were provincial ones. It is perhaps little wonder that Otago's three General Assembly representatives – two for Town of Dunedin, one for Dunedin Country – were elected unopposed.[48] Many leading men naturally recoiled from spending months on a sailing ship plodding along the tempestuous coast, especially when they had pressing business concerns at home. Otago was far more concerned with self-reliance and developing its local political

Otago's undisputed early leader, William Cargill (1784–1860), often referred to as Captain Cargill.

John Irvine, L52, Hocken Collections, Uare Taoka o Hākena, Dunedin

sphere. In this tiny electorate – the total population of Otago was only approximately 1500 – 78 votes were cast in the five-way tussle for the Town of Dunedin's three provincial vacancies.[49] There was a more substantial turnout for Dunedin Country, with at least 154 voters participating in the nine-way contest to elect six members.[50] This included seven votes cast in Tokomairiro and a whopping two in Waikouaiti. The rest were cast in Dunedin, including some particularly committed travellers who made a day-long trek from the Taieri to cast their ballot. Cargill supporters won all positions, provincial and central.[51] It is difficult to guess at the degree of participation had there been a contest for the General Assembly. However, the fact that 14 provincial council candidates could be found in extremely small electorates while only three came forward for national representation, allied to Otago's famous independent streak and well-established desire to do things its own way, surely speaks of a preference for provincial rather than central politics.

From north to south the superintendency was usually the focal point of contests. Even in Wellington and Otago, where superintendents were elected unopposed, the matter was still taken very seriously; these candidates had no challengers not because of a lack of interest, but because of their overwhelming popularity. The General Assembly elections were not deprecated – 1853 had the best turnout of voters to a national election in the entire provincial era[52] – but provincialism generated the greatest interest. It is unfair to suggest, as Atkinson does, that settlers, otherwise preoccupied, found the 1853 elections inconsequential.[53] His claim comes from a *Spectator* editorial published before Wellington's elections, which argued '[b]eyond the efforts made by certain *liberal* candidates and their friends … [the elections] seem to be regarded generally with indifference'.[54] The more popular and widely circulated *Independent*, however, had for some time been full of election matter favouring liberal candidates regarded by the *Spectator* as 'untried men, many of whom we only know as … agitators' from constitutional battles with Grey.[55] This was simply a broadside aimed at its competitor. A month later the paper readily acknowledged that elections had stimulated a week 'of unusual excitement'.[56] Some settlers may have failed to participate for a range of reasons – lack of eligibility, commitment to eking out an existence in a new colony, unfamiliarity with electoral politics or missing the narrow window to enrol or vote – but the elections were not received with indifference and contests were animated throughout the colony.

It should come as no surprise that, to satisfy the broad preference for local rule, the provincial councils met before the General Assembly. Every council sat by the end of December 1853 but the assembly did not gather in Auckland until May 1854. For this Grey has been roundly criticised, both by contemporaries and historians. Despite his democratic writings, Grey had undeniable autocratic tendencies and did not hurry to issue writs for the elections. After issuing financial circulars in August 1853 to enable the provinces to govern in the absence of either himself or the General Assembly, he left the colony on 31 December without summoning the assembly. Contemporary critics, always eager to stick the boot into their foe, condemned his 'shuffling endeavours to withhold from New Zealand the Constitution' via 'evasion, trickery, and cajolery'.[57] William Gisborne, the eminent public servant and politician for whom the city of Gisborne is named, was scathing about Grey's decisions when he wrote his influential portraits of New Zealand's colonial rulers and statesmen.[58] Even William Pember Reeves, New Zealand's first significant historian, expressed tame bemusement at 'the rather curious course of bringing the Provincial Councils into existence, and leaving the summoning of the central Parliament to his successor'.[59]

Yet this was not a curious course at all.[60] Grey always intended that the provincial councils should meet first. This was essential for his 1851 proposal that the councils elect the Legislative Council, each choosing three members, but after Pakington took over as colonial secretary, the upper house was turned into a miniature House of Lords.[61] The imposition of a nominated upper house was not enough to alter Grey's plans. He did not delay the assembly meeting out of any devious desire to avoid facing the colonists or to retain personal power – he wanted to return to England to visit his ailing mother.[62] Allowing the provinces to meet first was not to give them an artificial stimulus, but a response to the strong provincial feeling of the period. Grey's decision actually meant the provinces were restrained by a lack of powers or uncertainty about their extent, since the General Assembly was needed to clarify the boundaries of control.[63]

It is doubtful whether the provinces gained any real advantage by meeting first. As they struggled to define their powers, the earliest sessions could only hope the General Assembly would not overrule their decisions and budgets. As the *Taranaki Herald* wrote at the close of Taranaki's first session, 'all the provinces have been left to shift for themselves … assum[ing] what were considered necessary [powers] for useful legislation … [d]oubtless in some instances the letter of the Imperial act has been over-stepped.'[64] Whether such oversteps constituted practical necessity or flagrant opportunism was in the eye of the beholder. The reality was generally on the side of necessity, though emphatic provincialists took their chances. For instance, the tenor of Wellington politics changed markedly owing to the ultra-provincialists' fervent hatred of any power emanating from Auckland, imagined or real. Once so critical of Grey and his failure to summon the General Assembly, Isaac Featherston's party was struck mute as the council sought to enlarge provincial powers – only a small band of opponents led by E.G. Wakefield opposed this course of action.[65]

The real reason the provinces met first was not ideological but practical. The settlers wanted representative government – that much was obvious – and allowing the provinces to meet first was the quickest way of satisfying this demand. Provincial councils were constitutionally required to meet at least once a year and could be summoned swiftly after their election; there was no such requirement for the central government. Although the Colonial Office was later unhappy with Grey's course of action, Pakington, in his despatch transmitting the 1852 constitution, went so far as to note that 'under the present circumstances of New Zealand, and with a complete machinery of provincial councils, it was possible … that for some time [the General Assembly's] meetings will be occasional only'.[66] Without any constitutional stipulation for the General Assembly to meet first, Grey assumed the provinces could and should still take precedence, even if their role as electors of the upper house was denied. In addition, getting the General Assembly together required greater effort and inconvenience. After Grey's departure at the end of 1853 Wynyard summoned the assembly in January 1854 then allowed over four months to pass before its first meeting, for which the Otago members spent two arduous months travelling by sea. Better to get on with local government than be delayed by geography.

The first sessions had all the thrill of a novelty. Although many provincial councillors were prominent figures of the Crown colony period, they were newcomers to parliamentary procedures.[67] James Adam, an Otago councillor, felt these initial sessions presented 'the early legislators in a most primitive and unostentatious manner. Parliamentary forms were unknown to us, and we groped our way through these things like school-boys learning their lessons.'[68] Nevertheless, they embraced their new offices with enthusiasm, and pomp and ceremony surrounded the first sessions. Canterbury's council sought to transcend the simplicity of its first premises: the meeting room was 'papered for the occasion; the seats were covered with crimson cloth … [and] the house presented a very comfortable appearance.'[69] Not everybody was impressed. One councillor criticised Nelson Superintendent Edward Stafford's first address as 'courtly and patronizing', while Attorney-General William Swainson, an ardent centralist, deprecated all superintendents for their immodesty in 'opening the Council with a speech of presidential length'.[70] Such arguments carry only so much weight, often relying on a belief, not sustained by the constitution, that the provinces were intended to be little more than English municipalities. An over-abundance of pomp neither invalidates the councils' proceedings nor makes their existence questionable. It was unsurprising that after the lengthy campaign for representation, the colony's first representative bodies began with a sense of occasion.

Significant battles lay ahead. New Zealand politics of the 1850s emphasised three major related issues – control of land and the funds from its sale, attainment of responsible government and the balance between central and provincial power. Responsible government dominated, and in 1853–54 most provincial councils took steps to illustrate their commitment to it. The first ordinance of Otago's council created an executive of no more than three members, all of whom had to be councillors.[71] Wellington also immediately created an executive drawn from the council; appointees were required to resign their seats but could seek re-election.[72] Nelson passed a similar ordinance to Wellington's; Auckland and Canterbury created executives drawn at least in part from councillors; only Taranaki held out, not creating an executive until 1856.[73] Before the General Assembly met, a public meeting in Wellington, attended by all but one of the province's central representatives, unanimously passed a resolution that 'above all', the main object of Wellington's members was to secure the 'immediate establishment of ministerial

The 'Shedifice', the simple and cramped building that housed the General Assembly 1854–65 and then the Auckland Provincial Council until 1876. It was occupied by Auckland University College from 1890 and torn down in 1918–19. 7-A11714, Sir George Grey Special Collections, Auckland Libraries

responsibility'.[74] Although the balance of power between provincialism and centralism was also deemed important, proper representative government was not possible without ministerial responsibility – all other matters were subservient to this.

The first session of the General Assembly began in Auckland on 24 May 1854 on a miserable late autumn day of 'singularly unpropitious [weather]; continuous and heavy showers of rain'.[75] Similar adjectives could be applied to the session that followed. The House of Representatives featured only a handful of members who had not also stood for provincial election, although those who ran only for central office included three future premiers – Sewell, Frederick Whitaker and Frederick Weld.[76] Many members of the House of Representatives (MHRs) were also leading provincial councillors, or, in the cases of Featherston and FitzGerald, superintendents. Controversially, Wynyard was Auckland superintendent. Featherston and FitzGerald also illustrate another striking characteristic of early New Zealand politics: the close connection between parliamentarians and the press. Both had founded newspapers in their respective settlements, and other politicians owned, edited or wrote for various publications. This complex web of power relations set a trend for the whole provincial era.

Wynyard was caught in an unenviable bind. He was simultaneously unwilling to invite colonial anger by denying responsible government or to overstep his bounds by declaring it before a new governor arrived. The Colonial Office's failure to promptly replace Grey hobbled parliament. Wynyard's solution was distraction. In his opening address to the General Assembly, he did not touch on responsible government, instead raising the spectre of centralism. He could handle the debate over the balance of power between the central government and provincial councils; even if ground could not be won, some could be held. Swainson feared that, rather than uniting settlers, 'the new Constitution rather tended to perpetuate their isolation',[77] and his views featured prominently in Wynyard's address, which urged centralism. It was, he argued, up to the assembly 'whether New Zealand shall become one great nation, exercising a commanding influence in the Southern Seas, or a collection of insignificant, divided, and powerless petty States'.[78] This appeal was grounded in an assertion that the central government possessed power over the provinces 'almost without limitation or restriction, on certain specific subjects exclusive, and in all cases supreme', while provincial jurisdiction was 'liable to be controlled and modified by the power of the General Assembly ... [and] narrowed in its range'.[79] These were remarkable words from a man who doubled as a superintendent, but Wynyard's other prestigious appointments gave him the security – and the conflicting interests – to accept Swainson's contribution.

This was a radical departure from Grey's pro-provincial attitudes. Wellington was scathing of the address: '*because* the peculiar conditions of New Zealand require local self-government, *therefore* we will give it central government.'[80] Other provinces were more inclined to generosity, especially in little Taranaki where the pain of isolation was strong.[81] Nonetheless, the *Independent* had a point: although Wynyard's promotion of colonial unity was admirable, the present conditions demanded greater acknowledgement of the importance of provincial governments. Wynyard's address and Swainson's opinions set the tone for the attitude of New Zealand's highest authority for the rest of the decade. Governor Thomas Gore Browne endorsed their arguments when he arrived over a year later. A soldier since the age of 17, he had served in multiple British colonies and was a far-sighted and public-spirited man who travelled extensively during his first year in New Zealand in order to understand local conditions. Like Wynyard, Browne feared that concessions to provincialism would divide New Zealand into 'six insignificant colonies'.[82] From 1854 until conflict with Māori overshadowed all other concerns at the end of the decade, the promotion of central authority and a strong, unified colony at the expense of provincial power was one of the key objects of the Crown's representative in New Zealand.

This, though, proved to be a battle for the future. Wynyard failed to bait members into a central/provincial clash. After lengthy discussion Edward Gibbon Wakefield's motion in favour of responsible government was endorsed with only one dissenting vote. This Wynyard could not ignore. Douglas Adams' famous description in the *Hitchhiker's Guide to the Galaxy* of a machine that makes a form of tea almost, but not quite, entirely unlike tea, can also be applied to the form of responsible government Wynyard established. He expanded the executive council to include MHRs without removing existing officials and without granting any responsible powers to the new, elective members. Although Wakefield led the demand for responsible government, Wynyard called on FitzGerald and David Monro, a Nelson doctor and pastoralist active in politics since 1843, to form government in this 'mixed ministry' as they moved and seconded the House's response to Wynyard's opening address. Here, the central/provincial fault lines resurfaced. Monro wished to confirm the assembly's superiority over the provinces and to limit provincial powers; he could not formulate mutually agreeable policies with FitzGerald and chose to withdraw in acknowledgement that the latter's views were more likely to be supported.[83] Never mind that FitzGerald's provincialism was never going to receive approval from Swainson, who remained on the executive.

Confrontation soon ensued, but not over the extent of central control. The *Nelson Examiner* predicted correctly that 'if the wishes of the people in this matter [of responsible government] are neglected … [there will be] a fierce and irritating struggle'.[84] FitzGerald's ministry, frustrated by its lack of responsible powers, sparked a constitutional crisis when it resigned on 2 August. Wakefield accepted a request to become Wynyard's sole – unofficial – adviser, earning the opprobrium of the House for giving advice without accepting any responsibility to parliament. The legislative and executive functions of government became deadlocked. A stormy prorogation scene on 17 August produced enough colour and excitement to fill an entire book. A second irresponsible ministry, drawn from Wakefield's supporters when parliament resumed a fortnight after prorogation, failed to secure the confidence of the House.[85] Little was done and even less was achieved. Responsible government was not obtained; waste lands were not settled; provincial powers were not defined. In fact, the limited legislation addressed routine or petty matters: the assembly's very first act was to authorise the sale of alcoholic beverages on parliamentary premises for MHRs.[86] Wynyard's actions did, however, provoke a response in London. The Duke of Newcastle, who was colonial secretary from 1852 to 1854, oversaw an attitude shift whereby responsible government was seen as a normal British institution to which British populations overseas were entitled. He emphasised that new constitutions then under consideration for the Australian colonies must provide for responsible government.[87] The Colonial Office was not overly thrilled by Wynyard's unauthorised concession of some responsibility, but took it as a cue. Newcastle's successor George Grey – no relation of his colonial namesake, but an older cousin of the third Earl Grey, who had conferred the 1846 constitution – informed Wynyard in December 1854 that responsible government could be introduced.[88]

The outcome of the session was a stunning victory for provincialists – in the distraction caused by the furore over responsible government, provincial power was never called to account. A frustrated Swainson believed that the assembly's unwillingness to take the bait and place limits on the provinces meant that 'instead of controlling [the provinces], the Assembly was, in fact, itself controlled by the Local Councils'.[89] Meanwhile, the general public were infuriated, especially with Wakefield. Most newspapers – the *Spectator* was a notable exception – angrily denounced his readiness to abandon responsible government advocacy in favour of securing the ear of an irresponsible official. Even a flurry of letters and pamphlets by Wakefield and his supporters could not change popular opinion and electors 'turned in disgust from the secrecy and weakness of the general assembly to the visible strength of the provincial councils'.[90]

Fortunately, the General Assembly met only briefly in 1855 in a perfunctory session to dispense with necessary financial matters; all significant business was left to 1856. Attendance was so thin that Wynyard chose not to establish a responsible ministry in such an unrepresentative chamber. Twelve of the 19 members present at Wynyard's opening address on 8 August 1855 were from Auckland Province, while there were more letters of apology or resignation from the southern provinces than actual representatives. All three of the Otago members, for instance, refused to travel. William Henry Cutten, who was absent from Otago for almost seven months to attend the first session, fumed in his letter of resignation that the poor arrangements and hasty summoning of the assembly amounted 'intentionally to a disfranchisement of this Province'.[91] In a sketch James Brown, Cutten's colleague at the *Otago Witness*, suggested that the only way of reaching the General Assembly

James Brown's sketch of William Cargill travelling to Auckland. The famed collector Thomas Hocken captioned it: 'Almost the only way in the early days of reaching the Legislative Council at Auckland. Captain Cargill takes it.' (Cargill, it should be noted, actually sat in the House; Hocken dated the cartoon circa 1854 but it is likely from after 1855, the year Cargill was first elected to central office.) 7,733 a1406, Hocken Collections, Uare Taoka o Hākena, Dunedin

was witchcraft. Little wonder, then, that when Governor Browne arrived the following month, the session was promptly closed. The first responsible ministry and the anticipated central/provincial clash were deferred until after an election.

The provinces came to view themselves as the real sources of power, passing hundreds of items of legislation while the central government slumped from being an ineffective debating house to an unrepresentative, feeble chamber. Provincialism earned early praise overseas. As part of a campaign to achieve responsible government and access to more land in Victoria, the *Melbourne Morning Herald* happily invoked the New Zealand provincial system as a superior form of government. It described the superintendents as 'stand[ing] forward as quiet advocates of popular rights … [w]e do not find governors and governed arranged in hostility, as a matter of course'.[92] This latter point was an overkind assessment, since hostilities ebbed and flowed in most provinces, but the early superintendents did undoubtedly present themselves as champions of the people. As the 1850s progressed, superintendents became increasingly partisan and associated with one side of political fractures, but in the formative years up to 1856, they were able to position themselves relatively successfully as true local government, both against creeping power from the centre and against the memory of the unrepresentative Crown colony era.

But the provinces lived on shaky ground. Financially their dependence on the surplus of general revenue placed them in a vulnerable position that was liable to be upset by any change in central administration.[93] In October 1854, for instance, a government circular slashed the provincial share of customs and land revenue from two-thirds to half because central expenditure was greater than expected. The *Independent*, provincialist to a fault, hurled invective at the general government, accusing the miserable first session of the General Assembly of 'disgraceful extrava-gance'.[94] In practical terms this meant that Wellington lost £4,500 from an expected £18,000 – a severe hit to its ability to fund public works such as an expensive road over the Rimutaka Range to the Wairarapa. A resolution was necessary to put the provinces on a stable footing.

The forces of provincialism and centralism arranged themselves around the intertwined issues of colonial finances and the alienation and sale of land when the General Assembly met in April 1856, ready to govern responsibly. The chamber contained a wealth of political talent. All six superintendents were members and each faction had its eloquent champions, from Fox the ultra-provincialist to Stafford the moderate to Sewell the centralist. Few subsequent New Zealand parliaments were blessed with this session's depth of talent. Browne opened it with a pointed threat towards those members 'preferring the interests of a party or a province to that of the colony'; power would 'remain but a moment in their nerveless grasp'.[95] In official correspondence he fretted that any failure at this session to assert central authority could cause government to 'fall entirely into the hands of the provincial authorities'.[96] Browne first invited a member of FitzGerald's mixed ministry of 1854 to form a government. Because FitzGerald himself was yet to depart Canterbury owing to illness, Browne made the convenient and eminently suitable choice of Sewell.

Yet provincialism's forces were strong. Sewell and his Cabinet resolved 'to give battle at once to the enemy instead of fighting a series of petty skirmishes' and outlined a markedly centralist policy.[97] He did not hold back in his ministerial statement, describing the existing relationship between central and provincial governments as tending so much towards six independent colonies as to almost destroy the 'real aim of the Constitution', and alleging that to 'break up and divide the colony in this way is to deal treacherously with the institutions committed to our charge'.[98] This language was anathema to ultra-provincialists, some of whom – most notably Fox – entertained the idea of establishing New Zealand as a proper federation. Sewell knew they would react badly. In his journal he succinctly captured both his own proposals and his attempts to make the ultra-provincialists unhappily acquiesce to them:

> What we [Sewell's ministry] agreed upon was ... to administer the affairs of the General Government in the Provinces through the Superintendents, so making only one authority in the Provinces ... and prevent conflicts which are repeatedly going on between the Provinces and Officers of General Government Departments in the Provinces. But will the Provincial Authorities swallow this? To be made sub-administrators under the General Government is to lower them from their present high estate. We propose to soften this, by extending their patronage and right of control, to all the Departments whatever, except the Customs. All our Policy hangs on this.[99]

Hang on this it did. Fox was enraged and parliament devolved into a month-long whirlwind of cabals and intrigues. First Fox and the Wellington ultra-provincialists were able to secure enough votes to pass a motion of no confidence in Sewell and form their own shaky coalition ministry, including – to Sewell's considerable surprise – Ralph Richardson in the executive council. Richardson, whose wife had been a friend of Sewell's late first wife, was a Nelson landowner and a man 'who eschews Provincial Government in every possible form'.[100] Yet Fox persuaded him to join a coalition patched together from so many competing interests that it lacked coherence and proved unworkable. When two more Nelson members arrived to take their seats, the Fox ministry collapsed immediately. In its wake, a third ministry was formed, representing something of a return to the first without a centralist extreme. Although Sewell was treasurer, the ministry was led by the moderate, pragmatic and very able Stafford. It soon emerged from the fray of parliamentary backstabbing as a functional executive.[101]

With a stable government formed – Stafford served a five-year term as premier, the longest until Richard Seddon's reign of 1893–1906 – the business of parliament began in earnest. A complex web of financial problems faced Stafford's ministry.[102] The New Zealand Company had surrendered its charter of settlement back to

Britain after becoming insolvent as a result of maladministration. It owed the British taxpayer repayment for loans, and Auckland Province understandably refused to contribute as it contained no company settlements.[103] The central government had numerous other outstanding debts. The North Island provinces were united in their demands for the purchasing of more Māori land, but the South Island provinces were unwilling to share the bill. All provinces wanted control of revenue from land sales to fund provincial government activities. Receiving the land fund would not be without conditions. The Stafford ministry's solution to the colony's financial woes was, via the New Zealand Loan Act, to raise a loan of £500,000: £200,000 to pay off the New Zealand Company's debts, £120,000 to pay other debts and £180,000 to buy Māori land.

The parliament proposed 18 resolutions and an appropriation act to give the provinces their coveted land revenue – as well as at least three-eighths of customs revenue and other surplus revenues not spent by the central government – but to charge most of the loan against it. This became known as the compact of 1856, and although the permanence of the arrangements was not legally sacrosanct, it was established on the understanding that it should not be altered without provincial assent. The three southern provinces were to equally share the £200,000 bill to cover the New Zealand Company's debt; Auckland, Wellington and Taranaki were to receive the £180,000 for land purchases on a ratio of 5:3:2 respectively, and therefore to contribute to repayment in due proportion. Taranaki, which was in a parlous financial state, was given special dispensations to reduce its interest burden and to guarantee a level of income from land proceeds.[104] The remainder of the land fund was for the provinces to use as they pleased for 'Public Works, Immigration, and other local purposes, giving value to the Waste Lands, from the sale of which it is derived'.[105] This was a good, secure deal as far as the warring parties were concerned. The centralists had made concessions to provincial feeling without actually ceding significant ground, while the provincialists got their land fund.

Not everyone was happy. The ultra-provincialists wanted more, lots more, seeking revenue from more stable sources. Now that they were in opposition, they were also bitter about the demise of Fox's ministry. Featherston predictably spoke out against 'leaving the provinces almost entirely to the uncertain resources of the land revenue', an objection not without merit, and made a lengthy speech against the ministerial policy.[106] Fellow Wellingtonian Dudley Ward, a lawyer and the husband of temperance and women's franchise advocate Anne Ward, unleashed ferocious invective against the measure. It was 'one of the most nefarious schemes of plunder that were ever concocted'; the *Southern Cross* was unwilling to publish his 'unbecoming' tirade in its entirety.[107]

Taranaki's hopes rode on the achievement of special concessions in light of its stark lack of land or income, and the hostility of the province's Māori towards further land sales. Ultra-provincialists opposed these hopes. Fox described the concessions as one of the 'most bare-faced attempts at Provincial log-rolling' or trading of legislative favours, to howls of derision from the Taranaki press as 'blinded by selfish and partizan views [*sic*], show[ing] an entire want of true appreciation' for Taranaki's position.[108] Fox's objection, hypocritical from a man whose very election was based on boisterous provincial rhetoric, was not enough to deny Taranaki. It was lucky to have not only its superintendent, Charles Brown, to observe to the House that his troubled province had previously received 'little consideration', but also a receptive ear in the ministry.[109] The talented new member for New Plymouth, Christopher William Richmond, was colonial secretary. Richmond was a respected, scholarly man who refused to let his notoriously poor physical health – he was, among other things, a severe asthmatic – impede a rich intellectual life. Although he would later decry provincial parochialism and was a key architect of the New Provinces Act, in this case the special concessions stood.

Indeed the whole ministerial policy stood, passing the House by nine votes. Opposition came primarily from Wellington's ultra-provincialists and their Otago allies who wished to turn out Stafford's ministry. Sewell believed that, behind their bluster, the Otago members actually found the resolutions too good to be true.[110] From their perspective it was a great deal. Richly endowed with saleable land, they had much to gain from being granted the land revenue. When it was made, the deal was generally good for the entire colony; the main problem was that circumstances rapidly changed. Once made, the compact was difficult to alter. As one previous historian has concluded, the financial system localised the consequences of war, gold rushes and regional economic fluctuations, and 'no opportunity was afforded of striking a balance between the rampant prosperity of some provinces and the poverty of others'.[111] The compact reinforced but did not create the divide between prosperous and poor provinces. War retarded North Island settlement while gold furthered South Island growth, and as long as land revenue remained in the hands of the provinces, development would be uneven. These events were unforeseeable in 1856, but they meant the compact did not benefit the North Island. When war broke out, Māori were yet to sell nine-tenths of their land, and much of what could be sold to settlers was thickly wooded and not as valuable as the swathes of pastoral land in the south. Although the compact gave short-term security and was broadly satisfactory to the interests of both factions, in the long term it was far more advantageous to the southern provinces and became a source of jealousy. Much more than this was needed to bring down the provinces, however. The decisive battles would not revolve around complex colonial finances or occur in smoky parliamentary chambers. They would take place on muddy town streets and coveted pastoral land, on battered wharves and twisting mountain tracks, as electors worried about such everyday concerns as who governed the land and how provisions were made for settlement and development.

Chapter 4
Provincial Ineptitude

Provincialism began as a powerful system but a host of events during the 1850s stunted its growth. Many wounds were self-inflicted as provinces failed to drive home their manifest advantages or exploit their wide powers. Residents of capital towns were soon mortified by government scandals and disillusioned by bungling administration of public works, and a lack of investment in hinterlands fostered the rise of secession movements that destabilised provincialism. Naturally it was not just capital towns that required investment, though they needed improved roads, ports, drainage and other works. From the moment that provincial councils first met, Pākehā were pushing out from the earliest settlements – sometimes opening areas next to established centres, and sometimes from new coastal footholds. Control of the land fund preoccupied politicians but the task of developing acquired acres was of greater significance to settlers on the spot. Land had little value without public works to convey its produce to market profitably. Ports and jetties were required; roads, preferably all-weather, had to be formed; railways dominated settler visions of the future. All these needs and wants fell within the purview of the provinces.

Despite the proclaimed borders of the provinces, hinterland settlement was seen as provincial 'expansion'. Where land had been alienated – that is, acquired from Māori by the Crown – Pākehā civilisation had to be expanded into it; where land had not been alienated, it was coveted. The latter situation was especially common in Taranaki, where the provincial council felt Māori were retaining more land than they could possibly use, land that was essential for the province to grow and its economy to prosper.[1] As C.W. Richmond wrote in 1854, when he was clerk and attorney to the Taranaki Provincial Council, before his eminent careers in the central government and judiciary, provincial 'expansion [was] rendered impracticable from the unwillingness of our natives to alienate more of their lands'.[2]

Māori remained on the fringe of provincial society. Their connections to Pākehā were still predominantly negotiated through the central government, missionaries, and personal interaction rather than provincial organs. Johann Friedrich

Riemenschneider, a German missionary who spent much time in Taranaki and had a great affection for local Māori even as Māori nationalism conflicted with his conservative theology, provided both a valuable insight into indigenous attitudes and a rare Pākehā voice from the province's hinterland.[3] Many Māori, he wrote, believed that the constitution was 'an Act for the Europeans and for them only, and exclusively uniting them all throughout the country closely together, by concentrating all their combined will and power' with no similar arrangements for Māori.[4] It was an understandable perspective.

Except in Auckland, where Māori were more visible than in the south, their appearance in provincial capitals was viewed with wonder, even disgust. As late as 1862, Georgina Bowen, wife of Canterbury treasurer Charles Bowen, wrote disparagingly to her sister of encountering Māori in Christchurch.[5] Beyond the main towns Māori and Pākehā were thrust into close proximity and their contact could not be easily categorised, but in the provincial capitals race could be more readily labelled and organised to suit governmental and bureaucratic expedience.[6] The provinces answered to electors who were almost exclusively Pākehā, councils were expected to help develop territories into which Pākehā 'expanded', and both Pākehā and Māori understood that this development served Pākehā interests. Settlers' complaints focused on a lack of investment and a failure to support Pākehā growth.

Many lightly settled areas were so remote as to be practically out of government reach – central or provincial. The Golden Bay region (then Massacre Bay) to Nelson's northwest, for instance, remains an isolated part of New Zealand. In the 1850s it had no regular contact with the outside world. There were no roads to Nelson; no steamers called at its insignificant jetties; access was by either an arduous overland trek or a sea voyage at the mercy of the elements. Elizabeth Pringle Caldwell described the trip from Nelson to Golden Bay in the early 1850s as a 'tedious journey' by open boat to a place that was 'a mere "terra incognita" to the early settlers'. Government events, controversies and war 'did not affect our Bay' as late as the 1860s.[7] Conditions were extremely rough, and if the unsettled political climate of the 1860s did not affect the area, then the comparatively placid 1850s had no chance of touching its settlers. Inspired by a largely misplaced hope for gold, in 1857 Thomas Hewetson went to Golden Bay, where he recorded that the region's primitive roads would be covered by inches of mud after rainfall, worse than his family's stockyards in Nelson's backblocks.[8] However, neither Caldwell nor Hewetson blamed the government – this would have been unfair in such a sparsely settled area. In the 1850s the Golden Bay example held for other regions such as the Bay of Plenty, Poverty Bay and the mountainous interiors of Canterbury and Otago.

Conditions were very different in capitals and nearby country, where the advent of provincial councils was expected to lead to considerable advances. By the final days of Crown colony government, settlers the length of the country were dissatisfied with the handling of public works. In Auckland the *Southern Cross* fumed in March 1853 that everything attempted by the Crown 'afford[s] incontestible [*sic*] proof that they possess neither the ability to plan ... nor the capacity to execute public works'.[9] On 30 December 1852 Otago even hosted a public meeting on the atrocious state of its roads at which the province's leading men lamented a dearth of investment. John Hyde Harris, *Witness* founder and a future superintendent, feared settlers would have to wait until provincial governments were functioning for road improvements.[10] He was not wrong. The topic was almost ironic; some country settlers were unwilling to make the arduous journey into Dunedin simply to discuss the roads they had to endure.

The establishment of provincial councils did not prove the desired panacea, and this failure was evident even in provinces such as Canterbury, which went on to public works glories. Most Cantabrians in the early 1850s were clustered in three settlements – Christchurch, Lyttelton and Akaroa. Lyttelton, the original centre of population, possessed one of the colony's best deep-water harbours; on the other side of the rocky, formidable Port Hills was the provincial capital, Christchurch, beyond which the vast and fertile Canterbury Plains stretched to the Southern Alps. As plots of farmland around the city were taken up and cultivated, present-day suburbs such as Riccarton and Papanui began life as agricultural villages. The Avon River, tainted by sewage and clogged by imported watercress, graphically illustrated the effect of settlers on the environment even before major works were constructed. Meanwhile, almost forgotten near the tip of Banks Peninsula was Canterbury's oldest settlement. Akaroa was the first European colony in the South Island when French settlers landed in August 1840, mere months after Britain claimed the island. By 1853 it was idyllic yet unwanted, separated from other towns by a difficult overland trek or a lengthy coastal voyage. The main village was a motley collection of French and English settlers living together harmoniously, if slightly awkwardly.[11]

The locals wanted public works primarily to link Christchurch with Lyttelton. A road across the Port Hills was mooted but at the dawn of provincialism only the first section out of Christchurch was complete – and it was a poor road, neither stoned nor gravelled. The remainder was a rough bridle path, much to the disappointment of those arriving colonists who had believed that the road was complete.[12] Without proper access to the port, Canterbury could not readily reach outside markets. To increase agricultural productivity settlers also wanted improved communications with Akaroa and roads that extended onto the plains. The latter, they hoped, would stimulate the growth of Kaiapoi, north of Christchurch, sited near valuable woodland and the province's largest Māori settlement, and embryonic Rangiora and Timaru, both soon to thrive. Much of the high country was not explored until the mid-1850s, but safe river crossings were needed throughout the province, as Canterbury's swift and icy braided rivers were a serious hazard to travellers.[13] The necessity for road construction was a common theme at social organisations and in campaign speeches for provincial elections.[14]

Few men were available to construct roads. In September 1853 a public meeting to discuss the colony's labour shortage saw tempers flare and patience tested.[15] The *Lyttelton Times* was surprisingly quiet about the state of roads, although this was understandable as its editor, FitzGerald, was also superintendent. FitzGerald's priorities lay elsewhere, labour problems meant many works were unlikely to be completed swiftly and the paper with which he was still connected – even if he largely relinquished active duties upon election – was not going to build hopes he could not fulfil. Even his opponents helped to moderate expectations. Henry Tancred told the council's first session that money for roads 'could be raised without difficulty as soon as we obtain the administration of the land-fund'.[16] Until that point, however, the province's ability to fund improvements was doubtful.

At the end of the provincial council's second session in April 1854 FitzGerald issued an even more severe note of caution. The money 'voted for public works shall be expended with economy and care, but the scarcity and dearness of labour renders great caution necessary … lest too much labour be withdrawn from the more important operation of tilling the soil'. Until labour arrived from England, 'I rely on much forbearance on the part of the people should the Government be unable to accomplish all that you have contemplated'.[17] This did not satisfy everybody. Sewell, in his usual disagreeable fashion, wrote that '[s]ome people want the Government to do every thing. FitzGerald wants people to do everything for themselves.' He noted sarcastically that, for the present, 'roads must remain in their state of pristine mud'.[18]

Nonetheless, progress was made. At its second session the council established a road commission, which reported with commendable speed. The commissioners proposed minor expenditure on the bridle path since, in the short term, it 'must continue to be so great a convenience'. They were unwilling to endorse any long-term road option over the Port Hills, despite moderate enthusiasm for a route via Sumner. They concluded emphatically that the 'most advantageous mode of communication … would be by a line of railway'.[19] This option would take the longest to complete, and at the greatest expense.

Despite such an unambiguous and competent report, delays and indecision marked the next few years.[20] Numerous petitions were presented to the government and a resolution supporting the Sumner road advanced some way through the council in November 1854 before being withdrawn. Plans fell into disarray in 1855, with proposals modified, new surveys conducted and construction frustrated by the want of labour. At this point Canterbury's residents were willing to accept any temporary improvement while waiting impatiently for the funds and labour to build a railway. This impatience led to parochial, short-sighted proposals from Christchurch: first, in 1855, a tramway to replace the Christchurch side of the Sumner road, and then in 1856 a horse-drawn railway to do the same. This resulted in howls of protest from Lyttelton and Akaroa, thoroughly unimpressed that any money might be diverted for Christchurch's gain. As the province shuffled between schemes, the geological impediment to communication was nicknamed 'the Hill of Difficulty'.[21]

Henry W. Harper arrived in the colony late in late 1856 to find Canterbury still dependent on the bridle path. His father was Henry John Chitty Harper, the first bishop of Christchurch and later archbishop of New Zealand; he himself would become an archdeacon. Even for a young man at the peak of his strength, the bridle path was arduous. Leading horses laden with luggage down the rough and steep slope tested his strength and patience. Harper found himself navigating 'in and out of big chunks of rock, over slippery tussock grass, and places with a nasty foothold'.[22] Travellers and merchants importing large quantities of goods had to transfer them in Lyttelton to small coastal vessels that were capable of reaching river jetties in Christchurch and Kaiapoi. This was a costly inconvenience that even promotional material for potential migrants could not excuse or whitewash, and many boats came to grief on the notorious Sumner Bar at the outlet of the Avon Heathcote Estuary.[23] Finally, with an ostensibly temporary route over the summit of Evans Pass, the Sumner road was declared open for light traffic on 9 January 1858.[24] It had taken seven years to link port with plains. The *Lyttelton Times* wryly hoped that soon the road would also be open to heavy traffic 'if there is any perseverance left in the settlement'.[25]

Lyttelton and Christchurch were now connected, albeit unsatisfactorily, but the rest of the province had a pronounced shortage of roads or even bridle paths. Akaroa felt painful pangs of neglect. An allegedly fortnightly post was so intermittent that deliveries were sometimes spaced two months apart and a bridle path was useless economically; neither problem was properly resolved until a steamer service from Akaroa to Lyttelton began in 1858, each voyage taking eight hours. In the same year, a cross-peninsula foot track, started in 1854, was finally opened from Akaroa to Purau on the south side of Lyttelton Harbour.[26] This was a mere token. The *Lyttelton Times* was dissatisfied that more roads had not been constructed on Banks Peninsula to access its timber reserves and dairying potential. The need to metal main roads radiating from Christchurch was a further grievance, as was the lack of bridges over major rivers; ferries, wrote the newspaper, are 'primitive make-shifts on main lines of road'.[27] The meagre facilities for transportation in Canterbury were becoming more of an embarrassment by the year, especially to the eyes and the sensibilities of Britons accustomed to a high standard of roads and familiar with the benefits of railways. Fault lay with the provincial council; discontent soon followed.

Canterbury was not the only province experiencing public works difficulties. Wellington also suffered a shortage of labour in the construction of a road over the rugged Rimutaka Range separating Wellington from the fertile Wairarapa.[28] The *Spectator*, and especially its editor, Robert Stokes, never forgave the anti-Grey vitriol of the representative government campaign and gleefully reported every failing of the provincial government. The paper did not need to look further than public works to illustrate the hypocrisy of councillors: if 'any illustration were wanting of the hollowness of the professions of the Provincial Executive, or of their utter indifference to public opinion, the present state of the roads ... would furnish a sufficient example'.[29] For years many councillors campaigned on Grey's failure to provide such works, yet after the first lengthy council session, important roads were worse than ever. In neighbouring Taranaki, the governor's disallowance of a public works bill led ratepayers to question their liability to pay rates.[30] As was usual in the North Island, however, the relationship between provincial politicians and the provision of basic wants reached its nadir in Auckland.

Bitter factional strife in Auckland's provincial politics cast a shadow over the construction of public works. Superintendent Wynyard resigned abruptly in January 1855 without providing for a successor, which meant funds could not be spent legally on public works until an election two months away.[31] On 14 March 1855 William Brown, the founder of the *Southern Cross*, won the superintendency, but

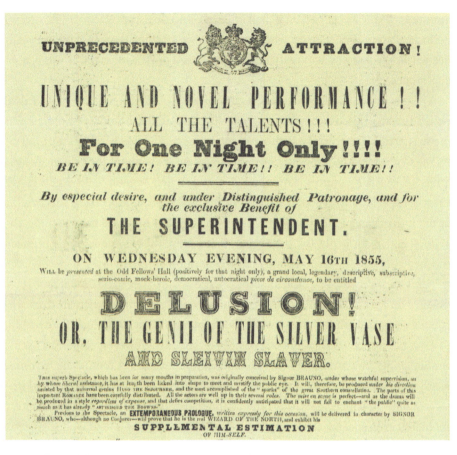

A satirical pamphlet from May 1855 criticising the policies of Auckland superintendent William Brown. Eph-D-POLITICS-1855-01, Alexander Turnbull Library, Wellington

inherited a council filled with the opponents of his Progress Party. They sought to undermine him by proposing to pass a budget for only three months, not a year, and then prorogue the council.[32] The consequences were obvious: without the necessary funds, public works would come to a halt. The *Southern Cross*, although a Progress Party mouthpiece, sagely urged all those involved to reconsider: '[p]arty strife and bitterness should be exhausted in some other way than in stopping or impeding the Public Works.'[33] Brown's expansive public works plans were scuppered, and by July he had to spend unauthorised money to maintain routine government activity. When fresh elections – for the superintendency, council and General Assembly – were held in October, Auckland's politics were toxic, with bribery, fraud and intimidation widespread.[34] The electoral rolls were scandalous, hostage to party interests, and hundreds of votes were cast on behalf of dead or non-existent electors.[35] Provincial politicians were preoccupied with personal power rather than providing much-needed works to a young colony in desperate need of development. It was a poor appearance.

Otago's Provincial Council discredited itself almost immediately. The initial policy directive raised by Superintendent William Cargill in his opening address was the 'urgent matter … [of] the state of our roads', suggesting that haste was necessary.[36] As the first session progressed, however, confusion arose about the province's legal limits to legislate before the General Assembly's first session.[37] Proceedings fell short of expectations, even though over £1,000 was approved for roads, surveys, the harbour department and public buildings – a start, but nowhere near enough. The *Witness* hoped, forlornly as it turned out, that at least 'the experience fairly initiated the members into the responsibility of their position as legislators'.[38]

The Otago Provincial Council's second session, which began on 31 October 1854, dragged on for a year thanks to poor attendance and prolonged adjournments. The council's membership of nine proved much too small but provisions to expand it to 19 could not be realised until it was dissolved. This, however, could not excuse the appalling standard of politics. The council met just four times in the first nine weeks of 1855, with lengthy adjournments ostensibly to allow members to read new legislation – of which there was little.[39] Councillors showed less and less interest. By March even speaker John Gillies did not always deign to attend, and this set an example: a 13 March meeting was postponed when neither member of the executive bothered to appear.[40] Some subsequent meetings proceeded without any executive representation. Indeed one of the two executives, Archibald Anderson, attended only one meeting in 1855.

Even the *Otago Witness* stopped reporting council proceedings. Editor William Cutten, a councillor, ceased to attend every meeting, and privately fell out with his father-in-law, Cargill, over an immigration policy dispute that flared publicly later that year.[41] In a *Witness* diatribe Cutten described the council as 'in a very languid state'.[42] Hardly better than a few bored men bickering in a pub, it was viewed with wonder elsewhere. To the *Lyttelton Times*, never one to miss an opportunity to deride its southern rival, Otago was 'hopelessly the same as we have always known them' and 'we do not pretend to understand the state of their affairs'.[43] Dissolution was justified. Cargill intimated as much in May: if the old Scottish parliament could complete its business in 10 days, 'there can be no reason why a Provincial Council … should not get through its Session within the same, or even a shorter, period'.[44]

This was pitched as a concession to rural members; implicitly, it was an attempt to avoid more members following Anderson's example and retiring to the country. Nonetheless the council met well into October. Wynyard was repeatedly requested to grant a dissolution, even by the council itself, but deferred action until Governor Browne's arrival.[45]

Dissolution was finally granted on 15 September, but in Auckland, meaning that news did not reach Otago until the start of November and the council's final six weeks were invalid.[46] Had the news arrived swiftly, it would have averted one final embarrassment. Against the wishes of council and public meetings, Cargill insisted that, in order to maintain Otago's Scottish character, immigrants should be drawn only from north of the River Tweed, part of which forms the traditional boundary between Scotland and England. Cutten, already sure that the superintendent's messages were 'not ... sufficiently interesting to call for their publication', turned the full force of the *Witness* on Cargill.[47] The *Lyttelton Times* felt the acrimonious squabbling 'should have read as a hoax' to anybody who did not know better.[48]

By this point the council was the subject of much disapproval. Cutten, weary from sitting on a 'languid' body and sick of criticism, lashed out. He accused residents of thinking that 'the Council is bound to do everything, and to pay for every public work out of some inexhaustible mine of wealth'.[49] His self-serving deflection did not wash, even though his attendance and conduct were superior to those of most of his colleagues. There were attempts to start a new newspaper in opposition to the *Witness*.[50] Through their poor attendance, mediocre conduct and public squabbles the councillors heaped shame upon the province. Roads were not improved, surveys were not done, public buildings were poor, education was unsatisfactory and complaints were numerous, especially as the council sat for so excruciatingly long and did so little. No wonder Otago was one of the provinces in which secessionism first flourished.

Although many of the problems the councils had to resolve were routine and mundane, this cannot excuse poor conduct or meagre outcomes for electors. Had councillors possessed more foresight, they could have laid foundations of popular support to withstand predictable challenges from central government. More successful councillors would have created a support base of local patriots, individuals who possessed more than a basic provincial identity, but also had confidence in the institutions of provincial government. They certainly would not have focused so narrowly on capital towns or personal gain, thereby alienating regions in which settlement was rapidly increasing. Instead the provinces made numerous mistakes and disappointed influential people, fostering grievances that formed the basis for future discontent.

It is no surprise that early on regional movements seeking secession from original provinces flourished. The three main 1850s secessionist movements were of Hawke's Bay from Wellington, Marlborough from Nelson and Southland from Otago. Rumblings that Wanganui should secede from Wellington possessed little influence until the next decade. All these movements emphasised inadequate investment in their region, but Marlborough differed from Hawke's Bay and Southland in that it gained momentum only when major landholders lost control of Nelson's provincial council. This was not a factor in the other two regions. It should also be noted that the settlers did not use the names 'Marlborough' and 'Southland'; they fought for secession of 'the Wairau' and 'Murihiku' respectively. Despite this apparent trend to replace Māori with English names, the province of New Plymouth changed its name to Taranaki in 1858.

Hawke's Bay was the only North Island region to achieve secession, although it was not alone in justifiably claiming neglect. Its secession is surprising yet little studied, despite the political upheaval it entailed and the social and economic forces marshalled in its support.[51] Pākehā presence was minimal when provincialism began: pastoralists had not arrived until the late 1840s, leasing land illegally from local Māori. To regulate settlement, government agent Donald McLean bought the Ahuriri block, within which Napier was built, on 17 November 1851.[52] Māori were soon marginalised as pastoralists swept across the Hawke's Bay plains during the 1850s.

Napier's location was unremarkable, huddled around Bluff Hill at the end of a sandy spit. Undoubtedly there were better sites for a township, but the region needed a harbour for wool exports. Town lots were first sold in 1855, by which point a motley collection of hotels already existed.[53] Soon a basic village developed. In late 1857 there were 60 or 70 houses and assorted shops on the flat ground below Bluff Hill, overlooked by a few more homes on higher ground. Although Napier boasted a magistrate's court, a school, a flourmill and a post office, among other amenities, it was a humble settlement – its prospects were discussed in the long term, not the short.[54] Laid out by Alfred Domett, it remained the sole notable settlement in Hawke's Bay until the 1860s, though even in 1858 its population was a mere 343.[55] On Wellington province's fringe, Napier hardly seemed the sort of place to become a political centre in its own right. Yet that is what happened.

Hawke's Bay settlers felt distanced from Wellington society and politics. It was stereotyped before settlement as the 'Alsatia of the colony', a colonial version of

London's historic haven for criminals where 'all disorderly and desperate characters resort to be out of the reach of the law'.[56] When settlement became regular and standardised, the region still struggled to have its case heard in the provincial council. It was not a lawless region – in 1856 Napier's two policemen enjoyed a light workload and the court sat infrequently, needing only one hotel room in which to perform its duties – but it barely appeared in Wellington's peripheral vision.[57] Never mind that it was already a major part of the economy. The number of sheep in Hawke's Bay was over a third of the province's total livestock, already exceeding the other major pastoral district, the Wairarapa.[58] Exports from Napier were predominantly wool – in 1856, the only year for which complete figures exist, £7,309.6.4 of the total exports of £8,912.14.0 came from wool, and settlers estimated 1858's wool export at £35,000.[59] Even allowing for exaggeration, the local economy was clearly booming, yet the region had only two provincial councillors, who until 1856 were shared with the Wairarapa, despite divergent interests and increasing antagonism.[60] Meagre roads were formed at private expense, but the council did not fund construction of a single yard of road anywhere in Hawke's Bay between 1853 and 1856.[61] In 1855 the council voted £1,000 for a road from the plains to Napier's port – and 'that is all we have heard of it since', reported one colonist over a year later.[62] His letter reflected great pride in Napier's development despite the Wellington government's invisibility. Settlers were growing restless.

Wellington offered Napier little more than empty gestures. Large runholders, who wanted to keep Hawke's Bay and the Wairarapa as big estates for personal profit, influenced the government. Fitzherbert and Fox visited in an attempt to calm Napier's disquiet, but this achieved only a 'hollow peace' and lasting animosity.[63] In December 1855 Featherston forecast investment in a road from Napier to the Wairarapa and Wellington, but at the same time he hoped that improving communications would keep Wellington city as 'the emporium of the trade of the whole province'.[64] This was not what Napier desired: it also wished to be an economic hub. Yet Featherston's policies continued to favour large runholders, who endeavoured to secure labour for their runs by making it difficult for men of modest means to become small freeholders.[65] Animosity grew. Wellington was quite obviously uninterested in Hawke's Bay except for economic exploitation, runholders sneered at Napier as a 'Little Peddlington', and the path was set for secession.[66]

Hawke's Bay settlers looked beyond the colony for inspiration. They encouraged new arrival James Wood to found the *Hawke's Bay Herald* in order to promote their own province. An enterprising newspaperman, Wood had honed his trade

THE Hawke's Bay Herald
AND AHURIRI ADVOCATE.

No. 3. | NAPIER, AHURIRI, OCTOBER 10, 1857. | Vol.

YOUNG & CO.'S LINE OF PACKETS
BETWEEN
LONDON & NEW ZEALAND.

Northfleet	N. Pentreath	1050
Duke of Portland	G. F. Seymour	870
Norman Morrison	C. L. Maundrell	1100
Royal Stuart	H. Tadman	957
Merchantman	W. Brown	1300
Oriental	W. C. Macey	600
Westminster	Westgarth	1500
Carnatic	J. Smith	880
Rose of Sharon	J. Southeron	1200
Heroes of Alma	T. Silk	1100
Kenilworth	J. Thorne	900
Solent (new)	M. Brooks	1050

The above are only a few of the vessels despatched by this line; and will be followed at intervals of about a month by equally favourite vessels, comprising some of the fastest and finest vessels afloat, all of the highest classification at Lloyd's and commanded by skilful and experienced Captains.

The undersigned, as agents of this line of packets, are prepared to make arrangements on liberal terms with parties in the AHURIRI DISTRICT wishing any of their friends to join them.

Goods or packages shipped by Young & Co.'s line for AHURIRI SETTLERS and consigned to our care will be promptly forwarded on arrival.

BAIN, GRAHAME, & Co.
Auckland,
25th August, 1857.

ORIENTAL BANK CORPORATION.

Incorporated by Royal Charter.

**Paid-up Capital, £1,260,000.
Reserve Fund, £252,000.**

RULES OF BUSINESS OBSERVED AT THE AUCKLAND BRANCH.

THE Corporation grant drafts on London Payable on demand, or at thirty days' sight, and drafts on Scotland and Ireland, on demand; also, circular notes negociable in Europe, on the Continent of Europe, India, and the Cape of Good Hope.

Drafts are also granted on the Branches and Agencies of the Corporation at Bombay Calcutta, Madras, Ceylon, Hongkong, Singapore, Mauritius, Melbourne, and Sydney, at the Exchange of the day.

The Corporation purchase or collect Bills payable in Europe, or in Bombay, Calcutta, Madras, Ceylon, Hongkong, Singapore, Mauritius, Melbourne or Sydney.

The Corporation also discount or make advances on private Bills and notes payable in Auckland, bearing at least two approved names, unconnected in general business and not having more than four months to run; or bearing only one name if accompanied by the deposit of adequate collateral security.

The Corporation grant CASH Credits on the same terms as above.

The Corporation collect Bills, Drafts, &c., payable in Auckland; take charge of Government or other securities; and realise interest and dividends for constituents.

The Corporation receive deposits on the

THE UNDERSIGNED begs to inform the Settlers and Mercantile Community of Ahuriri, that he has commenced business at the Port of Napier as MERCHANT and COMMISSION AGENT.

JOHN ALEXANDER SMITH.
Napier, September 21, 1857.

THE Attention of the Settlers and others at Ahuriri, is requested to the well assorted Stock of Supplies requisite for the District, viz. :—

Negrohead & Honey Dew Tobacco
Pampanga Sugar & Company's No. 1 Pieces
Crushed Loaf Sugar, Coffee
Congou Tea, in chests, halves, and bxs.
New South Wales & Liverpool Soap
Belmont No. 1 Sperm Candles, in 25 lb. boxes
Patna Rice, Black Pepper
Liverpool & Dairy Salt
Wybrow's Pint Pickles, in 2 doz. cases
London Bottled Vinegar
Olive Oil, in quarts and pints

Sydney made Town Drays
American Ploughs
Bullock Yokes & Chains, Cart harness
Horse Shoes, assorted
Foster's Spades and Shovels, Iron, assorted
Eubank's Nails, assorted, Shingle Nails
Galvanised Iron Wire, 9 & 10 in. blocks
Rope, assorted, ⅓, ¾, 1, and 1½ in.
White Lead, Paints, Boiled & Raw Oil
Stockholm Tar
Glassware and Earthenware, assorted

Blankets, 10/4, 11/4, and 12/4

OVERLAND MAIL
BETWEEN AUCKLAND & NAPIER

ARRANGEMENTS having been made for the conveyance of mails overland between Auckland and Napier, by way of Kangiawhia and Taupo, NOTICE IS HEREBY GIVEN from Auckland on Wednesday, the 23d September 1857; and the following Table showing the days on which Mail will be despatched from Auckland and Napier respectively during the remainder of the present year is published for general information.

Despatched from Auckland.		Despatched from Napier.	
Sept. 23		Oct. 7	
Oct. 7	Wednesday at 2 p.m.	Oct. 21	Wednesday at 2 p.m.
Oct. 21		Nov. 4	
Nov. 4		Nov. 18	
Nov. 18		Dec. 2	
Dec. 2		Dec. 16	
Dec. 16		Dec. 30	

EDWARD CATCHPOOL,
Deputy Postmaster

Post Office, Ahuriri,
Sept. 23, 1857.

EX DOLPHIN.

On Sale at the Stores of the Undersigned

2 NEW WOOL DRAYS of the best construction, complete.
Also
Bullock bows and yokes

3/4 Wool bales (the medium size)

The top of the front page of the third issue of the *Hawke's Bay Herald*, 10 October 1857. After two issues of advertising, this was the first to contain editorial content.

at the *Age* in Melbourne, where he witnessed the rise of Victoria after its successful campaign to be made a separate colony from New South Wales, and then became sub-editor of Auckland's *Southern Cross*.[67] There he worked under Hugh Carleton, a politician and pressman well versed in the arts of advancing political agendas through print.[68] Having learnt both the value of separation and the force of the pen, Wood eagerly accepted Hawke's Bay's cause. Conveniently, the *Spectator* had already laid the groundwork in Wellington. Ever keen to attack its opponents, it argued that 'professions of ultra-provincialism' from Featherston's faction meant only 'a centralized Provincial Government, in which every local matter is referrible [*sic*] to themselves'. It accurately characterised the government as 'profuse in their promises, but very niggardly in the performance of them', offering a 'specious make-believe' to far-flung citizens.[69] Featherston wanted 'Little Peddlington' to stop being a nuisance. He even circumvented proper channels to use the police as his 'eyes and ears' in Hawke's Bay.[70] In Wood's hands, however, Napier only became a stronger and more consistent nuisance.

Wood outlined the *Herald's* policy in its third issue on 10 October 1857. He marvelled that 'living as we do under a Constitution the very essence of which is Local Self Government, the lack of that very privilege should be [the] great grievance of the day. Strange, but true.'[71] A letter elaborated on the region's frustration that profit from the region's land sales had 'accidentally fallen' into the possession of Wellington.[72] In his next editorial Wood deepened this complaint by drawing explicitly upon his Australian experience, comparing Napier's plight with Melbourne under the rule of New South Wales. 'It contributes largely to the Provincial revenue; it has only a nominal voice in the expenditure of that revenue', and barely any money had been spent on public improvements.[73]

The next month Hawke's Bay got its chance to elect two provincial councillors. This was a much better opportunity to send a message to Wellington than the superintendency election of 1857, when Featherston's sole opponent alienated the local vote with radical opposition to pastoralism.[74] Hawke's Bay wanted to break the grip of absentee landlords and distant government, but it did not wish to impede the profitability of its largest industry. In the council election Hawke's Bay elected two secessionists. Settlers were increasingly frustrated with slow land sales, inadequate public works and the use of unsold Hawke's Bay land as security for Wellington's loans.[75] The *Herald* regarded the result as 'strikingly indicative of the feeling of the people … for local self-government … [and] tantamount to a vote of, at least, *very little* confidence in the Wellington Provincial Government'.[76] Little Peddlington was ready to move beyond its humble station. After all, observed one of the successful candidates while on the hustings, Taranaki had a similar population and less land open to settlement when provincialism began.[77] Crucially, some local runholders, fearing that Jerningham Wakefield's anti-pastoral faction would soon control the Wellington council, came over to the secession cause, though townspeople and smallholders remained the nucleus of the movement.[78] A secession petition circulated. It demonstrated that Hawke's Bay received just £1 of investment for every £10 it contributed to provincial revenue, dubiously appropriated an Earl Grey quote for support and presented statistics flaunting the region's wealth, before concluding with a plea for provincial independence.[79] Signed by 317 adult male residents, a considerable percentage of the total Pākehā population of 982, it was presented to parliament in April 1858.

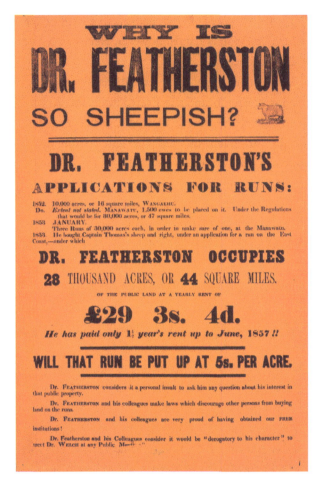

An anti-Featherston pamphlet from the 1857 Wellington superintendency election. Hawke's Bay was not receptive to this rhetoric as its economy was dependent on pastoralism.

Eph-D-POLITICS-Wellington-1857-01, Alexander Turnbull Library, Wellington

Hawke's Bay's petition was not the first; the Wairau had already got in on the act. Contemporaries who depicted the creation of new provinces as a sop to Hawke's Bay often overlooked this fact, but historians' neglect of the new province movements does mean that this myth has struggled for longevity. The Wairau presents an interesting contrast to Hawke's Bay, as there large runholders led secessionist agitation. The campaign began after Edward Stafford resigned Nelson's superintendency to focus on the colonial premiership. Electors replaced him with John Perry Robinson, whose ideology opposed the runholders' interests and whose appeal lay largely with the working classes. Born in England, Robinson was an ex-Chartist who saw in the colonies an opportunity for political achievement denied to him at home. As a woodturner by profession, he was well outside the social circle of the Nelson Supper Party, as the society of original landowners, runholders and other eminent Nelsonians was nicknamed.[80] Despite liberal professions in the 1853 elections, Stafford – and his supporter Charles Elliott of the *Examiner* – allied with the runholders, and for three years there was peace between the provincial capital and the Wairau. After Stafford's resignation, the Supper Party put up as its candidate, avowed centralist David Monro. Elliott initially strove for impartiality in the *Examiner*, but he became convinced that Robinson was a threat to the province's – or at least the Supper Party's – interests and abandoned any pretence of neutrality.[81] He exploited the *Examiner*'s position as Nelson's sole newspaper to promote Monro and ridicule Robinson and his supporters.[82]

Unfortunately for Elliott, runholders were out of step with the constituency. The efforts of Monro's advocates on the hustings provoked a response, both in print and on election day. One critic sarcastically highlighted the poor behaviour of Robinson's opponents as a lesson to the 'low-bred inhabitants of this province' in 'the etiquette of the higher classes in Nelson'.[83] Robinson won a close election and, far from destroying the province, served it well until his untimely death by drowning in January 1865. Elliott was appalled by Robinson's victory. Elections in the outlying Amuri district were conducted improperly and Elliott urged that the result be declared invalid, despite the fact that even if every Amuri elector voted for Monro this would be insufficient to change the outcome.[84] Robinson's 16-vote victory was finally declared six weeks after polling. Elliott fumed that the election of a lower-class man 'was an innovation on the customary and conventional mode of working' the constitution.[85] The Supper Party could not buy Robinson and in 1857 conflict erupted between Nelson and the Wairau.

Conveniently, runholder interests converged with those of small landowners and pioneering settlers in nascent Blenheim and Picton. All shared frustration with the provincial government for not servicing their needs – roads were few and impassable in winter, without a ferry or a bridge the Wairau River was the site of drownings, and there were no provisions for education or the maintenance of law.[86] If anything, the Wairau was regressing. It had once enjoyed the services of a magistrate and a constable but by April 1857 both had left the district and Elliott regaled the council with fears of violence and injustice.[87] Proper policing was re-established in May but it was too little, too late. The quest for secession was

Frederick Weld, later premier of New Zealand, painted the upper Wairau in 1855, capturing its wild and undeveloped character. A-269-007, Alexander Turnbull Library, Wellington

encouraged by Robinson's Waste Lands Bill, which sought to change conditions of purchasing and leasing land in a manner distasteful to runholders. Thomas Renwick, a major Wairau landowner, made the bold assertion that if the bill passed, 'the runholders, for self-protection, [would] use every legitimate means in their power to obtain separation'.[88] They had enough councillors to defy Robinson and defeat the bill, but Renwick voiced an increasingly popular sentiment and secessionism gained momentum.

Secession meetings held throughout 1857 fostered a campaign to secure the Wairau's independence from Nelson. There was little delay between Renwick's remarks and the first meeting in the Wairau on 14 May 1857, which voted unanimously for secession.[89] Upon learning that secessionist demands had been formalised, the *Examiner* agreed in principle that splitting the provinces into smaller units would be desirable when the colony's population was larger, but considered the present demands to be 'a very infantine cry'.[90] This did not impress the Wairau settlers, who sent a flurry of letters to the *Examiner* to persuade Elliott and the people of Nelson to support their campaign. This culminated in a letter issuing a veiled threat that 'in native swords and native ranks, the only hope of courage dwells' – a quote from Lord Byron's *The Isles of Greece*. It gave a concise summary of the Wairau's grievances, exploiting the southern provinces' disputes with Auckland to argue that '[w]hat Auckland has been to Nelson, Nelson is to us, and worse'.[91]

The increasingly vituperative language shocked some locals. Although the *Examiner* remained the primary theatre for secessionist debate, in October 1857 it gained a rival, the *Colonist*. One writer to described the Wairau contributions as 'really alarming' and only half-jokingly noted that the superintendent would have to use all his diplomatic skill to avoid 'internecine war'.[92] Another, with a good helping of sarcastic derision, retreated to the *Colonist*'s correspondence pages because 'Wairau settlers look so fierce, and write such clever letters … that I am almost afraid to say anything about them, particularly as they have the *Nelson Examiner* … on their side'.[93] This last claim was not entirely true. Elliott, despite his Wairau interests, never converted to outright secession. On the hustings for re-election as one of Wairau's councillors in October, he questioned the ability of the area and its low population to support the full machinery of provincial government. Instead he supported the devolution of local powers, a sort of sub-province or county with a cheap, streamlined administration.[94]

Elliott's alternative proposal, sensible though it was, came much too late and gained no traction. He never fettered secessionists in his pages – their ultimate goal was not far from his. By the time he was pressed on the matter of secession versus his county proposal, a pro-secession petition had already done the rounds. Signed by 180 men, all voters, it was forwarded to the General Assembly in mid-August 1857.[95] The signatories were unwilling to back down, and they had powerful friends in Auckland. Many Wairau runholders sat in the General Assembly, such as Monro, and one of them was the premier himself, Stafford. This was immensely valuable for Marlborough's borders when the New Provinces Act was drafted.

Of the three secessionist movements, the Murihiku campaign made the slowest progress before the act was debated in 1858. There was disquiet in Murihiku by early 1856 after the shambolic beginnings of Otago Provincial Council. Rumours circulated that the government was uninterested in Southland and wanted to confine land sales to Dunedin's hinterland – an impression promoted by the lack of land surveys and the failure to lay out a town at the port of Bluff.[96] In the General Assembly in June, John Cargill, son of William, accused Stafford of securing Otago members' support for his financial policy by threatening to dismember their province if they did not aquiesce.[97] Murihiku was infuriated by contradictory provisions of provincial land regulations and ordinances passed during 1856, culminating in a December ordinance that threw open a large tract of the region for sale in blocks of no less than 2000 acres (800 hectares) at 10s an acre.[98] This put the land well out of reach of smallholders and men of modest means. It was not long before Australian purchasers expressed interest in massive swathes of land, sales that would have been much to the detriment of existing settlers and small farmers.[99] Meanwhile those who actually lived in the area had to endure the frustration of travelling to Dunedin to sort out claims to small parcels of land, claims that had been thrown into utter confusion by the proliferation of legislation.

Murihiku's residents began entertaining a nebulous vision of their own province. The *Lyttelton Times*, happy to see its southern rival divided, threw support behind secession. Murihiku's settlers had 'the full hope' they were founding a separate province as the region was so different from 'what is commonly understood by Otago ... [that] Bluff is evidently an embryo Province.'[100] The first secession meeting was held in Invercargill on 28 March 1857. It was at such gatherings that James Alexander Robertson Menzies, a doctor and sheep farmer from the Scottish Highlands, came to the fore as Murihiku's political leader. He had originally migrated to Australia in 1853 but found the local climate too hot and the society unappealing. After proceeding on to New Zealand, he was profoundly impressed by Murihiku and settled there in early 1854.[101] Driven by a firm belief in the region's potential, Menzies at the March 1857 meeting led the adoption of a numerously signed petition to the governor and parliament requesting separation from Otago.[102]

At the *Witness* Cutten affected surprise. He described the meeting, quite incorrectly, as the 'first indication of anything like political life in the South.'[103] Obviously with the spoils of land sales in mind, he wrote that secession would be 'incalculably injurious to Dunedin', and that the expense of provincial administration would make secession disappointing to Murihiku as well. Cutten's scepticism was supported by Murihiku's meagre population; Otago's chief surveyor reported a population of 442 in January–March 1857: 253 Pākehā and 189 Māori and 'half-castes'.[104] The petition was unsuccessful but Menzies and his devoted compatriots were unwilling to concede. Their northern ally the *Lyttelton Times* remained confident Murihiku had the resources to support a great province and had 'good reason to pray for a separation' as they otherwise faced being 'squeezed like an orange [by Dunedin], so that its present possessors may leave nothing but the rind after them!'[105] The General Assembly's new provinces debate in 1858 was the motivation they needed to redouble their efforts.

Chapter 5
'Our Reactionary Policy'

At the General Assembly's 1858 session, the interests of centralists and secessionists achieved convenient harmony. While secessionist campaigns gained momentum, centralists had benefited from opportune decisions made at higher levels of government the previous year. The first was in response to the quite extraordinary actions of Wellington Province. Wellington Harbour is notoriously difficult to enter, especially on stormy nights. The constitution's nineteenth clause specifically excluded provincial governments from erecting and maintaining lighthouses, but the provincial government kept a light on Pencarrow Head at the harbour's entrance with the central government's permission. When this proved inadequate, and the central government would not pay for an upgrade, the provincial council read the constitution creatively – although it prohibited lighthouses *on the coast*, it made no mention of *harbour* lights. In this way the provincial council authorised a £25,000 loan for a lighthouse, and by the time Browne disallowed it, the finance was already raised.[1] Wellington's response was, in effect: too bad, we have the money and we are using it anyway. On 2 May Browne sent instructions to all superintendents that, in future, they were to reserve for his assent every bill for raising a loan.[2] This was a notable win for the centralists, placing important shackles on provincial legislatures. The second major victory came in September when Colonial Secretary Henry Labouchere instructed Browne to refuse assent to provincial loans except those of insignificant amounts for temporary purposes, or for emergencies.[3] This was a further blow to the independence and financial power of the provinces.

Hence, in 1858, the centralists' moment came. They had asserted their influence in 1856 but achieved little beyond quelling Wellington's ultra-provincialists. Now with a groundswell of dissatisfaction towards provincial governments, especially from rural areas, centralists had a prime opportunity to show the provincial councils who held the best cards by introducing legislation to carve new provinces out of the old. This New Provinces Act was a cunning piece of legislation. Not expressly designed to build up ferment for abolition, it *was* designed to divide and rule the provinces – which, in the end, encouraged abolition anyway. It robbed the six original provinces of a considerable degree of security, not to mention valuable land and revenue, and in its wake created disarray.

Worst of all for the ultra-provincialists, the act's passage through the General Assembly was partly the fault of Wellington's MHRs, who were so convinced of the importance of their province that they did not travel to Auckland. This was a fatal mistake. Provincial elections in 1857 returned Featherston as superintendent but elected a hostile council.[4] When the council opened in March 1858 deadlock ensued because Featherston was unwilling to accept the opposition's policies or executive. He sought to rule as if the election never happened and an acrimonious debate erupted. When the council replied to Featherston's opening address, Wellingtonians gathered en masse for the verbal stoush between William Fox, loyal to Featherston, and the 'Radical' Jerningham Wakefield, unofficial leader of the council's majority and Featherston's sworn opponent.[5] It was such a popular event that the council had to move to a larger room. Enjoying their celebrity status and unwilling to abandon such bitter politics, provincial councillors who doubled as central representatives refused to leave the fight. They believed that 'in all probability the Assembly will be occupied in routine business' and would pursue no major legislation. When the ship chartered to take them to Auckland departed on 24 March, they were still firmly on dry land, plotting against their provincial nemeses.[6] As one historian observes, the ultra-provincialists' 'deference to provincial politics above those of the colony appears to show considerable lack of political judgement', especially as they were aware a secession petition would be presented to the central government.[7]

Many South Island politicians also refused to attend. Five of Nelson's six members stayed home, convinced that the capital had to be moved south and unwilling to travel to Auckland at considerable inconvenience to their personal interests. Their absence, combined with numerous resignations from members throughout the colony, threatened parliament's ability to reach a quorum.[8] Some, such as Alfred Domett of the Town of Nelson, were willing to travel later once provincial council business was complete, sure that the absence of many southern members would hinder the House from 'serious business' until he could attend.[9] Parliament was meant to open on 31 March; the lack of a quorum meant this was delayed, and Aucklanders awaited the arrival of ships from the south.[10] There was considerable relief on 9 April when a quorum was finally achieved with the arrival of Speaker Charles Clifford, the sole Wellington representative.

The centralists could barely believe their luck – the absence of the ultra-provincialists combined with three secession appeals gave them the perfect opening. At the close of the session Stafford, on behalf of his ministers, wrote to Colonial Secretary Edward Bulwer-Lytton that the New Provinces Act was quite explicitly an attempt to quiet ultra-provincialist agitation: it 'may be regarded as the turning point in the struggle … between the Ultra-Provincialists, and those who maintain the authority of Her Majesty's Government'.[11] It was obvious that the constitution did not intend to forever restrict New Zealand to six provinces. After initially considering a system of municipalities much like that advocated for the Wairau by Charles Elliott, the ministry chose to expand the provincial system.[12] Furthermore, instead of dealing individually with secession requests, the ministry framed a general act.

C.W. Richmond, whose willingness to consider issues from a national rather than parochial perspective often led him to frustration with provincial councils, was one of the leading architects of the New Provinces Act. He articulated the spirit and object of the legislation in public and with even more frankness in private. At the second reading of the bill in parliament, he asserted boldly that in importance relative to other legislation, 'this yields to none'. Although the provincial system's 'cumbrous apparatus … [is] the evil we are all complaining of', the concept of municipalities was too vague; in drafting a bill for municipalities, 'we found that for all practical purposes we were creating provinces'.[13] He was supported by parliamentary ally Hugh Carleton, who described the act as striking at the 'very root' of ultra-provincialism and the tendency towards a 'hexarchy of six petty republics'.[14] It was convoluted logic to avoid saying the obvious. In private, Richmond got straight to the *real* point – and expressed shock that the ministry was succeeding:

> It is part of our policy, by multiplying provinces, to bring provincial powers within their due limits. When the size of the provinces is reduced they will necessarily confine themselves to local interests, leaving the general interests to the Genl. Government … Considering the strength of Ultra Provincial feeling in N.Z. I am perfectly astonished at the amount of success we have achieved in our reactionary policy. The leading Wellington politicians have been absent & there will be a dreadful howl of rage & grief from that quarter when they learn what we have done.[15]

Put simply, despite the opposition of members such as Domett and Cargill, the Stafford ministry successfully pursued a divide-and-rule policy. They were also innovating. In response to conflicts between superintendents and councils, especially in Auckland and Wellington, superintendents of new provinces were to be elected

NEW ZEALAND.

ANNO VICESIMO PRIMO ET VICESIMO SECUNDO

VICTORIÆ REGINÆ.

No. 70.

ANALYSIS:

AN ACT to provide for the establishment of new Provinces in New Zealand. [21st *August*, 1858.]

Title.

WHEREAS it is expedient to make better provision for Local Self-Government, and for that purpose, to provide for the establishment of new Provinces in certain cases,

Preamble.

BE IT THEREFORE ENACTED by the General Assembly of New Zealand, in Parliament assembled, and by the authority of the same, as follows :—

by the councils themselves, rather than by popular election. The superintendent did not have to be a member of the council, and if he was, his seat was to be deemed vacant – but he could recontest it and could even be appointed speaker.[16]

The creation of new provinces was essentially a formality.[17] The old provinces from which they were carved did not even have to be consulted, let alone grant approval. Secession would be granted upon receipt of a petition from at least three-fifths of the registered electors of a district that fulfilled certain criteria. A new province was required to possess a town (to be the capital) and a port, it had to be between 500,000 and 3 million acres (202,000 and 1.2 million hectares) in size and the petition needed at least 150 signatures of registered electors. Two points drove home the Pākehā nature of provincialism: the population of the district seeking secession was to be no less than 1000, *excluding* imperial troops and Māori, and Māori could not be counted towards the 150 required signatories on the petition, even if they were registered electors.

The governor would fix the boundaries of new provinces, which could deviate from the area requested in the petition, and no new province's boundaries were to come within 60 miles (95 km) of the capital of any other province, with two notable exceptions. One was made – and never used – for small Taranaki, allowing a new province to come within 35 miles (55 km) of New Plymouth. The other was the direct result of the Wairau having valuable supporters in parliament. Had the 60-mile limit been applied, almost all of the area seeking secession would have been denied: Blenheim is roughly 40 miles (65 km) from Nelson, and Picton even closer. The limit was waived and the border would follow the watershed separating Tasman Bay from adjacent territory to the east. The wishes of the Wairau were not to be thwarted by a technicality. Both it and Hawke's Bay soon completed the formalities. Hawke's Bay became independent of Wellington on 1 November 1858, followed by newly christened Marlborough exactly a year later.

As Richmond predicted, there was anger in the south. Wellington indulged the fiction that the New Provinces Act was aimed exclusively at it. The *Independent* argued farcically that the legislation did not meet the wishes of the Hawke's Bay settlers. Ignorant of the secessionist movements in the South Island, it claimed first that the act applied 'at the present time, solely to Wellington', then pronounced that 'we are mistaken if it has the effect of dismembering our Province, as was anticipated at Auckland'. In its view, Napier's 'object is certainly not to have a Superintendent

Opposite: The first page of the New Provinces Act.

and Council of their own; they want a municipality for their town and local boards for their country districts … [and] local self-government through the Wellington Provincial Government rather than through his Excellency'.[18] Apparently the *Independent* knew the desires of Napier better than its own memorialists. Some South Island papers also bought into this fiction. The *Canterbury Standard*, founded in 1854, criticised the act not so much on principle as for being used as a weapon of 'ultra-centralism' for 'the dismemberment of Wellington'.[19] Perhaps this was attributable to the lack of a secession threat in Canterbury, with Timaru's disquiet still a few years in the future. Superintendent William Sefton Moorhouse, on opening the provincial council after the act's passing, denounced it as 'disclosing an animus towards Provincial Institutions generally, foreshadowing the serious impairment of their Legislative functions, and a subsequent destruction of their usefulness' even though it was 'not much calculated to affect Canterbury'.[20] Moorhouse's criticisms were no doubt motivated by his belief in a powerful, independent superintendency and his opposition to the act's provision for councils to elect superintendents.[21]

The New Provinces Act was *not* written with just Wellington in mind, as was obvious from the Nelson boundary clause. When he arrived in London in April 1859 Stafford found that the Colonial Office's allowance of the act 'hung upon a thread'. Provincialists then in London, such as Clifford and FitzGerald, sought its disallowance, especially the latter, who was on good terms with Bulwer-Lytton.[22] They were unsuccessful and the legislation was left to operate without interference. Back in New Zealand Domett could not contain his fury when Marlborough's borders were defined. He vented his spleen in two extraordinary letters to Richmond, accusing the government of doing its 'best to quash the province of Nelson altogether … There was no occasion to *squeeze* into the new Province *every acre* of land you possibly could. You have left us only the worthless mountain tops with the expensive roads to be kept up … I do not see how you can escape the conclusion that you (some of you) have been actuated by some animus against the Nelson provincial Govt.'[23] In Domett's view the government gave 'the petitioners a larger extent of country even than they asked for' and 'you have made the new Province too large to carry out the true principle of the act … which was to divide the colony into something like counties'.[24] This was debatable, given Richmond's previous avowal that the ministry had moved away from municipalities to provinces, but time would, in a way, prove Domett right. Marlborough was too large *and* too small: its area was so big that a province of its small population struggled to sustain necessary public works.

Commercial buildings along Shakespeare Road, Napier, in 1862.

PA1-q-193-072, Alexander Turnbull Library, Wellington

The first test of the act came in Hawke's Bay. It had been most prominent in the new provinces debate, and if the expanded system could be confidently expected to work anywhere, it was there. But Hawke's Bay was embroiled in controversy almost from the outset. After winning secession, the alliance between most of the new province's leading political groups immediately divided into two factions: town and country – Napier and runholder.[25] The Stafford ministry hoped the act's provision for the superintendent to be chosen by the provincial council would reduce the unseemly clashes and time-wasting that occurred in other provinces between superintendents and hostile councils.[26] This decision was well intentioned, albeit framed to advance centralist goals by fashioning the superintendent as more of a chairperson or mayor of a municipality than a popularly elected quasi-governor. It would quickly backfire and show how fractious councils in small provinces could be, but from a longer-term perspective this would prove advantageous for abolitionists anyway.

The Hawke's Bay council made the selection of a superintendent scandalous. Its first sitting, on 23 April 1859, was preceded by considerable scheming behind the scenes. Most people in the crowded gallery, not privy to the intrigues, were astonished when Thomas Fitzgerald, member for Napier, was elected superintendent unanimously. Alfred Newman and J.C.L. Carter, both runholders and former soldiers, had been leading candidates, but the councillors found themselves deadlocked five-all. Accordingly both candidates withdrew before the first meeting. Donald McLean was offered the position but declined, citing his responsibilities to the central government. He had risen from being a police inspector and government agent to hold the combined offices of native secretary and chief land purchase commissioner, and enjoyed considerable mana with Māori on account of his command of their language and respect for social customs.[27] Fitzgerald, a surveyor who played a prominent role in secession, was advanced as a compromise candidate.[28] He did not enjoy widespread popularity; he was mockingly nicknamed 'Silky Tom' by some of the community, including future premier Domett, and considered a 'scheming Jesuit' by pioneering settler Alexander Alexander.[29] These slanderous opinions reflected bitter personal and factional conflict within Hawke's Bay's political class rather than serious sectarian division – Alexander was 'country', Fitzgerald was 'town'.[30] With no other viable compromise, however, Fitzgerald became superintendent. 'Silky Tom' vowed that he was a temporary candidate who took office solely to resolve the impasse and he 'did not seek a salaried office under government'.[31]

Fitzgerald's reputation as a schemer proved justified. He initially showed little enthusiasm for the superintendency, writing self-pityingly to McLean that he was unwilling to commit much time to the job lest it impinge upon his increasingly profitable personal business as a merchant.[32] However, he quickly warmed to the superintendency – or to its power. In November, having overseen the establishment of Hawke's Bay's provincial machinery and won the cordial support of much of the council, Fitzgerald indicated that he would resign the following month. He was not only earnestly requested to continue, but also voted an annual salary of £600 plus £200 for his previous service.[33] Fitzgerald's supporters stoutly rebuffed any suggestion his resignation had been offered with insincerity, but it was a clever ploy.[34] Despite his earlier pronouncements about taking the office in an honorary capacity, he was now receiving a considerable salary. The whole proceedings reflected poorly on Hawke's Bay, and cast doubt on the new method of electing a superintendent. Even as he took office Fitzgerald believed the position should have been popularly elected.[35]

Worse was to come the next year, when the province plunged into debt. The council sanctioned substantial public works, primarily Napier harbour improvements and rural roads. These were approved with an eye to runholder desires for better access to export markets; Fitzgerald described them as 'promoting the prosperity and rapid development' of Hawke's Bay.[36] He was wrong on both counts. Provincial funds were insufficient to meet demands and all government payments were suspended in July, the *Hawke's Bay Herald* ruing that this 'state of things … says very little for our business habits'.[37] Hawke's Bay became the first province to be overdrawn, to the tune of £3,500, and further public inconvenience was averted only when the bank provided an advance on the personal security of the provincial executive.[38] A petition was presented to the central government in September, requesting that local counties replace the whole provincial system in light of 'the grossest mismanagement' of Hawke's Bay's finances, conducted with 'neglect of the most ordinary rules of financial administration'.[39] Although it was not widely signed, a broad cross-section of Hawke's Bay society put their names to it. Less than two years into Hawke's Bay's provincial life, there was already an obvious undercurrent of dissatisfaction with both secession and provincialism.

If centralists wanted provincialism to suffer a swift blow, they could barely have hoped for better in Hawke's Bay. Provincialists, seeking to revoke the New Provinces Act and restore power to the original provinces, swooped on the September petition, but in truth the provincial system was beginning to come apart. Centralists blocked a provincialist attempt in 1860 to amend or repeal the act – just in time to allow Southland to secede and become another burden. The 1860 parliamentary debate and its reprise in 1861 focused on Hawke's Bay, with politicians on both sides of the debate unwilling to invoke fledgling Marlborough – less than a year old at the time of the first debate.

In signifying royal assent to the act back in 1859, Lord Carnarvon, colonial under-secretary to Bulwer-Lytton, informed Governor Browne that the Colonial Office firmly recommended an amendment. This, however, was to satisfy creditors who had lent money to a province on the basis of its security before any secession that they would continue to enjoy the same security.[40] Carnarvon dismissed the concerns of Wellington members absent from the vote. This was not what provincialists wanted to read. In October 1860 a motion to repeal the act was put before the House by Otago's Thomas Gillies, a formidable politician determined to leave a mark during his first parliamentary session. He later became a leading separatist and then superintendent of Auckland. To a packed gallery – one of the most crowded of the session – Gillies introduced the second reading of the New Provinces Act Amendment Bill with a fiery speech on 12 October 1860.

The bill would render inoperative the key features of the original act. After much bluster that the New Provinces Act was a 'political blunder' and 'a worm … eat[ing] out the core of the greatness of this country', Gillies got down to business.[41] He tore into the act for allowing provinces to secede without any discretionary powers; he accused the ministry of deviously withholding objections from the Colonial Office until the act had already received assent, including a series of resolutions by Otago Provincial Council; he argued – correctly – that the act did not promote local self-government, reduced the efficiency of provinces in opening up New Zealand and had brought provincial institutions into contempt. It was a stirring speech that skewered the centralists. Moorhouse, Canterbury's superintendent, followed it with more of the same, insulting the new provinces as the spread of a disease and denouncing Hawke's Bay's financial mismanagement. This language enraged 'Silky Tom' Fitzgerald. He derided Moorhouse, the anti-provincial petition, Wellington's provincial council and any other perceived enemies of Hawke's Bay and the act that gave it life.[42] After the debate was adjourned for five days, it emerged that the other Otago member present would oppose Gillies' motion. Francis Dillon Bell was pledged to the electors of Wallace – the electorate encompassing Southland – to defend the act and their right to secede.[43] Ultimately a vote to kill the bill succeeded by a single vote.

This was not the end of the matter. After Stafford's government fell in 1861, a New Provinces Act Amendment Act was approved under the new Fox ministry. It passed only in a neutered form, however. The debate reprised similar themes to 1860, with the added fear of further secession – Southland had just left Otago, and where would be next? The Bay of Islands, Wanganui and especially Timaru were all names on members' lips. Fox originally wanted to repeal the New Provinces Act's first two clauses to stop the automatic creation of new provinces, but lengthy debate revealed the House was unwilling to do so without providing some recourse for outlying districts. There were also demands that a clause be added to allow the reannexation of provinces.[44] All that the ministry could pass was a watered-down, ineffective amendment of the New Provinces Act. A district seeking secession now had to present a petition signed in duplicate by 201 electors, not 150, thus limiting – at least marginally – the ability of very small districts to secede. It also introduced a requirement that before any secession petition was presented to the governor, it had to be forwarded to the superintendent of the affected province and published at least once a week for eight weeks in any newspaper in the affected province's principal town.[45] Yet there was no provision to act upon objections. Rather than being scrapped, the automatic secession clause was simply made a little stiffer.

As intended by Stafford's centralists, the edifice of provincialism began crumbling almost from the inauguration of new provinces. The original form of the provincial system had struggled to respond to the opening of hinterlands, and now the expansion of the system, in step with the spread of settlement, also proved to be flawed. The new provinces functioned poorly and showed that the settlers' cherished goal of administering local affairs themselves could not be achieved through a cumbrous political system unsuited to the requirements of small, isolated settlements. Within old provinces, these new settlements were ignored; within their own provinces, new settlements found it difficult to support the demands of provincial institutions – and soon became liable to complaints of neglect from their own hinterlands. Most significantly for provincialism's fate, centralists weathered the stormy first few years of the New Provinces Act's operation with little concession, despite widespread discontent. As the *New Zealander* noted, small districts 'may erect themselves into a separate State, where, powerless, poor, without credit or money, burthened it may be with debt, they must take upon themselves the charge of the maintenance of officials and departments, of harbours, police, gaols, schools, hospitals, charities, and those inevitable establishments under which the older Governments are gradually being bowed down'.[46] What it failed to mention was that all these burdens and costs were exacerbated by ill-informed policy and staggeringly petty political one-upmanship that stymied the real work of colonial government – the widening and deepening of settlement. This was soon to become most pronounced in Hawke's Bay's younger siblings, Marlborough and Southland.

Chapter 6
Marlborough and Southland Implode

To understand the downward spiral of provincialism, it is necessary to comprehend the self-inflicted wounds of two of the smallest provinces. Marlborough seceded before Southland and should have perhaps been a cautionary tale, since it demonstrated, to a greater degree, both of Hawke's Bay's tendencies – scandalous politics and overestimation of the capacity to develop infrastructure. Yet none of the provinces, confident in their own ability to succeed, seemed willing or able to learn lessons from any other. One reason for Marlborough's enthusiastic divorce from Nelson was lack of investment in infrastructure, so it rushed to entertain grand road and railway proposals. Within days of secession there were popular rumours – at that point baseless – about government plans to borrow money immediately for a railway or tramway.[1] The *Marlborough Press*, founded in Blenheim in January 1860 as the province's first newspaper, soon published proposals for an iron ore railway to Tophouse, a trunk road to other provinces that would enable Picton to act as the key port to the North Island, and a road and/or railway for general freight between Picton and Blenheim.[2]

The author of one proposal cast his ideas as a means of civilising Marlborough and raising it out of an infantile state. 'Roads of one sort or other' – he meant both highways and railways – 'must, of course, exist in every country emerged from barbarism … [their construction] contributes more powerfully than anything else to the progress of improvement.'[3] Only one contributor to the debate, surveyor William Budge, sought to counter the 'zealous, if not numerous supporters' of the railway by pointing out the obstacles of 'the material element of cost'.[4] Budge had professional expertise on England's railways, but had ceased such employment 18 years before. None of his assertions dissuaded Marlborough's railway zealots from the belief that recent technological advances worked in their financial favour and that they could support a railway. They overlooked that fact that Marlborough's Pākehā population was even lower than the 1500 stated in the 1857 secession petition. Of 1151 Pākehā, a mere 163 were actually registered electors.[5] Blenheim, the largest settlement, was a quiet country village, described by the *Marlborough*

Press as making 'rapid strides towards the appearance of a town. Houses are still going up, extending the street lines.'[6] By 1861 Marlborough had grown to 2299, 516 of whom were registered electors at the next election in 1862, but this was still a strikingly small settlement.[7]

Two bills, one for railway construction and another for a loan of £60,000, dominated the 1861 session of the provincial council. The *Marlborough Press*, the only source of advocacy in Marlborough outside personal persuasion, quelled objections and cajoled support for a railway to run from Picton's splendid harbour to Blenheim. It was the loudest voice amid a chorus of idealistic boosters. The railway was not conceived as a profitable enterprise; it would be constructed by the government as trustee for the people and operated for the public benefit.[8] This was not necessarily abnormal. Governments had cheaper access to finance than private borrowers, and railways in colonial New Zealand were constructed and constrained to serve settler interests rather than as independent economic enterprises.[9] Projected population growth and the resulting increased traffic justified high capital costs. Marlborough, though, had not yet learned to walk. Vague references to hypothetical future prosperity were inadequate. Neither the *Marlborough Press* nor any of the railway's other supporters could demonstrate how such a small province, with such modest means, would achieve the speculated growth and pay off the huge cost of the railway. Opposition, some of which came from selfish Blenheim interests seeking to preserve its status as a river port, was hastily dismissed as distasteful; railway proposals 'ought to have united every well-wisher to the province in its favour'.[10]

The provincial council, at this stage dominated by Picton residents, approved both bills with an eye to Picton's development as a centre of trade, but central government approval was necessary because the railway required Crown land. When the Picton Railway Bill went before parliament, Blenheim's river port interests had their own eye to outsmarting their opponent – William Henry Eyes, a man who hated Picton so much that he vowed to make it a deserted village.[11] Eyes migrated from England in 1838, first to an unprofitable cattle station in New South Wales, and then to New Zealand. As the owner of a successful Wairau Valley sheep run he would not brook any challenge by Picton against Blenheim. The Stafford ministry had been friendly to Picton, whose representative was the speaker, Monro, but Fox's new ministry owed its existence to Eyes, who was also the MHR for Wairau. The bill passed parliament, assisted by a petition with hundreds of signatures, including the Picton faction of the provincial council, and a favourable select committee report.[12] At this point, Eyes exerted his influence.

First, the loan that Marlborough had authorised was vetoed. Labouchere's 1857 instructions that Governor Browne should veto most provincial loans had not been followed scrupulously – the friendly Stafford ministry probably would have endorsed the loan – but now they proved convenient for the Fox ministry. Browne was advised to exercise his veto. Fox justified the decision by fears the loan would damage the credit of the whole colony, especially as he was critical of Marlborough's lack of financial data; the figures for expected returns and maintenance expenditure were conjectural and Fox could not adequately assess the province's ability to repay the loan.[13] Yet neither governor nor ministry wanted to be fully responsible for dashing Marlborough's hopes, so the Picton Railway Bill was reserved for imperial assent. It went to London, accompanied by the buck-passing caveat that the ministry did not feel 'warranted in recommending the confirmation of it' unless the Colonial Office could conjure a 'prudent and practical scheme ... for raising the requisite funds'.[14] No scheme was forthcoming and assent was denied, one of just five times Britain refused assent to a New Zealand bill.[15] Fox was partly motivated by enmity towards Monro, but it was Eyes' influence that persuaded the ministry to this course of action, and he was perfectly happy to boast about it.[16] Monro, enraged, denounced Eyes for holding 'blind and bigoted hostility'– the 'name of Picton operated on Mr Eyes like a red rag upon a bull'.[17] It was an accurate depiction and the whole affair foreshadowed much similar petty conflict led by Eyes.

A happy by-product of Eyes' hostility towards Picton was that the province avoided expenditure it could not afford, but Marlborough's railway boosters would not yield. The council sought a £75,000 loan in 1863, and when this was rebuffed, £60,000. Marlborough originally applied for the loan during the administration of Domett's ministry, which was favourably disposed to provincial loans, but while the loan was under consideration there was a change of ministry to one led by Frederick Whitaker with Fox as colonial secretary. Fox repeated his previous reasons for rejecting a loan – light population, meagre revenue, vague budgets – and judged that Marlborough offered insufficient land as security. It put up land ostensibly worth £87,500, but Fox had serious reservations, especially when gold was discovered. He was convinced that a goldfield would be a source of expense rather than revenue because of the extra services and infrastructure the provincial government would need to provide. To a final plea from Thomas Carter, Marlborough's frustrated superintendent, that railway construction would provide employment for destitute men, Fox curtly replied that this was 'not the proper object for a loan', and even if it were, 'there does not appear any probability of negotiating it in the present state of the money market'.[18]

There the matter should have ended, but Marlborough pursued one more doomed scheme. In 1865 it approved a hopelessly optimistic proposal by William Long Wrey to raise money in England and build the railway as a private enterprise. Once a Cornish miner, by 1853 Wrey began to make a name for himself in Nelson as a railway booster.[19] He was central to the opening of New Zealand's first railway in 1862, the private Dun Mountain Railway in Nelson. By 1865 this was struggling and Wrey saw an opportunity in Marlborough. He took £1,000 from the provincial council on the condition that, if he secured a contract, he would keep the money as remuneration for expenses, and if he failed, he would return the money.[20] As security, the council took out a mortgage over some of Wrey's possessions. In keeping with the province's misfortunes, Wrey not only failed to find investors but also did not pay back the £1,000, and the mortgaged property raised just £135 at auction.[21] Marlborough's shambling railway hopes were finally halted, but only because the conduct and management of the provincial government had become so embarrassing and expensive that no further attempt could possibly be entertained.

It was bad enough for the long-suffering locals that their provincial government could not provide basic public works to stimulate the economy and open markets for export; they did not need the humiliation of a council that was more dysfunctional, acrimonious and petty than any other in New Zealand. It was riven by a dispute about whether Blenheim, the established inland centre, or Picton, the port, should be the capital, and tempers flared as soon as the proclamation of Marlborough's independent existence affirmed Picton as capital.[22] This dispute so consumed Marlborough politics that by the middle of the 1860s few other issues were even considered and competent governance was cast aside. Neither the townsmen and small farmers of Blenheim nor the runholders who held property in Picton were willing to give an inch – either their town should be the capital, or they would destroy the other.

Because Picton was then little more than a few meagre houses on the shores of Queen Charlotte Sound, connected to the rest of the province by a rough road and singularly unsuited to hosting a legislative chamber, the first council met at Blenheim in April 1860. Rather conveniently, James Sinclair, councillor for The Beaver, as Blenheim was then known,[23] and a member of Eyes' rabidly anti-Picton faction, owned the Blenheim courthouse, so the provincial council met there. Throughout its existence the council hosted an unending series of controversies, and the most dramatic disputes meant Marlborough did more than its fair share to bring the provincial system into disrepute.[24] The capital moved to Picton in April

1861 only after angry public debates in Blenheim, which sought to erect public buildings and keep the council.[25]

The Blenheim supporters, led by Eyes, seized their opportunity at the first meeting of the second council on 20 September 1862.[26] The incumbent superintendent, William Douglas Hall Baillie of the Picton faction, knew he lacked the numbers to win re-election from the council. As soon as the first meeting began, and before it had time to elect a speaker and superintendent, Baillie rose and prorogued the council. Technically, he was within the letter of the law, since he remained superintendent until the council chose a new one, but it was a cynical move, attempting to buy time while he and his faction challenged the results of the recent election. The gallery, full to capacity, burst into laughter, and Baillie departed with his supporters, believing himself victorious. The remainder of the council, however, ignored the prorogation and elected Eyes superintendent. Suddenly Marlborough had two men claiming to hold the province's highest office, and Baillie refused to hand over the keys to the council or any other instruments of government.

Eyes and his faction, unable to meet in the provincial chamber, gathered in the Tasmanian Hotel across the road and resolved to move the council to Blenheim, where they next met on 24 October. The farce was not over.[27] In accordance with the New Provinces Act, Eyes resigned his seat when he was elected superintendent, but was unable to sit in the council as he could not issue writs for his re-election while Baillie held the provincial seal. With the provincial records also firmly in Baillie's possession, Eyes could not prepare any business for the council, and although he travelled to Wellington to initiate legal proceedings, the machinery of justice moved slowly. Neither superintendent could access public funds since the bank, naturally, was unwilling to advance any money until a decision was made on who rightfully held office. All public works and government activity ground to a humiliating halt, leaving provincial employees such as the Marlborough police unpaid for months.[28] The fiasco continued until the governor dissolved the council and new elections were held – after which the council met in Picton, partly because that was still required by law and partly because the Picton party won the election.

The next attempt to relocate the capital to Blenheim would not fail, but it again came at the cost of Marlborough's dignity. In 1865 Marlborough found itself not with two competing superintendents, but with two opposing councils – an astonishing situation that represented the lowest ebb of provincial politics. When the council met in Picton in late June it fervidly debated whether the superintendent had the exclusive right to determine where the council met. The Picton supporters of the superintendent, Arthur Seymour, resented Blenheim's renewed attempts to move the capital and emphasised the superintendent's constitutional right to fix the time and place of the council's sitting. Eyes, however, arrogantly asserted that the council could decide any question before it, and was supported by James Sinclair, who argued that if the Picton faction was right then the council could be convened 'at the top of some hill'.[29] The Blenheim group, in the majority after securing an alliance with disenchanted former supporters of Seymour,[30] commanded 11 of the council's 20 votes and carried a motion to hold the next meeting in Blenheim.

Frustrated at this attempt to usurp his constitutional authority, Seymour ignored the vote and summoned the council to meet again in Picton. His nine supporters continued to meet in Picton, happily defiant of the Blenheim resolution.[31] They did not even deign to notice the Blenheim faction's absence and quietly proceeded with their business.[32] Meanwhile, the 11 seceding members met at the Blenheim courthouse and held their own session, assuming full legislative functions and passing estimates that, among other things, slashed the superintendent's salary. The situation could not last, and on 5 July, the Blenheim party marched on Picton, entered the provincial chambers, to the astonishment of the members there, and attempted to substitute their own minutes into the record.

What happened next is unique in provincial history. Both sides made increasingly vicious and aggressive speeches, including an attempt by Eyes to have the packed public gallery expelled, and the Blenheim group sought to pass a motion of no confidence in Seymour. Lacking the numbers to defend itself from such attacks, the Picton faction needed a hero. It found one in author Katherine Mansfield's grandfather, Arthur Beauchamp, a man who then possessed less than a year's political experience. In a spectacular act of public speaking, he stonewalled with a ten-and-a-half hour speech through the night. This was enough to tire the Blenheim councillors, many of whom withdrew to the Tasmanian Hotel. The no confidence motion was withdrawn and the council adjourned to October. Beauchamp won the battle, but it was a Pyrrhic victory.

New Zealand was scandalised and Marlborough was viewed as a joke. The scenes in the provincial chamber had been accompanied by a mob in the gallery hooting the Blenheim members, and then pelting them with stones outside.[33] The *Nelson Examiner* delighted in the apparent foresight of Charles Elliott, who in 1859 predicted 'two parties would spring up … [that] would fight and scratch each other until nothing would be left of either'.[34] The *Press* of Christchurch, which had been founded in 1861, summed up the popular impression: 'Marlborough, in the absence of any other mode of achieving fame, resolves to do so by making itself infinitely ridiculous.'[35] The most insightful comment, however, came from the soul-searching of the *Marlborough Press* as it came to grips with the province's position: 'Politically, what are we? Our whole population barely numbers that of a village in England or a suburb of Melbourne, and yet we aspire to so much. The wretchedness of provincial institutions has a wonderful exemplification in this little Province of Marlborough.'[36]

The horrified governor dissolved the council, hoping new elections would bring some order. Seymour was bundled out of both the superintendency and the council and, to the profound disappointment of Picton, Eyes had sufficient support to become the new superintendent. In November 1865 he achieved the removal of the provincial government to Blenheim and left Picton hurriedly with the instruments of government before aggrieved locals could attempt to retain them.[37]

Hawke's Bay stumbled from the outset, but Marlborough collapsed beneath the weight of ambition and petty rivalries. The vitriol of Marlborough's internal conflict and the public works aspirations of both provinces were at manifest odds with their minuscule populations. Although provincial government was clearly not suitable for such small communities, the system had already proved defective when Hawke's Bay and Marlborough were part of larger, more sustainable provinces. 'The opposers of Provincial Institutions', wrote the *Independent* in 1862, 'have an additional cause for rejoicing; another province [Marlborough] having been added to the number of those whose machinery has come to a dead lock.'[38] As other threats to provincial institutions developed through the 1860s, it did not help that the newest provinces were crumbling faster than the original six. One, though, fared worse than the others. Neither Hawke's Bay nor Marlborough experienced the lows of their younger sibling, Southland. More than any other scandal, Southland's experience demonstrated the deficiencies and poverty of the provincial system.

Back when Southland was known as Murihiku, its future appeared hopeful and bright. The passage of the New Provinces Act renewed Murihiku's hopes of leaving Otago and its enthusiasm was stoked by ham-fisted attempts by Otago politicians, especially Superintendent William Cargill, to stall secession in the late 1850s. As his biographer noted, Cargill 'overestimated his influence outside Otago and underestimated the determination of the southerners'.[39] He presented a personal petition to parliament decrying secession as injurious to Otago and in debate he dismissed the Murihiku settlers as 'the remnant of a Sydney Whaling Station', a few 'hardy squatters', and a 'clamorous' Melbourne party.[40] Cargill did not act alone. His provincial council in 1858 endorsed a report denouncing Murihiku secessionism – further proof to the secessionists that Otago was hostile to Murihiku's interests.[41]

James Alexander Robertson
Menzies, the leading public
figure in early Southland, always
wore items of Highland dress.
PAColl-0785-1-207-03, Alexander Turnbull
Library, Wellington

Cargill's visit to Invercargill to address a public meeting in July 1859 was decisive. He was obdurate on secession: a 'wilder or more destructive course, as regards the progress of New Zealand' was inconceivable.[42] This poorly chosen language was more than enough to maintain the motivation of secessionists, especially their leader, James Menzies.

Finally, in April 1861, Murihiku won secession. It was a close-run affair. Menzies, along with the newly founded *Southern News* – later the *Southland News* – kept passions alive through 1860 and early 1861.[43] The successful petition to the central government requesting secession barely satisfied the criteria of the New Provinces Act and it would have failed had the amendments of 1860 been successful. James Macandrew, Cargill's successor as superintendent, made stern representations to Browne about the number of invalid signatures on the petition.[44] Many objections, however, were petty, including such pedantry as signatory 'Alexander Clark of Waikiwi' being registered as 'Alexander T. Clark' on the electoral roll.[45] Sufficient signatures survived investigation for Murihiku to be declared an independent province by order-in-council on 25 March 1861. The news was not all good. Otago MHRs used their influence to limit the bounds of the new province, keeping Fiordland and the eastern Mataura for Otago, and foisted upon it the name 'Southland'.[46] Southland's local member, Francis Dillon Bell, wrote furiously to Menzies that the ministry was almost totally lacking in taste: 'I did not however anticipate such a villainous name for the new Province. Of all the names that could have been invented, to take an unpronounceable heap of consonants!'[47] There was nothing to be done: the name was gazetted and Murihiku learnt to live as Southland.

There was also nothing to be done about Southland's bad timing. Its independent existence began on 1 April; less than two months later, Gabriel Read made his famous discovery of gold near Lawrence, sparking the Otago gold rush. Immigrants and wealth flooded into Otago, completely transforming the province and enriching the merchant and pastoral classes. Southland entertained dreams of discovering a goldfield within its own borders to transform Bluff into the 'New Zealand Melbourne',[48] yet the young province could only watch jealously when, in August 1862, Horatio Hartley and Christopher Reilly registered in Dunedin their discovery of gold on the Dunstan River in Central Otago. A few months later, on 23 November, Southland's fortunes appeared to change dramatically. When gold was struck on the Arrow River, the successful prospectors made for Invercargill, not Dunedin. The *Invercargill Times*, founded earlier that year as a more conservative rival to the *News*, was jubilant: '[the prospectors] were strangers to Invercargill, they went up to the Dunstan via Dunedin, and they were consequently acquainted with that route; their interests were connected with that city, and yet … they make for Invercargill in order to obtain supplies'.[49] Invercargill, closer to the Central Otago goldfields than Dunedin, considered itself better placed to supply the rush's needs and thereby profit from this trade.

To supply the goldfields Southland required reliable transportation, which did not exist. Organised Pākehā settlement was less than a decade old, Invercargill was surrounded by swamp for the first 18 miles (30 km) of the route to Central Otago, the route south to Bluff was equally swampy, and rudimentary roads kept sinking into the voracious soil.[50] The need for a railway was clear even before the Central gold rush, and Menzies – predictably elected superintendent of the province he helped establish – emphasised this theme in the provincial council during 1862.[51] By early 1863 Invercargill was rife with discussion about the best infrastructure to build to access Central Otago. This was particularly animated because Southlanders believed they had already lost much trade and wealth to Dunedin through sluggish involvement in the goldfields.[52] Menzies brought two proposals before the provincial council, one of which was approved: a conventional railway between Invercargill and Bluff to provide a much-needed link between capital and port. It rejected his other proposal, a poorly detailed and hastily prepared suggestion for a horse tramway north to the gravelly plains beyond Winton.[53] Money was instead voted for the upkeep of a road through the swamp and northbound travellers had to endure another muddy winter.

At the end of July the province's chief surveyor, Theophilus Heale, presented his preliminary report into a northern railway. Heale, originally one of Wellington's first settlers, was a well-regarded, thorough surveyor and a capable mathematician.[54] He emphasised that time was of the essence, as the 'primary object [was] … securing to this Province the great traffic which has sprung up with the Whakatipu Lake [sic]'.[55] Work had to be complete by May 1864 to beat the next winter when the road would become an 'adhesive bog'. The Bluff railway was already under construction with iron rails, but Heale did not believe it possible to obtain a sufficient quantity from England in time for the northern line. James R. Davies, a Bluff railway contractor who had recently arrived from Victoria, proposed a solution: he would quickly and cheaply build the northern line with wooden rails. According to his figures, the superstructure of an iron railway cost £2187 per mile while wood cost only £460.[56] He imported a demonstration locomotive to run on a short length of track, and Heale endorsed the plan in the belief that it 'involves no danger, and affords every probability of success'.[57] The locomotive *Lady Barkly* became the first to raise steam in New Zealand when it shuttled back and forth along a temporary track laid on the Invercargill jetty on 8 August 1863. The demonstration, under the watchful eye of Menzies and other government officials, was 'extremely gratifying'.[58] Enthusiasm subsumed scepticism and the demonstration was all the impetus Southland needed to choose wooden rails.

By October preliminary works were under way and the provincial council approved two loans to cover costs. One, for £140,000, was passed in April to cover the Bluff railway, and the second in October sought £110,000 for the first 18 miles (30 km) of the wooden railway to Winton.[59] Both received the assent of the governor on the advice of his responsible ministers. The Domett ministry, which had a relaxed attitude towards provincial loans, approved the Bluff loan and informed Menzies that northern railway proposals would receive a favourable hearing in Auckland. Domett believed Southland was pursuing 'good policy' on sound reasoning.[60] His ministry fell before considering the second loan, but the new Whitaker ministry also granted approval. Both April and October's debentures had an interest rate of 6 per cent; these were handed in full to banks to cover advances – the first £140,000 to the Bank of New South Wales and then £110,000 to the Bank of Otago. The banks charged Southland 7 per cent interest on the advances and sold the debentures on the London market.[61] In the absence of Menzies, who was attending the Legislative

The bold railway ambitions of Southland: a regular iron-railed line from Invercargill to Bluff (opened 1867) and an experimental wooden-railed line from Invercargill to Kingston via Winton. Some versions of the latter scheme had the railway ending in Winton with a road from there to Kingston. Only the first stage to Makarewa opened, in 1864.

Lady Barkly, built by the Hunt and Opie Victoria Foundry in Ballarat, Victoria.

VPRS 12800/P1, item H 1655, Public Record Office Victoria. Reproduced by permission of the Keeper of Public Records

Council in Auckland, Deputy Superintendent Nathaniel Chalmers had the honour of turning the first sod of the wooden railway at a ceremony on 25 November 1863.[62] Many businesses closed for the day and Southlanders anticipated that the wealth of Otago's goldfields would soon flow south.

The cost of construction spiralled out of control but ambitious optimism went unquestioned in public. By January 1864 the Bluff railway had exceeded costs by over £35,000 and the construction of roads and the railway to the north had incurred liabilities of almost £100,000.[63] The next month the provincial council sought two new loans to cover debts and fund the remaining costs necessary to complete both railways. By now, however, the Whitaker ministry's willingness to accommodate provincial borrowing had narrowed; it was seeking a central loan for £3 million in London. It reluctantly approved one of Southland's proposed loans, £40,000 for the Bluff railway, but categorically rejected a £120,000 loan for the wooden railway.[64] Despite financial concerns, Heale spoke glowingly of the railways at a banquet celebrating Southland's secession. He forecast that the first 10 miles (16 km) would be open soon and hoped that 36 miles (58 km) would be operational within three months.[65] The main Invercargill railway station, equipped with commodious passenger and goods facilities, was nearing completion. The *Daily News* – the rechristened *Southland News*, which had become a daily on the back of Invercargill's growth – echoed Heale's belief the railway would be open to Bluff and Winton within three months. It was sure that '[a]t present nothing threatens any untoward delay in opening the line'.[66]

Nonetheless rumours about the province's finances were afoot by late April and in early May the *Daily News* called for 'a Treasurer, possessing something of the quality of statesmanship' to deal with provincial finances – but calmed nerves with the assurance that 'the Government has fulfilled its engagements and maintained its credit, and we have no reason to apprehend that it will fail to do so'.[67] At this critical juncture the *Daily News* was the only public voice in the capital; the *Invercargill Times*' offices had been destroyed by fire and it did not return until June, renamed the *Southland Times*. Through the following fortnight the *Daily News* espoused optimism while demanding, increasingly aggressively, an emergency meeting of the council to resolve provincial finances. It struggled to understand how there could be a crisis when the money required was a 'mere bagatelle' compared with the millions of acres of land Southland could offer as security.[68]

Behind the scenes the provincial executive scrambled to avert financial collapse under the weight of railway costs and misappropriated expenditure, but only succeeded in scandalising the province at the hands of the *Otago Daily Times* and its editor Julius Vogel. The entrepreneurial Vogel was an English Jew who had emigrated first to Victoria at the age of 17 in 1852, where he entered business on the goldfields first as a merchant and then as a newspaperman, before following gold seekers across the Tasman to Otago in October 1861. He continued plying his newspaper trade and founded the *Otago Daily Times*, New Zealand's first daily paper, only a month after arriving in Dunedin. A talented writer with strong political interests, Vogel was only too happy to publish a scoop on Southland's dealings. The *Otago Daily Times* revealed that the banks had refused any further overdraft or accommodation to the Southland government, so the executive 'prepared to issue Treasury notes, printed in imitation of bank notes, and which the unwary might mistake for them'.[69] Samuel Beaven, a member of the executive, was sent to Dunedin on an emergency mission to secure more funds from the Bank of Otago. Provincial Treasurer William Tarlton confirmed to another paper that the executive briefly contemplated, as a last resort, an issue of 'convertible Treasury notes', but that 'they never *entertained the question of actually issuing them*'.[70] Beaven apparently felt himself authorised to order a note plate for a test pressing, allowed the design to closely resemble bank notes, had copies struck in blue and pink and one found its way to Vogel.[71] This was possibly the least helpful news the province could have received. Instead of carefully negotiating to win emergency concessions, the executive had committed a calamitous, if not quite criminal, blunder.

A few days later, on 20 May, the *Daily News* announced that '[t]he public works are now actually stopped!'[72] The northern railway was nowhere near Winton, let alone Lake Wakatipu, and the Bluff railway was similarly incomplete. Invercargill, already entering a commercial depression, felt acutely the collapse of public works that employed many men and kept numerous businesses afloat. The *Daily News* was furious that a few thousand pounds could not be found to complete the railways 8 miles (13 km) north to Makarewa to meet the road to Central Otago or 16 miles (26 km) south to Mokomoko jetty, where there was deep water, if not quite the desirable Bluff harbour. The revived *Southland Times* insisted that the railways were affordable if expensive and blamed the collapse of provincial finances on wasteful expense and mismanagement.[73] Outside Invercargill, rage had been palpable ever since the provincial council had sought new loans in February. Riverton – an older settlement than Invercargill and still bitter about being passed over as capital and principal port – took a particularly dim view of Invercargill's dealings.[74] The *Riverton Times* captured Southland's folly by asking pointedly 'are the goldfields at the Wakatip [*sic*], unlike all other goldfields yet discovered, inexhaustible, and is the lead of the gold always sure to follow the line of the railway?'[75]

With neither railway even close to finished, the provincial government was starved of revenue with which to repay its debts. Unable to negotiate any further overdraft from the banks and prohibited from raising a new loan, Southland became reliant on the central government, which advanced money reluctantly – £15,000 per month for four months – on the security of Southland's waste land revenue.[76] More bad news was to come, which imperilled the success of the wooden railway when work finally resumed. At a terse and damning exchange in council, it emerged that Chalmers, in an attempt to save money, had authorised the use of inferior wood for the northern railway. Kahikatea, a soft wood best known as the material for butter boxes in the early days of refrigerated exports, and other cheap timber had been used instead of the contractually mandated and more expensive kauri, matai, totara and Tasmanian blue gum.[77] Nonetheless, construction resumed on the wooden railway in August 1864 in a desperate attempt to open part of it, generate income and salvage a modicum of dignity. The Central Otago rush was past its peak and the feverish excitement of new discoveries would soon move to the West Coast,

Invercargill railway station c. 1864, with the wooden rails clearly visible.
Box 087-002, Hocken Collections, Uare Taoka o Hākena, Dunedin

but even before construction began, Heale had emphasised another purpose for a railway. It would open prime agricultural land where railways, 'the best means of communication', were 'required for purely local purposes'.[78] It would also drain produce from the province's north and northeast, and open up the northwest and Fiordland. If Southland could not have Otago's gold, it might at least exploit its own resources.

The calamitous opening of the Southland railway showed just how spectacularly it had failed. The grand opening on 18 October 1864 was meant to be a day of achievement and celebration, but the train to Makarewa was reserved for invited guests, leaving the rest of the populace furious on the platform.[79] To calm popular dissatisfaction, a second grand opening with trains open to the public was planned for a week later. Three days before these new festivities, a pall was cast over proceedings by the first death of a railway worker in New Zealand: young Alfred Gasket died instantly when he fell beneath a train shunting in Makarewa.[80] When the big day came, Southlanders enjoyed a public holiday and turned out in large numbers to ride to Makarewa, where a picnic and sporting events were held. The morning passed without incident, but afternoon rain left the tracks coated in clay. In a shower of sparks and smoke, the locomotive struggled for traction as it hauled trainloads of tired passengers home to Invercargill. It was also too heavy for the poor quality wood used to make the rails and had already carved out splinters. Some disgruntled travellers were left to fend for themselves, either walking home to Invercargill damp and tired, or staying the night in Makarewa.[81] The poor planning and foolhardiness behind Southland's wooden railway was clear and the line was unready for regular traffic.

What was a province to do? Southland drifted into a malaise. The railway was an omnishambles: even its rare operational periods were beset by problems, such as cinders from the locomotive setting fire to the wooden rails in December 1866.[82] The opening of the Bluff railway in 1867 could do little to salvage the province's pride or prosperity. It had been accompanied by yet more controversy, notably when police seized government property on 20 December 1864 to repay debts. The contractors who had constructed Bluff's railway pier received a judgement of over £15,500 against the provincial council. To pay the debt, the Invercargill sheriff took possession of the government offices, books and railway plant, which were only returned two days later when Menzies indemnified the sheriff personally.[83] This occurrence highlighted a discrepancy between colonial and provincial law: central government property could not be seized, but provincial property could, and the spectre of further litigation over Southland's debts remained. As the province's anniversary of separation from Otago fell on 1 April 1865, the *Southland News* sarcastically wondered whether an 'All Fool's Day' separation banquet would be held.[84] The paper had reason to be bitter: it had reverted to its former name because it was no longer a daily publication. Invercargill's commercial depression, exacerbated if not caused by the wooden railway, had many victims and the press was not immune from hardship.

Ambition cost Southland dearly. It personally hurt Menzies' political career. After fresh elections the council, by a narrow margin, chose not to give him a second term as superintendent; it then elected Heale, but his election was struck out on a technicality.[85] On business in Auckland at the time, Heale never returned to Invercargill.[86] John Parkin Taylor, whose initial election on 12 January 1865 was also struck out, was finally declared superintendent on 13 March after a revolving door of acting superintendents. Taylor, one of Southland's longest residents and a prominent Riverton citizen, inherited a heavily indebted government and implemented a programme of sweeping retrenchment and austerity.[87] The province had liabilities of over £400,000; its assets were a meagre £34,865, including almost £8,000 of overdue immigration bills, and the banks were now threatening to charge interest of 12 per cent on their advances.[88]

James Menzies sketched by James Brown, c. 1865, annotated by Hocken: 'Refers to the disastrous separation of Southland from the Province of Otago of which it formed part. Dr Menzies, fishing for the superintendency, "catches crabs".'

11,600, Hocken Collections, Uare Taoka o Hākena, Dunedin

Southland was bankrupt. Besides its debts to the banks and the central government, more and more private creditors were clamouring for payment. According to a central government report, Southland's only hope of raising the money independently was its land fund, but land sales had stalled.[89] The *Southland News* argued despondently that if Southland could survive only by delaying repayments with tedious applications of the law, then 'the sooner our individual being as a Province is blotted out, the better'.[90] Both the province and its creditors looked to the General Assembly for a solution. In October 1865 it passed the Southland Provincial Debt Act, which had far-reaching consequences. To avoid any more disasters, the final clause of the legislation required the governor to approve provincial loans only if they received the General Assembly's assent. To rectify the immediate difficulty, the superintendent and the central auditor-general would certify Southland's debts, which would become claims on the colony as a whole. They would then bear 6 per cent interest until they were paid – by the central government with debentures also bearing 6 per cent interest, with the principal to be repaid within 30 years. Although these debentures were made a charge on the ordinary revenue of the colony, Southland's land revenue was impounded to cover costs.

Chapter 7
The End of Secession

Despite Marlborough and Southland's experiences, other outlying regions remained confident in their ability to secede and govern themselves. South Canterbury was the most likely site of another new province, even though its regional centre, Timaru, barely existed when the New Provinces Act was passed. In 1858 it contained little more than a homestead and a pub, but by January 1861 its population was roughly 300 and growing rapidly.[1] In December that year the population of the region between the Rangitata River and the Otago border had passed 1200.[2] South Canterbury was probably short of the number of electors required by the act but its residents believed firmly in the region's prospects. By August 1861 secessionist desire had taken hold of Timaru, based on the usual grievances of neglect, underrepresentation and frustration that local revenue was spent elsewhere – such as on Canterbury's ambitious railway tunnel.[3]

That month Moorhouse fronted the largest public meeting in Timaru's short history. Fearing the 'dismemberment' of his province, the Canterbury superintendent, in an able and conciliatory address, reached out to southern Cantabrians. He promised to make Timaru a port of entry and forecast a railway network for all of Canterbury, of which the tunnel was a necessary first step.[4] Afterwards many retired to the Royal Hotel, where Alfred Cox, an Australian-born runholder who had cut a prominent figure at the meeting, recalled that 'the representatives of both sides of the question met, ate, drank, and made merry; all agreeing that William Sefton Moorhouse was a right good fellow'.[5] This conciliation and merriment did not stop over 100 residents signing a petition against the act's repeal, but Moorhouse had successfully calmed immediate agitation and neutralised local anger ahead of the passage of the New Provinces Act Amendment Act the next month.[6]

Secessionist fervour was revived in early 1862. Some settlers threatened to leave the province if their grievances were not addressed, while others wanted secession 'at any cost and whatever may be the consequence'.[7] Yet it was not until 1864 that South Canterbury secession entered its most passionate phase. The *Timaru Herald* was

> ### TIMARU SEPARATION.
>
> ———
>
> Tune—King of the Cannibal Islands.
>
> Oh ! have you heard the news of late ?
> We've wanted it long, but we've had to wait,
> But we're coming forward now in state—
>   For Timaru Separation.
>
> For long we've been like a pig in a poke ;
> Our money and lands have gone like smoke—
> Expostulation is thought a joke,
>   So we must have Separation.
>
> Our roads, ankle deep in mud are laid,
> Tho' lots of money for them we've paid ;
> To save us from being bankrupt made,
>   We must have Separation.
>
> To see our money go, 'tis pretty,—
> To build for Lyttelton a jetty ;
> There's only one thing now will fit ye,—
>   And that is Separation.
>
> Fifty thousand acres go—how fine !
> To Holmes, for the Rakaia line—
> If you won't be ruined, you must combine,
>   For immediate Separation.
>
> And then there's another famous bore,
> Williamson's patent bonded store,—
> Why, the sea there for years will roar,
>   If we don't have Separation.
>
> Sutter and Turnbull both have told
> How only we can save our gold,—
> And this is just by going in bold,
>   For downright Separation.
>
> Oh ! Separation is all a hoax—
> So say the squatters, led by Cox,
> But I hope that they'll be in the wrong box,
>   When we get Separation.
>
> Then, there's "silent Simms" who looks so glum,
> On every subject he is dumb—
> To him, I think we should say " come,"
>   "'Tis time we separated."
>
> Then let us heart and hand unite,
> To free ourselves from our bondage-light—
> To OUR OWN, we surely have BEST right ;
>   So, good luck to Separation !
>
>   TRUE BLUE.
>   Timaru, June 12, 1865.

The secessionist author of these song lyrics ('True Blue') was 'going in bold for downright separation'.

founded in June 1864 to advocate for the easiest and cheapest method of securing the region's interests – which essentially meant secession – and by January 1865 a petition to secede was doing the rounds.[8] The electoral roll was now large enough to satisfy the amended act: 317 of the region's 2000 inhabitants were enrolled and more were expected to do so if it would aid secession.[9] Songs were even written to support the cause:

for long we've been like a pig in a poke
our money and lands have gone like smoke
expostulation is thought a joke
so we must have separation.[10]

The creation of South Canterbury as New Zealand's tenth province had become distinctly probable.

Other regions, too, wanted to secede. Rumours of a secession movement in the Bay of Islands were strong enough to be discussed in the Auckland Provincial Council in March 1865, where they became the subject of a disapproving motion.[11] Hugh Carleton, a former and future Bay of Islands member then representing Newton, supported secession but denied the existence of a movement, and the sitting Bay of Islands member, J.W. Williams, said there was no secession petition.[12] A Wanganui secession movement had been on the rise since the start of the 1860s and, like South Canterbury, reached its peak in 1864–65. Its appeal, however, was predominantly confined to Wanganui township and its immediate hinterland. In the Manawatu, Rangitikei and Turakina regions, which Wanganui wanted to include within its borders, opposition to secession was strong. Petitions for and against secession were circulated, including one against that was signed by all 44 adult male Pākehā in the Manawatu, and the Wellington newspapers made no attempt to hide their opposition.[13] One pro-secession petition in 1864 would have succeeded had some signatories not withdrawn their names before it was presented to the governor.[14]

The North Otago region also became more assertive. The *Oamaru Times* was founded in February 1864 with the express purpose of advocating for the region's interests and proper administration of public finances.[15] The *Lyttelton Times* argued that if Timaru and Oamaru must secede from their provinces, the General Assembly should combine them as one strong province rather than allowing the New Provinces Act to create two weak provinces.[16] This sensible proposal deserved more consideration than it received, but Oamaru was disenchanted with provincialism and 582 signatories petitioned the General Assembly to replace provinces with local boards sustained by a portion of their land fund.[17]

These rumblings for secession or complete restructuring made provincialists in the General Assembly nervous. Fearing further damage to the system, they finally seized the opportunity to repeal the New Provinces Act in 1865. Not everybody took the secessionists seriously. Writing specifically about Timaru, but in terms applicable to all the movements, the *Lyttelton Times* was dismissive: 'If they want attention paid them, they give notice of a separation meeting, and talk a great deal about the New Provinces Act. By this means they at least get a visit from some members of the government, which results a little later in a good round vote of money in the Provincial Council for the aggrieved district.'[18] However, the act's automatic secession clause meant that threats could not be ignored – any region could secede in a fit of popular excitement. Moreover the lack of any provisions for reunion meant that a hasty secession could not be easily reversed. Nelson's *Colonist* captured much of the popular frustration when it wondered bitterly '[h]ow long is this iniquitous act which permits of such divisions and such unnecessary multiplying of governments and officials, to continue to disgrace the statute-book of the colony?'[19] There was a distinct concern throughout New Zealand that new provinces would follow the example of Marlborough and Southland and plunge headlong into debt.[20] 'Provincialism,' it seemed to the *Press*, 'is being gradually extinguished, and nothing has more surely tended to this result that the conduct of some of the new provinces.'[21]

Two bills were proposed in 1865, one compromise bill and one for repeal. The latter succeeded just after Edward Stafford returned to the premiership. Although he was premier when the New Provinces Act passed in 1858, his new ministry was weak. The previous ministry, led by Frederick Weld, had been thrown out by provincialists, but they lacked a man of sufficient standing to become premier. This left Stafford to form a compromise ministry, one that the leaders of both centralism and provincialism were disinclined to join.[22] Hence the new provinces debate did not follow a government/opposition divide. Otago and Auckland politicians were suspected of scheming to weaken their opponents, especially in Canterbury and Wellington, by allowing those provinces to be dismembered under the continued operation of the act.[23] Wellington was particularly keen to halt the legislation before Wanganui could secede.

The first bill proposed simply to limit the powers of secession. The New Provinces Act Limitation Bill would have allowed the governor-in-council to declare that an outlying district was sufficiently provided for if the provincial council permanently appropriated to it at least a quarter of the district's nett territorial revenue. Once this declaration was made, a district would be unable to secede.[24] However, this bill and similar proposals received opposition from many fronts. It frustrated those regions aspiring to secession,[25] it did not suit the North Island, where provinces had poor territorial revenue because of the lack of alienated lands, and, finally, the act's most enthusiastic supporters and opponents were united in their distaste for compromise legislation, and unwilling to make a deal.[26] The Limitation Bill was dismissed on its second reading.

Attention turned to the New Provinces Regulation Bill, which would effectively repeal the act and require new provinces to be created only by the decision of the General Assembly.[27] This bill did not contain any awkward requirements to appropriate revenue, and it united those willing to settle for the Limitation compromise with those who wanted nothing short of repeal. It successfully passed the House of Representatives and dodged a Legislative Council attempt to insert an amendment allowing the creation of counties that would absorb a portion of the local land fund.[28] The act was a lean piece of legislation with just two clauses, one giving its short title and one requiring all new provinces to be created by an act of parliament.[29]

Timaru, livid, unsuccessfully petitioned the governor to withhold assent.[30] It was forced to maintain the rage for two years before receiving any satisfaction. By August 1867 enthusiasm in the town for secession could no longer be ignored because it was prepared to use the measures of the revised act.[31] Parliament remained unwilling to acquiesce to this demand but ultimately framed a measure not dissimilar from the Legislative Council's unsuccessful amendment of the failed Limitation Bill. The Timaru and Gladstone Board of Works was created by legislation and endowed with the power to perform works of 'general utility' in the district, funded by a quarter of gross territorial revenue.[32] Not even Moorhouse's attempts to filibuster in the House could stop the measure.[33] It did not appease all secessionists – another attempt was made in 1869 to achieve greater separation from Canterbury – but it mollified agitation sufficiently that South Canterbury's political structure remained unchanged until the end of the provincial period.[34]

Despite Timaru's disdain, the era of automatic secession was over. Provincialists had successfully repealed an act that, for seven years, substantially weakened and destabilised the provincial system. Three new provinces had been created, none of which could be considered successful. Hawke's Bay had been a 'butterfly ... flutter[ing] in the sunshine of prosperity while they had lands to sell', according to one Auckland newspaper, 'but when there were no more lands to sell ... it was suddenly transformed to a chrysalis, without a wing to fly with'.[35] It survived during the 1860s because of the alliance between Donald McLean, who had been superintendent since 1863 (having resigned his central post as native secretary some two years earlier), and his friend and valuable political ally, John Ormond,

The Timaru and Gladstone Board of Works was housed in this handsome bluestone building on Stafford Street, Timaru. Francis Vallance

whose knowledge of public business placed the province's finances on a decent footing.[36] Marlborough and Southland were complete embarrassments. They were dysfunctional, rash and overambitious, believing blindly that a glorious future was within their grasp. Either through inability or incompetence, they did not perform their basic duties: public works and immigration. Worse still, in their failures, the new provinces dragged down the entire colony and dashed the hopes of other regions aspiring to an independent provincial existence. Southland's bankruptcy caused an already unsteady system to stumble, and it never regained a firm footing. The early 1860s witnessed overborrowing, both provincial and colonial. Now the colony was grossly indebted, and the new provinces were obviously incapable of performing the jobs they existed to do.

The one public network successfully implemented and expanded throughout the colony in the 1860s was not even a provincial success. In the decade and a half of the provinces' existence, their citizens had gained little from the operation and expense of provincial machinery. Roads, especially outside the capitals, remained rudimentary; regional ports were poorly maintained; railways were a distant dream,

In the 1860s telegraph offices were established throughout New Zealand. Pictured at left is Westport's office in 1868, adjoining the post office as was common practice.

1/4-017414, Alexander Turnbull Library, Wellington

except in Canterbury, and a nightmare in Southland; settlers in rural towns and on the land lacked the infrastructure they needed to participate fully in the economy. The central government, however, led the rapid spread of telegraphy. Some provinces, notably Canterbury and Otago, were involved in its implementation, but the central Telegraph Department pursued a vigorous policy of taking over provincial lines. It bought Southland's Invercargill to Bluff telegraph and extended it to meet Otago's growing network, and when a military telegraph in Auckland reverted to civilian control, it came under the authority of the Telegraph Department rather than Auckland Province.[37]

This was a significant and serious example of the central government infringing on the provinces' public works duties. A network of trunk telegraph routes was important for the central government's communications, and with enthusiastic support from newspapers and the police, the Telegraph Department took the lead – especially to cross Cook Strait.[38] This arrangement suited provinces in financial difficulty. It was also a foretaste of the dramatic public works centralisation that lay a few years in the future. Provincial administration of public works was a costly mistake, while under central control the telegraph network expanded quickly.

Chapter 8
Life during Wartime

The 1860s were difficult for provincialism as its foundations were eroded by a whirlwind of events. The New Provinces Act was just one part of the process; also significant were the effects of the New Zealand Wars and the implementation of the New Zealand Settlements Act. The provinces had not been seriously unequal in 1853, and the compact of 1856 appeared to provide a reasonable – if somewhat unstable – financial foundation. When the North Island was ravaged by war in the 1860s, the compact came to favour South Island provinces blessed with large land funds, and the experience of the North Island provinces began to diverge dramatically from richly endowed Otago and Canterbury. Apart from the obvious human toll, war impaired development, discouraged investment in essential peacetime services, and shifted both provincial and central emphasis away from policies that would shape long-term development. Two questions loom large: What role, if any, were the provinces expected to take in prosecuting the war, and how serious were the consequences of warfare for the entire provincial system?

The provinces, as institutions run by Pākehā for Pākehā, were not expected to determine Māori relations. As Pākehā settlement expanded, provinces were expected to serve only Pākehā wants and needs. This was in line with the original approach to central government. When Governor Browne implemented responsible government in 1856, he expressly limited the General Assembly's responsibility to the Pākehā community it governed and reserved Māori affairs to himself since they were, in his view, an imperial rather than domestic concern. This decision appears to have been Browne's alone – the Colonial Office gave no explicit instructions on the matter – but once he made it, London supported him fully.[1] And his action was not without precedent. The violent treatment of Aboriginal peoples by settlers in the Australian colonies concerned the Colonial Office and influential British humanitarians, especially from the late 1830s. Protectors were appointed to represent Aboriginal interests and a proportion of land funds were secured for Aboriginal affairs via imperial legislation, although these protections fell away in

Thomas Gore Browne, c. 1859, seated with (from left) daughter Mabyl, private secretary F.G. Steward, wife Harriet and son Harold. PA1-q-250-06, Alexander Turnbull Library, Wellington

the 1850s as Britain became increasingly reluctant to let Aboriginal welfare stymie self-government.[2]

The General Assembly, believing that its responsibility should not be limited, regarded Māori affairs as a domestic rather than an imperial concern. This complaint was not new: prominent men such as John Robert Godley had criticised London's control over Māori affairs from the dawn of the constitution, echoing Australian complaints about unelected protectors representing Aboriginal peoples.[3] In 1858 Browne conceded to the Stafford ministry's pressure, granting *some* responsibility for Māori affairs. In a despatch to the Colonial Office he outlined his policy:

> ... *those who possess the confidence of the Assembly [have been admitted] to a participation in the management of native affairs, as a matter of expediency ... I admit the right of the Assembly to legislate in the manner it thinks proper, reserving to myself the right of veto, as provided for by the Constitution Act. I retain to myself the executive and administrative part of native affairs, admitting my responsible advisers to full information, and granting them the right to advise me, but reserving to myself the right to act upon my own judgment when I differ from them.*[4]

An eloquent memorandum by C.W. Richmond expressing the ministry's contrary views accompanied Browne's remarks, but the Colonial Office supported the governor. Under-Secretary Lord Carnarvon refused to relinquish full control of Māori affairs to the central government, especially while British troops remained in New Zealand:

> Her Majesty's Government wish to give the fullest effect to the system of responsible Government, and to leave all [Pākehā] questions of domestic and internal interest to be decided by the Colonial Government, but they cannot, either for the sake of the colonists or for that of the natives, or for Imperial interests, surrender the control over native affairs … whilst Her Majesty's Government feel themselves constrained to justify to Parliament the large expense which every year is incurred for the maintenance of a military force in New Zealand … they must retain in their hands the administration of those affairs …[5]

The General Assembly was unimpressed. It was reluctant to approve money for Māori affairs to be spent by a governor and staff who were not accountable to the electorate, and a stalemate developed between governor and parliament.[6] In light of such events, it is not surprising that the provinces were never granted control over Māori policy. Both governor and parliament coveted what powers London conceded and were reluctant to give them up. Neither was likely to delegate any powers to provincial councils, especially as these were dominated by settlers whose declared objectives and hunger for land would antagonise already wary Māori and potentially require the use of British troops.

It is possible that Māori could have been brought into the provincial system. In 1858 the Kīngitanga or Māori King movement coalesced under inaugural king Pōtatau Te Wherowhero as an endeavour to unite Māori under a single monarch on equal footing with Queen Victoria and to stand against rampant alienation of land. To accommodate the Kīngitanga and resolve increasing tensions, some leading Pākehā proposed one or more Māori provinces. This drew on ideas expressed both in the 1852 constitution and in the 1858 parliament, that Māori be provided with 'native districts' or some form of annual assembly to govern their affairs. George Augustus Selwyn, the Anglican Bishop of New Zealand, pressed Governor Browne on the issue in 1859 and again in 1860. He believed Māori were 'thirsting for better government' than that offered by Pākehā provincial councils, which were a 'public danger' through their covetous view of Māori land as a source of profit and an outlet for migrant settlement. Hence, he argued, Māori might accept the creation of one or more central North Island provinces of their own as a 'simple system of elective and representative Government under the immediate sanction of the Governor' to grant them equal status within the political system and guard their interests.[7]

James Edward FitzGerald, in one of the earliest issues of the Christchurch *Press*, asserted that Māori provinces would 'absorb' the Kīngitanga. 'The *chieftainship* would become the origin of a *Superintendency*, and the *Runanga* [traditional tribal assembly] would form the basis of a *Provincial Council*.'[8] The Duke of Newcastle, as colonial secretary, also endorsed the idea, proposing in June 1861 that Māori districts be withdrawn from the provinces in which they were 'nominally included' and provided with their own legislature and administration. In March 1862 he suggested that the Māori King, now Pōtatau's son Tāwhiao, or other chiefs, could assent to laws of the rūnanga before receiving the governor's assent, akin to a superintendent assenting to provincial council legislation.[9] However, this proposal was condemned in parliament by Premier William Fox and appears to have lapsed later in 1862 with little to show for it.[10] In any case, having Tāwhiao subordinate to the governor was unlikely to be acceptable to the Kīngitanga. Newspaper editors and letter writers occasionally resuscitated variations on the province idea later in the decade but none gained momentum. One editor condemned a correspondent's proposal as 'simply another dream'.[11] A province may have put Māori on a relatively equal legislative footing with Pākehā, but it would also have imposed settler political institutions on Māori without providing anything approaching the status or authority they sought.

With existing provinces focused on settlers, and proposals for Māori provinces stillborn, the interactions between Māori and provincial governments were not central to the evolution of the provincial system. Māori rarely possessed direct influence on the way the provinces operated. Yet warfare between settlers and Māori in the North Island inevitably affected the system – both through the hardships of war and, more indirectly, by straining New Zealand's finances. The conflict profoundly disturbed the fledgling Pākehā economy. It disrupted regular trade, inhibited the North Island's economic growth and demanded expenditure – the central government had to pay for the war and the public services provided by the provinces were placed under great stress. This had severe implications for the colony's finances and came at a time when some provinces were running into financial problems, entertaining grand expenditure or both. Furthermore, the South Island increasingly saw the demand for war expenditure as a hardship, and one barely related to their interests. Although they sympathised with the difficulties of their fellow settlers in the North Island, they did not believe the war should come at a cost to southern development.

Even before the fighting began, New Zealand had numerous debts to service. At the end of 1859 the national government and all six original provinces held outstanding loans, and even greater borrowing had been avoided only by Labouchere's 1857 instructions. The national government, with the luxury of an imperial guarantee, had borrowed £500,000 at 4 per cent interest via the Union Bank of Australia as part of the 1856 compact.[12] The Union Bank was well established in New Zealand and typically negotiated provincial loans on the London money market where, without imperial or colonial guarantee, they did not enjoy such favourable interest rates. The largest provincial loans were two separate ones of £50,000 each for Wellington, including the controversial lighthouse loan from the Union Bank.[13] Between their inauguration and 1859 the provinces collectively had borrowed £310,239 at interest rates between 6 and 8 per cent – or in the case of one Auckland loan, 10 per cent.[14] The interest payments on these loans were a substantial commitment for a colony with a total Pākehā population of approximately 80,000.

Open combat started in March 1860 after Taranaki Māori disputed the sale to the Crown of a block of land at Waitara, northeast of New Plymouth, and obstructed the work of Pākehā surveyors. Pākehā forces comprised local militia and imperial troops and it was soon apparent that New Zealand had to bear the burden of considerable military expenditure. Initially the central government sought to make Britain pay for the war, arguing that New Zealand could not afford it. The House, which by 1860 was home to a provincialist majority as a result of resignations and by-elections, resisted the Stafford ministry's attempts to pay for the war out of surplus revenues that by law were meant to go to the provinces.[15] However, as Britain was increasingly unwilling to subsidise a colonial war, the costs would soon come home to roost one way or another, and when they did they would have consequences for the provincial system.

Taranaki was profoundly affected by the war. It became a desperate, impoverished polity much like the new provinces.[16] Even before the conflict it was the smallest province by area and the most vulnerable to upheaval. As a result of its weakness, Taranaki was often favourably disposed towards centralist policies, though it jealously guarded its independence whenever cynical Auckland politicians mooted annexation.[17] In 1858 it was home to 2650 Pākehā who were outnumbered by 3015 Māori.[18] By late 1860 an exodus from the fighting meant the Pākehā civilian

This ambrotype of New Plymouth, taken between 1855 and 1860, is one of the earliest photographs of the town. The Marsland Hill Barracks are prominent at top right.
A77.528, Puke Ariki

population had plummeted to 1239 and Māori now outnumbered them three to one.[19] This meant Taranaki's population was smaller than that of nascent Hawke's Bay, or equivalent to that of Marlborough, which was expanding.

No province was more poorly positioned to withstand the pressures and costs of war than Taranaki. It was already so impoverished that the £150 expense to replace losses when the provincial chambers caught fire in August 1859 was 'more than we can afford with our poor shrinking revenue'.[20] Yet when war broke out the local population – eager to open up more land, frustrated by what they perceived as Māori intransigence and grossly underestimating Māori military skill – were supportive, anticipating a quick victory. One commentator, in an 1878 history of Taranaki, unleashed a stream of racial invective that reflected the attitudes of many settlers who felt they had 'received every kind of insolence' from Māori and had been denied the province's best land. The war was 'necessary … for the sake of ultimate peace and prosperity … and [to] let the tyrannical barbarians learn once and for ever the royalty of the Pākehā race'.[21] Martial law over the whole province was proclaimed on 22 February 1860 and open warfare soon followed.[22]

The results were calamitous. New Plymouth, normally home to 937 people, suddenly became crowded with British troops and almost the entire population of the province. In such a tense situation relations were strained between troops, civilians and the provincial authorities.[23] Rural settlers fled into town for safety and the military assumed control of the countryside, which meant that the territory under the control of the provincial government shrank to the town and a tiny hinterland. The province and its police struggled to deal with the problems caused by such close living – fire and health hazards, perceived 'moral' problems, fear and panic when bad news arrived and settler dissatisfaction with military measures considered insufficiently decisive.[24] This overcrowding and confusion, along with the provincial government's difficulty in maintaining rations for dependent civilians, led to the evacuation of hundreds of women and children to Nelson from August 1860.[25] New Plymouth lacked an adequate hospital and open sewers exacerbated the spread of sickness. Fevers, diarrhoea and diphtheria were prevalent, not just among those in New Plymouth but also among the Nelson refugees, and the civilian deaths in Taranaki for 1861 were over five times higher than the average of previous years.[26] Māori suffered even more heavily, although their plight was little known or understood except by a handful of sympathetic doctors.[27]

Basic provincial functions were suspended, including meetings of the council. When it finally met on 16 November 1860, almost a year after the end of its previous sitting, Superintendent George Cutfield informed the members that the 'complete derangement of ordinary business which the state of war has brought with it has made it useless and impossible to enter on legislative work'.[28] Instead the provincial government devoted its funds and machinery to the support of those suffering hardship, and in October 1860 the General Assembly approved £25,000 to compensate settlers for losses – an inadequate sum that was quickly supplemented with another grant of £30,000.[29] This meant that the council, in part thanks to the revenue accrued from the military's presence, actually had some funds at its disposal to carry on essential business. The province survived and the central government took out a loan of £150,000 to cover war-related expenditure, of which £10,000 was paid to the Taranaki provincial government for refugee expenses.[30]

Given its poverty and uncertainty about how long war would last, Taranaki could not hope to raise a loan of any amount; it was entirely dependent on the credit of the central government. The longer the unsettled conditions lasted, the worse the province's situation became. In 1862 the superintendent – now Charles Brown, returned to the position he first won in 1853 – and the council asked the governor for a loan of £200,000, raised on colonial security, to compensate Taranaki settlers for their continuing hardships.[31] This was accompanied by an extract from the council's minutes that all 'agricultural pursuits and trade hav[e] long ago ceased to exist' and the majority of the population were reliant on government support.[32]

The provision of charitable aid and welfare was a provincial matter. Although there have been many studies of later 'social experiments' and the rise of the welfare state, provincial charity and welfare have received minimal attention. Bill Sutch, for instance, who pays careful attention to provincial provision of services such as education and welfare, characterises the era as one of struggle for New Zealand's poor. To him, the 'absence of unemployment payments or of a Poor Law … meant that for months and sometimes years on end, many of the people of New Zealand in the [eighteen] fifties and sixties suffered hardships'.[33] This is not wholly inaccurate since social welfare was not then regarded as a function of the government. Families were expected to be self-reliant or assisted by private charity.[34] Yet, as Margaret Tennant writes, the provincial period saw a 'progressive elaboration of welfare structures and institutions', even with the necessary qualifications that 'welfare spending was meagre' and 'attitudes toward welfare were still very ambivalent'. She notes that Taranaki's per capita welfare spending in the 1870s was only just below Canterbury's, even though the latter was much larger and wealthier.[35]

Taranaki's commitment to welfare in this decade reflected its wartime circumstances; parts of the community endured long-term suffering and poverty. Immediate relief came in the early 1860s when the government agreed with Taranaki's request for aid; £200,000 of its £3 million loan of 1863, discussed in depth below, was designated for Taranaki relief. This arrived slowly – the £55,000 previously voted for Taranaki was subtracted from the award, and full payment took until 1868, primarily because of central government sluggishness.[36] The war accentuated the problem of poor provinces being dependent on the central government for survival – in Taranaki's case, not just the survival of institutions but of citizens too. If nothing else, Taranaki proved that an original province was susceptible to destitution, not just the new provinces created with half an eye to failure.

More significantly for the fortunes of provincialism as a whole, the war justified the central government's first substantial entry into the provincial domains of immigration, settlement and public works. At first this happened through the construction of public works required by the military, a job conducted by both colonial and imperial authorities. As the war dragged on, however, two connected themes emerged: the need to pay for the war, and the desire not just to win the war but to ensure it could never recur. Opening the central North Island with public works and settlement would achieve both ends. The New Zealand Settlements Act was passed to achieve this under the direction of the central government in conjunction with affected provinces. Because the North Island provinces, lacking the South Island's large land funds and enduring wartime hardship, were dependent on outside support, it was not difficult for the central government to enter the provincial domain. Valuable tracts of land such as Taranaki's hinterland and Auckland's Waikato region remained in Māori possession. The provinces could not develop this land unless the governor was willing to alienate it, and Browne had been unwilling to sanction every demand. He even rebuffed a Māori request in 1860 to allow direct land sales to settlers, fearing it would create isolated pockets of settlement and lead to misunderstandings and provocation.[37] This far-sighted decision avoided the creation of a New Zealand equivalent of isolated Israeli settlements in Gaza and the West Bank, but it did nothing to help the provinces open up their territory. As the war raged, responsibility for Māori affairs was increasingly transferred to responsible ministers, and as the central government confiscated land, it sought to make these acres productive in order to repay the cost of the war.

This has led some historians to argue that the war initiated the centralising forces that fatally encroached upon the provinces in the 1870s. B.J. Dalton puts this argument concisely: 'more important in redressing the imbalance [between central and provincial governments] was the great expansion in the central government's activities which proved necessary to match the new responsibilities of native policy and war from 1860 onwards. Immigration and public works … rapidly passed into central control.'[38] Similarly, Tony Ballantyne argues the 'key engine for political transformation was the conflict over land and sovereignty that raged from the end of the 1850s through to the early 1870s'. The wars, he claims, were 'an important impetus towards the centralisation of power in New Zealand' by enlarging the central state and shifting emphasis away from the provinces.[39] The reality is more complex. Bernard Attard has criticised the warfare-as-centralisation argument by emphasising the provinces' inability to borrow as the prime force for change,[40] but provincial difficulties ran deeper still: the difficulties of borrowing were symptomatic of difficulties of development. The encroachments of the central government were limited by the boundaries and costs of war.

Damon Salesa asserts that war 'forged the new self-governing colonial polity, [and] critically shaped settler subjectivities and institutions', especially as a 'workshop' for 'projects of racial amalgamation'.[41] He is not wrong, and the reverberations of war are still felt in New Zealand's race relations today. It is essential, however, to remember that the colonial polity was not a monolith. Events that forged and critically affected some facets of colonial life had less crucial consequences elsewhere. The survival of the provincial system was based on its ability to advance the colonial progress industry. To what extent did the war enable the central government to encroach upon this?

For the first time in the provincial era, the war involved other parties heavily in public works. Military roads out of Wellington had been constructed under the governor's auspices in the 1840s, but after 1853 roadmaking was a provincial responsibility. In Taranaki, however, and especially in Auckland, imperial and colonial authorities oversaw some wartime public works as the need for military roads ran ahead of provincial development. When George Grey resumed the title of governor in 1861, he was acutely aware that although Taranaki was nominally at peace, fighting could spread quickly to the Kīngitanga's stronghold, the Waikato region. This was of grave concern, as the approach from the Waikato into southern Auckland was poorly defended, and the Kīngitanga controlled the Waikato River, the one 'highway' suitable for a Pākehā assault. Grey therefore authorised the construction of a military road, the Great South Road, ostensibly for defence but with the clear double purpose of facilitating a Waikato invasion.[42]

This move does not represent expansion of the central state at the expense of the provinces. The justification for this foray into a normally provincial domain was military – it could never have occurred without the justification of war. In the words of John Larkins Cheese Richardson, a government minister appointed as commissioner into imperial claims against the central government, although roads like the Great South Road would be 'of benefit to the Colony, [they] would not … have been undertaken by it for many years to come'.[43] The Great South Road was originally constructed with imperial military funds, then with a contribution upon sufferance by the central government. This was drawn from the £3 million loan authorised in conjunction with the Settlements Act.[44]

The Great South Road was the most notable and enduring military route, serving for decades after the war as the arterial link between Auckland and the Waikato, but other military roads were constructed in Auckland and Taranaki. Although these offered future civilian benefits, they were built solely for military purposes. In June 1862 the military expressly ordered that troops were 'on no account to be employed on roads designed for the convenience of private individuals, but only on roads … constructed for the defence of the settlement, or with reference to future

Alfred Domett, c. 1870.
1/1-001298-F, Alexander Turnbull Library, Wellington

military operations'.[45] This was written specifically about Taranaki but also applied to Auckland. This policy could never have affected the construction of public works in the South Island, or even in other parts of the North Island, such as the bulk of Wellington Province or north of Auckland city. Minor calls from Wellington for Grey to oversee ostensibly military-related roadworks that would have been of far more civil than military benefit were not answered.[46] A generalised fear of the war spreading further south was insufficient reason for roadmaking outside the war zone.

Because the war was not a provincial concern, it made sense for imperial and colonial funds to be used for constructing the necessary works. These actions did not wrest any powers from the provinces, though they provided beneficial development for Auckland and Taranaki. On the basis of restoring peace and prosperity after the war, the central government did *attempt* to usurp some provincial power, originally through a proposal of Domett's ministry and then through the Settlements Act. This did not prove to be a particularly successful usurpation of provincial power, nor did it drive much centralisation, but it did show the central government's willingness to engage in some public works ahead of the provinces. It was a harbinger of what was to come.

When the Domett ministry fell at the end of October 1863, it was considering a vast plan for military roads and settlements throughout the North Island.

This idea was conceived not just to end the current war, but to make any future conflict impossible by creating a network of roads linking chains of settlement that would occupy and populate Māori land with Pākehā colonists. The goal was not a temporary military victory that could evaporate when troops were withdrawn, but the complete subjection of the Māori world to Pākehā through a programme of immense land confiscation.[47] The concept derived at least in part from policies Grey implemented as governor of the Cape Colony in South Africa, modified to suit New Zealand's circumstances. However, Grey's increasing opposition to confiscation in subsequent years indicated that Domett and his ministers were the primary authors.[48] Domett's influence is apparent; despite a 20-year residency in New Zealand, he was profoundly ignorant of Māori culture. His stern, confrontational approach was activated by the mistaken belief that 'might is right' was the only diplomacy Māori understood.[49]

The Domett ministry was replaced by an alliance between Whitaker and Fox, with the former as premier. The new ministry was dominated by the aggressive Māori policy of Auckland businessmen and land speculators, notably Whitaker himself and his talented legal partner, Thomas Russell, who founded the Bank of New Zealand in 1861. Both had much to gain by confiscating land.[50] On entering office Whitaker assumed full responsibility for Māori affairs, placing Grey in the weakest constitutional position he had occupied in New Zealand. Yet the continued presence of imperial troops meant Grey had an undefined veto over defence matters, creating uncertainty between Whitaker and Grey over who held ultimate power.[51] Three items of legislation defined Whitaker's policy and Grey assented to them, despite personal qualms – the Suppression of Rebellion Act, which suspended habeas corpus; the New Zealand Settlements Act, to confiscate swathes of Māori land; and the New Zealand Loan Act, known hereafter as the £3 million loan and raised to pay for the first two acts and the cost of the war. The latter two acts are significant for provincialism, and as the colonial treasurer prepared budgets during this period with assistance but not guidance from permanent officials, responsibility for the financial details lay with Whitaker's treasurer, Reader Wood.[52] The Settlements Act was not an anomalous act of land-hungry settler politics; it was based on a long British legal history of military pacification and settlement, drawing especially on Irish and southern African precedent.[53] It was also based on another history, this one only months old: Domett's proposals, which survived the ministerial transition. This is unsurprising, since Russell was in Domett's ministry and Whitaker may also have exercised influence via Russell.[54]

The Settlements Act was not designed simply to confiscate Māori land through-out the North Island, but also to settle it – under the auspices of the central gov-ernment but with provincial involvement. It provided for the governor-in-council to reserve for settlement any land in any district in which Māori had fought against the Crown, with compensation granted to Māori who had supported the Crown. The Loan Act authorised £3 million to be raised in Britain at an interest rate of 5 per cent, and the accompanying Loan Appropriation Act specified the manner in which the money was to be spent.[55] The government believed it could repay the whole loan by selling 1.5 million acres (607,000 hectares) at £2 an acre.[56] The relevant charges for the settlement programme were £300,000 for the introduction of settlers to the North Island and £900,000 for surveys and public works – and, crucially, the provinces were to be involved. This point has often been overlooked in arguments that assume the war was, in Ballantyne's words, the 'key engine' for centralisation. Because the provinces were the agents of immigration and public works, the Loan Appropriation Act delegated the money raised to the provinces in which the set-tlement would occur – primarily Auckland, with Taranaki a distant second. If land sale revenue was insufficient to repay the interest and sinking fund to the central government for 'all sums expended in any Province for the permanent advantage of such Province', it would be made a charge on the province's general revenue.[57] To achieve its objective, the central government still had to work with the provinces.

The scheme was not successful either as a driver of centralisation or as a creator of settlement. It *did* lead to vast swathes of confiscation in a legally dubious process that has left a harsh legacy for Māori.[58] Confiscating land was one part of the equation; settling it was another. There was little dissent when the acts were passed. FitzGerald opposed them in parliament as unconstitutional and inhumane; Sewell condemned them in print, alleging that they had been hurried through parliament with poor oversight, no detailed estimates and insufficient time for members to consider the proposal.[59] The subsequent difficulties substantiate FitzGerald and Sewell's fears. As other historians have indicated at length, it was hard to carry out the scheme when neither Grey nor the Colonial Office was willing to give full support to the ministry.[60] In short, the Colonial Office urged caution, and the inability of Grey and Whitaker to agree on the details of confiscation delayed the process. Whitaker wanted to proceed quickly and saw confiscation as a means of defraying wartime expenses; Grey viewed confiscation as a form of punishment. Their differences were irreconcilable and the ministry resigned. It was replaced by a ministry led by Frederick Weld, whose dislike for Grey was decidedly reciprocated,

Military settlers of No. 9 Company at the blockhouse in Pukearuhe, northern Taranaki.
PHO2009-118, Puke Ariki

and this did not bode well for the new premier's policy of New Zealand being 'self-reliant' and taking on all costs of war and settlement.[61]

Worse still were the arrangements for immigration. John Gorst, who had served as Grey's resident magistrate in the Waikato, condemned the plan: 'From whence are the 20,000 settlers, who are to occupy the frontier, to come? When colonies in every part of the world are competing for labourers, will a grant of fifty acres of land, overlooked by a rugged forest, the lurking-place of evicted and revengeful proprietors, induce a preference for the North Island of New Zealand?'[62] Liberal terms of enlistment helped to attract recruits, but in haste the government chose quantity over quality. Ross Hamilton emphasises the scheme's personnel failings. His study reveals that the men had 'neither the means, experience nor inclination to become farmers'.[63] Military settlers swept into Auckland and Taranaki before the war was even over: 5124 arrived in Auckland by the December 1864 census, comprising over 8 per cent of the province's population of 42,132.[64] Many experienced lengthy stays in barracks and were even used as auxiliary troops. Once the settlers were sent onto the land, they received inadequate provisions and complained of neglect.[65] Those who were granted Waikato land near Cambridge and Pirongia soon called for military protection, leading to howls of derision from the south – instead of civilian settlers quickly following, the military settlers wanted military protection of their own.[66] Periodic fears that war would resume caused many settlers to retreat to the safety of townships until the scare passed, hobbling the success of their farms. Many soon sold or abandoned their properties. By the early 1870s much good land granted to military settlers lay idle.[67]

The scheme collapsed in execution, as did its finances. Both central and provincial governments struggled to maintain their ends of the bargain. Weld was able to confiscate 1.2 million acres (485,000 hectares) because Grey did not mistrust his intent. Rather than taking Whitaker's attitude that confiscation was a financial boon, Weld, like Grey, saw it as a deterrent and a punitive measure. However, the ministry found New Zealand almost bankrupt in the wake of difficulties associated with the £3 million loan and confiscation; only extra custom duties and protracted negotiations with the Bank of New Zealand saved the day.[68] By November 1864 emigration agents were complaining that they had not received enough money and that a plan to raise £20,000 with the Bank of New Zealand had no prospect of success; in January 1865, they suspended operations owing to a lack of funds.[69] In a compromise, confiscated Waikato land was transferred to Auckland Province's control with a small royalty per acre paid to the central government, but the province was unable to maintain the expenses of surveying, constructing public works and employing the settlers. A similar scheme for Taranaki was abandoned, Auckland could not raise a loan to cover its costs except at a ruinous discount, and the Waikato land reverted to the management of the central government.[70] By mid-1867, far from recouping the loan, land sales had earned just £25,000.[71]

The whole shambles casts neither central nor provincial government in a good light. It is hard to sustain Morrell's conclusion that the Weld ministry 'had tried hard to make Auckland, like the Southern provinces, responsible for its own colonisation, but circumstances had proved too strong for them. Yet if the northern Provincial Governments could not colonise, was not the strongest argument for their existence taken away?'[72] Much of the responsibility for the scheme's poor implementation lay with the central government – successive ministries had attempted to carry out its bold vision with little obvious competence – and Auckland had inherited it on the brink of collapse. It foreshadowed the struggle of central and provincial authorities to co-operate on a vast colonising scheme in the 1870s, but it was an ideological dead end. The later centralisation was born of different, largely disconnected reasons. As a geographically isolated programme, settlement under the Settlements Act did not allow a significant degree of central encroachment on the provincial domain, especially those outside the war zone; as a botched programme, it did not achieve significant centralisation in the provinces it affected; as the source of a centralising impulse, it is not terribly compelling.

The failure lay partly in the difficulties encountered by the central government in raising the £3 million loan – difficulties that would have serious consequences for provincial finances and public works. The Whitaker ministry, confident in the success of the loan, began spending money with advances from the Bank of New Zealand while Reader Wood was sent to London to negotiate the loan proper. The British parliament refused his request for a guarantee of the full loan; it would guarantee only £1 million, covering the portion of the loan for military expenses but not the Settlements Act.[73] Worse followed when the first £1 million of debentures were placed on sale. Only £6,100 were bought on the first day, increasing to approximately £30,000 during the next 10 days.[74] The loan was affected by numerous factors: the general state of the money market, recent criticisms of New Zealand aired in parliament and the press during the debate on guaranteeing the loan, the shift of the main theatre of war to the Bay of Plenty, and, as the Crown agents described it, 'the unfortunate manner in which some of the Provincial Loans have been dealt with in this market'.[75]

The forces of provincial public works and central government expenditure were now colliding spectacularly on the British money market. The process of raising the loan was slow: the interest rate was increased from 5 to 6 per cent a year later to make it a more attractive investment, and authority was given for £1 million of short-dated debentures to be issued at 8 per cent to provide a quick injection of funds. In the meantime the government was forced to rely on an overdraft with the Bank of New Zealand that reached as high as £818,000 and caused the bank considerable problems.[76] The provinces were facing their own challenges. Otago failed to negotiate £650,000 of debentures in London. Superintendent John Hyde Harris blamed not only competition with the £3 million loan and others, but also the lack of a guarantee from the colonial government and a perceived misapprehension by British investors of the security offered by the provinces.[77] These were common complaints among the South Island provinces, eager for more money to further their development. In Invercargill the *Daily News* repeated the charges multiple times before Southland's financial collapse became public knowledge.[78] In Canterbury the *Press* argued angrily that, with its loan, the central government had 'killed our credit'.[79] Both central and provincial governments saw the other as stepping on the toes of their own borrowing. Of course the expenditure of central loans concentrated on the North Island fostered southern discontent.

The direct results of the war for the provinces and centralisation were slighter than the arguments by Ballantyne and Dalton suggest. War did play a part in provincialism's decline, but it was not a leading factor. Taranaki accentuated the problem of provincial governments becoming dependent upon the central government and being incapable of performing the key tasks of immigration and public works. The construction of the military road to the Waikato was a notable demonstration that public works need not be exclusively provincial, but implementation of the Settlements Act reflected badly on both levels of government. The war compounded inequality between the northern provinces, which remained largely unsettled and poor, and those in the south, which tried to proceed quickly with development. In no regard, however, was the provincial system undermined. It managed that by itself.

Chapter 9
Separation: Provincialism's Apogee?

Provincial aspirations were often unrealistic and grand, and perhaps the grandest were campaigns to separate a province – or provinces – from New Zealand to form a new, distinct colony. South Island separatism flourished during the early 1860s, stoked by discontent in some provinces with the travails of war, but the desire to create new colonies in the archipelago was nothing new. Auckland Province was first to experience agitation for separation from the rest of New Zealand, led by James Busby, a provincial representative for Bay of Islands from 1853 to 1855 and again from 1857 to 1863. In his youth Busby founded the Australasian wine industry while living in the Hunter Valley of New South Wales and published multiple papers on viticulture. His career took a turn when he was given the responsibility of being British resident in New Zealand in 1832, a role in which he was expected to apprehend escaped convicts from New South Wales, protect law-abiding traders and prevent violence against Māori by Pākehā. It was an unenviable, poorly resourced job but he approached it as a welcome challenge and performed it until the Treaty of Waitangi was signed in 1840. During the 1840s, however, Busby became bitter, primarily over difficulties he encountered in securing land claims in the Bay of Islands. When the provincial era dawned, he was a largely bald man with a severe countenance, armed with an ear trumpet to combat increasing deafness. Busby had few friends, and the relentless pursuit of his claims and his 'enemies' alienated him from many influential Aucklanders. He came to view himself as the central architect of the Treaty of Waitangi and was not impressed with the changes inaugurated by the constitution.[1]

Unable to conceal his indignation, Busby wasted no time in promoting Auckland's separation, heading a select committee in 1853 that endorsed this move.[2] Such proposals were not unique to Auckland – in 1854 Henry Sewell alienated many moderates and North Islanders by hinting at South Island separation[3] – but it was only in Auckland, thanks to Busby's energy, that any form of separation became a major and ongoing subject for a New Zealand legislature in the 1850s. On no less

James Busby, 1860s.

7-A5804, Sir George Grey Special Collections, Auckland Libraries

than four occasions – 1853, 1855, 1858 and 1862 – he occupied council and committee time with motions and petitions on the topic. To popularise his viewpoint, he issued a stream of publications throughout the 1850s.[4] These glorified political pamphlets were often reproductions of council speeches or letters authored by Busby, and typically printed independently owing to his distrust of the Auckland press.[5]

In making his arguments Busby ran counter to political reality. He inaccurately considered that the six settlements were separate British colonies and that the constitution had effected a federation of dependencies. There was, in his view, 'no greater abuse of language' than to call New Zealand itself a single colony. 'You might, with as much truth say that England is a city, or Auckland a street.'[6] He firmly believed the physical obstacles between the six settlements presented 'impediments to a *real* union of Auckland with the Southern Settlements [that] are insurmountable.'[7] The only political relations between the provinces, he argued, were those foisted upon them by the General Assembly, an illegitimate and meddlesome body seeking inordinate taxation to sustain itself.[8] As central legislation overrode provincial legislation, Busby felt this created 'perpetual uncertainty' in the validity and efficacy of provincial powers and fostered institutional 'Anarchy'.[9] Consequently he blamed all New Zealand's political inefficiencies on the constitution.

Busby therefore sought the establishment of Auckland as a separate British colony with responsible government. The council was reasonably positive about his ideas and passed motions to petition the Queen for separation. Morrell attributes the authorship of these to Busby rather than committee collaboration or any collective council initiative, and their passage to his influence rather than any strong public opinion.[10] Both major newspapers refused their support. After the first petition's failure, the *Southern Cross* urged that Auckland should 'live comfortably with our partners ... [and] not place it in a state of isolation'.[11] John Williamson, *New Zealander* editor and Auckland superintendent, even sued Busby for libel in 1860. The latter then took the unbecoming step of giving his private communication with Williamson's lawyer to the rival *Southern Cross* for publication.[12]

One newspaper, though, vehemently supported separation: the *Auckland Examiner*, founded in December 1856 by Charles Southwell, an anti-clerical iconoclast and populist who had been imprisoned in 1841 in England for blasphemy. He enjoyed mocking his rivals in the press and oversaw a paper that aspired to respectability despite muckraking tendencies. In 1858 he eagerly threw in his lot with Busby's agitation. Separation was *the* article of the *Examiner*'s political faith: 'until Auckland pronounces for Separation, and insists upon it, no New Zealand Province can be Governed upon Sound Principles or made Progressively Prosperous.'[13] Southwell largely ignored the new provinces debate and most other central events to editorialise repeatedly about separation in late 1858, urging Aucklanders that the other provinces 'are not so much friends as rivals'.[14] The *Examiner* cornered the market for pro-separatists, but this and Southwell's blatant populism were not enough for it to survive beyond July 1860. It perished amid bitter claims that it would have remained solvent had subscriptions been paid on time, though the reasons probably ran deeper because of a controversial April 1860 leader about Browne's Māori policy.[15]

Separation did not excite much of Auckland's political class and was met with indifference further afield. Nelson's *Colonist* suggested derisively that Busby should pen another petition to improve his writing skills.[16] Separation petitions that emphasised land policy reflected Busby's misfortunes with the commissioner of land claims. By 1860 his arguments and petitioning – both of the Queen by official channels and the governor by private means – were largely subsumed by questions of land sales and revenue.[17] He could not capture the imagination of Queen or country; none of his petitions succeeded and his own attempt to fill the void left by the *Auckland Examiner* with the *Aucklander* was unpopular, lasting only from 1861 to 1863.[18]

As a result of Busby's constant agitation, he and the rest of the Auckland Provincial Council came in for considerable criticism. FitzGerald felt Auckland's early councillors were unfit for provincial government, let alone colonial government. He had 'never seen any set of public men so politically ignorant'.[19] The *Nelson Examiner* echoed this opinion, with reference to Busby, when the 1855 motion was put to council: Busby possessed 'remarkable ignorance of the colony saving the northern portion of it … [and is] quite incapable of taking an extended view of its interests'.[20] Busby's reputation outside of Auckland never recovered. While in England during the 1860s, he republished his old arguments in London. When word reached New Zealand, the *Wellington Independent* responded venomously. Describing Busby as a 'particularly dirty bird', the paper quickly connected his arguments with his failed land claims. '[D]isappointment often makes a man bilious' and Busby had 'vented his spleen on everything and everybody connected with New Zealand, except Auckland and the Aucklanders'.[21]

Busby was also criticised within Auckland. William Atkin, pioneer settler and prominent figure in the early Anglican community, wrote a scathing letter to the *Southern Cross* in 1858 challenging Busby's desire to replace local responsible government with a nominee system administered from London. Concerned that the provincial council would support Busby's motion, he stressed that members 'could only represent their own individual opinions – their constituency never having been consulted in the matter'.[22] It had never been an election issue, and Atkin's allegation highlighted not only the personal agenda of Busby and his allied councillors, but also Busby's hypocrisy. One of Busby's own publications had asserted that the constitution was drafted without any advice 'represent[ing] the interests and wishes of the people of Auckland'.[23] He had made little effort to do this either, acting as if his interests and wishes, and those of Auckland, were one and the same. The council passed the 1858 motion 13 to three with one abstention, and one of the three opposing votes stands out: that of Daniel Pollen, then provincial secretary.[24] Pollen became premier in 1875, leading the central government while Julius Vogel was overseas – and his ministry oversaw the vote on provincial abolition.

In the 1860s much more popular and potent separation movements emerged, mainly stimulated in both Otago and Auckland by the war, and especially its cost. The Otago movement sought, but never achieved, broader South Island support; the Auckland movement was largely a kneejerk reaction to threats of moving the national capital to Wellington, and enjoyed wider appeal than any of Busby's separation attempts. Both movements have vanished into the historical fog and been little researched or analysed.[25] An authoritative history awaits a future author, but important aspects of separatism are relevant to an understanding of the provinces and their demise. Separatism was a prominent outgrowth of provincialism, reflecting fervent contemporary localism, and was at its strongest between 1862 and 1865 before fading in the late 1860s. The movements left a legacy of lively advocacy but little accomplishment. They did not achieve a remodelling of provincial government, let alone the desired separation of New Zealand into two colonies; they were not agents of abolition. Three points, however, demand attention – the theme of centralism within some arguments for Otago separation; the consequences for provincialism of relocating the national capital; and the role of separation as a distraction in parliament from advancing the interests of provincialism.

Two strands existed within Otago separatism: the ultra-provincialism preached by James Macandrew, and Julius Vogel's demand for separation with little regard for how provincialism would function in a hypothetical South Island colony. Relocating the national capital from Auckland to Wellington in 1865 not only took the sting out of separatism; it also weakened the viability of provincialist arguments and played into the overarching process that undermined the provinces: the relationship between geography, distance and travel. Both separation movements distracted provincialists in the General Assembly. Their fruitless campaigns took energy away from asserting provincial interests against centralism, and divided those provincialist politicians who demanded separation from more moderate provincialists who wanted to restrict central encroachment on provincial powers. When provincialism was under attack and needed a strong, united force in the General Assembly, it was weakened by the separation campaigns.

As justification for provincialism disintegrated with the new provinces during the 1860s, why did these movements gain power? The circumstances of war in the north and a passionate desire for more localised government featured prominently, though for different reasons in Auckland and Otago. The South Island movement was fundamentally an expression of settlers' desires that the focus of colonisation – development through public works – be sped up, and that the fortunes of one region should not be shackled to the tribulations of any other. In Auckland similar demands were tied up with the province's desire for more control over Māori policy and the war. By 1867, however, separatism had waned in both provinces as passions cooled. It is worth noting that Dunedin rarely enjoyed much interprovincial support, and secessionist Otago hinterlands were suspicious of the city's intentions.

In 1861, after articles of peace were signed and Taranaki entered into an uneasy truce, the South Island – which had previously supported the war effort while disclaiming any direct interest – became increasingly unhappy with the Fox ministry's pacification policy.[26] Southerners believed that attempts to establish institutions among Māori and to engage in lengthy negotiations would benefit only Māori and their immediate Pākehā neighbours, and that the cost of salvaging peace in the North Island would fall unduly upon the South. Thus arose the vocal movement seeking the establishment of the South Island – or, at its most radical extreme, Otago Province alone – as a free-standing colony, so that it could use its revenue to stimulate its own development rather than pay the North Island's bills. Vogel spearheaded the movement and emerged as the leader of separation through his persistent editorialising in the *Otago Daily Times*. Historians agree that Victoria's separation from New South Wales in 1851 was significant in shaping Vogel's separatist beliefs.[27] Although he did not arrive there until December 1852, Victoria offered proof that separation could succeed and Vogel witnessed the dramatic strides it made as an individual colony. Queensland, which achieved separation from New South Wales in 1859, was also an inspiration, and Vogel invoked both as examples of what Otago could achieve.[28] If new Australian colonies could leave their past masters and become successful, then what was stopping this new, gold-rich province from doing the same?

Dunedin's separation campaign, or at least the desire for a remodelling of Otago's relationship with the North Island, did not begin with Vogel and the *Otago Daily Times*, but he became its most vocal proponent. An undercurrent of discontent grew from the 1850s, stoked by Otago's disgust with the New Provinces Act and fears that Otago would be divided into multiple inconsequential municipalities.[29] Emphasis on the South Island's distinctive differences from the North even led to the use of militaristic language. In October 1861 the *Otago Colonist*, a newspaper backed by Macandrew, drew a comparison between New Zealand and the civil war in America, which had begun a few months before and, in its view, was caused by the artificial union of countries deemed separate by nature.[30] It is possible Vogel was responsible for the argument, as he was then on the staff, having just crossed the Tasman.[31] The next month, Vogel founded the *Otago Daily Times* with William Cutten, the editor of the *Otago Colonist*'s rival weekly, the *Otago Witness*. From the second issue of the *Times*, on 16 November 1861, Vogel maintained a forceful argument that the 'Northern and Middle Islands have nothing in common'.[32] He routinely emphasised the lack of shared interests between the two islands, the distance between Otago and the seat of government in Auckland, the South Island's lack of parliamentary representation (especially Otago's mere five seats) and the continued unwillingness of leading men – despite the steamships now plying New

Zealand's coasts – to commit to the expensive and protracted trips required to attend parliament in Auckland. To Vogel, the people of Otago were 'hourly brought in contact with abuses, the redress of which [was] prevented by the distance from the seat of Government'.[33]

Yet in all of this vociferous argumentation, provincialism featured very infrequently. Vogel never pitched separatism as an extension or outgrowth of ultra-provincialism, and when he *did* invoke provincialism, it was to air dissatisfaction or urge reform. His strand of separatism was actually an expression of discontent with the existing provincial system – frustration with provincial jealousies, squabbles, ineptitude and inequalities – and of a belief in more centralised government. Vogel first wrote at length about his complaints with provincialism and their relationship with separation in a March 1862 editorial:

> *The separation of the two Islands will have the paradoxical effect of enlarging, as far as the inhabitants are concerned, instead of reducing the colony in which they feel themselves interested. With an Imperial representative on the Middle Island that love of country which now expends itself on Provincialism will draw its inspiration from the whole Island. The jealousies between the Provinces will be forgotten in the one feeling of attachment to the new colony, Southern New Zealand. We write now from the whole Island point of view, believing, as we do, that Otago would be the first to hail the consolidation of the various Provinces.*[34]

Vogel, not always willing to stay grounded in reality, was clearly over-optimistic about the willingness of South Islanders to forsake their regional differences and come together as Southern New Zealanders. The interests of Nelson were unmistakably different from those of Invercargill, and disagreements both within provinces and between immediate neighbours – Nelson and Marlborough, Southland and Otago – were even more passionate than disagreements between the island's extremities. Canterbury would have been a useful ally but its people preferred not to support a plan as drastic as separation and favoured minimal interference from a distant central government.[35] All this caused Vogel some consternation. When the separation movement failed to catch on outside Dunedin, he blamed the provincialist media: 'the machinery for [separatist] agitation has been wanting. The press throughout New Zealand is devoted to Provincial politics, anything outside the charmed circle of provincial party difference is regarded by them with dulled attention.'[36]

Vogel was not a provincialist but a centralising separatist. Without the interfering North Island provinces, their war and the distant location of the national capital, the South Island could be more centralised and more able to manage its common interests without the distraction of petty local jealousies. Vogel did not, however, want to alienate provincialist support for separation. In June 1862 he emphasised that 'nothing in the Separation asked for [is] necessarily antagonistic to Provincialism', but that 'in the Act of Separation … the opportunity no doubt will be afforded of re-adjusting the present constitution. The advocates of provincialism must be concious [sic] of some inherent weakness in their cause when they object to this test.'[37] He did not venture an opinion on how provincialism would survive in a separated South Island until 1863 when – in an echo of Pakington's 1852 expectation – he forecast the evolution of the provinces into powerful municipalities led by a strong central government that would 'break down the exclusiveness of provincialism.'[38] This was the logical development of Vogel's separatist twist on the popular ultra-provincial catchcry that provincial areas should continue to enjoy the receipt and control of their own land funds even if the political machinery of provincialism were refashioned or discarded.[39] The spirit of localism so crucial to provincialism was also alive in Vogel's separatism, and a clear portent that localism and centralism were not incompatible.

Under the Domett ministry in late 1862 the South Island made gains that both temporarily hampered the separation movement and indicated that the central government was willing to act upon the negative influence of provincial jealousies. Otago won a number of concessions, thus reducing the grievances upon which Vogel could draw to promote separation. The Representation Act gave Otago four new members in the expanded 57-seat House of Representatives, increasing its total representation to nine.[40] A Supreme Court judge was appointed for Dunedin to silence allegations that justice was poorly administered in Otago. The appointee was none other than C.W. Richmond, who had not enjoyed his time in politics despite his success with the New Provinces Act, and had recently moved to Dunedin to establish a lucrative law practice.[41] Most significantly, steamship services were improved, a central telegraphic engineer was appointed to advise and oversee Canterbury and Otago's infant provincial telegraphic networks with an eye to integrating them as an island-wide network, and proposals were made to lay a telegraphic cable across Cook Strait to link the South Island with the principal northern centres.[42] Telegraphy was important in nullifying the complaint that the seat of government was too distant from Otago, and the central government was not willing to let its plans be scuppered by any lack of provincial co-operation in establishing cross-border telegraph routes.

These results, along with the renewed state of warfare in the north, interminable land policy debates in the Otago Provincial Council and further gold discoveries in Central Otago, overshadowed the separation debate.[43] The separation movement largely went into abeyance until late 1863.

After the fall of the Domett ministry separation re-emerged as a key political issue. It became entwined with the debate over relocating the national capital from Auckland. This, not arguments about localism, parliamentary underrepresentation or paucity of common interests, united Otago and Auckland separatists. If they worked together, they could secure separation from each other and rule individual colonies in each island. Auckland feared that, without the status of capital, it would also lose a strong military presence and suffer a business recession, and its support for separation was a handy stimulant for the movement in Dunedin.[44] This odd couple came together out of self-interest: Auckland to protect its present status and Otago to enhance its future prospects. After a couple of years of operating largely alone, Otago's separatists gained a powerful ally in parliament, as Auckland's 12 members were of one mind on this subject.

Attempts to reach out to other provinces bore little fruit. Some prominent papers and individuals expressed support for South Island separation, but there was never a popular campaign. In Nelson the *Examiner* had offered some very guarded support for – potentially temporary – separation in light of wartime circumstances,[45] but remained sceptical about most separatist arguments, especially as Nelson was 'nearer to Wellington, and more accessible to Auckland, than to Otago or even Canterbury'.[46] The political concerns of Nelson Province in the early 1860s were gold, coal and public works, especially railways; separation, justifiably, does not rate a mention in Jim McAloon's able account of the period.[47] In Canterbury the *Lyttelton Times* supported separation, as did some leading politicians, including Superintendent Moorhouse, but the *Press* was hostile and the cause gained little public momentum.[48] Opinion in Southland was divided. The *Invercargill Times* pronounced itself separatist, while the *Daily News* suspected that Otago aspired to great power as 'the metropolitan and governing province of the Middle Island'.[49] Southland's talk, like Canterbury's, did not translate into action. Even Otago's hinterlands were not sold on separation, with the goldfields in particular mistrustful of Dunedin's motives. The *Lake Wakatip Mail* saw through Vogel's separatism, lashing out at the Dunedin elite and press for their 'over-powering belief in the value of centralisation', which meant the concentration of Otago's and the South Island's business and governance in Dunedin.[50]

The Whitaker–Fox ministry in November 1863 attempted to appease the South Island's dissatisfaction with the colony's financial arrangements. Fox proposed a lieutenant-governor to expand and oversee the island's governmental machinery, though he was unwilling to make it a matter of confidence in the ministry.[51] This plan was very similar to the Eyre and Grey arrangement of the 1840s, right down to the detail that if the governor went south, the lieutenant-governor would travel north to handle the affairs of the North Island. It met with little enthusiasm from either side of the separation debate. Edward Cargill, son of Dunedin's founder and an opponent of separation, perceived the plan as a clever ploy to calm Auckland's fear of losing the capital rather than to improve southern governance. The ministry's proposals would, he argued, lead to 'the shelving for the present of the removal of the seat of government from Auckland'.[52] Vogel, who accused Cargill of not being a true South Island representative, argued that if the question was removal of the capital to Wellington *or* semi-separation, then the latter was preferable; he supported Fox's motion.[53] The separatist *Invercargill Times* opposed both options: it rejected Fox's 'compromise' motion since it failed to give the South Island pre-eminence, and it felt that giving Wellington the status of capital would 'suit nobody but the Wellington people'.[54] The southern separatists saw the capital's relocation as a paltry response to their complaints and continued to demand separation, or at least greater steps towards it. Fox struggled to gain support and quietly dropped his motion.[55]

Instead the Cook Strait members successfully passed a motion to relocate the capital.[56] Previous attempts to move the capital were foiled by the inability of southerners to agree which settlement should receive the title. Nelson, for instance, would not support a Wellington bid, and vice versa. In 1863, however, the members representing Marlborough, Nelson and Wellington agreed to unite and press for an independent commission to determine the capital. Accordingly, with Fox's motion dead, Domett of Nelson advanced resolutions in favour of removing the seat of government that were supported by all Cook Strait members except Stafford.[57] The resolutions came from outside the ministry, which was divided on the issue: there was little common ground between Whitaker of Auckland and Fox of Wellington.[58] Both Domett's resolutions and a subsequent address to Grey praying for the resolutions to be given effect, advanced by FitzGerald, passed easily.[59]

Opposition was restricted almost entirely to Auckland and Otago members – and Otago's parliamentary support of separatism was weakened by the presence of anti-separatists such as J.L.C. Richardson and Cargill. Auckland and Otago harboured frustration with the resolutions. Auckland argued vehemently that it was the best site for government, especially for handling Māori affairs while the war continued. Removing the capital to a central location was likened derisively to a man 'select[ing] his navel as the receptacle of his brains, because that happened to be the centre of an ordinary mortal's body'.[60] According to a petition to the Queen, endorsed by a crowded public meeting in January 1864, it was 'imperative that the seat of government should not be removed' during wartime and that Auckland was 'equally well adapted [for government] … in times of peace'.[61] There were even outlandish proposals to relocate the capital *within* Auckland Province to Ngaruawahia in the Waikato to subdue Māori and promote peace.[62] At a turbulent and unruly Dunedin public meeting Otago's provincialists and separatists denounced the parliamentary defeat of separation as a self-interested political trick by Wellington to secure the capital. Vogel continued to emphasise that relocation to Wellington would be no better for Otago than if the capital were on the Chatham Islands.[63]

Despite this anger, and in accordance with parliament's resolutions, three independent commissioners were appointed. They were drawn from the Australian colonies – Francis Murphy, speaker of Victoria's Legislative Assembly; Joseph Docker, a member of the New South Wales Legislative Assembly; and Ronald Campbell Gunn, a distinguished Tasmanian public servant and former parliamentarian. In October 1864, after a lengthy tour, the commissioners presented their report, unanimously recommending Wellington ahead of Wanganui, Picton, Port Underwood, Havelock and Nelson.[64] Relocation became an established fact when the Weld ministry adopted the commissioners' decision as part of its platform and successfully fended off amendments to postpone any relocation until after Auckland was declared a separate colony, an election or the end of war.[65] The failure of these amendments can be partly attributed to their separatist affiliation. The *New Zealand Herald*, founded by ex-*New Zealander* partner William Chisholm Wilson in 1863 and soon Auckland's premier publication, turned on the province's separatists. It blamed 'ill-advised and ill-timed' references to separation for alienating parliamentarians from outside Auckland and Otago who did not want 'indecent haste exhibited in the removal of the seat of Government'.[66]

Amid outrage and separatist unrest at both ends of New Zealand, the capital was moved to Wellington and the provinces won no concessions. The relocation, on the basis that it provided more convenient, efficient national government, could have been coupled with strengthening or reforming the provincial system, but there was no impetus for this. The central provinces would not lead the charge: a changed seat of government was the reform they wanted. Once parliament was more centrally located, provincialist arguments about distance from the national government were no longer so compelling. Distance ceased to be Wellington's concern. Auckland continued to make ineffectual noise about how its allegedly unique ability to handle Māori affairs required the capital to remain in the north. Some newspaper editors, perhaps with an eye to sales, promoted fears that Auckland had been abandoned to a 'war of extermination' with Māori, unable to rely on support from a suddenly distant central government.[67] In light of Auckland's belief that it was the 'natural capital' of the North Island, if not the colony, the predictable disruptions experienced during the relocation of the capital were exaggerated to be an increase in the 'evil' of which the South Island complained – inefficient, distant government.[68] Retaining the capital and potential separation were the topics of the day, not provincial reform.

Otago kept demanding separation, and separatists with a centralising impulse such as Vogel were not going to push for stronger provincialism. Macandrew tried to whip up provincialist fervour, blaming New Zealand's ills on the failure of the central government to pursue provincialist policy.[69] Neither Vogel's nor Macandrew's forms of advocacy succeeded. Otago hoped in 1866 that the Stafford ministry would give it some concessions, but fiery speeches and extremist motions in parliament did not win any friends and the opportunity for reform was lost.[70] Separation survived through 1867 thanks to controversy. Macandrew, who lost office in 1861 when he was arrested for bankruptcy, was re-elected to the superintendency in 1867 but Stafford denied him the goldfields powers normally delegated to superintendents because of his past indiscretions. Outrage with this decision drew Macandrew and Vogel closer together as they railed against central interference in provincial affairs. This, however, was a last gasp. The dispute cast Vogel as an ultra-provincialist but he had lost his passion for the separation cause; he realised it was no longer the means of achieving his primary object of economic growth.[71]

Separation was at a dead end. Neither Auckland nor the South Island became separate colonies, nor did the movement secure concessions to strengthen provincialism or remodel New Zealand's constitution into an explicitly federal one. When the moment for agitation to enhance the position of the provinces arrived, the two most frustrated provinces were committed to uncompromising separatist campaigns that had little appeal elsewhere and alienated moderates. The only achievement after the removal of the capital was the suspension of the New Provinces Act, which merely bandaged provincialism's most obvious wound. It was not one of the concessions the separatists wanted. Furthermore, at least in Otago, separation was not intrinsically tied to a belief in provincialism. Vogel was not going to fight for improvements to a provincial system that he believed was at best a temporary measure that would fade away, and at worst a hindrance to economic growth. Separation announced Vogel as a talented, influential politician, but its long-term consequences for provincialism were few. It was a distraction, most valuable now as an insight into the genesis and development of Vogel's centralising impulses. It is a mistake to use 'separatist' and 'provincialist' as synonyms, as A.H. McLintock did when writing his history of Otago, and depictions of Vogel as a flip-flopper or a 'provincialist … converted to centralisation' are unsubstantiated.[72] His lack of commitment to provincialism, and his passion for remodelling any political institutions that obstructed his faith in economic growth or technological advances, were readily apparent in his separatist agitation as early as 1862.

Chapter 10
'Provincialism Will Soon Only Exist in History'

War and separation were major issues of the 1860s, but they masked a more fundamental problem: provinces from north to south were coming apart at the seams. It was not only the new provinces that failed to provide public works – almost all the original six experienced significant failures. Taranaki was hobbled by war, but the others had no such excuses. Their experiences demonstrate the full scale of provincial debt and show how popular discontent with provincialism spread beyond Invercargill, Blenheim and Napier to the original provincial strongholds. The pace of development languished behind settler expectations even in Canterbury, the one province to achieve success with a grand public works scheme. The push for railways throughout New Zealand was strong. In Australian colonies, where public investment in railways was rising steeply, towns that became railheads experienced a sudden increase in both population and business, an economic boom that eminent historians Stuart Macintyre and Sean Scalmer have likened to a gold rush.[1] New Zealand's settlers expected the same results. The provincial system struggled for popularity and viability as public works failures mounted across the colony.

As has been mentioned, the first railway in New Zealand was opened not in Southland, despite frequent boasts, or in high-achieving Canterbury, but in Nelson Province. Unlike almost all subsequent New Zealand railways, it was private. William Long Wrey, a former Cornish miner, and William Thomas Locke Travers, a prominent lawyer and politician, promoted the venture. The Dun Mountain Railway shared the fate of most other provincial railways. Wrey and Travers were enthusiastic promoters of copper mining in the Nelson Mineral Belt, coaxing prominent Nelsonians, including Edward Stafford, to invest in their schemes in the mid-1850s.[2] Wrey pushed the belief that the Dun Mountain behind Nelson contained substantial copper deposits, but in early 1858 it emerged that there were only commercial quantities of chrome ore, not copper; chrome was a very new mineral, used mainly in the manufacture of dyes and pigments.[3] To carry chrome to port, Wrey needed his company to construct a horse-drawn railway.

The opening celebrations of the Dun Mountain Railway. Men with flags stand on the horse-drawn wagons. C2641, Nelson Provincial Museum

In May 1858 the Nelson Provincial Council passed the Dun Mountain Railway Ordinance, which required the governor's assent.[4] However, London had recently disallowed the central Waste Lands Act of 1856, which would have given control over the sale of Crown lands to the provinces, because it threatened the imperial guarantee of New Zealand's £500,000 loan.[5] Since the railway ordinance empowered the company to make use of Crown lands for construction, Governor Browne had no power to give assent.[6] Later in 1858 a new Waste Lands Act was passed, appeasing – with some difficulty – London's qualms about the former act and forbidding provincial land legislation.[7] The door was now open for the company to seek permission for a railway and central government approval was given in August 1861.[8] The line was finished a month ahead of schedule and within budget, but it was built hastily and to low standards.[9] The Dun Mountain Railway opened on 3 February 1862, two days after Nelson celebrated its twentieth anniversary. Nelsonians thronged the streets to witness the first train, with the Nelson brass band performing on the leading wagon.[10] It was a day of feasts, speechmaking and celebration.

The railway soon ran into troubles when the chrome market became depressed in January 1863. The market was saturated; the American Civil War disrupted cotton supply to Lancashire textile mills, in turn reducing demand for chrome dyes; synthetic dyes became more popular at the expense of chrome; and the company struggled to sell its product in the face of monopolistic practices overseas. Worse followed. In February 1866 flooding damaged the line and the company struggled to afford maintenance. Although repairs were made, the company wanted to sell and by 1867 traffic was almost non-existent.[11] Part of the line remained in use because the railway was legally required to operate a daily passenger service between central Nelson and its port.[12] This service, really a horse-drawn tram, became known as the City Bus. It was the first railed public passenger service in New Zealand, and although the Dun Mountain Railway failed in its original objective, the passenger service operated reliably for decades.[13] The freight line up Dun Mountain was dismantled in 1872 but the City Bus ran until 1901.

Unfortunately for Nelson, the provincial council's attempts to push ahead with public transportation proved less successful than the modest but dependable City Bus. In 1862 Waimea East provincial councillor Fedor Kelling led agitation for a railway from Nelson to the Waimea Valley.[14] The Nelson Examiner extended its support and council viewed the proposal favourably, but the province's financial position was precarious.[15] No action was taken until 1866, when a gold rush in Nelson's southwestern Buller region sparked enthusiasm for a railway from Nelson to Cobden, on the north (Nelsonian) bank of the Grey River opposite Greymouth, with a branch to Westport. This enthusiasm led to the passage of central legislation authorising the superintendent to reserve Crown land for a railway.[16]

There was a prominent current of scepticism in the community, some fearing that the province lacked the financial capacity to build a railway, especially in light of interprovincial failures.[17] Sceptics included Alfred Saunders, superintendent between March 1865 and February 1867. In his intensely political history of New Zealand, Saunders criticised the railway-related 'incredible epidemic of borrowing' and 'imprudence' of provincial councils.[18] In June 1868 another attempt to secure approval for a railway from Nelson to Cobden was endorsed by a select committee but rejected by the whole council.[19] Apart from the Dun Mountain Railway, therefore, Nelson saw little transport development in the 1860s. Railways did not open up the interior and roads remained inadequate. One writer argues that 'procrastination was a godsend', allowing Nelson to avoid the failures of other

Nelson often awaited public works and rarely had its ambitions fulfilled. This 1868 view looks west along Bridge Street with the provincial buildings prominent in the middle, viewed from the side. They sat in Albion Square with a Bridge Street frontage; today only a small matching fire engine house remains to recall their design. The original fire engine was purchased to protect the chambers. C941, Nelson Provincial Museum Collection

provinces and take advantage of Vogel's centralisation after 1870.[20] Yet it was not a godsend to merchants or hinterland settlers who wished to open up the province's interior and develop its economy, nor to a provincial council that could not bring Nelson into the modern age of railways. Nelson did not even gain much from the Vogel years – it was never connected to the rest of New Zealand's railway network, and at least one historian of Nelson's politics has blamed this failure on the transfer of public works from a provincial council in tune with the region's needs to an uninterested central government.[21]

Wealthy Otago also failed to become a leader in land transport development. The province was poorly developed and isolated before the gold rush, though by the late 1850s serviceable roads were slowly extending their tentacles into the hinterland, even the most remote districts had a weekly or fortnightly postal service, and mechanisation started to reach the region's farms.[22] As superintendent in 1860 Macandrew, with an eye to the future, split the Surveying and Public Works Department into two and made lavish public works proposals that stunned Otago, including main roads, steam navigation on inland waterways and land reclamations of Otago Harbour.[23] He considered a railway or tramway to the Taieri and Tokomairiro regions and proposed to reserve land in the belief the province would soon be 'in a position to indulge in railroads'.[24] The reality was quite different. Roads were inadequate and railways existed only in imagination. One close study reveals the tardiness with which the province constructed roads to the goldfields, much to the exasperation of residents of Otago's interior.[25] Nonetheless a favourable select committee report in 1863 did lead to the passing of resolutions that endorsed the preparation of a plan for railways, including a line to the Wakatipu goldfields. The *Otago Witness* believed 'the Province ought to have a central line opened' within three or four years.[26] The committee also sternly criticised the province's roadmaking, urging an overhaul of construction management as poor quality roads were being built at a 'ruinous rate' of £3,000 per mile.[27]

The report resulted in little action. Plans for two railways from Dunedin, one to Port Chalmers and another to the Clutha region, proceeded slowly through the council, with guarantees of 6 per cent returns offered in 1864 to any companies willing to construct the lines.[28] In 1865 the matter was taken to the General Assembly for approval to build on Crown land, and in October 1866 the Otago Southern Trunk Railway Act received assent. But the central government was unwilling to support a railway loan, leaving Otago's provincial council to entertain forlorn hopes that improved conditions on the London money market would stimulate the formation of a private company to construct the lines under the terms of the provincial guarantee.[29] More positively, the superintendent could inform the council that some major rivers – the Clutha, Mataura and Shotover – had been bridged and new schools constructed. Public works were proceeding, albeit much more slowly than the province's swelling population wished.

The development of works was hampered during 1866–67 by a pronounced scarcity of labour and a lack of new immigrants.[30] After much discussion of railways and telegraphs, the province remained dependent on primitive roads often made

John Turnbull Thomson, the famed surveyor, was also a talented artist. This 1870 painting depicts the new Clutha River bridge in Balclutha, one of Otago Province's public works achievements. It was destroyed by floods in 1878. 92/1338, Hocken Collections, Uare Taoka o Hākena, Dunedin

impassable by bad weather. Even at this late date in the province's history, its poor infrastructure acted as a barrier between Dunedin and Otago's small towns; this may have encouraged the towns to flourish as local economic and industrial centres, but it did not foster an integrated provincial economy.[31] In February 1867 Macandrew achieved a spectacular victory in the superintendent election after a campaign that capitalised on Otago's frustration with the slow development of infrastructure and the continued isolation of hinterlands. In the words of one of Otago's most celebrated historians, Erik Olssen, 'Macandrew incarnated boosterism' with rhetoric of boundless public works, investment and immigration.[32] His campaign was popular even in Southland, where the emphasis on railways and other public works spurred popular cries of 'reunion and Macandrew'.[33] Thus, come 1867, Otago was all talk and little action – men like Macandrew touted wealth and development, the slow pace of development fostered discontent, boosters exploited this through even more wildly optimistic solutions and Otago fell in behind them. After all, any booster could blame a lack of results on laggards in provincial government.

This was especially the case in 1866–67, when the administration of Macandrew's predecessor, Thomas Dick, 'was in danger of collapsing from sheer boredom'.[34] Firm plans, let alone results, remained elusive.

Instead it was Canterbury that became the beacon of provincial development. When it began railway construction, it had no gold rush to generate funds. Canterbury's first railway featured a 2.6 km tunnel on the route from Christchurch to Lyttelton and resolved the province's struggle with the Port Hills. Visionary superintendent William Sefton Moorhouse led this conquest over geography. Moorhouse was elected in 1857 in a mild contest between himself, a man of action, and Joseph Brittan, a man of ideas who was seen as inaugural superintendent FitzGerald's legitimate successor. The election was a matter of personalities not policies, and although public works featured in the campaign, neither man gave more than vague indications of policy.[35] When Moorhouse defeated Brittan, there was no sign that he would lead Canterbury to public works success, yet once he took office he never wavered in his conviction that a railway tunnel was essential to the province's prosperity.[36]

In October 1858 Moorhouse put the tunnel proposal before the provincial council. His timing was impeccable. The province was primed to accept a visionary project as its economy was flourishing; in the first half of the year, land sales brought in £9,000 a month and exports exceeded £100,000 in value, nearly double the return for all of 1857.[37] When Moorhouse asked his councillors 'whether the ultimate advantage … would or would not justify the required disbursement' of a large outlay of money, they readily approved the plan, backed by popular enthusiasm.[38] A commission appointed to handle the proposal conferred in England with George Robert Stephenson, nephew of railway pioneer George Stephenson, who unequivocally endorsed the direct tunnel over more circuitous alternatives.[39]

Canterbury's first attempt to authorise a railway failed on a technicality. On the basis of Stephenson's recommendation, and ignoring unexpected opposition from FitzGerald, the council passed a railway ordinance in December 1859.[40] It granted £235,000 to make the railway, of which £70,000 was to be raised via debentures under a loan ordinance passed on the same day.[41] However, the governor withheld assent to both as the railway ordinance contravened the Constitution Act's nineteenth clause prohibiting provinces from passing legislation affecting Crown lands.[42] Moorhouse, also a central parliamentarian, therefore had to put forward a bill at the next meeting of the House in 1860. His pressure and the help of well-known surveyor Edward Jollie, member for Cheviot, ensured that

William Sefton Moorhouse,
superintendent of Canterbury
1857–63 and again 1866–68.

35mm-00151-C-F, Alexander Turnbull Library,
Wellington

the Lyttelton and Christchurch Railway Act, framed along the same lines as the original ordinance, was first to pass the House that session.[43] Between the rejection of the original ordinance and the passage of the act, Canterbury boldly authorised a new loan for £300,000.[44] This was intended to fund the whole railway, leaving provincial revenue free to fund ordinary public works. Moorhouse believed this course of action would allow wider exploitation of the province's resources, thereby increasing revenue.[45]

Construction of the Lyttelton railway began on 17 July 1861. Not everybody was thrilled. John Hall, a future premier, placed greater importance on establishing links with outlying areas such as Timaru, rightly fearing neglect would breed secessionism.[46] FitzGerald went further. After weeks of quietly fuming on his Canterbury sheep run, FitzGerald savaged Moorhouse in a letter to the *Lyttelton Times*, accusing both the superintendent and large parts of the community of 'financial insanity' and a delusion that 'this [economic] progress ... would last forever'.[47] He invoked the spectre of England's railway mania, clearly fearing a colonial repeat of the financial chaos of 1847 when speculative investment in British railways created a bubble that inevitably burst.[48] FitzGerald's outrage was no temporary passion: he founded the *Press* to oppose the tunnel. In its first issue he asked whether the government's estimates that the railway would be profitable were the creation 'of *folly* or of *fraud*'.[49] These libellous attacks were beneath FitzGerald's dignity. His friends felt he was hurting rather than helping his cause and after a few weeks he assumed a more measured and reasonable approach.[50] It was to no avail. The public eagerly endorsed the project, and despite bad weather between 1500 and 2000 of Canterbury's 16,000 citizens attended the first sod ceremony in the Heathcote Valley.[51] The province's biggest occasion yet, it featured lavish festivities – parades, a banquet and a very lively ball. Poor weather could not overshadow the sense of achievement and optimism.

The railway's construction was not without controversy or difficulty.[52] On several occasions the province came close to financial disaster. A brief recession in mid-1860 left the provincial government with barely enough revenue to satisfy ordinary expenditure but this did not dent local confidence, and Moorhouse's personal standing was not seriously tarnished by his indiscretions in privately acquiring land for the railway and then being repaid by the council.[53] By 1862 the province was again so prosperous that it expanded its railway ambitions. Through the Canterbury Loan Ordinance it authorised borrowings of £500,000 to fund public works and immigration. Moorhouse was passionate about securing migrants who could develop Canterbury's natural resources and its public works, and the ordinance was a provincial harbinger of Vogel's Great Public Works Policy.[54] It did not, however, have the chance to achieve the same degree of transformation.

In 1864 Canterbury decided to build railways north and south of Christchurch to link to the tunnel when it was completed and to open up land. Construction on the southern route started the next year, but Canterbury's boom collapsed into another more pronounced recession.[55] The previously discussed competition between provincial and central debentures in Britain meant Canterbury struggled to raise money. New Zealand's government agent in London wrote privately that the money market was in 'a singular state' and Canterbury loans were 'in a mess', sold at a discount because of the stock exchange's refusal to recognise provincial securities on its official list.[56] The precise reasons for this refusal are unclear, but colonial loans had fallen out of favour after Canada refused to take responsibility for an 1863 default by the City of Hamilton in what is now Ontario.[57] By 1866, funding for road construction through the Southern Alps to Westland also clashed with the railway projects and Canterbury was in a rough position. Over half of the £500,000 loan was yet to be raised when the central government consolidated provincial loans. Nonetheless, the province persevered, and the central government's acquisition of unsold debentures proved a boon.

Nelson may have opened the first horse-drawn railway, and the *Lady Barkly* in Southland may have been the first locomotive to raise steam in New Zealand, but the first public steam railway was in Canterbury. This wood engraving by Richard Seymour Kelly for the *Illustrated London News* shows the festivities on opening day. PUBL-0033-1864-241, Alexander Turnbull Library, Wellington

Canterbury was rewarded for its exertions when in 1863 it became the first province in New Zealand to open a steam railway – to Ferrymead, on the Avon Heathcote Estuary, below the Port Hills – and then finished the Lyttelton tunnel and first stage of the southern railway in 1867. These were momentous achievements for Canterbury – and, in retrospect, for New Zealand, though there were few hints of a unified colony at the time. The branch to Ferrymead was approved in 1862 to link the city with Ferrymead's rivermouth wharf, improving communications and allowing easier transport of supplies while the tunnel was being built. Its opening on 1 December 1863 was lauded by the *Lyttelton Times* as '[o]ne of those great events which form an epoch in the history of a people'.[58] The *Press* also rejoiced in the sense of occasion, despite snide comments about petty inconveniences and Moorhouse's appearance.[59] Not even dusty conditions and a howling nor'wester could dampen spirits; Cantabrians dressed in their Sunday best, railway buildings were decorated with bunting and flowers, food and beverage sellers made considerable profits and flags flew throughout Christchurch. By noon the largest crowd ever assembled in Canterbury gathered at the railway station. Moorhouse had retired from the superintendency earlier that year but was given the honour of riding aboard the locomotive for the first of many trips that day – the train conveyed approximately 3500 people between Christchurch and Ferrymead.

New Zealand's first railway was celebrated not as a national accomplishment, but as a provincial achievement within an international empire. Canterbury and its British character were emphasised. Formal festivities, featuring hundreds of invited guests and numerous opportunists, were held inside the goods shed, which was adorned with evergreens and flags, the Canterbury and British coats of arms and slogans such as 'God save the Queen' and 'Advance Canterbury'. Speechmaking was the order of the day, with toasts honouring the royal family, Moorhouse, his successor Samuel Bealey and many others. The closest to an acknowledgement of the colony was a toast to Governor Grey. The railway was fundamentally a provincial project; Moorhouse, whose speech more than any looked into the future, spoke of neither New Zealand nor interprovincial links, but of breakfasting in Christchurch and dining in Timaru – 'in fact they would journey to the extreme limit of the province, transact business and return to town in a day'.[60] Provincial initiative had no national vision and the idea of connecting the Bay of Islands with Bluff was very far from the public mind.[61]

The only railway event to feature a similar celebration was the beginning of work on the southern railway; its opening and that of the Lyttelton tunnel were treated in a more sober and utilitarian manner. By the time these ceremonies occurred in the mid-1860s, the *Press* was settling comfortably into its role as a premier journal of record; its antagonism to the railway had dissipated and FitzGerald's dwindling association with the paper concluded in 1867.[62] The southern railway ceremony, held to coincide with the Queen's Birthday public holiday on 24 May 1865, celebrated New Zealand more overtly than the Ferrymead festivities but retained a Canterbury emphasis. The public had 'been eagerly looking forward' to work on the southern railway starting; hundreds attended the ceremony in Christchurch, which was 'decked in its gayest holiday apparel' and interest in the holiday was greatly magnified by its dual function of honouring the Queen and turning the railway's first sod.[63] At the grand banquet this time there were toasts to the General Assembly as well as to provincial and imperial authorities. Apart from the changed circumstances in the colony, under which the central government was becoming more important and had moved closer to the southern provinces, there were political factors at play. The explanation belongs to FitzGerald himself, now happy to toast the railway and the House: 'I should have had far less pleasure in replying to this toast any time during the last two or three years, because I felt that they [the House] had been pursuing a policy which had been detrimental to the interests of the Middle Island and of this province.'[64] Now, he believed, the House was more in tune with southern interests, Canterbury would no longer be subject to neglect from the centre, and the province would be able to reach its potential.

FitzGerald was not entirely correct. The southern railway's first section was opened to the then inconsequential destination of Rolleston in October 1866 with only minor celebrations. Its most interesting feature, according to the *Press*, was a 60-foot (18-metre) well that had been sunk for the railway.[65] Construction stalled on the banks of the Selwyn River the next year, while the Lyttelton tunnel failed to meet its 1866 deadline. The province, impatient for the benefits the tunnel would bring, grew frustrated. As a consequence, the tunnel's grand inauguration event was not the running of the first train, but the chance to walk through it on foot as soon as the two ends met – a privilege allowed to dignitaries in late May 1867, followed by 2000 people on 10 June, equivalent to a third of Christchurch's population.[66] The first train, on 9 December 1867, was packed with curious travellers, and although there were many services for excursionists throughout the day, there was no formal demonstration or ceremony.[67] Now Canterbury had an operational railway from Lyttelton to Selwyn via Christchurch. It carried thousands of passengers per month and up to 400 tons of freight per day, though the recession hid the railway's immediate benefits. The saving on imports and exports during 1868 was at least £24,500, a welcome if not impressive outcome.[68] By 1870 Canterbury's 32 miles (50 km) of railway earned a 3 per cent profit.[69] Municipalities and town boards were improving Canterbury's roads and other local facilities, and the province's rapid telegraph advancements had made Christchurch, in the early 1860s, the colony's unofficial telegraph headquarters.[70] Canterbury had been through economic turbulence and unexpected slumps like the rest of the colony, yet it alone oversaw a range of successful public works.

Public works were pressing elsewhere. By the early 1860s Wellington Province aspired to grand projects both for economic development and provincial pride. The Wairarapa was now largely owned by Pākehā or was actively being negotiated for release from Māori, especially fertile river valley farmland, but the region's communication with the capital had improved little since 1840. Only a rudimentary road crossed the Rimutaka Range and coastal shipping was unreliable, especially since the Wairarapa lacked a good harbour. The bitter dispute between Featherston and his opposition in the provincial council in the late 1850s had caused a halt to public works spending. There was considerable unrest in the province, especially

Charles Barraud's 1869 watercolour of the difficult road across the Rimutaka Range.
C-003-005, Alexander Turnbull Library, Wellington

from new immigrants who were promised employment, only to find there was none.[71] Locals were stung by interprovincial critics for whom it had 'become customary to underrate and sneer at Wellington'.[72] Finally, in 1861, Featherston's allies won control of the provincial council and public works could resume.

Calls for some sort of railway or tramway, no matter how rudimentary, became increasingly common and popular. The *Spectator* was surprised that Wellington could not count a railway as one of its accomplishments; Robert Stokes, its proprietor and a member of the provincial council, had for some years been advocating a railway to the Hutt Valley and Wairarapa.[73] James Coutts Crawford, a pioneer Wellingtonian of many talents – he was, among other things, a geologist, explorer and politician – put forward a plan more ambitious than any proposed by Stokes. He published a pamphlet promoting a railway network throughout Wellington Province to develop the timber trade in the northern Wairarapa and to form the start of an interprovincial network.[74] The *Independent*, although hoping that Crawford's aspirations might be realised, feared this would not happen for many years and that the pamphlet was 'one of those day dreams in which men of leisure sometimes indulge'.[75] Crawford himself later acknowledged that the 'time was not ripe' because of Wellington's depressed commercial conditions and that his appeal was 'premature'.[76]

Yet in 1863 railways came to the forefront of Wellington's public agenda and both newspapers were behind the proposal – the *Spectator* as Stokes' organ and the *Independent* as Featherston's ally. Featherston has often been depicted as maintaining consistent scepticism and even hostility towards railways.[77] In early 1863 he appeared to have mellowed. At the opening of a new session of the provincial council in April, Featherston forecast the potential development of railways, with a memorandum on the topic to be introduced by Stokes.[78] Frustrated with the Rimutaka road, and believing that the Wairarapa's resources were 'comparatively useless from want of a cheap and expeditious means of transit' to Wellington, the *Independent* eagerly supported Featherston with the blind optimism so common to colonial boosters.[79] It believed that a short tunnel cut through the summit of the Rimutakas would then enable an easy descent to the Wairarapa – the very route that would ultimately be traversed by the steepest and most arduous railway line ever built in New Zealand, the Rimutaka Incline.[80] A select committee endorsed Stokes' proposal for a £500,000 railway from Wellington via the Wairarapa to the Hawke's Bay, with a branch through the Manawatu Gorge to the west coast, and plans were made to approach contractors in England.[81] Predictably but accurately this was derided in Auckland. One newspaper wondered if 'some patent rolling machine must have been recently employed between the City of Wellington and the Wairarapa Valley'.[82] Wellington was resolute. As the *Independent* put it, the 'time never would come for anything great and new if it were not that some men are in advance of their age'.[83]

Unfortunately Wellington's railway boosters remained too far in advance of their age. Settlers in the Wairarapa, rather than receiving a railway to convey their goods to town and harbour, were left to complain about the inadequacy of the weekly post.[84] When the provincial council sat in 1864 Stokes blamed hostilities in the Waikato for the province's failure to act on his recommendations – under such conditions, it was impossible to interest British capitalists.[85] By 1866, however, the council stirred into action. The province's London agent, who had previously been despondent about raising money for provincial purposes, believed that English capitalists were becoming more favourable towards financing the railway – and even more promisingly, a local proposal to build the railway was submitted to the provincial government.[86] Robert Mudge Marchant put in an offer to build the first 18 miles (30 km) of the railway for £150,000 if the government would sanction a guarantee of 7 per cent on his outlay. Marchant had trained in England under his cousin, Isambard Kingdom Brunel, the famed transport engineer, and plied his trade in Brazil, Victoria and – less auspiciously – Southland. Yet he was apparently not professionally disgraced by his association with Southland's wooden railway. Wellington's provincial council authorised Featherston to enter into a contract for construction with Marchant. However, the recommendations of 1863 had offered a guarantee of only 6 per cent and negotiations between Marchant and Featherston collapsed in September 1866.[87]

By 1867, therefore, Wellington found itself wanting in public works. Local businessmen made further attempts to form a company to build a railway to the Wairarapa, but other leading figures, including the Anglican Bishop of Wellington, Charles Abraham, aired their concerns about the project and like all previous proposals it proved fruitless.[88] Other public works were also deficient. Sanitation was poor, Lambton Quay was dotted with cesspools, a fire brigade was formed in 1865 but received no public assistance, roads were typically poorly made, surface drainage was a constant problem and lamps above hotel doors provided the only public lighting.[89] Despite its ambitions and its acquisition of the seat of government, Wellington in 1867 was a very rudimentary capital, lacking many of the basic public works that provincial governments were expected to provide. Interprovincial sneering continued. When Wellington's first railway finally opened in 1874, celebrations were subdued, with one author suggesting that lavish festivities were considered inappropriate in light of how long the work had taken.[90]

Although Auckland derided Wellington's belief that steam locomotion could easily conquer the Rimutakas, Auckland itself became the subject of mockery when its railway ambitions faltered. A comprehensive history of Auckland's public transport accurately depicts transport provision in this period as chaotic and poorly organised.[91] The provincial council had problems providing many services, especially roads and education in outlying districts. Ambitious plans for a road network went unrealised, leaving Auckland dependent on muddy cart tracks and rotten bridges in the 1860s.[92] The Coromandel became particularly disgruntled about these matters in 1867 and Kaipara settlers alluded to opening trade with Sydney if they did not receive better communications with the provincial capital.[93] Railways, though, were the province's biggest failure. A desire to exploit resources south of Auckland and to integrate the Waikato into the provincial economy motivated proposals to build a railway south from Auckland to Drury, with the long-term aim of extending it to the Waikato River. In January 1862 the provincial council endorsed a resolution in favour of the railway, asserting that it would both increase the province's prosperity and promote friendly relations with Māori.[94] Drury, then as now a small village south of Papakura, was proposed as terminus because of nearby coal deposits and its location as a junction with the Great South Road being built by the military.[95] A wooden tramway to convey Drury coal to a nearby arm of Manukau Harbour was completed in May 1862, but the railway proposals had to wait.[96] The tramway was uneconomic and closed within a year, but it helped to motivate enthusiasm for a railway.

Aucklanders were also aware of the strategic potential of railways, especially as fear of war grew. The role of the railway in shaping the American Civil War, where it was essential to military strategy and transport, was not lost on Aucklanders.[97] Their newspapers described the control and use of railways in America as battles raged and troops were transferred from one theatre to another.[98] Auckland's railways, however, did not play a role in wartime offensives, although they might have been convenient for military commanders. In a country with poorly developed infrastructure, roads were needed, and built, first. The railway was envisaged as a post-war tool of civilisation and pacification, a means not of achieving victory, but of securing peace.

Although approved in 1863, the railway soon ran into difficulties. Approval itself was delayed by the resumption of open combat. The proposed railway's route was well publicised by February, but the provincial council did not approve a loan ordinance until September, with almost two-fifths of the £500,000 loan allocated to public works, and authorisation did not pass the central parliament until December.[99] In 1864 the provincial council appropriated £100,000 of the public works portion of the loan for the railway and established a board of five commissioners to oversee construction and expenditure. In an ominous sign, the commissioners' first report alluded to a power struggle with the province's executive.[100] Both the *Daily Southern Cross* and the *New Zealand Herald* threw their support behind the railway. Keen for an extension into the Waikato to open its land to settlement, they urged that Drury should not be a permanent terminus.[101] Auckland began to dream large – the railway was occasionally pitched as the start of an interprovincial trunk route to Wellington, but it was typically seen as a means of intraprovincial economic development.[102]

The first sod was turned in February 1865 but within months the press was publishing complaints of inexplicably slow construction.[103] The project coincided with Auckland's entry into commercial depression, caused by the transfer of troops out of the province following the end of the Waikato campaign in 1864 and the

The Parnell railway tunnel under construction in 1865, before work ground to a halt. It was replaced in 1915 by a new double-track tunnel and used as a temporary air-raid shelter in World War II. 4-126, Sir George Grey Special Collections, Auckland Libraries

removal of the seat of government in early 1865. The property market fell sharply, a commercial panic developed as businesses collapsed and soon the provincial treasury was bare.[104] The board of commissioners was scrapped to cut costs and by mid-1867 the project was lacking in oversight and visibly disintegrating owing to mounting expenses, slipping embankments, tunnels filling with water and fences succumbing to disrepair. The *Daily Southern Cross*, still enthusiastic about a railway, angrily turned on the way construction had been handled:

> It is hardly possible to write anything regarding the Auckland and Drury Railway unless in the way of complaint. There is absolutely nothing to be said in favour of it except that the project is a good one … of the railway works – their cost, condition, and prospective extension – the less one says the better … a more discreditable instance of squandering public money it has never been our misfortune to witness.[105]

The newspaper was so outraged by the mismanagement, incompetence and possible corruption that it sought an inquiry. Work ground to a halt and did not resume until the Vogel era. Aucklanders might have mocked Wellington's railway aspirations, but at least that province had not borrowed and wasted vast sums of money on an unfinished line. Even debt-stricken Southland managed to open an operational section of railway.

Despite being hobbled by war, Taranaki, too, entertained railway proposals. Far too weak to develop railways on its own and lacking a vast hinterland for the construction of a rural network, it focused on plans for interprovincial trunk railways. In July 1864 William Hulke, a former provincial councillor, proposed the building of a railway from New Plymouth to Wanganui as soon as conditions allowed – in other words, the defeat of the South Taranaki Māori and acquisition of their land.[106] Hulke presented his proposal to the provincial government in conjunction with contractors from Melbourne. The *Taranaki Herald*, in announcing the scheme, wondered if the provincial council could not do it more cheaply, but cast aside these doubts in light of the council's ineptitude at road construction: despite expenditure equalling that of a railway, only 6 miles (10 km) of a road intended to reach Wanganui had been formed, and less than four of those were metalled.[107]

Taranaki's dreams quickly expanded from a Wanganui railway to an interprovincial trunk route linking Wellington and Auckland via New Plymouth. A resolution adopted by the provincial council in late July 1864 requested that Taranaki's superintendent hold a conference with Auckland and Wellington's superintendents.[108] Wanganui viewed this proposal very favourably, believing a railway would improve its claims for the seat of government.[109] Others regarded it with suspicion. Although thinking it 'full early to bring the scheme forward' as 'the country … is still in the hands of an unconquered enemy', one Taranaki correspondent to the *Otago Witness* hoped the proposal would eventually be approved.[110] For the next year, both Taranaki and Wanganui debated the details and merits of railway proposals, but nothing came of this discussion.[111] In all this interprovincial chatter, however, one interesting shot was fired across the bow of provincialism. The *Wanganui Chronicle* urged the North Island provinces to unite in bringing the railway to fruition, for instance by collectively appointing one engineer rather than each having their own. With such an approach there could be provincial co-operation without provincial mergers or abolition, but 'unless there be so, provincialism will soon only exist in history'.[112]

There were already warning signs that the provinces would struggle to co-operate. Most provincial roads and railways had been conceived only as local developments rather than as arteries of interprovincial communication and integration. Since provincial expansion generally fanned outwards from coastal capitals, most provinces were yet to face immediate questions of cross-border co-operation. There was clearly a problem in different provinces selecting different railway gauges, the distance between the rails: this would create inconvenient and costly breaks-of-gauge when one network met another.[113] Canterbury pushed ahead with a broad gauge of 5′ 3″ (1600 mm) for its network, based on precedent in Ireland and Victoria, while other provinces either used the international standard gauge of 4′ 8½″ (1435 mm) or contemplated the cheaper narrow gauge of 3′ 6″ (1067 mm) that later became New Zealand's national gauge. In 1867 a central government select committee was appointed to consider the necessity of a uniform gauge for the South Island.[114] It lacked urgency because no railways were close to meeting and, since the committee did not believe there was evidence to recommend any particular gauge, it resolved that 'it would not be desirable … to insist upon uniformity'.[115] In an extraordinarily provincialist finding, perhaps influenced by the presence of such men as Macandrew and Moorhouse, the committee also asserted that New Zealand's scattered population made a single trunk line of railway inapplicable to present requirements. Both of these findings were rebuked in subsequent years.

Two provinces had already clashed over a different form of interprovincial link: Canterbury and Otago were utterly incapable of reaching an agreement to fund a bridge across the Waitaki River that formed their border. Petty local jealousies intervened, especially Timaru's fear that the Waimate region, until then tied to Timaru's port, would start exporting through Oamaru if a bridge were built.[116] The difficulties of breaks-of-gauge – or agreeing to a uniform gauge – and local parochialism meant serious problems lay ahead. Canterbury and Otago proved these difficulties were not limited to the railway network, but to any public works co-operation.

If the provinces were so inept at developing their own public works and at managing their finances, how could they be expected to work together constructively and efficiently when necessary? As has been mentioned, the central government had entered the telegraphic field rapidly: by 1867 it had built or bought all significant telegraphic routes.[117] Provincial capitals, harbours and goldfields were linked by wire. Ron Palenski and Eric Pawson both emphasise that the rapid expansion of the telegraph shaped national identity and was the primary cause for the introduction of

New Zealand Mean Time, the first national standard time zone in the world.[118] The telegraph enabled near-instant exchange of news and ideas between centres that had been separated by weeks of travel, and facilitated the rise of national standardisation over provincial distinctiveness. National railway development, with its capacity to move people and goods as well as words, would be even more revolutionary.

Chapter 11
The Watershed of 1867 and the Westland Experiment

Despite its gluttonous financial borrowings, in 1867 New Zealand entered economic stagnation with underdeveloped infrastructure. Most provinces, although they had accrued sizeable debts, had squandered the popular goodwill of 1853 by their systematic failure to provide the public works so necessary in a fledgling colony. Even Otago, the beacon of provincialism, had suffered during the mid-1860s and had made inadequate progress. The debt crisis had not been inevitable, nor was it rooted in structural flaws; arguments that London capitalists drove colonial expansion and development overlook what actually happened within New Zealand.[1] Administrative bungling by the provinces meant money was frittered away on incomplete and botched projects, and this had created a strong desire for reform among politicians and electors. The dire financial position of the provinces was simply the most obvious symptom of a deeper malaise within provincialism. It meant, though, that the matter of debt was tackled first – and in a way that would allow Julius Vogel to enter the scene with his public works policy.

Provincial loans amounted to £2,739,000, almost half of the colony's entire debt of £6,389,000.[2] Annual charges for interest and sinking funds occupied half of the £850,000 customs revenue, and the *New Zealand Times* highlighted that debt per (Pākehā) head in New Zealand was £28.10.0, almost £1 higher than in Britain and more than double any continental European power.[3] Debt per head in Australian colonies in the same period was, with the exception of Queensland, also well below New Zealand's level. Queensland in 1870 had debt per head of almost £34 – by which point New Zealand's debt had passed that level – but only New South Wales broke the £21 barrier in 1871, with South Australia, Tasmania and Victoria grouped between £11 and £17 per head.[4] The *Times* presented its figures as part of a plea for political frugality and a simplification of New Zealand's governmental machinery. It was clear something needed to be done.

Premier Edward Stafford had recently bolstered his position against the provincialists, oddly because of a controversy that featured a stunning provincialist

Edward Stafford, who enjoyed
respect across factional lines.

326883, Nelson Historical Society Collection,
Nelson Provincial Museum

victory. On 8 August 1866 Francis Jollie – the weak treasurer of a weak ministry thoroughly dominated by Stafford – delivered a financial statement arguing that it was 'no longer possible … to continue the old arrangement of subsidizing the Provinces with three-eighths of the Customs' and that the provinces must rely more upon themselves and their own resources.[5] The provincialist backlash was swift and sharp: Moorhouse moved a motion of no confidence that was endorsed 47–14. Crucially, the motion expressed no confidence in the *ministry*, not in Stafford personally. The opposition leadership was in disarray – Isaac Featherston was unwilling to give up Wellington's superintendency for an insecure colonial position and young Vogel, although rising fast, was not yet a viable option. Even Moorhouse wished Stafford to form a new ministry, one that could possess the confidence of the House. Nobody enjoyed the same level of backbench support as Stafford, and he was able to form a new ministry of extraordinary individual talent, a pragmatic Cabinet drawn from across 'party' lines – it even featured, after significant persuasion, Wellington provincialist William Fitzherbert as treasurer.[6]

The scene was not yet set for a reorganisation of New Zealand's political structure, especially as the wealthier South Island provinces maintained self-belief, but a consolidation of provincial and national debts was needed to avoid any weaker provinces collapsing. When the reconstituted ministry began its duties on 24 August 1866 Stafford acted as if it was a new ministry that had just swept into office.[7] In his ministerial statement he forecast the consolidation of existing colonial and provincial loans and a reconsideration – this part was never acted upon – of how 'any further provincial loans should be raised, regulated, and charged'.[8] The following year the Stafford ministry acted decisively to consolidate loans. Provincial finances remained stagnant and their debentures unsaleable, while the central government's credit had been steadily improving since its nadir of 1866.[9] Happily war expenditure was declining at the same time as ordinary revenue was increasing.[10] It was time to implement a solution for the poor credit of the provinces using the improving credit and security of the colony as a whole. The provinces were at a considerable disadvantage; they were marginalised on the London market as obscure borrowers and treated like mere colonial municipalities.[11] The central government enjoyed the benefits of sovereignty that the provinces lacked, and the collision between provincial and central loans in London noted earlier resulted in the central government becoming a much more creditworthy and powerful borrower. This meant consolidation was implemented on terms favourable to centralism.

Fitzherbert put forward the consolidation plan in his financial statement of August 1867. He was dissatisfied with the state of colonisation in New Zealand, particularly by the failure of the provinces to carry out immigration and public works, and was – temporarily, anyway – drifting from provincialist ideology.[12] This was not the first time Fitzherbert had proposed consolidation: a different plan in 1865 was thwarted by the removal of the Weld ministry. Nor was he the only individual proposing solutions. Numerous other people, including Vogel, had weighed in and offered various ideas, typically framed to avoid a simple conversion of provincial debentures into colonial bonds that would make the South Island liable for the debts of the North.[13] Fitzherbert's proposals of 1867 were strikingly centralist. Although he emphasised that the government wished to 'maintain existing institutions in a state of efficiency', it was 'unwilling that the unity of the Colony should remain a mere idle name', and desired 'that the powerful combination expressed in that term should be made to yield its legitimate financial results, by putting in motion the vast power of a common credit, which is now frittered away and wasted by being exercised provincially'.[14]

The consolidation offered colonial securities in exchange for provincial, with a loan raised to finance the conversion; the provincial debts thus became charges by

William Fitzherbert, one of
Wellington's 'Three Fs' with
Featherston and Fox.

1/2-025518-F, Alexander Turnbull Library,
Wellington

the central government upon the provincial governments that had incurred them.
Provincial debenture holders were given three years to come in. The provincial share
of consolidated revenue was paid over to the provinces only after the deduction
of annual charges for the consolidated loan.[15] This scheme was enshrined in two
associated acts – the Public Debts Act and the Consolidated Loan Act.[16] There was
initial outrage, with Featherston leading provincialist condemnation of the proposal
as a nefarious plot to benefit Bank of New Zealand shareholders, and Stafford
faced a considerable challenge persuading a hostile Legislative Council to pass the
acts. He prevailed, however, and the London money market viewed consolidation
favourably.[17] British financiers may not have had sufficient influence to effect an
absolute structural transformation, but they gave centralists valuable support in the
face of provincialist outrage. Fitzherbert himself performed the detailed work of
consolidating all the loans manually, without 'even a clerk … let alone a calculator'.[18]

Consolidating New Zealand's debts, as enshrined in the fourth clause of the
Public Debts Act, meant that the provinces would no longer be permitted to borrow
at all. Further loans would undermine the entire purpose of consolidation. As
described previously, borrowing had already been restricted in 1865 by a clause in the
Southland Provincial Debt Act that required provincial loans to be sanctioned by the
General Assembly.[19] Since most provinces were already in difficulty, this restriction
had affected only two small Wellington loans, allowing one to be negotiated at a

better interest rate than if it had not received General Assembly approval. However, as Morrell indicates, this law 'offered such an obvious inducement to log-rolling in the Assembly that it might have become dangerous'.[20] Now even this avenue to loans was closed. From 10 October 1867, when the Public Debts Act was signed into law, the provinces were completely barred from borrowing money. Although they had other regular revenue streams through rates, fees, licences and their allocation of customs, these were insufficiently lucrative and now represented the sole source of income for assisted immigration, public works and any other activities to promote colonisation. The provinces' tasks had not been circumscribed but their governments were suddenly placed in a very vulnerable position, much to the consternation and resentment of some, especially Canterbury and Otago.

Alongside debt consolidation, another prominent reform during 1867–68 was that of local government. After provincialists killed the New Provinces Act in 1865, outlying communities remained dissatisfied with their treatment and Stafford had not lost his centralising tendencies. Public works shortcomings further enraged the hinterlands: not only had much time been spent discussing proposals and large sums been borrowed to fund works primarily beneficial for provincial capitals, but the failure of these projects meant there was little to show for all that time and money. Certainly not much wealth was flowing to regional towns and rural communities. Settlers petitioned the central government frequently to alter New Zealand's political structure, be it via reorganisation of the provincial system or the creation of local bodies beneath provinces as a third level of government.[21]

From the early 1860s, as provinces grew and councils could no longer act as the local authority for the capital without infuriating the hinterlands or overburdening councillors and public servants, there was a clear need for some form of more localised government. In 1861 Canterbury adopted a municipal council ordinance, under which any town could be established as a municipality with a nine-member local council upon presentation of a petition of at least 100 residents.[22] Cantabrians were slow to exercise this new power because of fears of the financial burdens it might entail.[23] New ordinances were prepared specifically for the needs of Christchurch in 1862 and Lyttelton the next year, while Kaiapoi in 1864, Timaru in 1865 and Hokitika in 1866 availed themselves of the general ordinance.[24] With the machinery for municipalities enacted, rural road boards followed in 1863. The provincial public works department was by this point stretched much too thin: not a single properly macadamised highway was said to exist in Canterbury. The Roads Districts Ordinance of 1863 divided Canterbury into 27 local boards. These swiftly established road and bridge tolls to fund their work rather than enforcing local rates – the burden of rates, many colonists believed, had been left behind on emigration from England.[25] Otago had also established a full system of nine municipalities, subsidised by provincial revenue.[26] Although the other provinces had not established general systems, most passed ordinances to provide main towns with municipal powers.[27]

It was up to the central government to extend a consistent municipal system to the entire country. The 1867 session of the General Assembly was a watershed not only for the colony's finances, but also for the conflict between centralism and provincialism over local government. In August the ministry introduced two related items of legislation, the Local Government Bill and the Municipal Corporations Bill, though it did not make their passage a question of confidence. The former sought to establish road boards and district councils throughout rural New Zealand, the latter to allow towns to incorporate as municipalities; both would be created by residents' petitions to the governor rather than to provincial councils. The Local Government Bill included a provision that the central government would contribute a subsidy of £2 of colonial revenue for every £1 of local rates raised, and that each district would receive an endowment from the land fund.[28] The provinces were thus entirely bypassed.

Edmund Bohan is undoubtedly correct when he suggests that Stafford 'could not have chosen a worse moment' to introduce this legislation.[29] Provincialists had already been on the defensive after a controversy surrounding the election of Macandrew as Otago's superintendent in February. The Stafford government, as punishment for Macandrew's past sins, refused to bestow upon him the usual goldfields powers that went with the superintendency and instead appointed James Bradshaw, MHR for the Goldfields and a staunch centralist, as government agent.[30] It was a brazen attempt to usurp control of the goldfields and push back at the power of provincialists, especially the charismatic Macandrew, but it did not succeed. Otago rallied around Macandrew and provincialists elsewhere joined the cause, fearing the central government would seek control of other goldfields. The Stafford government was forced into an embarrassing retreat, vesting the delegated powers in provincial executives, and the provincialists were wary of any further encroachment on their turf. Otago in particular was set against any central incursion on local government, fearing that it would not only represent a return of the New Provinces Act, but be 'more likely to attain the object ... of undermining the Provinces ... [and] break up the Provincial system'.[31]

Indignation in the most powerful provinces killed the Local Government Bill. The ghost of the New Provinces Act was readily evoked by the *New Zealand Herald* to condemn the bill as 'cutting up the provinces into a number of little independent districts ... [that] would be made to look to the central Government at Wellington as their source of power'.[32] Provincialists in Wellington likewise saw the bill as 'being framed to strike a fatal blow at the powers of Provincial Governments'.[33] Vogel at the *Otago Daily Times* forcibly expressed the general Otago belief that the bill was a 'deadly invasion on the integrity of Provincial institutions' since it vested the most important powers in the governor rather than superintendents, and its principles would be compulsorily enforced rather than accepted or rejected by provincial councils.[34] This was the closest Vogel would ever be to earning the 'provincialist' label so often bestowed upon him, despite his centralising tendencies. Opinion was more divided in Canterbury than Otago, but even the *Press*, despite its belief some powers should be devolved to outlying regions, felt the Local Government Bill 'went too far, and provided an organization more elaborate than could be brought into use'.[35]

The bill perished on its second reading, 27 votes for and 36 against. Some of the latter even came from outside the opposition's ranks, because of the members' unwillingness to endorse such a sweeping measure.[36] These votes were heavily concentrated in the cities where provincialists held most power – and 15 of them came from members who also held provincial offices.[37] Auckland and Otago by themselves provided 22 of the votes against.[38] The majority of votes in favour came either from small provinces – the five members from Taranaki and Hawke's Bay all voted yea – or from outlying districts of the larger provinces. The bill's defeat was received with particular disappointment in Timaru, where an indignation meeting laid the groundwork for the creation of the Timaru and Gladstone Board of Works.[39] Meanwhile, some government critics, delighted by their success, called for the ministry to resign. The *Independent* was unimpressed by protestations that the bill was not a ministerial question – 'when a policy is set aside, its framers share the same fate' – but later acknowledged 'the opposition were not quite prepared to go in. The latter party is numerically strong, but it lacks leading men who are in a position to form a new Government.'[40] Again Stafford survived less on his own strength and more on provincialist inability to find a parliamentary leader.

Stafford's survival allowed the Municipal Corporations Bill, the counterpart of the Local Government Bill, to proceed. John Hall, then postmaster-general, introduced it. He had resigned from Canterbury provincial politics on joining Stafford's ministry and was passionate about solving the problem of regional government.[41] The bill, he argued, was necessary as 'the circumstances of the different towns throughout the colony are not by any means so dissimilar as to render necessary such a great variety of legislation' by the provinces and one uniform system could be applied to all.[42] He sought to distance the bill from provincialist agitation surrounding the Local Government Bill, but his argument was explicitly against the proliferation of provincial legislation and against the very logic of provincialism: that some matters were best resolved locally. Hall's argument did not, however, live or die on a centralist's desire for national consistency – he also emphasised concerns that municipalities sought or deserved powers that provincial governments could not confer upon them constitutionally.

The bill faced some hostility, with provincialist fears that it would be a 'ministerial abortion' like the Local Government Bill.[43] Early reports suggested the government was preparing a scheme under which the smaller provinces might abandon provincialism by petitioning the governor to make them under the direct control of the central government as a sort of county or municipality.[44] This scheme, which would have aroused vociferous anger, did not eventuate and the bill introduced by Hall received much less provincial opposition than its local government counterpart. Some saw it as the 'twin brother' to the Local Government Bill and others felt 'Provincial Legislatures are the proper bodies to bestow corporations upon the towns in the districts under their control', but these arguments did not carry the day.[45] The Municipal Corporations Bill left some power in provincial hands – for instance, superintendents could veto bylaws, and a new municipality could not be established if both superintendent and provincial council objected.[46] Some opponents of the Local Government Bill regarded this measure favourably. The *New Zealand Herald*, for instance, felt that it was 'a step in the right direction'.[47] The bill therefore faced a less hostile parliament and was passed. The Stafford ministry may not have been able to secure all of its local government policy but it had been able to implement part of it. Interestingly, municipalities were given legislative permission to borrow money in limited circumstances for 'public works or undertakings', meaning that in the same session as provinces were barred from borrowing, towns gained the ability to raise small amounts for local works.[48]

The demise of the Local Government Bill had left two problems that could not be resolved by the Municipal Corporations Act – the respective positions of South Canterbury and Westland. South Canterbury's needs were met with the creation of the Timaru and Gladstone Board of Works. The West Coast, essentially unsettled by Pākehā before the mid-1860s, was split administratively at the mouth of the Grey River by the border between Canterbury and Nelson. That portion north of the Grey, incorporating Buller and the northern part of what is now the Grey District, was known at the time as Nelson Southwest, while the Cantabrian stretch of the Coast was dubbed Westland or, sometimes, West Canterbury. Provincial surveyor Arthur Dudley Dobson was impressed by the region's wild and heavily wooded contrast to Canterbury's sweeping plains.[49] By 1863 knowledge of the West Coast's gold deposits began to spread and the work of surveyors such as Dobson caused a growth of interest, leading Samuel Bealey's provincial executive to contemplate opening up Westland as part of Canterbury proper.[50] A Canterbury government depot was established at Greymouth and by the second half of 1864 the trickle of surveyors, explorers and prospectors into the area was increasing. Not all Cantabrians were thrilled. The *Lyttelton Times*, not entirely without tongue in cheek, grumbled that a goldfield would be 'forced upon Canterbury, without the consent and contrary to the expressed desire of the settlers'.[51] It urged caution in opening up a territory so wild, hostile and difficult to supply. But when in December 1864 the steamer *Nelson* proved that the intimidating bar at the mouth of the Hokitika River could be crossed safely, the door to the rush burst open. Hokitika, closer to the richest diggings than Greymouth, grew quickly and the cost of provisions, previously a hindrance to large-scale exploitation of Westland's wealth, plummeted.[52]

With the commercial viability of Hokitika came not only the gold rush, but also additional pressures on the provincial system created by the sudden development of a large new centre. From a population of 830 in December 1864, Westland exploded to 7000 in April 1865, by which time the Banks of New South Wales and New Zealand had established themselves, the Canterbury government had chosen Hokitika over Greymouth as its administrative hub, and new goldfields were either being exploited or about to be discovered.[53] As a result Westland's population expanded further, reaching 16,000 in September 1865 and 50,000 by the end of 1866.[54] This boom was not confined to Hokitika. In 1866, hotels, home to many itinerant miners and a test of prosperity, were abundant: 100 in Hokitika, 57 in Greymouth, 34 in Stafford and 24 in Ross.[55] Publicans, merchants, prostitutes and other traders came along with the miners. All these people and businesses needed administrative services, public works, law and order and governance.

What was the effect of Westland upon the provincial system? The West Coast gold rushes have been studied widely, and Philip Ross May's remarkable scholarship is authoritative.[56] As he argues, Westland's political demands were 'shaped less by

Despite the treacherous river bar, Hokitika quickly became one of New Zealand's busiest ports. Here, 41 ships are seen in port on 16 September 1867. 270, Hokitika Museum

the gold-rush ethos than by the unresolved tensions in New Zealand's provincial system.[57] It was a completely new population centre, existing by chance within Canterbury, separated from the rest of the province by New Zealand's most imposing mountain range. The *Press* dubbed the Southern Alps a 'stupendous barrier' and espoused geographic determinism, predicting that Canterbury's agricultural and pastoral eastern half would cultivate a society with institutions, occupations and habits different from the mining and logging western half.[58] This notion was not without some justification. Trade between the two regions was inherently difficult, and Westland developed more as a suburb of Melbourne in Victoria than as part of Canterbury. The *Press* heralded the debates that occupied Canterbury and Westland politicians from 1865 to 1868 with its insistence that the two regions 'cannot be kept under the same local Government' and that the Canterbury provincial government keep 'very careful account' of Westland expenditure so that 'every penny may be charged against the future province'.[59]

A movement to separate Westland from Canterbury developed during 1865. Westland was granted two provincial councillors and one central parliamentarian (growing to five councillors in 1866). Canterbury's council allocated all Westland's revenue to local works and work began on a road linking east and west. Clearly there was a desire to avoid repeating the mistakes that enraged South Canterbury.[60] Nonetheless, grievances grew quickly. The *West Coast Times*, one of Hokitika's leading newspapers and a rare steady presence among the unstable goldfields press, spearheaded secessionism. It lamented that Westland's revenue was 'expended strictly on the requirements of the West Coast – from a Christchurch point of view'.[61]

The road, meant to bring the two regions together, instead did just the opposite. It was, said the *West Coast Times*, an 'unprincipled trick' to divert people and trade via Christchurch. 'Melbourne, Sydney, Wellington, Nelson ... are within a few days' sail; our stores are replenished from these sources'; Hokitika port improvements would be more beneficial and cost one-tenth of a road.[62] Not everybody shared the paper's agitation. A competitor, the *Hokitika Evening Star*, although critical of Christchurch, merely sought greater provincial and central representation, urged the public that 'the expense of the road cannot be made ... a cause of separation' and hoped that both the trans-alpine antagonism and the secession question would abate.[63] Moreover, Canterbury did not entirely neglect Westland. In early 1865 Hokitika's roads were devoid of footpaths and routinely became channels of knee-deep mud after rain, but by 1866 one well-travelled Briton reported that they exceeded those of any American mining town.[64] Yet expenditure became an increasing burden. By early 1867 Canterbury politicians dropped pretences of preserving provincial unity and spoke angrily about Westland's debt to the east.[65]

Into the picture came Hall, whose passion for local government reform was stimulated in part by his interest in Westland's position. The isolated localism and distinct founding identities that defined the six original settlements meant little to a mobile goldfields community unattached to provincialism and unsympathetic to its bureaucratic pedantries.[66] Hall sympathised with Westland's desire for more effective local governance and its lack of interest in provincialism. He also corresponded at length with leading Westland figures, which gave him almost unparalleled knowledge of the region's issues.[67] He felt New Zealand had enough provinces and would not make any more, but that an adaptation of the failed Local Government Bill to Westland's peculiar circumstances would be appropriate and receive parliament's approval.[68] He therefore crafted his own scheme: a county directly under the authority of the central government, possessing an elected council that controlled local revenue and distributed it among road boards for public works. A nominated chairman would lead the council and the General Assembly would legislate for Westland on the advice of council resolutions. Hall emphasised that this was to suit Westland's need for 'some machinery less cumbrous and costly than that of the Provincial Governments'.[69]

The scheme was criticised by provincialists in provincial capitals, but widely lauded in Westland. Wanganui also looked favourably upon a county system to satisfy its secessionist desires.[70] Undoubtedly this stoked Wellington's rage, where the *Independent* derided Hall's plan as reviving the Local Government Bill in miniature

Revell Street on 2 March 1868, not long after Hokitika became capital of the new Westland County. Daniel Mundy, PA1-f-041-38, Alexander Turnbull Library, Wellington

despite the House rejecting that scheme.[71] Moorhouse, who was Westland's MHR as well as Canterbury superintendent, could not reconcile the competing interests of his dual status and pursued the agenda of the latter in opposing secession. He pushed through the House an amendment dividing Canterbury and Westland's debt on the basis of their customs revenue. This placed a greater burden upon Westland and its bustling ports than Hall intended – and he was notably the only Canterbury member to oppose the amendment.[72] Moorhouse, who enjoyed personal popularity and respect in Westland right up until early 1867, was now disdained in Greymouth and burnt in effigy by outraged Hokitika residents.[73] This aspect aside, most citizens were delighted by the creation of Westland County, with the Hokitika press united in praise.[74] The Greymouth district in northern Westland was more ambivalent. In the manner typical of New Zealand's early settlements, it maintained a vigorous parochial distaste for Hokitika. It had sought annexation by Nelson because its hinterland was cut in half by the provincial border, causing considerable inconvenience for both miners and merchants. When the new county was created, Greymouth acquiesced to the measure at least temporarily, especially when it learnt that it would have control of its own revenue for public works expenses.[75]

When the county of Westland formally came into existence on 1 January 1868, a heavily populated part of New Zealand was removed from the provincial system and placed under a centrally controlled experimental system of local government. Previously, the two main islands and most of the smaller ones fell within the provincial system, though provincial governments struggled to manage outlying areas and remote islands. One pioneering family, for example, suffered considerable hardship as a result of Auckland Province's difficulty in administering Great Barrier Island.[76] Stewart Island was the largest part of New Zealand previously excluded from the provincial system. It remained under central control – insofar as any control was necessary for its tiny population – until it became part of Southland in 1863.[77] This annexation was motivated not by provincialist ideology but by the reality that Southland's administration was cheaper and more convenient than establishing a central government outpost for a few hundred irregular settlers.[78] Southland was so uninterested in its acquisition that the island experienced only slight legal and political changes.[79] Excising New Zealand's wealthiest goldfield from the provincial system as part of a centralist experiment was certainly noticed. Much as provincialists were disgusted, the centralists were not without justification. The system had never been designed to face the challenges created by a sizeable transient population unsuited to bureaucracy. Westland's needs could not be handled by a distant capital, but it could not sustain provincial machinery – and New Zealand in 1867 was, sensibly, unwilling to give the creation of new provinces another chance. Hall's county plan came at exactly the right time to be approved – centralists and Westlanders were united in their willingness to attempt a new system of local government. Hall's connection with Westland was strengthened by his appointment as the county's first chairman.[80] Whether or not the county proved a success, it was obvious that provincialism's days were numbered.

Apart from 1875, the year of abolition, 1867 was the most momentous and calamitous year for provincialism. The provinces had accrued vast debts, gaining little but frustrated citizens in the process, and the development of infrastructure had essentially stagnated. The solution to provincial indebtedness was presented in a manner that not only favoured centralism, but also blocked provincial borrowing. Yet loans were necessary if the provinces were to pursue immigration and public works. Moreover, centralists succeeded in overcoming provincialist opposition and passed part of their local government reforms, including the creation of Westland as an experimental county. No matter how powerful the provincialists were in opposition, they could not secure power or stem provincial blood-letting.

From 1867 provincialism subsisted on borrowed time. At the start of his tenure as Legislative Council speaker Richardson lamented that New Zealand 'might have been traversed by well-formed and well-designed roads or railroads' if development had been overseen nationally, not provincially.[81] As Wanganui's *Evening Herald* wrote, with shades of drama but not without justification, 'provincialists cannot close their eyes to the slow but sure process of strangulation which is going on. Almost daily the cordon is being drawn tighter around the provinces.'[82]

Chapter 12
The Great Public Works Policy

The provinces were neutered by the events of 1867 but they remained a constitutional part of New Zealand's geopolitical landscape. They still had vocal adherents the length of the colony, and many other political institutions have lingered for decades after outliving their usefulness. New Zealand's Legislative Council is a key example: unnecessary by the 1890s, the nominated upper house of parliament lingered until 1950.[1] Abolishing the provinces was a measure not taken lightly, and to make it desirable – or at least palatable – to the voting public, such radical upheaval had to be accompanied by a great national vision. In 1870 Julius Vogel provided this vision. Other historians have already charted the political and parliamentary machinations admirably. However, politicians enjoyed their power only at the pleasure of electors, who were a demanding lot – provincial councils had learnt this the hard way. How did Vogel and his contemporaries capitalise on existing discontent to sell their visionary policies?

If the basic work of colonisation was bumbling and inefficient before loan consolidation, afterwards it almost ground to a halt. Existing projects for which money had been raised and allocated could continue, but new projects remained talking points unless they were minute enough to be funded by regular revenue. The provinces could not find more money and public works were not the central government's domain. The Stafford government failed to come up with new conditions under which provinces could be allowed to borrow, and a solution to the stalemate was urgently needed if the colony were to avoid long-term stagnation. In June 1869 William Fox finally succeeded in ousting Stafford, who had recently dismissed Hawke's Bay superintendent Donald McLean from the position as government agent on the North Island's east coast. McLean had considerable mana with Māori and the ensuing controversy over his dismissal united Stafford's opponents in a no-confidence motion; Fox carefully avoided articulating alternative policy to avoid any split.[2] The new Fox ministry was small. McLean was appointed native minister, Vogel received his prized position of treasurer, eminent statesman

William Fox, four-time premier of New Zealand during the provincial era, photographed in the 1880s. 1/4-004154-G, Alexander Turnbull Library, Wellington

William Gisborne became colonial secretary, and Francis Dillon Bell joined Cabinet despite an independent streak. Soon the addition of Isaac Featherston and Henry Sewell expanded the ministry.

Fox's government faced many challenges. Financial recession had set in; the mid-1860s decline had not been reversed. The South Island goldfields, which had been the primary source of immigration and wealth that decade, were beginning to be worked out. Although new fields were discovered in Westland and Nelson Southwest in 1867, evoking boosterism and fanciful beliefs of gold towns rapidly evolving into great cities, these fields were not as rich as the older, increasingly depleted ones and the heady days of the West Coast's rush were over.[3] In 1868 Nelson's superintendent had to announce a curtailment of public works expenditure; by early 1869 public works had effectively come to a halt throughout the province, inciting secessionist desires in the southwest.[4] Other provinces also led a precarious existence in the late 1860s. Some struggled with regular administrative costs, others were forced to repeal costly legislation and Marlborough received a late stay of execution only after the province rose up against a bill to have it reannexed by Nelson.[5] Vogel was frustrated by Marlborough's insolvency, deriding the locals for 'not car[ing] to tax themselves sufficiently to maintain the expense of a separate Government'.[6]

Unlike Marlborough, Southland perished. The province was haunted by the spectre of its railway debt, unable to recover from financial despondency and incapable of satisfying demands for more railways.[7] In October 1869 Southlanders were so disenchanted with their province and its prospects that they elected a council with three-quarters of its members in favour of reunification with Otago.[8] Reunion suited both provinces. Southland's debts would be repaid, while Otago, which had the capacity to cover the debt, would soon be enriched by Southland land sales.[9] Commissioners from both provinces met and devised a scheme that was endorsed by strong majorities of both councils and brought into law by an act of the General Assembly.[10] Southland's existence as a province formally ceased on 6 October 1870. The *Southland Times* bemoaned as 'unpardonable' the province's 'vapid state of public feeling' in its dying days; thus with a whimper one of the sorriest chapters of provincial history was closed.[11] Woeful provincial failures, gold rush mobility and new migrants who had not been part of the secessionist fight had all washed away the provincialism and provincial independence so important to early Southlanders.

Popular discourse on the provincial system and the colony's settlement turned in the late 1860s to reorganising New Zealand's political structure and pursuing development with a national emphasis. Vogel was not the first to propose a major national development plan. Stafford, when he spoke to the House after Vogel announced his scheme in June 1870, was only exaggerating slightly when he asserted it 'is no new idea ... older than many of the members who sit around me'.[12] Plans such as the Domett and Whitaker-Fox ministries' network of North Island roads and Canterbury's pursuit of public works hand in hand with immigration pointed the way. Vogel's proposals were also prefigured in the press, though sometimes underpinned by financial measures amenable only to the interests of local readers.[13] Stafford in 1869 had advanced palatable financial initiatives. He spoke to parliament about the need to pursue large-scale public works by means of foreign capital, invested on the basis of colonial security, and employing immigrants for construction.[14] He developed these ideas further in an April 1870 speech in Timaru, when he urged a system of arterial transport routes to 'ensure that every dangerous river between Southland and Auckland should be bridged' and to 'open and people all parts of the country simultaneously'.[15] This was a clear enunciation of the idea of the progress industry, expanding the breadth and depth of settlement. William Rolleston, when he succeeded Moorhouse as Canterbury's superintendent, also spoke of the need to pair public works with immigration so that major projects would not sap labour from the province's established industries – though he was later harshly criticised by his rivals for not implementing such a plan swiftly.[16]

Some pundits advocated private enterprise rather than government investment to secure sufficient immigration to make railways remunerative.[17] This was not an unreasonable perspective. Some of the best developed land transport in New Zealand was private bush tramways throughout Westland. Built as part of a tramway bubble accompanying the gold rush, they were rudimentary lines of a low quality, not expected to operate for decades or to provide all-purpose heavy haulage.[18] They nonetheless provided an important means of goldfields transportation and sometimes shaped the layout of the towns they served.[19] However, in a small colony of limited capital and remote from international capitalists, private enterprise would play no significant role in public works and immigration schemes. The question of who would fund these was not a matter of public versus private, but of one level of government versus another.

Discussion of public works schemes became linked with reshaping or abolishing the provinces. Richardson, who had been a Clutha provincial councillor, told a large public meeting in Balclutha during 1868 that he wanted the complete remodelling of the provincial system. He called it abolition, though he wished to retain provincial borders and a sort of council to act as a local administrator for the central government.[20] Rolleston went further at an April 1870 meeting in Timaru, stating there were 'looming great constitutional changes, which must come sooner or later …' He wanted 'to localise government, and to give to outlying districts … a system of a localised form of general government'.[21] With particular reference to the North Island, he felt provincialism 'which at first was admirably adapted to the wants of the country, was now inadequate … [and on the Assembly] alone should devolve the inauguration of large works'. As isolation between the provinces was breaking down, superintendents, in his view, should be administrators, not visionaries. Even in Wellington, the former provincialists at the *Independent* began advocating central incursions into provincial responsibilities such as immigration, although rebutting total abolition.[22] One contemporary in Greytown was irked that almost all the Wairarapa's land fund went to defraying provincial expenses and salaries rather than local works: 'it [is] high time for the Provincial system to cease unless it can be carried on more efficiently … we ask how long is this system to continue?'[23] Abolitionism was yet to coalesce as a political imperative, yet noises from politicians and press for substantial reform were becoming louder.

When parliament met in June 1870 it was no secret that Fox's ministry planned to announce a major immigration and public works policy to revitalise the stagnant economy. Vogel foreshadowed it in his 1869 financial statement: the ministry could 'not see our way to deal with [immigration] this Session' but would 'propose next year a comprehensive plan which, without violating constitutional conditions, will extend the benefits of regular and systematic Immigration [throughout] the Colony.[24] In February 1870 Vogel began planning his policy. Although Fox was ostensibly the head of the ministry, he was outshone by the talent and ambition of his young treasurer. Fellow ministers Bell and Featherston had investigated large-scale European immigration, and in the process of unsuccessful negotiations with the Colonial Office to retain British troops in New Zealand they scored a valuable concession: the British government promised to guarantee a £1 million loan for development. Now Vogel worked largely alone.[25] His centralising impulse, once reserved for the South Island, acquired a national character. Vogel was no longer an Otago councillor, nor even an Otago resident, having relocated to Auckland – though as recently as 1868 he had, with Macandrew, considered a plan for infrastructural expansion and immigration to Otago, a plan the province lacked the funds to implement.[26] No doubt his experiences in Otago influenced his thought. What he had not accomplished while in power provincially, he now had the opportunity to accomplish on a grander scale.

The plan Vogel devised, the Great Public Works Policy, was the most momentous and revolutionary yet advanced in New Zealand, irrevocably changing the country's character. The policy was introduced in Vogel's financial statement just 12 days into the 1870 session on 28 June – an extraordinarily early date, two days before the end of the financial year, in response to demands from the House for an early statement.[27] In 1869 Vogel had delivered his first statement so hesitatingly and inaudibly that he had raised Stafford's ire.[28] Circumstances were much different in 1870. Vogel detailed the previous year's accounts and then proceeded to his works policy. The packed House, incredulous, hung on every word. Referring to the past three years of developmental stagnation, Vogel emphasised that 'the time has arrived when we must set ourselves afresh to the task of actively promoting the settlement of the country'.[29] This meant addressing 'the great wants of the Colony … Public Works, in the shape of Roads and Railways; and Immigration', with Vogel emphasising that 'the two are, or ought to be, inseparably united'.

The works proposals were broadly similar to national schemes already advanced, yet this was the first time they were put forward as ministerial policy and with concrete financial details. Past plans had been idealistic sketches. Now Vogel asked the House to join him in a tangible, structured scheme. The first step was to provide the North Island with £400,000 for trunk roads to open up lightly settled regions to closer settlement (and an equivalent sum for South Island railways), and to acquire at the current market value a public estate – land near the roads to sell later and enable the colony to share in the improved land values that resulted from public works. The land would cost £200,000, charged provincially, and profits accrued by the provinces were to go to railway and immigration purposes, along with any profits from confiscated Māori land. The government, Vogel argued, could safely assume that, since each province possessed a landed estate, it had some means to promote settlement and induce immigration. Now he could proceed to the meat of his policy.

Vogel articulated a comprehensive plan for trunk railways throughout New Zealand that would shape its economic fortunes for decades and play an instrumental role in bringing down the provinces. The network he proposed was extensive:

> *Auckland to Wanganui by Taupo, with connections to Napier and New Plymouth. Wanganui to Wellington. Nelson to Greymouth, and Hokitika, with connection to Westport. Picton to Amuri, Christchurch, Timaru, Oamaru, Waikouaiti, Dunedin, Tokomairiro, Molyneux, and Winton, with connections to Tuapeka, Clyde, Cromwell, Arrow, and Queenstown. These railways should be commenced from a number of different points, and be constructed as cheaply as possible – the works being continued as traffic demanded.*[30]

This national network would, Vogel emphasised, be developed in partnership with provincial governments. They would select routes according to the nature of present traffic, and the central government would contract and construct the lines as part of a broader national scheme. In other words, the central government would take responsibility for the national vision while provinces received railways to service their immediate needs. The central government's concurrent expansion of the national telegraph network would also be funded by £60,000 of the loan.

A total of £10 million was required over a decade: £8.5 million for public works and land purchases and the remainder for immigration, £6 million of which would be borrowed and the rest met from land grants and profits. Although some have suggested otherwise, no loan for the full £10 million was ever contemplated.[31] Total borrowings for public works only reached this level later in the decade when additional loans were approved. Vogel wanted a 6-million-acre reservation of land as a railway fund to defray costs, and he mooted taxing land that benefited directly from the works policy. Although the scheme would be a partnership with the provinces, he fired a shot across the bow of provincialism: 'if the existence of the present [provincial] institutions of the country are inconsistent with the promotion of Public Works and Immigration … I would infinitely prefer the total remodelling of those institutions to abandoning that stimulating aid which, as I believe, the condition of the Colony absolutely demands.' In deference to provincial sensibilities, he noted that 'violent political changes are much to be deprecated' and acknowledged that the genuine provincial sentiment in New Zealand could not be destroyed simply by sweeping away the institutions. His message was unambiguous: the survival of the provinces was dependent upon how they adapted to the works policy.

The first reaction in the House was shock and condemnation. Vogel's speech ran over three hours, punctuated by 'bursts of laughter and ironical cheers'.[32] The press emphasised the lack of enthusiasm: the *Otago Daily Times* reporter 'never saw any important Ministerial statement so very coldly received'.[33] Reader Wood, instrumental in the £3 million loan of 1863, now had no time for vast borrowing. In what has become his most quoted remark, he denounced 'the wildest, most visionary, unpractical, and impracticable [policy] to which he had ever listened'.[34] Thomas Gillies, who had sought to overturn the New Provinces Act in 1860 and had been Vogel's ally in the Otago separation movement, supported Wood. Recently elected Auckland's superintendent, Gillies felt these 'wild extravagant proposals' would be a 'signal for every man, who had respect for himself or his property, to leave the Colony'.[35] Discussion, though, was brief. As one historian has astutely observed, 'members in general refrained from comment until they had mastered the details of the scheme. Possibly, they wished to study the reactions of their constituents before committing themselves.'[36]

Vogel's speech was not for the House; it was for the country. After all, it was electors rather than the politicians who would determine the policy's fate. The news quickly spread throughout the nation. Wanganui's *Evening Herald* praised the 'Herculean task' of the local telegraphic operator, performing the 'quickest telegraphing that has ever been performed in the Colony' in transcribing the financial statement.[37] By midnight the message was even being received in the deep south in Balclutha.[38] The telegraph was already breaking down isolation, and the works policy promised to end it completely.

There were some prophets of doom. Wellington's *Evening Post* decried the policy as an 'astounding scheme … [of] uncontrolled expenditure of fabulous sums of money'.[39] Nelson's *Examiner* accused Vogel of trying to 'distract attention from the frightful state' of colonial finances with 'a wild scheme of borrowing and expenditure, which it would be utterly impossible to carry out'.[40] The *Timaru Herald* was bereft of foresight when it considered the plan. It failed to comprehend why railway lines along the coast were necessary; railways, to its mind, were a mere conveyance

Staff of the Wanganui post and telegraph office in the 1870s, who, like their counterparts nationwide, performed admirably telegraphing government news rapidly.

1/1-000093-G, Alexander Turnbull Library, Wellington

from farm to port and it could not conceive of interprovincial railway links that were much swifter, safer or more reliable than New Zealand's tempestuous sea. It concluded that a scheme as extraordinary as Vogel's 'gambling transactions' had never been 'presented to intelligent beings' and that any man audacious enough to make such proposals in the Australian colonies would be committed to an asylum.[41] Otago, of course, raised the war cry of provincialism and even rehashed old arguments used to advocate separation.[42] Hokitika took an especially parochial view. It feared incurring greater burdens than the rest of the colony because of its unusual political status, and criticised Greymouth for being slow to express similar small-minded outrage.[43] The peculiarities of local or provincial economies influenced some reactions: unimaginative local scribes struggled to view the national plan with national perspective.

Generally, however, the response was enthusiastic and excited. Vogel now had a stake in Auckland's *Daily Southern Cross*, which predictably editorialised favourably and rebutted negative reactions.[44] His former press mouthpiece, the *Otago Daily Times*, wanted more moderate measures and considered the works policy 'specious', but acknowledged that 'Public Works and Immigration at any cost is the favourite cry from one end of the colony to the other' and that the scheme would receive public approval.[45] The *Wellington Independent*, supportive of the Fox ministry, was impressed. It argued that the scheme was a blow against *anti*-provincial politicians who tried to break down localism and create national sentiment through 'arbitrary political provisions' such as the New Provinces Act. The works policy would encourage colonisation to dismantle 'the natural barriers which at present prevent the political, social, or commercial union of the different divisions of the colony'.[46] The *Independent* was correct when it forecast that Vogel's plan would do more for colonial unity than any centralist scheme of the previous 17 years.

The works policy also demonstrated that the influence of newspapermen had reached its limit. The negative editorials of some portions of the press made little impression. Public meetings were held throughout New Zealand to debate the policy. Charles Elliott of the *Nelson Examiner* called a public meeting in Nelson and proposed a condemnatory motion, but a supportive amendment won by a considerable majority.[47] The Nelson press may have been largely opposed to the policy but Nelsonians were not. At a public meeting in Christchurch William Montgomery, Canterbury's deputy superintendent during 1868–69, advanced a motion that 'cordially approve[d]' of the 'able and comprehensive financial scheme'. His initial reaction had been 'astonishment and surprise … [at a] reckless and extravagant scheme', but the more he considered it, the more he realised it would 'infuse new life into a colony which for the last five years had been in a state of stagnation and collapse'.[48] Jerningham Wakefield sought an amendment that the meeting not commit to an opinion, positive or negative, but this found only 13 supporters while Montgomery's motion was carried amid applause and cheers. The people of Christchurch were definitely taken with the policy. Moorhouse spoke at the meeting, praising the scheme as the start of 'a good state of things for New Zealand' and intimated a return to national politics. This he did in August, elected on the express understanding that he would support Vogel.[49] Emotion ran so high in Napier that an initial public meeting – called to support the government – voted for a resolution seeking a much smaller loan than the works policy, followed by an even more crowded meeting the next night that condemned the first meeting's outcome and almost unanimously supported favourable motions.[50]

Two newspapers openly acknowledged the attitude shift that occurred more quietly throughout the media and the wider population. The *Taranaki Herald* wrote that the policy at first 'appeared somewhat startling', but upon an examination of its details, 'our amazement subsided'.[51] Placed in the context of a decade-long programme, the £10 million expenditure meant a more modest outlay of £500,000 per island per year. The *Hawke's Bay Herald* also emphasised that the public did not anticipate a scheme so vast, hence the first unfavourable responses, but as the details were more thoroughly digested, the more thoroughly they were appreciated. The editor concluded that 'however extensive and (at first sight) startling may be the Government plan, we should be glad to see something of the kind'.[52] Positivity replaced shock and surprise, and as the public fell in behind Vogel, so did their parliamentary representatives. As the *Oamaru Times* stressed, Vogel offered something to every class of colonial society.[53] The figure of £10 million might have initially dazzled, but upon sober reflection Vogel was correct to expect support for the scheme.

Some compromises were necessary to push the policy through parliament. Vogel had the support of George Bowen, who had been governor since replacing Grey in February 1868. Bowen felt the policy would open the colony and that 'the pickaxe and the spade are the true weapons for the pacification' of the North Island Māori.[54] This support counted for little, though, if Vogel could not reach across the floor in parliament. His policy inaugurated a shift in parliament's nominal parties; one scholar has defined it aptly as a split between 'bold' members who supported the policy and a 'cautious' grouping that sought to either limit or oppose borrowing.[55] To have his plan passed, Vogel had to court moderately cautious members and the centralist opposition led by Stafford. Some cautious members such as Rolleston, fearing the loss of provincial agency, voted for the second reading only in the hope that modifications would be made.[56] They were. Vogel was conscious his position was weak even among his front bench colleagues and that provincialists in the government could vote against the ministry; he faced the awkward scenario where one of the government whips opposed the policy while both opposition whips supported it. He conferred with Stafford, who was willing to co-operate. Stafford readily acknowledged that the policy embodied many principles he had advocated for years and he helped Vogel to modify the scheme to make it more acceptable.[57] The £6 million loan was cut to £4 million, safeguards were implemented to ensure it was spent on the purposes for which it was raised, a central London agency would be established to manage immigration, and money borrowed for defence purposes would be subject to annual appropriation.[58]

Not all the modifications were positive. Gisborne, a key Vogel Cabinet ally, later lamented the loss of proposals to use land as security for the central government's loans at the hands of provincialists and 'the political constitution' of the time; in old age Vogel described this loss as disastrous.[59] One lucid analysis of the scheme's introduction emphasises that provincial and personal jealousies inhibited members from seeing their interests as connected with those of far-flung districts. In particular Vogel's provisions to use land as security were shot down by some wealthy South Island landowners in the House.[60] Southern anger about colonising the north at their expense justified the transfer of £100,000 from North Island land purchases to South Island goldfields water supply. Most unfortunately, Vogel retreated from fixing railways during the 1870 session, instead allowing that the provinces be consulted on routes before the House voted on them in 1871. This opened the door to annual, piecemeal construction instead of focusing energy on creating a core trunk network. This decision made a general plan of development difficult to implement and gave rise to the curse of political railway lines as MHRs tried to appease their constituents with unprofitable branch lines to small country towns rather than vigorously pursuing main lines to link regions. Many of the gaps and failings of New Zealand's current railway network can be traced to the selfish narrow-mindedness of provincialists in 1870 and their trading of political favours.

Vogel persisted boldly in the face of petty opposition and the modified policy met with general approval. He had captivated the colony, and politicians realised their careers would be in jeopardy if they failed to reflect the widespread excitement of their constituents. Smart political opponents of Vogel, such as Rolleston and Stafford, knew that working with the scheme to secure modifications was a far better course of action than destroying it altogether. The passage of the acts embodying the policy became a formality.[61] The Immigration and Public Works Act provided the key machinery and powers to undertake the policy; clause nine, in keeping with Vogel's compromise to approve railways piecemeal, required the General Assembly to pass acts authorising individual railways. Logrolling began immediately, as the superintendents of Auckland, Nelson, Marlborough, Canterbury and Otago pressed their cases for local railways.[62] The most tangible offerings for settlers were embodied in a separate Railways Act. It empowered the governor to enter into contracts for construction of some railways and surveys of others, encompassing a series of lines throughout every province (though not Westland County). Most were trunk routes, including initial sections of the Main South Line from Christchurch to Invercargill via Dunedin and a network linking New Plymouth, Wanganui, Napier and Wellington. The superintendents generally wrote of their railways in terms of local needs, even those that would become trunk routes, though Gillies of Auckland emphasised the national benefits that could accrue from a short railway linking the Kaipara and Waitemata harbours.[63]

The Railways Act also settled the national gauge at 3′ 6″ (1067 mm), on the recommendation of a select committee more decisive than its 1867 predecessor. An exception was allowed for Canterbury, but the Canterbury Gauge Act limited the extent to which it could construct 5′ 3″ (1600 mm)-gauge railways and required that, if narrow gauge railways met the broad gauge line, a third rail had to be laid into Christchurch for the use of 3′ 6″-gauge trains. The Railways Act ended the era of provinces passing their own railway legislation, choosing their own gauge and contracting for railways. No more lines would be built under purely provincial auspices. The most important aspect of New Zealand's infrastructure had passed out of provincial hands, and clause 91 of the Immigration and Public Works Act created the central position of minister of works to oversee implementation of the policy. Gisborne was appointed to the position. Although he served for only a year, he gave the Public Works Department an administrative form that endured for over six decades.[64]

The governor and some perceptive newspapermen understood just what a dramatic change the policy inaugurated. In proroguing parliament, Bowen, despite intense personal dislike for Vogel, described the policy in glowing terms. He made a thinly veiled threat at provincialism by emphasising that the financial policy and the reunification of Otago and Southland 'afford[ed] proof of the elasticity of the existing institutions of the country, and of the readiness with which modifications to suit changes of circumstances can be effected'.[65] The *Press* editorialised that this statement was 'an ominous hint to those … who look upon the present Government as devoted to the maintenance of provincialism'. The session marked 'a fresh starting point in the history of New Zealand', with Māori–Pākehā conflict for the first time overshadowed by a policy of peaceful colonisation.[66] The *Otago Daily Times* did not mince words about the drama of the change, though its frank language underestimated the fighting spirit of Otago's provincialists. The policy was a 'social revolution' and '[t]he current of our history … [has] entered into a new channel'. The debate between provincialism and centralism was dead; '[t]he whole system of Provincialism is virtually abolished. Its utter disappearance is a mere question of time'.[67] The policy afforded New Zealanders previously inconceivable social and economic possibilities. 'We are already in imagination travelling by express trains,' wrote Daniel Pollen in Auckland; 'a cloud of seedy looking Civil Engineers hangs about the Superintendent's office in waiting for the good time coming'.[68]

Chapter 13
Suffocation of the Provinces

The people of New Zealand received their opportunity to cast a verdict on the Great Public Works Policy at the 1871 general election, held over January and February. It received a ringing endorsement. Vogel himself was easily able to secure a new Auckland seat, despite hostility from Superintendent Thomas Gillies.[1] The ministry found support nationwide, even in the opposition's Nelson heartland and in powerful Canterbury, the latter of which might have been expected to join Otago in fearing the policy but instead was keen to continue developing its extensive public works.[2] Not every region was fixated on the policy – the Central Otago goldfields campaign, for instance, emphasised local discontent with squatters and Chinese – but in general it shaped the national outcome.[3] James Crowe Richmond, younger brother of Christopher William and a vehement opponent of the policy, would not modify his views and was defeated in both Wellington City and Nelson by government supporters. Six of the nine defeated sitting members were vocal opponents of Vogel, while many newly elected members – occupying 39 of the 78 seats – endorsed increased public works spending.[4] Vogel's policy was assured.

Spirited opposition was restricted to Otago, yet its ultra-provincialists were split at the most inopportune moment. Superintendent James Macandrew and Provincial Secretary Donald Reid were already hostile opponents on the matter of provincial land legislation, and their responses to the policy were diametrically opposed. Reid raised the old criticism of colonising the North Island at the South's expense. Macandrew, torn between provincialism and populist advocacy of large-scale public works, fell in with his old ally Vogel. Despite suspicion of the central government, Macandrew was keen to see Otago's railways constructed.[5] The provincial council, however, refused to recommend railways for construction to the central government by a 23:13 margin in November 1870, and Reid even tried to persuade another member to advance a motion of no confidence in the central government.[6] Macandrew and Reid waged a vicious contest for the superintendency in February 1871. Amid allegations of irregularities, Macandrew won by fewer than 300 votes, thanks to Southland's support.[7] Had these two men put aside their differences to advance a common platform of ultra-provincialism and Otago particularism, they would have secured the support of most of the province and been a more formidable force.

Instead, at the 1871 parliamentary session, Vogel pushed for more central authority. Fox lost control of policymaking and Vogel, with Gisborne as his right-hand man, was effectively head of government, devising and changing policies as circumstances required.[8] The works policy was too young to have achieved significant results; Gisborne's public works statement contained many surveys but construction was less extensive.[9] Facing a budgetary deficit, Vogel proposed alterations to the policy that removed even more provincial powers. The provinces had struggled to play their assigned role in immigration, so he made immigration a central responsibility. To cover costs, the provinces were deprived of some of their central funding.[10] Thus they found themselves stripped of a key legislative and administrative role and deprived of income. Even Vogel's abortive plan to establish an independent board of works centralised authority.[11] The powers this was meant to acquire, of determining and recommending railway routes, were not returned to the provinces.

A scramble for railways began in the General Assembly, fulfilling Vogel's worst fears. Settlers keen for public works no longer looked to their province for construction, advocacy or recommendation; pressure to secure improvements now fell upon central representatives. The 1871 Railways Act authorised railways in every province and Westland – a total of 23 main, branch and coalfield lines.[12] Every settler thought their railway the most deserving of construction. The act appropriated provincial waste lands to fund North Island railways, but complaints of colonising the North at the South's expense drove parochial rhetoric demanding that southern railways be built first. This caused the last serious demands for South Island separation, led in parliament by Macandrew, and calls for the consolidation of the South Island provinces. Timaru and Hokitika both flirted with the notion of annexation by Otago, Otago's provincial council viewed favourably union with Canterbury to create a provincial powerhouse, and Greymouth continued to seek annexation by Nelson.[13] However, this agitation received only vague assurances from Vogel that in the next session he would formulate plans to reorganise provincial and local government, 'a new Constitution Act'.[14] This was also influenced by Vogel losing a measure to reduce provincial council sizes and make superintendents ex officio members of councils. The latter innovation was later introduced to Marlborough by

The start of railway construction was a major civic occasion. This photograph depicts the ceremony held in Timaru on 4 October 1871. Jane Cain, wife of the mayor Henry Cain, had the honour of turning the first sod and can be seen holding the spade.

1/2-020116-F, Alexander Turnbull Library, Wellington

parliament in 1872, then to Taranaki in 1873; another act permitted it in Hawke's Bay if petitioned by a majority of electors – but this never occurred.[15] Vogel found the 1871 session trying, but the ministry did seek to proceed urgently with his policy.

Construction remained slow, but rather than turning on the policy, the public became all the more vociferous about receiving its benefits. There was impatience for progress across New Zealand, from Wanganui and New Plymouth to South Otago, while in Nelson no candidate opposed to railway construction had a hope of success in a by-election.[16] Every development was eagerly awaited and Vogelite newspapers took any good news as a sign of action.[17] The *Daily Southern Cross* flagged the Auckland–Waikato railway as 'the most important … of all the public works embraced in the scheme of colonisation' because of its perceived role as a civilising mission towards Māori, and hoped its construction would be 'considerably advanced' during 1872.[18] John Davies Ormond, having succeeded his friend Donald McLean as superintendent of Hawke's Bay while also holding the central seat of

Clive, observed that with the popularity of the ministry and the unpopularity of provincial institutions 'a very great deal depends upon how Public Works succeed – the difficulty is that so short a time is allowed us to set things going'.[19] Although written specifically about Auckland, the comment can fairly be generalised to all New Zealand.

The tumultuous parliamentary session of 1872 ultimately reinforced national support for the works policy. Immigration had been as slow as construction, though this was excusable. After the provinces' failure to secure migrants co-operatively, Featherston had to build an agency from scratch after his appointment as agent-general in London in August 1871. He faced difficulty working with provincial agents, especially Otago's.[20] It was impossible to manage immigration while provinces enforced their own conditions, so Featherston created a uniform scheme in December 1871.[21] His subsequent pursuit of migrants was vigorous, if not always successful. Ormond, who took over from William Gisborne as minister of works, was at least able to report to parliament that 247 miles (398 km) of new railways were under construction and that 2758 immigrants had either arrived or were en route.[22] Another development, surprisingly not emphasised by Ormond, was the telegraphic connection of Auckland with the rest of New Zealand in April 1872.[23] Vogel did not bring forth his planned 'new Constitution Act', believing the central–provincial relationship was becoming more harmonious as each found their place, but as one paper emphasised, 'this apparent harmony has been compulsory' since legislation 'deprived the Provinces of the voice in the administration of Railways and Immigration that they previously possessed'.[24]

Provincialists wanted a greater role in the works policy. Fitzherbert, now Wellington's superintendent and back on the ultra-provincial bandwagon, sought an alliance with Stafford, but the opposition's unifying feature was merely opposition to Vogel.[25] Stafford was the clear opposition leader and his centralism was unquestioned, while Fitzherbert wanted a federation in which provinces led public works. Although Stafford was able to achieve a vote of no confidence in the Fox ministry and cobbled together a new ministry headed by himself, he could not form a stable government from such a clash of views. His minister of works, Donald Reid, announced that the government would proceed with constructing 'those [railway] lines which may be considered likely at the earliest date to yield the largest results to the Colony', even though 'some districts … expected that the works in their own localities would be amongst those to be commenced during this year'.[26]

Reid's affirmation of the works policy made no concessions to provincial or parochial sentiment, alienating the ultra-provincial faction of the ministry and frustrating centralist members inclined to trading favours. The biggest problem was that the ministry offered no new policy and its modifications ran counter to increasing public confidence in large borrowings.[27] A majority of members supported the policy; they just happened to be split between Vogel's opposition and those government supporters loyal to Stafford and centralism. Vogel and McLean worked to regain support from some members and then Vogel launched a vicious attack on the ministry. He won the subsequent vote of no confidence and Stafford, after just three months in government, departed from the premiership for the third and final time.[28] At the end of 1872 Vogel's position was more powerful than ever. The session confirmed general support for the works policy and, most astonishingly, Stafford soon moved further into Vogel's orbit as their public works aspirations and exasperation with provincialism became increasingly shared. Vogel did not take office immediately; he was young, Governor Bowen disliked him, and he was still seen as a journeyman. George Waterhouse of the Legislative Council, who had previous experience as premier of South Australia, was called upon to become premier, with Vogel managing government business in the House. The arrangement could not last. Gisborne diplomatically described Waterhouse as 'cautious and deliberative', unable to 'harmonise' with Vogel and lacking 'requisite parliamentary status to secure his proper ministerial position.'[29] His imperial career counted for little among his colleagues. Historians have been more scathing about this 'able but sensitive and rather vain' man who was 'naïve enough' to think he could control Vogel.[30] Waterhouse resigned after only five months and, with Bowen's commission over, Vogel ascended to the premiership in April 1873 at the age of 38.

The last meaningful attempt to salvage provincial agency occurred during 1873, and its failure signified that provincialism's days were numbered. The opposition was in disarray after the fall of Stafford; Rolleston, a committed opponent of Vogel, emphasised that 'there will be *no change* of ministry as no one is prepared to take office.'[31] Stafford lost interest in leading the opposition and took an independent role in parliament, at times advising Vogel. New governor James Fergusson quickly developed a good relationship with Vogel through similar interests and temperaments.[32] Vogel's power was assured but his ability to pass legislation was not. He advanced a policy that he called a 'search after equilibrium' between provincialism and centralism.[33] The central government would retain responsibility for trunk railways and immigration, while the provinces would be allowed to raise loans within the Australasian colonies for specific local public works including branch railways, harbour works, hospitals and schools. Land values were rising rapidly as the colony's development proceeded, and Vogel recognised this could be a valuable asset for the government to repay railway loans, shifting some of the debt burden from consolidated revenue to the land fund. He therefore revived his railway reserve plans, proposing to take parcels of land from South Island provinces and two-thirds of land purchased from Māori in the North Island.[34]

Again provincialists stood in Vogel's way. Wanganui's *Evening Herald* noted sagely that if the provinces could 'settle themselves down' and work with the central government on creating and promoting settlement of the railway reserves, 'they will yet be able to occupy a sphere of usefulness for a few years'; if they could not, 'our trust lies in the stronger power setting them aside'.[35] This warning was ignored. Immediately there were protestations that 'Canterbury and Otago will be seriously injured' by the railway reserve plans.[36] North Island provincialists joined the chorus. Their eagerness to control Māori land was no secret, so any suggestion that it would become a railway reserve rankled. Fitzherbert condemned the policy as a blatant land-grab, a raid on the provinces.[37] The policy was lost and all Vogel could do was secure a loan of £500,000 for the purchase of Māori land to develop a landed estate for the North Island provinces.

A bill allowing provincial loans to be raised within Australasia was lost in the Legislative Council, despite enthusiasm from some provinces for a return to borrowing. The bill passed the House with the help of votes from members who opposed provincial borrowing but feared a backlash from electors.[38] Before the Legislative Council even considered the bill, six provinces – Auckland, Hawke's Bay, Marlborough, Nelson, Otago and Wellington – brought forward proposals for providing security for public works loans.[39] As nominated members, legislative councillors had no electors to worry about. As soon as Daniel Pollen introduced the bill, preaching the government policy of 'equilibrium', it became apparent there was a majority against it. Waterhouse and other prominent members feared a return to unfettered provincial use of 'such dangerous powers'.[40] In the wake of the loan bill's failure, the ministry abandoned its plan and allowed provinces to come to parliament individually for authority to borrow. The six aforementioned provinces and Taranaki submitted a package of seven individual bills. These were rushed through the House, but again mustered little support and came unstuck in the council. Great interest surrounded the council's dealings, with the gallery packed by ordinary citizens and members from the lower house. The council's swift rejection of the bills was described as a 'slaughter', with Auckland's *Evening Star* announcing:

> Fresh pork! fresh pork! fresh pork! seven little sucking pigs all in a row.
> Behold the little grunters have ceased to squeak, and Vogel's heart is sad![41]

Vogel may have been sad, but this was the matter's end. Provincial borrowing was not resumed. The end of the provinces was nigh – they could not borrow, and the continued intransigence of provincialists was an irritant Vogel would not suffer indefinitely.

Abolition sentiment was gathering steam, especially in hinterlands. The *Evening Herald*, in forecasting provincialism's demise favourably, spoke for much of the Wanganui district, chafing under Wellington rule. The *Tuapeka Times* gave voice to goldfields dissatisfaction with provincialism and Otago's administration, while the *Southland Times* perceived an 'unmitigated weariness and disgust [held] by most thinking men' about provincialism.[42] The issue permeated Auckland's super-intendency election of 1873. Public meetings debated it, letter writers urged that candidates be asked their views on abolition, and the *New Zealand Herald* progressed fairly rapidly from advocating reform to outright abolition.[43] Abolitionist agitation found strongest support in Auckland's hinterlands. Ngaruawahia electors, for instance, cheered one candidate's assertion that provinces were 'a temporary expedient' and it 'would be easy now to conduct the whole business of the colony from a common centre'.[44] Throughout 1873 the tide was turning decisively against provincialism.

Before year's end, in what may appear a startling occurrence for a system teetering on the brink of destruction, Westland was upgraded from a county to a province. Yet this did not reflect any belief in provincial viability or vitality. Experimentation with a centrally administered county did not last long. During 1868 Stafford's ministry, acting largely upon local recommendations and seeking to appease the parliamentary unrest that ultimately unseated it, allowed Westland's council to elect its own chairman and exercise full control over revenue.[45] Bernard Conradson, the one historian who has studied the county in detail, concludes that 'the distinctiveness of county government was largely removed' by these reforms, and even though Westland still lacked legislative competence, this restriction was 'more apparent than real'.[46] From the start of the council's third session Westland enjoyed most privileges of the provinces.

Westland County struggled to handle its affairs responsibly, however. From the outset, influential figures sought expenditure. James Bonar, Hokitika's inaugural mayor, telegraphed county chairman John Hall in 1868 that 'revenue [is] accumulating in your hands' and 'it would be a pity that so much money should be lying idle'.[47] The tone was set and money did not lie idle for long. By 1870 Westland had endured scandals regarding bribery, embezzlement, financial irregularities and unfair dismissals, and its position deteriorated further during the early 1870s. Although criminal misuse of funds ceased, the county had no shortage of financial difficulties; in 1873, it had £10,000 of assets offset by liabilities of £45,000.[48] Members were often unsuited to office, merely seeking status and rewards. Their inevitable ineptitude led to lamentations that 'the whole Colony is a witness to our degradation'.[49] Greymouth's leading newspaper, the *Grey River Argus*, revelled in the scandals, hoping they would expose the 'utter rottenness of the Council' and persuade electors to vote for councillors interested in Westland's future rather than those 'regard[ing] politics as a profitable trade'.[50] A central select committee viewed favourably Greymouth's proposals for annexation by Nelson in 1870,[51] but fervour waned over the next two years. Even the greatest champion of the cause, William Henry Harrison of Greymouth, vacillated between annexation and a proposal to unite all West Coast goldfields in one province.[52] In the end Oswald Curtis, superintendent of Nelson, quashed any border adjustment when he secured parliamentary support for a motion that 'hasty changes in the boundaries of provinces ... tend to uncertainty and confusion in government' and changes would be inadvisable unless there was 'some definite and permanent scheme applicable to the whole Colony'.[53] This motion tapped into the wider constitutional debate about the position of the provinces in the Vogel era. The system was clearly inadequate and parliament was ready to consider a new one.

Westland required immediate attention and the impetus for the conversion to provincial status came from above. Vogel proposed the change to Westland politicians as a solution to the county's administrative problems. Full legislative competence might allow Westland to dig itself out of a financial hole. Conradson makes the plausible argument that Vogel probably had ulterior – and devious – motives; frustrated by provincialists, he knew '[a]nother struggling province would do little to enhance the image of provincial institutions'.[54] It was a change hard for provincialists to reject. The county system, created in acknowledgement of Westland's transient needs of the 1860s, was less suited to the post-rush reality of increasingly permanent, fixed settlement. Westland, with the backing of its representatives,

The fruits of the Great Public Works Policy in the North Island: the Parnell tunnel, first started in 1865, is seen nearing completion under central auspices c. 1873 (top); the first train ran from Auckland to Onehunga on Christmas Eve 1873.

therefore became New Zealand's tenth and final province.[55] As Morrell observes, this was no radical change but the completion of a process of assimilation.[56] From 1 January 1874 Westland took its place among the community of provinces, with the superintendent popularly elected but also ex officio a provincial council member.

Despite the lessons of the previous years, parliamentary provincialists neither fully grasped the strength of abolitionist feeling nor understood that Vogel was not a man with whom to trifle. The works policy was starting to bear fruit and the 'wisdom or otherwise of the Colonial policy is not now in question … it would cost us more to retrace our steps than to go forward'.[57] In October 1873 Vogel proposed by circular to the superintendents that the provinces should be responsible for immigrants once they landed in New Zealand, and by February 1874 this plan was endorsed by all the provinces.[58] Between July 1873 and May 1874 15,102 immigrants arrived in New Zealand. The benefits were spread unevenly – Taranaki, Nelson, Marlborough and Westland together received only 191 – but it still represented a surge in the colony's population and labour force.[59] A total of 542 miles (336 km) of railway were opened in 1874. The first Vogel lines in the North Island had been completed: the inaugural stage of Auckland's southern railway opened to Onehunga in December 1873 under central auspices, a whole decade after Auckland Province began work, while in Wellington Province a light line between Foxton and Palmerston North was operational from September 1873, and the initial stage of the Wairarapa railway opened from Wellington to Lower Hutt in April 1874. In the South Island, during 1872, Otago joined Canterbury and Southland in the railway age with a line between Dunedin and Port Chalmers. One consequence of opening new railways was a diversion of revenue from the provinces to the central government on some transport routes where railways duplicated the routes taken by toll roads, further weakening provincial income. In Hawke's Bay, for example, receipts from a provincially managed toll road declined significantly after the new centrally operated railway from Napier to Pakipaki, southwest of Hastings, began to carry much of the traffic that formerly went by road.[60]

Now the central government was earning a return on its investment; initial revenue was modest but represented an important beginning.[61] Canterbury's experience since 1867 afforded proof that a humble start would lead to increasing rewards. In addition to the operational network, by 1874 another 58 miles (92 km) of railway nationwide were ready for traffic, 525 miles (845 km) were under construction and 337 miles (542 km) were still to be let.[62] Work was under way in every province; lines – either operational or under construction – spread out from

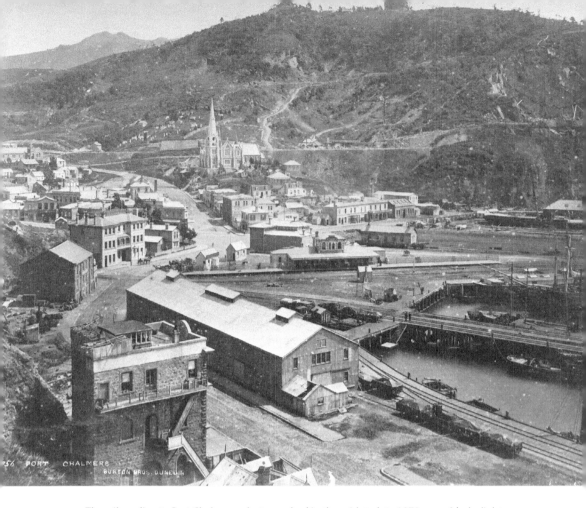

The railway line to Port Chalmers, photographed in the mid- to late 1870s, provided a link to export markets for the regions opened by Vogel's works policy.

every port and capital towards productive hinterlands; the physical and political landscapes of New Zealand were being changed radically. Improved access to resources and demand for wooden railway sleepers fostered a related boom: the rapid penetration of New Zealand's forests by bush tramways to serve sawmills. By the end of the provincial era, forest exploitation – a major part of the economy – was almost unimaginable without rail access.[63]

Yet nobody foresaw the turmoil that would ensue in parliament over forest policy. Previews of the session, which began on 3 July 1874, emphasised that '[n]ot much in the shape of legislation was expected by the public from the Government in the session now begun' and predicted similar disputes to those that defined the previous session.[64] Vogel's newfound interest in forest policy received little coverage beforehand. Forests had been only a minor political issue. Recent environmental historians have shown that the transformation of the natural landscape through the exploitation of grasslands and forests was a significant but hitherto underappreciated aspect of colonialism.[65] New Zealand's environment had to be 'tamed' and integrated into the imperial economy. The inevitable result was the destruction of native forests to create farmland and to serve the burgeoning timber industry. Forestry regulations, weak and made at provincial level, were subservient to settler aspirations for land and industry and often hostage to the belief that timber was an inexhaustible resource. Canterbury and Otago were notable exceptions, but especially in the North Island and Westland local challenges with seemingly impenetrable bush fostered large-scale destruction.[66]

The 1874 New Zealand Forests Act, which responded to increasingly rampant exploitation, had been preceded by similar attempts. Thomas Potts, appalled by the destruction and waste of forests in the South Island, secured the passage of a parliamentary motion in favour of forest conservation in 1868. It passed by one vote in the face of opponents who saw forests as obstructing settlement. Even then, however, there was recognition that the motion lacked practical consequence – all it enabled was dialogue between central and provincial governments on the subject.[67] Charles O'Neill, who supported Potts in 1868, emerged as a champion of conservation, pushing it in 1871 and again in 1873, when he sought a royal commission on the state of New Zealand's forests.[68] Vogel, opposed to Potts in 1868, came around to the cause in 1873–74 after a South Island visit that revealed the devastating effects of deforestation. In the words of Raewyn Dalziel, Vogel 'took up the cause with the convert's enthusiasm'.[69] He recognised that the railway and telegraphic networks of his works policy required large amounts of timber. Vogel hoped to provide a positive spin: the act would allow up to 3 per cent of each province's land area to be designated as state forests, with the revenues from such forests dedicated to relieving the public debt, which was of course consumed by the works policy.

Provincialists immediately saw this as another central encroachment on their jealously guarded land, but their cries were one obstruction too many for Vogel. Led by Wellington's Fitzherbert, his right-hand man Henry Bunny, and Canterbury's Rolleston, the provincialists protested loudly and noisily. Personal interests in maintaining provincial power and wealth hijacked the debate; the provincialists saw conservation as a flimsy pretext for the central government to make money from land.[70] The matter had particular implications for the North Island, which possessed the most valuable forests and hence had most to lose. This resulted in a sudden reversal of the cliché fear that one island's wealth would pay the other's debts, illustrated by the *Wanganui Chronicle's* hysterics that the 'whole burthen would fall upon the North Island Provinces' as a concession to the southern vote.[71] Yet some in the south leapt up and down too. The *Press* cynically, though not entirely unfairly, saw state forests as a resurrection of Vogel's desire to pay for railways with a landed estate, and ridiculed his conversion to the conservation movement.[72] Provincialist opposition in parliament meant the final act was a butchered shadow of Vogel's original. It inaugurated a voluntary process under which superintendents could request areas to be set aside as state forests. Vogel was livid and, unwilling to deal with any more provincial intransigence towards his proposals, called for the abolition of the North Island provinces. The die was cast.

It is nevertheless a mistake to view forests as *the* issue that brought about abolition. Vogel's contemporaries overplayed this aspect. Some newspapers saw abolition proposals as part of a power struggle between Vogel and Fitzherbert, while the *Press* claimed hastily that Vogel's 'sudden fancy for tree-planting threatens to bring about a change in the constitution'.[73] Variations on this theme have seeped into some scholarship.[74] It is also erroneous to dismiss forests entirely. Dalziel's nuanced analysis shows that forestry was not only 'the straw that broke the camel's back … [but] must also be seen in a political and economic context … [as] Vogel could sense the way the wind was blowing'.[75] Vogel's immigration reforms showed his willingness to work with the provinces, but continued obstruction and the surging current of abolitionism led him to act. Vogel would not sit on his hands waiting for the 'right' moment. He was a visionary, and in keeping with his usual temperament he moved decisively.

The provinces had become pensioners. The Provincial Public Works Advances Act of 1874 confirmed this perception. It provided special allowances of £25,000 to Auckland, £10,000 to Nelson and £5,000 to Westland – as well as 2s 6d for every head of population in Westland – to allow them to maintain basic functions. In addition, the legislation granted loans out of consolidated revenue to multiple provinces, the largest of which was £40,000 to Auckland. According to the *Daily Southern Cross*, Auckland looked south at the 'embarrassment of riches' in Canterbury and Otago while forced to 'visit her kindly relation at Wellington, and borrow from the Colonial Government a paltry £40,000, doled out by instalments'.[76] The *Press*, entirely unembarrassed about its riches, was scathing about Auckland – ever since the collapse of the military settlements scheme and the removal of the seat of government, the northern province had been in 'a state of chronic embarrassment'.[77] As harsh as this language may be, it illustrates the contempt in which Auckland was held. The other North Island provinces were little better – Taranaki's dependence on the central government since the outbreak of war was no secret; Hawke's Bay was simply functional; Wellington had emerged from the depression of the late 1860s but was by no means prosperous.

So Vogel proposed abolition of the North Island provinces. The tide had turned very quickly. The *Southland Times* in 1873 observed that, because abolition could be effected only by the General Assembly, 'he would certainly be a somewhat adventurous politician who would stake the existence of his Government on the carrying of such a measure' when so many members also received provincial salaries and therefore had vested interests in provincialism's survival.[78] Vogel did not shrink from the policy, and after the passage of the forests bill's second reading, a head count confirmed that he had a majority in favour of abolition.[79] Vogel, of course, was a very adventurous politician.

Reactions quickly revealed popular support for the move. Prosperous Christchurch and Dunedin were unwilling to denounce South Island provincialism, but the *Press* emphasised that in the North Island 'Provincial Government has long been the sorriest of faces. Any well considered plan which will sweep the whole thing away ... will be a real blessing.'[80] Others wished to go further. Taranaki wondered why North Island provinces should be abolished without the measure being extended to the South.[81] The abolition of Taranaki would merely acknowledge the reality that it was already governed predominantly by local boards or central support. Marlborough, too, was in deplorable financial straits; most locals viewed secession as a mistake and supported local member Arthur Seymour in siding with Vogel.[82] South Cantabrians were heartily in favour of total abolition, while the rest of the province showed little interest in the constitutional struggle so long as the land fund remained localised.[83] Other discontented regions, from north to south, goldfields to pastoral, endorsed Vogel's plan. They either explicitly wanted total abolition or saw the extension of northern abolition to the south as inevitable and positive.[84] Even Vogel's former critics such as the *Thames Advertiser* were on board, despite fears he would abandon abolition once his passion cooled.[85] The mayors of some towns, such as Hokitika and Greymouth, convened enthusiastic meetings to carry resolutions supporting abolition and condemning any local members who did not support Vogel.[86] When the *West Coast Times* wished Vogel 'God-speed' in his 'anti-provincialist course', it spoke for many both in Westland and beyond.[87]

Naturally some opponents appeared. They included Vogel's intractable adversary, Wellington's *Evening Post*, which alleged that he wanted to alter the constitution 'to suit individual caprice or feelings' and demanded he resign in favour of somebody willing to work with the provinces.[88] The *Marlborough Express*, on the editor's initiative, fought a losing battle to convince locals to oppose 'this radical change … [from] Local Self-Government to a Central autocracy'.[89] Otago had considerable interests to protect. An emergency caucus of 15 Otago members met, led by Macandrew. Some had no objections to Vogel's policy if the South Island land fund remained secure, but most feared that abolition in the north would swiftly become national.[90] The *Otago Daily Times* correspondent reported events colourfully, noting that the 'Southern Provincialists are thoroughly alarmed'.[91] Even former advocates of abolition jumped ship. Richardson, for instance, was appalled by the haste of Vogel's action.[92] A breach developed between Vogel and his old friend Macandrew. One telegram described the latter as 'wild at Mr Vogel, and well he may be. He has been completely sold.'[93] But was there anything that provincialists could do? Vogel had all the momentum.

Chapter 14

Provincialism's Fortress is Burning

Vogel may have had the impetus, but he had yet to work out how to actually replace provincialism. Hence, rather than legislation, three resolutions were put before the House in 1874. These were to abolish the North Island provinces, to confirm Wellington as the seat of government, and to continue localisation of land revenue in line with the compact of 1856. Although one Cabinet minister resigned in protest, the resolutions were carried decisively, 46:21. Representatives from the small provinces of Hawke's Bay, Marlborough and Taranaki all voted for the resolutions while the larger provinces were divided, with practically every hinterland representative supporting abolition.[1] Opponents were predictably clustered in the main centres, and all but five held provincial office – including the superintendents of Auckland, Canterbury, Nelson, Otago and Wellington. The main parliamentary party divide changed from supporters and opponents of the works policy to abolitionists versus provincialists, allowing the policy to continue quietly while parliament debated abolition.[2]

The Vogel ministry now had to devise an acceptable, popular plan for abolition in the recess before parliament's 1875 sitting. Immediately after the passage of the resolutions, it became clear electors did not want half-measures – if abolition were to be proposed and debated, it should be a national scheme. Some North Islanders, including a large meeting of Aucklanders on 20 August 1874, felt their pride was at stake and were indignant about their financial woes being singled out when some South Island provinces were also insolvent.[3] They therefore sought national abolition. When Vogel addressed Auckland on 15 September, his attempts to justify the abolition of the northern provinces did not wash with the large crowd; their feeling was 'unmistakably to be this: The total abolition of the provinces of both Islands, but not the one without the other.'[4] Arguments for northern abolition could readily be applied to all provinces. A comprehensive measure was clearly needed.

By this point, the central government completely dominated the provision of services. The works policy caused the public share of total investment to rise from

George Grey in 1875, the year of his return to politics.

1/1-001345-G, Alexander Turnbull Library, Wellington

under two-fifths in 1871 to over half three years later, with railways the single largest component of gross capital formation.[5] This was not an abnormal share: railway construction in Australian colonies was booming at the same time and government capital outlays, primarily for railways, accounted for up to half of all capital outlays.[6] New Zealand's public expenditure for 1874 was £5,715,000, of which £1,553,000 went to public works – £1,115,000, essentially a fifth of total expenditure, to railways alone.[7] Borrowing for the works policy reached £10 million and total national debt £17,400,000, amounting to 62.14 per cent of New Zealand's gross domestic product of £28 million.[8] With the central government responsible both for services and the resultant financial burden, the provinces were a hindrance serving little useful purpose.

Yet the provinces would not go silently. Into the mix came the resurgence of the leading figure of New Zealand politics between 1845 and 1868: former governor George Grey, architect of the provinces. Unwilling to see provincialism dismantled so swiftly, Grey was stirred from his retirement on Kawau Island north of Auckland. Until then Vogel's most intimidating opponent had been James Macandrew, a man whose command of Otago was not replicated throughout the country. Grey still held influence and respect, and a deputation led by William Chisholm Wilson, proprietor of the *New Zealand Herald*, secured his return to politics.[9] For its part, the *Herald* now harboured doubts about abolition: provincialism protected Auckland against being charged for loans that were spent predominantly in the South Island. Abolition, if

An indication of the respect some communities held for George Grey – as well as of the social significance railways had already acquired – is this locomotive decorated in his honour.
661-114, Sir George Grey Special Collections, Auckland Libraries

implemented without appropriate safeguards, would result in Auckland's customs revenue going to consolidated revenue and being used to repay loans; the *Herald* believed this would be 'more injurious [to Auckland] than the so-called compact of 1856'.[10] Fergusson retired as governor in December 1874 to pursue his political career in England and was replaced by the Marquess of Normanby. Less than a year into Normanby's term, on 14 October 1875, his famous predecessor Grey petitioned him to summon parliament immediately to consider the abolition question.[11] Grey was effusive about the virtues of the provinces, presenting them as idyllic bastions of political and social virtue, defenders of liberty against the central government. The petition was one of the most eloquent and thorough defences of provincialism ever made, yet it was not uncompromising. Grey emphasised that institutional change should not occur rapidly or without extensive national consultation. If the provinces were to disappear, the General Assembly should be made more representative – this was a criticism of the Legislative Council and governor being nominees. He was still bitter that his proposal for an elective upper house had been denied.

Normanby rejected Grey's suggestion that parliament be summoned as a move independent of – even in opposition to – the governor's responsible ministers, but this appeal was just one component of Grey's foray back into politics.[12] He continued, fruitlessly, to petition both Normanby and the Colonial Office. Wellington rejected Grey's claims while London officials held a low opinion of him and saw no reason to intervene.[13] When Auckland's superintendent, John Williamson, died in February 1875, Grey was elected to the office in March; for all his involvement in colonial politics, it was his first taste of representative authority. He found, however, that his views had not yet caught on widely. In May his provincial council passed a resolution in favour of abolition by 19:14. Not happy with having his authority brazenly defied, Grey the next day secured the passage of resolutions that did not support abolition, at least not until the presentation of an alternative scheme of local government to be applied to the whole country.[14] But while Auckland's voters and provincial council were susceptible to Grey's influence, he – like Macandrew before him – struggled to extend his influence across provincial borders. Even in Otago the *Daily Times* dismissed his petition as the 'plaintive whine of an inventor who sees his ingenious device about to be superseded by more practically useful improvements'.[15]

The inhabitants of Otago, for all their provincial passion, had not been seriously stirred. Dunedin did not yet believe that abolition of the North Island provinces also meant Otago's abolition, and as late as May 1875 it was content with promises that the land fund would remain localised with a sufficient degree of local administration.[16] This state of southern apathy was perhaps influenced by the declaration of Charles Bowen, a member of Vogel's ministry, that when there is 'almost a legislative revolution, it is better to begin at the end where the demand is most needed for a change [the North Island]' rather than in the south, where Canterbury and Otago were still solvent.[17] Bowen, a former *Lyttelton Times* editor who was profoundly suspicious of ultra-provincialism, had earned much respect in Canterbury for his provincial administrative work since the 1850s and his word carried weight.

The south was roused, however, when parliament met in July 1875 and the final great battle between centralism and provincialism began. Vogel, who had travelled to England to negotiate further loans and attend to other government business, was detained there by a severe attack of gout. In his absence, the ministry was reorganised with Daniel Pollen at its head, though Treasurer Harry Atkinson was the most powerful member. Atkinson was not Vogel's truest ally since he feared

Harry Atkinson, 1860s.

PAColl-1802-1-29, Alexander Turnbull Library, Wellington

excessive borrowing, and his ability to appreciate the strengths and weaknesses of both sides of most issues meant he rarely settled on a position. But as would be expected of a Taranaki member, Atkinson was an ardent centralist who believed the works policy made the provinces superfluous and his accession to power guaranteed the ministry would continue to pursue abolition.[18] Hometown support even came from a Taranaki provincial councillor who felt it would be good if superintendents or 'Despots' had 'their heads taken off' – this was written by Charles Brown, a former superintendent himself.[19] On 6 August 1875 Atkinson introduced the second reading of the Abolition of Provinces Bill – and that was abolition of *all* the provinces. In Atkinson's words, 'the more the Government considered the subject, and the more they became acquainted with the feelings of the people, the more clearly it became apparent to them that nothing but a complete measure would satisfy the country.'[20] There was no longer any illusion that the southern provinces would survive. After all, as Atkinson emphasised, most provincial powers had either been assumed by the central government or had, by the provinces themselves, been devolved to single-purpose local bodies such as harbour and road boards. The only functions left to the provinces were legislative, surely unnecessary when 'the legislation of this Assembly is amply sufficient for a population of four hundred thousand', and as pensioners, 'getting money out of this Assembly'.[21]

Atkinson's argument that 'the power which raises the taxes should be the spending power' was undoubtedly persuasive. Despite howls of protest from provincialists during the parliamentary debate, their arguments were weak and unconvincing. Before the session, Grey tried to argue that the colonial parliament had no power to abolish the provinces.[22] Both the attorney-general and solicitor-general disagreed: the power to abolish any province in the Constitution Act meant 'one, or more, or all' provinces and that 'the power to abolish Provinces is absolute'.[23] The Earl of Carnarvon, Colonial Secretary, concurred and noted that this subject fell within Wellington's competency, not Westminster's.[24] The debate was a domestic matter for New Zealand to resolve. No amount of pleading by provincialists could persuade a majority of the House that provinces still met the country's requirements. Even cries from people such as Macandrew for a consolidation of provinces into two or four fell on deaf ears.[25] The debate took a largely financial character with little time given to higher points of political theory. Although the opposition contained such eminent figures as Fitzherbert, Grey, Macandrew, Rolleston and Reader Wood, and enjoyed the services of rising star Robert Stout, it was numerically weak.[26] On 29 September the provincial cause was lost decisively, 40:21.

The provincialists did, however, negotiate valuable concessions, including a clause in the Abolition of Provinces Act that it not come into force until after the next parliamentary session. This was a device to allow the country a voice: a general election was due. New Zealand's electors would have the final say on abolition. The concession was fair and indeed necessary; there was general support for abolition, but the public had not been given a say on what system should replace it. The provincialists' call for an election essentially as a referendum elicited sympathy.[27] The government proposed a system of road boards, which could apply to be amalgamated as shires, but this was unpopular and their Local Government Bill was dropped. It had been derided as a plot to secure 'complete centralization of all real authority and administrative power' since the road boards were not granted any powers they did not already possess – indeed fewer than those already existing in Canterbury and Otago – and some saw the bill's abandonment as a government attempt to have 'the powers of local government ... transferred to the General Government'.[28] Both to gauge public support for abolition and to allow time to draft a new local government measure, abolition would not occur for another year. In that time provincial councils were prohibited from meeting.[29]

In keeping with the usual theme of Māori being ignored or excluded from provincialism, the parliamentary debate and election campaign were conducted with little reference to them. Māori politicians, occupying the four seats created for them in 1867, occasionally expressed opinions on abolition. In 1875 Wiremu

Katene, the member for Northern Māori, and the first Māori appointed to the Executive Council, pithily informed parliament that 'I have not heard a word' about Māori.[30] Although Māori members did not influence the debate substantially, they felt their constituents understood provincialism poorly and had little involvement with or fondness for it.[31] Karaitiana Takamoana, representing Eastern Māori, blamed some of this ignorance upon the government's failure to translate the Abolition Bill into Māori.[32] He followed George Grey on account of the latter's mana and feared abolition was 'something aimed at the Maoris' to dubiously appropriate land.[33] This fear was also related to Takamoana's role in the Hawke's Bay Repudiation movement, which rejected all Crown and private land deals as fraud.

Takamoana's statement provoked a short debate with Wiremu Parata (Western Māori) and Hori Kerei Taiaroa (Southern Māori), who saw no connection between abolition and land, but there was no deep reflection on the consequences for Māori autonomy or governance.[34] *Te Waka Maori o Niu Tirani*, a government publication, and *Te Wananga*, an independent opposition paper, were printed in both Māori and English. They gave scant attention to the issue beyond reprinting parliamentary speeches that discussed abolition.[35] The greatest reaction came from a *Te Wananga* editorial frustrated that the act was not operational for a year. 'Pass it, if you have agreed that it shall be passed, and have done with it. To keep "bothering" over it is a waste of time and trouble that might be turned to much better account.'[36] The clear theme was that Māori were little affected by abolition and its dominance of current political discourse interfered with timely action for more relevant and important matters.

The election was a victory for abolition – barely a provincialist was elected outside the strongholds of Auckland and Otago. The election was fought predominantly on abolition and practically every newspaper reduced election results to whether or not 'abolition' candidates defeated 'opposition' or 'provincial' candidates. Of 88 members in the new House, 53 were pro-abolition, 26 anti-abolition and nine doubtful; of the anti-abolitionists, only one supported the status quo, with the rest proposing reforms.[37] The small provinces of Hawke's Bay, Marlborough, Taranaki and Westland were naturally abolitionist; Westland's electors in particular, disgusted by its previous representatives not supporting abolition, promptly turned them out. Allegations that Vogel depended on 'remote impecunious provinces' for support were, however, inaccurate.[38] Nelson joined the abolition chorus, and in Wellington even ultra-provincialists had to change their tune. Fitzherbert, bluntly realistic in his assessment that the 'provinces could not be resuscitated', felt 'it would be ridiculous to try to repeal the Abolition Bill, because the Upper House … passed it almost unanimously, and they would support it again'.[39] Nonetheless, he remained critical of the government for not bringing down a practicable local government bill, and vowed to seek robust local administration. Bunny perceived that Wellington, especially his Wairarapa electorate, was strongly for abolition and put himself forward as 'prepared to assist in building up a new system … to give the people the best form of local self-government'.[40]

The result was not a walkover. Auckland and Otago between them elected 39 of the 84 Pākehā members, and many electorates returned provincialists, though there were extenuating circumstances in a number of these cases. It is incorrect to suggest that both provinces were solid in opposition to centralism or to characterise Auckland's new members, as at least two leading historians have, as 'a solid phalanx of supporters of Sir George Grey'.[41] Grey's policies were ridiculed in southern Auckland Province as ambiguous and mysterious.[42] Anti-abolitionists did not even stand in a number of rural Auckland electorates. In urban electorates, Greyites leveraged class conflict in a manner that responded to the particularities of Auckland's division between the interests of capital and labour.[43] Meanwhile the goldfields election for Thames was farcical, and it is hard to suggest its support for Grey's 'phalanx' was sound.[44] Thames during 1875 came out for abolition, yet in November a requisition was sent to Grey himself, who agreed to stand. Both leading newspapers were baffled, speculating the requisition was signed because of personal respect for Grey rather than 'any modification of the views of the public of the Thames [on abolition]'.[45] Much of Thames's discontent was caused by the ministry's failure to open land for miners to farm or to provide subsidies to the goldfields in line with subsidies to other local bodies. Pollen was consequently seen as a 'shuffler'.[46] In the end, Thames chose provincialists as its two members, with Grey at the head of the vote. Vogel, still in England and nominated by friends, finished third – but fortunately secured election a few days later in Wanganui. Absurd scenes followed the Thames outcome, with protests proposed against every candidate's result.[47] Thames seemed more interested in controversy than political institutions, and its vote was more a vote against the government than for provincialism.

Meanwhile, even in the provincialist stronghold of Auckland city, there were prominent undercurrents of dissent. As election returns came in the *New Zealand Herald* desperately tried to believe that the ministry was 'in a small and hopeless minority', but not everybody was listening.[48] James George, chairman of Auckland's 'Progress Party' in the 1850s and provincial councillor in the 1860s, wrote that although 'Sir G Grey may become Cheif [sic] mourner' of the provinces, few in Auckland were particularly attached to his 'expencive [sic] bantling'.[49] (A bantling is a young child.) George had a long-standing distaste for Grey and obviously did not speak for a majority of voters, but he was certainly not the only person in Auckland who recalled 'old officialdom' disdainfully. Southern sentiments that provincialism was a burden had some currency in Auckland. Influential businessmen such as John Logan Campbell favoured abolition and in Auckland City East, for example, a pro-abolition candidate lost only narrowly.[50]

As for Otago, some of its results deserve qualification. Any suggestion that the election results show the entire province, with the exclusion of some goldfields, in favour of retaining some form of provincialism is a misrepresentation.[51] Linda M. Cowan's study has provided a measure of clarification, in particular that in country districts personality rather than ideology was central to a candidate's success or rejection, and that electoral turnout was poor even in provincialist strongholds.[52] However, the nature of the results was even more complex than her analysis suggests. Provincialists banded together in a well-organised Anti-Centralist League to campaign throughout the province. Oamaru's was the most remarkable outcome, since in 1875 it had been anxious that William Steward, the popular member for Waitaki, support abolition and at the end of the session publicly expressed satisfaction with his conduct. On election day, though, Oamaru rejected Steward. In this election Waitaki was expanded into a two-member electorate and provincialists won both positions. They ran together effectively on a joint ticket and enjoyed a boost when Robert Stout of the Anti-Centralist League visited Oamaru to assist their campaign.[53] The *North Otago Times* railed that Oamaru had been swayed by provincialists suggesting that abolition threatened the land fund and education reserves, despite the fact that Oamaru had sought a new system of local government for years.[54] This lent some weight to the frustrated reflections of one anti-provincial West Coast paper that 'Auckland and Otago did not know they had been so badly treated until they heard their advocates addressing them on the hustings'.[55] A brief spurt of eloquent populism in Oamaru swayed its vote away from the long-term sentiment of the district. The *Southland Times*, at least to a degree, shared this sentiment about its own region, feeling that Southland would have elected a better calibre of candidates '[h]ad the Macandrew counsels been rejected' and the abolition debate not become such a defining issue.[56]

Southland, of course, had already rejected provincialism utterly. So why did it join the general Otago trend of electing provincialists? Erik Olssen's argument

The 1875–76 election brought out political satirists in force. This bill, purporting to promote a concert, comments on the Kaiapoi contest between Charles Bowen and Joseph Beswick.

Eph-E-POLITICS-1875-01, Alexander Turnbull Library, Wellington

is strong: some Southlanders 'hoped to make Dunedin more responsive to their complaints, if abolition failed, or, if it passed, wanted to retain local control over local matters' and thought defenders of provincialism would secure a superior level of local self-government.[57] Another study adds depth: Southlanders viewed abolition as a fait accompli, and provincialists won votes by campaigning on parochial issues, invoking class divisions.[58] To this must be added the reality that Southlanders had been susceptible to Macandrew's rhetoric ever since the late-1860s cry of 'reunion and Macandrew', and he ceaselessly offered visions of future prosperity to southern New Zealand. Rumours also circulated that provincialists intentionally brought forward multiple abolitionist candidates to split the abolition vote.[59] The 1875–76 election results did not mean that Otago's previously secessionist hinterlands had suddenly made peace with provincialism. They continued to oppose it and they did not follow Dunedin's lead in lamenting its demise. Steward was even soon elected as Oamaru's mayor.

The abolitionists did not have everything their own way, but the provincialists' hopes of last-minute salvation were forlorn. Some Canterbury electorates, for instance, were surprisingly close – abolitionist Edward Wakefield, the nephew of Edward Gibbon, won Geraldine on the returning officer's deciding vote, while much was made of Cabinet minister Bowen's reduced margin in Kaiapoi.[60] None of this, however, could justify delusions that Vogel, upon returning from England, would repudiate his colleagues for going too far and either chart a middle course or join the opposition. The *Otago Guardian* believed 'the hope of the Provincialist party is in Sir Julius'. One more astute observer rubbished the *Guardian*: 'never perhaps was any hope indulged with less reason'.[61] Macandrew himself wrote to the *Clutha Leader* to pour cold water on such fanciful dreams after a candidate on the Clutha hustings expressed similar views.[62]

Another provincial delusion was that the result was insufficiently conclusive. Unlike the provincialists, who were well organised in Auckland and Otago, the government did not conduct an organised campaign anywhere and still won a sound majority.[63] Some provincialists, including the editor of the *Clutha Leader*, made sweeping claims: since 'the country is about equally divided on this question, the proper course to take is to let things remain as they are. This is no ordinary question … [as it affects] the constitution of the country, no change should be made unless at least two-thirds of the House are agreeable to it'.[64] This argument had no constitutional basis and could not be sustained. Provincialism was completely divided. The *Press* made one of the most perceptive insights when it noted that Canterbury and Otago provincialists argued provincialism was the only protector of local land funds, while Auckland's provincialists were the most eager to make the land fund colonial revenue. 'It is from provincialists that the danger to the land fund comes; how in the world then can adherence to provincialism suffice to avert it?'[65] Auckland and Otago advanced provincialism for different reasons and agreed on little; there was no hope of Grey and Macandrew working together to protect and strengthen the system, even if they had the numbers to take office. Vogel returned to find an opposition in disarray and Pollen keen to return the mantle of premier. When Vogel resumed the premiership in February 1876 abolition was assured.

The only question was what kind of local government would follow? The election made clear that although voters supported abolition, they wanted strong local government to replace it. This was a much-desired and well-developed part of New Zealand's political landscape: each locality's primary interest was to 'see their patch properly settled and given the trappings that a decent life required'.[66] The *Taranaki Herald*, for instance, was delighted that 'Provincialism as a mode of local government is a system of the past' but was wary of the central government 'grasping with a too arbitrary hand the higher administrative duties which are still performed by the Superintendents and Executives'.[67] The ministry, led by Atkinson from 1 September after Vogel again departed for London, this time to become agent-general, did not repeat 1875's mistakes and provided a broader scheme – although one that was still hasty in its conception. A plethora of bills were dutifully passed into law – the key acts were the Counties Act and Municipal Corporations Act, accompanied by a series of acts creating a swathe of single-purpose local boards to oversee education, harbours, rivers and roads. This provided the strong local self-government desired by Fitzherbert, Bunny, Southland's electors, the *Taranaki Herald* and most of the country. Main centres were established as boroughs, while the rest of the country was covered with 63 counties. (The six most sparsely populated could not become operational until authorised by a General Assembly resolution.) The counties and boards largely followed the boundaries of pre-existing local authorities, proving that 'the country was well enough stocked with local bodies to make the abolition of the provinces of little account in terms of local government'.[68] Localism was, and remains, a potent theme in New Zealand politics.

Parliament rose on 31 October 1876 and the Abolition of Provinces Act came into effect the next day. On 1 November 1876 provincialism disappeared from New Zealand's political landscape with little more than a whimper. Few mourned the provinces. Invercargill and Riverton observed a public holiday with scenes of jubilation on their streets, proving Southland was abolitionist at heart.[69] The *Thames Advertiser*, noting such festivities, wrote that Thames 'prefer[s] a less demonstrative mode of welcoming the new system of local government' and expressed hope for the 'machinery of more modern construction' while paying 'a tribute of respect to defunct Provincialism – bur[ying] our dead decently out of our sight'.[70] For some, the provinces presented instructive lessons for the future, especially in hinterlands newly blessed with self-government. On Banks Peninsula the *Akaroa Mail* took the provincial system, especially the county of Westland, as a warning of excesses to avoid for itself and other rural areas, while taking comfort that the new counties were 'differently constituted … [with] well defined administrative powers'.[71] The *Grey River Argus* noted pithily that abolition came into force 'without producing any of the serious results apprehended by Sir George Grey', while the *Daily Southern Cross* simply observed that 'people in town and country see no difference. Everything has gone on as before.'[72] Ebenezer Fox, secretary to the Cabinet, expressed surprise about the quiet state of affairs to his close friend Vogel: 'I confess I expected to see more immediate inconvenience.'[73]

It was now time to look to the future. Nelson's *Colonist* issued a stern warning against sore winners and losers.[74] The father of Southland provincialism, James Menzies, counselled that evil would not come of abolition and urged support for the newly constituted local bodies.[75] This good advice evidently did not reach some in Otago and Auckland, where there was a healthy crop of sour grapes. Abolitionists in Balclutha tried to organise a holiday as in nearby Southland but bitter provincialists thwarted these plans, destroying posters announcing the festivities.[76] Grey took the extraordinary step of petitioning the Colonial Office in June and October pleading for disallowance of the Abolition Act lest there be disturbances in Auckland.[77] Governor Normanby attached a cover letter to the June missive ruing that 'it is hard to convince Sir George Grey that any decision can be right which does not coincide with his own pre-conceived opinion', while Vogel wrote a ministerial memorandum to Carnarvon, clearly infuriated by Grey's 'irresponsible desire … [for] harping upon fancied grievances and baseless rumours'. Grey received a stern rebuke from Carnarvon: the act would not and could not be disallowed.

Macandrew had a modicum more tact, but his energies also came to naught. He did not seek revolution – though the fantasies of 'President Macandrew' penned by a Wellington satirist may have appealed.[78] Before parliament sat, he denied co-operation to ministerial commissioners involved in smoothing the administrative transition.[79] During the session he and other provincialists sought special concessions that would have essentially retained Otago's existence as a province within a system of counties; after parliament he held an Otago Convention that petitioned the Queen to proclaim Otago a separate colony.[80] Carnarvon, when he received the petition outside the normal channels, simply expressed surprise that 'the memorialists have thought fit to ask for the interference of Her Majesty in a matter within the competency of the Colonial Legislature, and on which the Legislature and constituencies have long since expressed a decided opinion'.[81]

Despite the sound and fury in Auckland and Otago, New Zealand had endorsed abolition and the Colonial Office was unwilling to interfere. Provincial government was dead. As if to ram home the point, Marlborough's provincial council chambers in Blenheim caught fire on the evening of 1 November. An inquest was unable to

The contradictions of the era: James Macandrew, with barrow in hand, turns the first sod of the centrally funded Invercargill–Riverton railway in 1875, the same year he fought vigorously to save the provinces. P1998-028/09-001, Hocken Collections, Uare Taoka o Hākena, Dunedin

Henry Howard Molyneux Herbert, fourth Earl Carnarvon, who in rejecting provincialist arguments confirmed Wellington's competence to legislate on New Zealand's domestic political structure. Carnarvon was colonial secretary in 1866–67 and 1874–78, and is pictured here in the first year of his second term. He previously served in the junior post of colonial under-secretary during 1858–59.

x15592, London Stereoscopic & Photographic Company, National Portrait Gallery, London

locate the cause or culprit but did not consider the event an accident. Whatever the fire's origins, it spread rapidly through the town and the chambers burned to the ground along with over 20 businesses and homes.[82] There could not have been a more dramatic end in a more dysfunctional province.

***

So what happened to provincialism? The 1875–76 election had been fought over abolition and won by its advocates, but this did not give a party platform for the creation of a ministry. The election had been a single-issue vote, more a referendum than anything else, with few politicians or voters casting an eye even to the near future. The election result itself settled the abolition question, and a new alignment of parties arose by 1877. The machinations and decisions of this new parliament pointed towards a fresh post-provincial direction in New Zealand in which central government intervention became increasingly prominent and frequent.[83]

Newspapers that had forecast a lack of common interests among those elected to support abolition were proven right. Once the abolitionists repelled the final attempts of the provincialists to stop or delay abolition, they lost their main bond. By contrast, ex-provincialists survived the demise of their original issue, uniting as a vigorous opposition that stood for liberal principles. Just too late to save his provinces, George Grey, pursuing a more moderate course than in 1875, came to power in 1877 with a provincialist ministry in an abolitionist parliament. The historian of the Grey ministry has emphasised that once 'the abolition question had slipped completely into the background … it became possible for the Government's opponents to challenge the [Atkinson] Ministry'.[84] Grey may have failed in halting abolition but he secured the consolidation of the land fund, a proposal that won support across 'party' lines, despite the opposition of most Canterbury and Otago members.[85] For all the bluster of Greyites during the 1875–76 election, abolition and land revenue were not inextricably linked. Even that most staunch provincialist and opponent of consolidation, James Macandrew, joined Grey's ministry and enjoyed national power for the first time. His willingness to move on from the provincial cause and participate in national government is ample evidence of Herron's argument that politicians' allegiances were often determined by what offices they held.

From this time, the battlelines of the provincial era faded, new issues gained prominence and politics turned towards a liberal future. Long-term political alignments fragmented and collapsed as familiar, even stereotypical, provincial rivalries disappeared.[86] Although some politicians feared Grey would revive the provincial system, it was never resuscitated.[87] The demise of provincialism had both immediate and long-term consequences. Matters that had been handled on a provincial level now acquired a national quality; abolition removed the legal basis for legislative diversity. Grey's land fund consolidation was just one example. Education historians have credited abolition with clearing the way for the 1877 Education

Act that made primary education free, secular and compulsory throughout New Zealand.[88] Harry Atkinson gave brief consideration to a measure in 1876 that would have effectively kept the separate provincial education systems intact, but it was quickly abandoned in favour of a uniform system.[89]

Local government came under the authority of a plethora of councils and single-issue boards. Bill Sutch savaged these 'Lilliputian local authorities' as 'too weak, too apathetic, and too short-sighted', their shortcomings ultimately fostering greater centralisation.[90] Another critic rightly noted that the new system 'bore the impress of imperfection'; like provincialism in the 1840s, it was crafted not by ideology but by parochialism and improvisation.[91] For some minorities, the replacement of provinces with counties and local boards was a particularly negative development. Otago's Chinese population, who received a welcome and a guarantee of equal protection from the provincial council, experienced racial discrimination in employment and legal rights from some county councils.[92] Nonetheless, the counties in general reflected a greater awareness of local needs and wants, even if the lessons of provincialism were grasped inadequately. The new bodies flourished and multiplied, serving New Zealand for over a century until their replacement by the current system of regional and territorial authorities in 1989.[93]

Provincialism did not, however, disappear immediately. Its fading echoes were felt for years; one historian, appropriating Tennyson's words, has described it as a 'slowly dying cause'. Some adherents continued to fight, especially those from Otago. Regional envy and rivalry retained a major role in New Zealand's political life, but even Otago had little affection for the former provincial system, and its defence of provincialism was born of very local, sometimes selfish, motives.[94] Otago provincialists sought what they felt was their province's share of revenue – inevitably, a fair share meant more than what was given – and continued to destabilise parliament with petty jealousies and logrolling. Auckland also demonstrated this behaviour. The defection of the four 'Auckland Rats' from the nascent liberal party in 1879 after the fall of Grey remains a controversial moment in New Zealand politics, activated by striking provincialism; their main concern was not progressive reform but Auckland's provincial development.[95] Relentless negativity, unbridled parochialism and appeals to nostalgia were not the basis for an enduring party and Auckland and Otago provincialists failed to agree on an alternative system of local government to offer electors. As A.H. Cook has suggested, 'since Provincialism was derived from the jealousies and rivalries of Provincial interests, any attempted united action was foredoomed to failure'.[96] Had Auckland and Otago been able to co-operate, and had they been able to cultivate provincialist support elsewhere, the cause may have endured, but their interests were irreconcilable. Both sought to prosper at the expense of the rest of the colony, including each other. Provincialism slowly but surely perished as a political force during the 1880s.

Localism rather than provincialism remained persistent and local identity continues to possess significance in New Zealand, but it no longer relates to sub-national political entities with legislative powers. Regional identity and politics have been largely divorced since 1876. The national parliament may now be a theatre for local needs, grievances and parochialism, but localism and regionalism are subservient to national identity. The provinces, metaphorically and literally, were railroaded by the central state.

Page 240: This 1883 map shows the rapid growth of North Island railways, none of which were operational in 1870. It shows railways open (crossed lines and highlighted), under construction (thick lines), authorised but not begun (dashed lines), and exploratory surveys for the main trunk between Wellington and Auckland (dotted lines). Note the private Wellington and Manawatu Railway under construction (dashed and crossed line); it would be the only significant private railway to operate in New Zealand. Not all authorised railways were built, such as the line depicted from Rotorua to Tauranga. A. Koch, NZ Map 191, Sir George Grey Special Collections, Auckland Libraries

Page 241: This 1883 map shows the rapid growth of South Island railways, of which only Lyttelton–Christchurch–Selwyn was operational in 1870 (and Invercargill–Makarewa was in the process of conversion from wooden to iron rails). It shows railways open (crossed lines and highlighted), under construction (thick lines), authorised but not begun (dashed lines), and a couple of small private railways (crossed lines not highlighted). Not all authorised railways were built. This map shows two notable railways-that-never-were: the Canterbury Interior Main Line from Sheffield to Temuka, and the extension of the Otago Central Railway beyond Cromwell to Lake Hawea. A. Koch, NZ Map 2602, Sir George Grey Special Collections, Auckland Libraries

NORTH ISLAND
NEW ZEALAND
1883.

John Blackett. M. Inst. C.E.
Engineer in Charge

GREAT BARRIER I.

HAURAKI GULF

KAIPARA H.

MANUKAU H.

BAY OF PLENTY

TE UREWERA COUNTRY

Taupo Moana

NORTH TARANAKI BIGHT

HAWKE BAY

MARIA PENA

SOUTH TARANAKI BIGHT

HAWKE'S BAY

COOK STRAIT

TASMAN B.

REFERENCE

Authorized Railways made
under construction
not begun
Private Railways
Explorations for Main Trunk
Railway Line

Scale of Miles.

Conclusion

Provincial government perished in New Zealand not for a want of provincialist sympathy or identity. Provincialism was born from the peculiar circumstances of the late 1840s, when geography demanded separate provinces for New Zealand's dispersed settlements. A small population meant that the country could not be divided into separate colonies, as in Australia, but this approach – as well as the influence of recent local government reforms in England – offered inspiration for the devolution of some power to provincial level. The arduous, unpredictable nature of transport between the six main Pākehā centres meant that local and regional matters were best determined locally, including immigration and public works, the two most important requirements of a young colony. Earl Grey as colonial secretary endorsed federations, believing they fostered the values of free trade he held dear, though his proposals of 1846 did not meet New Zealand's needs. In the end, it still proved easier to implement a quasi-federal structure in such a young colony than to herd the cats of Australia and Canada into federal arrangements. The production of the provincial system makes clear the primacy of settler initiative: the counter-proposals of Governor George Grey, based on colonial observations and advice, were largely accepted in London.

The identity of New Zealand's settlers was bound up with the success of their new home. This fostered passionate localism, which became stronger as boosterism proclaimed each settlement's allegedly unique virtues. Even Nelson, once sceptical of provincial government, was won over to the system when it was implemented. To Pākehā in the 1850s, provincialism represented the most accessible form of politics, continuing a number of English traditions of local government but with greater authority – particularly through the possession of legislative powers – and wider popular participation. But because the provincial system was conceived as a response to the needs of the late 1840s, it lacked a lasting foundation. As time and space were transformed, so were the roles of New Zealand's tiers of government.

The centralising actions of Edward Stafford's ministry in the late 1850s played a major role in destabilising the system. Its New Provinces Act created small, poor, ineffectual provinces while striking at the political power base of Stafford's opponents. Meanwhile, by handing over management of the land fund to individual provinces, the compact of 1856 meant that land-poor provinces, especially in the North Island, lacked the money to proceed with development schemes while land-rich provinces, especially Canterbury and Otago, were able to surge ahead, creating marked inequality within the provincial system.

Complicated questions of political and economic reform were often removed from the daily lives of settlers, who looked for more practical measures. For the colony to develop, public works were essential, especially access to railways and roads. Only these could overcome isolation and artificial distance – and promote economic and social growth. New Zealand's light population and lack of wealthy capitalists meant private enterprise could not meet these needs, so settlers looked to their provincial governments, which possessed the will, legal power and capacity to raise the necessary money on the Australian and London money markets.

The six original provinces proved a disappointment, especially to hinterland settlers, and secessionist ferment led to the creation of new provinces. Hawke's Bay, Marlborough and Southland, established between 1858 and 1861, were not successful. Hawke's Bay struggled from the outset but settled down into a mundane, if not particularly auspicious, existence. Marlborough and Southland were profound embarrassments to their citizens. Both entertained ambitious plans of development but were unable to play their required role in the progress industry. Marlborough could not afford to maintain the machinery of provincial government for its tiny population and illustrated the worst evils of localism through petty disputes and rival councils. Southland presented the direst example of provincial failure. In haste it experimented with a wooden railway that bankrupted the province and forced it to reunite with Otago. The new provinces were a sorry chapter in the provincial saga, doing more to discredit provincialism than their centralist creators could have envisaged. The old provinces were also largely incapable of achieving their goals. By the mid-1860s the provinces were heavily indebted and had few tangible results to show for their effort.

Other factors also played a role in undermining provincialism. Warfare had significant but not dire consequences for the system. Powers assumed by the central state were either limited to the theatre of war and lacked national or long-term applicability, or had little relevance to provincialism in the first place. The difficulties that the central state and Auckland Province experienced in implementing the

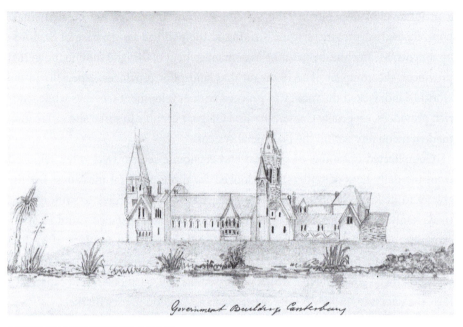

A-210-016, Alexander Turnbull Library, Wellington

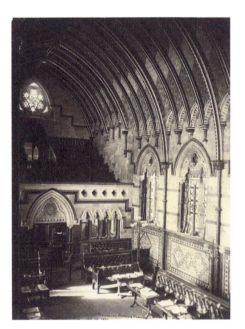

661-137, Sir George Grey Special Collections, Auckland Libraries

Only one purpose-built provincial council building survives, but it is the most splendid: that of Canterbury. Seen here are James West Stack's charming 1860 sketch of the building (above) and an 1870 photo of the interior, which was badly damaged in the devastating Canterbury earthquakes of 2010 and 2011. The photo opposite shows repairs under way in 2013. The building that housed Southland's council, originally built as a Masonic Hall, also still stands on Kelvin Street, Invercargill.

André Brett

New Zealand Settlements Act prefigured the difficulties that would beset Vogel's Great Public Works Policy in its first years, but they did not undermine the system. Postulating a direct connection between wartime expansion of the central state and the works policy is simplistic and unjustifiable. War also stimulated the South Island separation movement, notable not for what it did but for who it involved: Julius Vogel. This movement facilitated his entry to New Zealand politics, and his separatism had a centralising impulse. Vogel harboured a visionary's fascination with the potential of new technology such as railways. At the end of the 1860s he became a major national political figure – he was the main policymaker of the Fox ministry of 1869–72 – and his centralising impulse came to encompass the entire country. Rather than being strictly provincialist or centralist in ideology, he pursued policy in accordance with his possession of provincial or central power.

Provincialism experienced a watershed year in 1867. War's most significant effect on provincialism occurred on the London money market, when provincial loans for public works competed with central loans to fund the fighting. London's preference for central loans was a serious problem for the provinces, but the provincial financial difficulties would have existed without this collision, and if anything it prevented some provinces from borrowing even greater sums – which they could not repay. By 1866 New Zealand's finances, nationally and especially provincially, were stagnant, and in 1867 the central parliament banned further provincial loans as part of its consolidation of provincial and central debt. The obvious result was a halt to development. Railways and other works remained a provincial responsibility, but no province could undertake them without loans.

A way out was essential, and Julius Vogel provided it. His Great Public Works Policy transformed New Zealand. As it was implemented, regional development and population increases went hand in hand with railway expansion.[1] In just a decade, over a third of New Zealand's railway network was constructed. The policy responded to the persistent failures of provincialism to develop the colony, and averted the perils of province-based development – perils that were realised fully in Australia with the use of incompatible railway gauges. Vogel's plan deprived the provinces of their two main functions, public works and immigration, and imposed a national form on infrastructural planning. Provincial borders quickly became irrelevant and the compression of time and space shrank the provinces. Provincial councils had already devolved many minor tasks to local boards and municipal councils and now their major tasks were assumed by the central government. It was only a matter of time before they vanished from the New Zealand landscape, which now looked dramatically different from that of the 1840s.

Provincialism's swift disappearance nonetheless remains remarkable. It is testimony to the fervour of the abolitionist cause and to the belief that the central state was fitted to fulfil the settlers' urgent demands. Although a national trunk railway network was still decades away and some of Vogel's vision was never realised,[2] it provided a clear programme and the central government achieved more in five years than the provinces had in two decades. Provincial inadequacy, already so evident, was brought into stark relief by central competence. Provincial politicians, aware that their comfortable superintendencies and executive offices were under threat, quickly feared the worst and from 1870 to 1875 stood persistently in the way of Vogel's policies. This obstinacy backfired. Vogel could sense the mood of the colony had turned against provincialism, and when his forest conservation policy was neutered by provincialist interference in 1874, he sensed an opportunity. The response from constituents to his proposals for abolition of North Island provinces was unmistakeable: New Zealanders wanted total abolition. Resolute opposition came from Auckland and Otago, but even some of their outlying areas had long since boarded the abolition train. Electors cast their vote for abolition at the 1875–76 election, and on 1 November 1876 the provinces disappeared for ever from New Zealand's political landscape.

New Zealand's commitment to unitary statehood marks it out from Britain's other former settler colonies. Earl Grey's plan for a quasi-federal structure in New Zealand, distinctive though it was, fits within a broader pattern: his push for federation of the Australian colonies in the wake of the union of Upper and Lower Canada.[3] From 1876, however, New Zealand diverged from the Canadian experience, while Australia and South Africa converged on it as they eventually followed the example of Canada's 1867 confederation. Those three dominions were all created as federations and to this day are divided into provinces or states, albeit with attenuated powers. The US had markedly different origins, but it too began as a federation of former British settler colonies and its constituent states remain prominent and potent. New Zealand represents a striking reversal of the trend from colonial statehood to independent federation.

The provincial experience did not, however, pass without mention or consequence for the federation of settler colonies. Thomas D'Arcy McGee, one of the fathers of Canadian confederation, published a pamphlet in 1865 that praised New Zealand's provincial system. New Zealand offered an example to Canada, especially as a fellow British settler society; the presence of a central government with wide powers above provinces appealed to McGee, who believed the best federations were those with a strong centre.[4] For this reason, though, New Zealand's system did not appeal to other Canadians – either for failing to sufficiently protect the powers of each province or, in the case of William Ross of Nova Scotia, for illustrating the ills of federalism through an expensive multiplicity of government organs.[5] New Zealand's system ultimately had little influence on Canada, where confederation granted a greater degree of provincial autonomy to ensure the support of the Maritime provinces.[6]

There is a stronger link between provincialism and the federation of Australia's six colonies in 1901 – not in the design of the federation but in its composition. New Zealand stayed distant while Australia federated. Australia had been nudged in the direction of federation first by Earl Grey and then from the 1880s by indefatigable local campaigners such as Henry Parkes, Edmund Barton and Alfred Deakin. The Australian world then was really an Australasian world that encompassed New Zealand. It is often forgotten today that in the second half of the nineteenth century the relationship between Victoria and Tasmania, for example, was no different from that between Victoria and New Zealand – a memory lapse resulting from what Tony Ballantyne eloquently calls the anachronistic deployment of the nation-state.[7] New Zealand was invited to join the Australian federation but persistently declined. The most compelling reasons were a loss of independence; fears that a

The cartoonist Scatz, in the *New Zealand Graphic* of 22 December 1900, depicts Father Christmas making a 'federal plum pudding'. He has already included the six Australian colonies and looks quizzically at New Zealand on the shelf.

J-040-008, Alexander Turnbull Library, Wellington

federal parliament would impose protective tariffs on trade; distance, with the 1200 miles (1930 km) of the Tasman Sea described famously as 1200 impediments; and misgivings about white Australia's relations with Aboriginal peoples, which lagged behind those between Pākehā and Māori.[8] The provinces also reared their heads. Might Australia produce its own Vogel who would abolish the states, robbing New Zealand of whatever autonomy it might initially possess within a federation? Some provincialists, pushing their slowly dying cause in the 1880s, suggested that a provincial system be revived within New Zealand as an alternative to federating with the Australian colonies.[9] At the 1891 Australasian federation conference an elderly George Grey sang the praises of the 1852 New Zealand constitution that he had written. With a predictable lack of success, he even proposed that the Australian constitution replace nominated state governors with an elected executive akin to the provincial superintendents.[10]

The fear of distance, as Ged Martin notes, represented a continuation of the current of localism so pervasive in New Zealand since the 1840s.[11] Each of the Australian colonies, apart from Queensland and Tasmania, had one clearly dominant social, political and economic hub that served as capital and transport centre. New Zealand, on the other hand, was still reconciling itself to post-provincial life as a unitary colony, seeking to balance the demands of competing regions of comparable size and power. A New Zealand national identity was only nascent and many Pākehā were accustomed to identifying with their region first. Being subsumed as part of a federation – especially one with a political centre of gravity on the other side of an ocean – was not a particularly compelling prospect.[12] If hinterlands had been mistreated by governments within New Zealand, how much more ignorant would a government across the Tasman be? Provincialism may not have been the most prominent argument in the debate about New Zealand's participation in Australian federation, but the negative experience of one quasi-federal system provided New Zealanders with reasons to resist when considering another federal proposal.

The abolition of the provinces does not fit neatly within Norman Davies' categories of state demise introduced at the beginning of this book.[13] Was provincialism's demise simply a case of infant mortality? No. There were no vultures circling at provincialism's birth, just a few opportunistic centralist seagulls. The provinces, despite the imprecise manner in which they were framed, possessed a full governmental toolkit and, most importantly, enjoyed the primary loyalty of electors. They were not doomed from the outset; their advantages were squandered, not stolen. Was provincialism's demise little more than liquidation? This concept of political failure explains the demise of a state through the consensual separation of its constituent components or, veering into the realm of merger, the acquisition of one state by another. It does not explain the elimination of an intermediate level of government within a single country. It is possible to shoehorn the provinces into either category but they fit uncomfortably and a better category can be framed.

Rather than succumbing to infant mortality or disappearing through liquidation, the provinces were the subject of amputation. In the same way as a formerly healthy limb can become irreparably damaged and discarded while the rest of the body continues to live, grow and thrive, the once powerful provinces became irredeemable failures and were discarded unceremoniously while New

Zealand continued to develop, expand and prosper. The removal of provinces became necessary for the long-term health of the New Zealand body politic. An objection may be that amputation leaves a disfiguring stump. This can be answered readily: the 'false limb' of hundreds of local government bodies that stood in for provincialism became more unwieldy than the one it replaced. Yet as artificial legs have evolved from clunky wooden pegs of pirate clichés to the technological sophistication of prosthetic limbs, so too has New Zealand's local government undergone improvements to meet the changing needs of cities, towns and regions.

History is testament to the difficulties of fashioning appropriate sub-national government for New Zealand in the wake of abolition. Unfortunately, these difficulties and their solutions are poorly understood as a result of inattention from historians and political scientists.[14] Achieving a balance between local control of local affairs, shifting demographics and the dictates of geography is a formidable juggling act and the balls have often been dropped. Some regions may be small in population but possess interests markedly different from those of their neighbours. This was captured vividly by the discord in some of New Zealand's smallest provinces – Picton and Blenheim squabbling over which would be capital of Marlborough, and Greymouth's persistent threats to separate from Hokitika-led Westland. Such problems endure. Any attempt to create new province-like authorities encompassing large amounts of territory and people would form political units that grouped together regions with divergent expectations and needs. The answer from 1876 to 1989 was to devolve government to as local a level as possible, with new authorities created, reformed and terminated frequently, but this generated excessive bureaucracy for a country whose population did not reach even three million until 1974.

The key lesson of provincialism is that a uniform system of local government is impractical for New Zealand. Its economy, geography and patterns of settlement require flexible solutions and administration to respond to changing demands and demographics. What worked for Canterbury and Otago in the provincial era did not work for Marlborough or Southland; what worked for Westland during the gold rush was unsuitable when its heyday passed; demographic shifts of the twentieth century that saw the North Island's population surge at the expense of the South would have posed serious difficulties had provincialism remained operative. Abolishing the provinces allowed New Zealand to avoid some of the problems that have afflicted Australia and Canada. Both have had to employ elaborate fiscal equalisation measures within their federations, engendering an imbalance between the responsibilities and the financial capacity of their states or provinces. Canada has shown modest flexibility in adjusting borders and creating new provinces or territories as regions developed, mainly in the first four decades after confederation, but regional aspirations for statehood have been consistently thwarted in Australia. It has been described as representing a constitutional 'frozen continent'.[15] No new state has been introduced to the federation even as demographics have shifted and local needs changed, much to the displeasure of regions such as North Queensland. A uniform system can be difficult to craft and maintain anywhere; New Zealand, had it retained provincialism, would have faced great challenges.

Abolishing the provinces was not a cure-all, however, and local government has undergone many changes since 1876. A balance must be struck between a narrowly prescriptive or functional approach to sub-national government, where local bodies exist only to provide activities predetermined by the central state, and an exaggerated emphasis on local autonomy that demands so much devolution of power that consistency and cohesion between regions are lost. The provincial period fell victim to the latter, as the provinces became too much of a threat for the central government to tolerate – and too much of a liability to accept. New Zealand has since experienced arrangements that are often contradictory in their aims. The 1876–1989 counties were intended to be closer to home for electors, to provide a greater level of local autonomy in decisionmaking, yet they were designed to administer narrow, specific functions delegated by Wellington.[16] By the second half of the twentieth century, local government required wide-ranging reforms to resolve the contradictions and shortcomings of the counties.

The current system of regional and territorial authorities is by no means static. At first sight it appears to be a well-considered response to New Zealand's distinctive problems. Sixty-seven city and district councils (the territorial authorities) are responsible for local concerns such as building consents, libraries, sewerage and local roads. These are overlaid with 16 complementary regional councils for wider issues, including environmental management and public transport. Five of the regions and the Chatham Islands are unitary authorities, possessing the responsibilities of both a regional and a territorial authority. Yet this system has not settled. Less than 20 years after the upheavals of 1989, a reform programme began in 2007 that created the Auckland 'supercity' in 2010, a unitary authority that merged the Auckland Regional Council with seven city and district councils.

In the wake of Auckland's reorganisation there has been a push to create supercities or enlarged unitary authorities in Hawke's Bay, Nelson–Tasman, Northland

and Wellington.[17] Provincialism echoes throughout these proposals as some New Zealanders look for larger, more powerful authorities in response to perceived shortcomings and failures of a system with authority split between multiple smaller bodies. In 2012 the National government of John Key commenced the Better Local Government programme of reforms.[18] These place a premium on achieving economic efficiencies by increasing centralisation, limiting local autonomy and prioritising a very functional interpretation of local government. As part of this programme the Local Government Act 2002 was amended in December 2012 to alter significantly the process for reorganising local authorities. The Local Government Commission, which has operated since 1947, passed judgement on three possible amalgamations in 2015. It rejected those in Northland and Wellington; that for Hawke's Bay went to a local referendum, at which it was defeated. Central Hawke's Bay, Napier and Wairoa voted firmly against amalgamation; only Hastings, by a narrow margin, endorsed it.[19] This replicated the fate of a plan to merge Nelson and Tasman, initiated in 2010 prior to the Key government's reforms. At an April 2012 referendum a majority of Nelson electors voted in favour but Tasman was unequivocally opposed and the amalgamation failed.[20] There is scope to save money within the current system, but reforms should not be fixated on narrowly defined economic indicators, become blind to the broader causes of discontent with local government, or overlook the fears of neglect when administration is insufficiently localised. The potential to form supercities where required indicates that the current system may possess some of the flexibility necessary in New Zealand, but an emphasis on centralisation ignores the historical need for freedom to make local adaptations.

How can abolition inform planning in the twenty-first century? New Zealanders are concerned with efficiency and achieving results, but not necessarily in accordance with a neoliberal understanding of those terms. They want meaningful engagement with local administration but they do not want a plethora of authorities that possess overlapping responsibilities and competing, even mutually exclusive priorities. Objectives are sometimes in conflict: electors are disdainful of an inability to co-operate on matters of national or regional importance but remain fiercely determined that their locality receives its 'fair share' of resources and is not disadvantaged. The vote to abolish the provinces was not a vote in favour of small government; it was a vote to replace a failed intermediate tier of government with an increasingly large central state with wide responsibilities and exclusive legislative competence, augmented by a well-stocked system of local bodies.

An understanding of 'efficiency' as streamlined authority based on small government and user-pays principles ignores a lengthy history of New Zealanders seeking community gains through the activity, administration and intervention of governments at all levels. New Zealanders judge their local governments not by theoretical frameworks or ideologies, but by tangible outcomes. Are roads safe and usable? Is public transport accessible and convenient? Do councils pay attention to all electors or do they bicker among themselves and with neighbours? Little has changed in this regard since the 1850s.

Support or rejection of sub-national governments cannot be boiled down to narrow goals of economic reform, be they pursued by right- or left-wing politicians. New Zealanders are concerned with regional distribution that is fair and equitable, and with development that confers social and cultural benefits as well as economic gains. In the provincial era development was understood as the state providing necessary services in a young society without the private means to sustain large infrastructural projects. Today that passion for development is understood as providing measures that are environmentally friendly, socially inclusive and technologically advanced. In a small country without the economies of scale that attract private provision of services in larger nations, the public continues to see sub-national government as having a frontline responsibility for developmental needs. Attempts to reduce local government to small and feeble authorities under Wellington's control are doomed to unpopularity. It is false to assume that dissatisfaction with local bodies because of poor outcomes indicates deeper dissatisfaction with the role of government in society. If the abolition of the provinces in the nineteenth century and the drive for amalgamations and supercities in the early twenty-first century are indicative of anything, it is that New Zealanders have limited patience for authorities that lack vision and become mired in petty squabbles. Institutions must be able to co-operate if they want support from electors.

It is no surprise, therefore, that public works, especially railways, provide a common thread throughout provincial history. This theme gets to the heart of what New Zealanders wanted from their provinces, why they did not get it, what alternatives were offered and how they responded. Explanations that rely on warfare as a driver of centralisation are inadequate. They fail to recognise the condition of the provinces themselves or to acknowledge the forces that most affected the popularity of the provincial system in the minds of electors. A fixation on forest conservation policy misses the bigger picture; by taking this one policy in isolation, it is mistaken for a cause, when it was a single event in a much wider context.

The appeal of a financial explanation is obvious – the provinces, by and large, were insolvent and New Zealand wanted better conditions on the London money market to finance its lofty developmental ambitions – but this explanation is also too superficial. It fails to recognise how the provinces became insolvent in the first place, or why electors asked their provincial governments to raise so much money. Assumptions of London's influence are misdirected; the initiative came from settlers themselves and the Colonial Office declined to intervene. In any case, boosters such as James Macandrew drove provincial politics to a significant degree with their unceasing confidence that, whatever the current circumstances, riches lay just ahead. Loans and insolvency were products of public works policy and indicative of deeper problems. Present and future reformers would do well to avoid mistaking symptoms for the disease or their reforms will lack staying power. Effective reforms cannot be restricted to short-term needs, as when the provinces were created; or to controversies, such as those creating impecunious new provinces; or be drafted on the run, in the case of the county system. They must meet the core expectations of electors.

The demand for public works, for investment and for development in essential services made the provinces sufficiently destitute for abolition to become compelling. When New Zealanders cast their ballots in 1875–76 they were not going to be persuaded by abstract financial considerations; they voted on the basis of everyday experience. Roads that became impassable seas of mud in winter, splintered and inoperable wooden railways, other railway projects abandoned in the course of construction, shabby wharves, incomplete surveys and inadequate public lighting were very persuasive. The neglect of hinterlands, denied even basic amenities by distant and seemingly forgetful councils, fostered deep resentment. Settlers could not ignore the realities they experienced whenever they stepped outside. They wanted to improve their lot, and this required the prompt and competent provision of public works. The provinces failed this test. Vogel gave New Zealanders an alternative vision and they embraced it. Abolition, once unthinkable, became a reality when electors went to the polls dreaming on a railway track.

Have we ever been here before,
rushing headlong at the floor?
Leave me dreaming on a railway track …

'PURE NARCOTIC', PORCUPINE TREE

Appendices

APPENDIX A: Population of the Provinces[1]

	1854	1858 (Pākehā)	1858 (Māori)	1861	1864	1867	1871[2]	1874
Auckland	11,919	18,177	38,269	24,420	42,132	48,321	62,335	67,451
Taranaki	2094	2650	3015	2044	4374	4359	4480	5465
Wellington	6231	11,753	11,772	12,566	14,987	21,950	24,001	29,790
Hawke's Bay	—	1514	—	2611	3770	5283	6059	9228
Nelson	5858	9272	1120	9952	11,910	23,814	22,501	22,558
Marlborough	—	—	—	2299	5519	4371	5235	6145
Canterbury	3895	8967	638	16,040	32,276[3]	38,333	46,801	58,775
Westland	—	—	—	—	—	15,533	15,357	14,860
Otago	2557	6944	525	27,163[4]	49,019	48,577	60,722	85,113
Southland	—	—	—	1820	8085	7943	8769	—
NAT'L TOTAL[5]	32,554	59,328	56,049	99,021	172,158	218,668	256,393	299,514

Totals for the individual provinces and 'national total' represent the Pākehā civilian population, i.e. exclusive of British soldiers. Until the end of the 1860s these soldiers contributed an additional population of approximately 2000 to 12,000, peaking in the 1864 census. Civilian figures for 1853 were unfortunately incomplete because of a lack of returns from Wellington and Canterbury. At the dawn of the provinces, however, the Pākehā civilian population in Auckland was 10,833; Taranaki 1985; Nelson 5148; Otago 2391.

Māori were not included in the census. However, a specific Māori census was undertaken in 1857–58, the numbers of which are given. The Nelson figures are from 1855; the Wellington figure includes Hawke's Bay. Because of the inconsistent time period, Pākehā and Māori totals are not combined.

Notes

1   Data compiled from relevant years of *Statistics of New Zealand*. All years represent official census returns except 1854, which represents official estimates.
2   Figures for Otago and Southland reflect their pre-reunion borders.
3   This figure reflects the sudden spike in population due to the start of the West Coast gold rush; Canterbury's population in 1863 was 20,432.
4   This figure was estimated to exclude 3000 miners 'in different gullies and on the roads, on the day when the Census was taken'.
5   The national total is higher than the total for the several provinces from 1858 because of Stewart Island and the Chatham Islands. Stewart Island was counted separately 1858–61; it is included in Southland from 1864. The Chatham Islands were counted in the 1858 Māori census, and then in Pākehā censuses from 1861.

APPENDIX B: Colonial Revenue, Expenditure and Indebtedness[1]

Reliable and complete expenditure and indebtedness figures are not available for 1853–61; railway expenditure by the central government did not begin in earnest until 1871. Figures for debt before the loan consolidation of 1867 include provincial debt.

Year	Revenue (£ 000)	Expenditure (total, £ 000)	Expenditure (railways, £ 000)[2]	Indebtedness (£ 000)[3]
1853	80			
1854	111			
1855	111			
1856	108			
1857	154			
1858	179			
1859	208			
1860	233			
1861	324			
1862	761	752		876
1863	1,317	1,331		1,290
1864	2,928	2,758		2,219
1865	3,253	3,335		4,369
1866	2,784	2,497		5,436
1867	3,779	3,531		5,781
1868	4,386	4,228		7,183
1869	5,971	6,369		7,361
1870	1,980	2,090		7,842
1871	2,293	1,745	101	8,901
1872	2,311	2,239	212	9,985
1873	3,951	4,100	632	10,914
1874	5,879	5,715	1,115	13,367
1875	7,733	6,366	1,997	17,400

Notes
1 Data from G.T. Bloomfield, *New Zealand: A handbook of historical statistics* (Boston: G.K. Hall & Co., 1984) and cross-checked with selected years of *Statistics of New Zealand* for accuracy.
2 These figures represent central expenditure only; Canterbury and Otago's expenditure is not included. Unlike the other figures, which are for the calendar year, these figures are for the financial year ending on 30 June of the next year.
3 These figures are the total debentures in circulation, not the total debentures authorised, which in many years was much greater.

APPENDIX C: Provincial Revenue and Expenditure

The following tables present the annual revenue and expenditure for the 10 provinces. The primary purpose is to illustrate provincial expenditure on public works, and this is subdivided into two categories: 'roads, railways, telegraphs' to capture expenditure on opening up land and creating hinterland and interprovincial links; and 'other public works' to capture all other expenditure on the progress industry. *Statistics of New Zealand* published provincial revenue from 1853, but did not include expenditure until 1862. Consequently, each table presents full figures for 1862 and then in three-year intervals from 1864 to abolition. For some provinces, I have accessed or calculated expenditure for earlier years for comparison, or provided the provincial estimates of expenditure. For other provinces, revenue before 1862 is listed in three-year intervals.

Revenue and Expenditure for Auckland Province[1]

Early revenue: £74,964.3.5 (1853); £71,699.16.3 (1856); £80,511.7.10 (1859).

	1862 (£)	1864 (£)	1867 (£)	1870 (£)	1873 (£)	1876 (£)[2]
REVENUE	80,514.8.5	269,815.10.6	168,707.6.1	147,885.15.2	90,468.4.10	139,893.7.5
Expenditure:						
Interest, sinking fund	4,500.0.0	9,705.15.6	31,575.1.11	0	0	0
Executive, legislative, judicial[3]	13,648.10.9	22,668.10.1	20,680.0.10	11,032.14.8	14,777.7.6	20,028.0.3
Roads, railways, telegraphs[4]	11,885.10.3	98,456.19.11	42,675.6.11	15,410.15.0	12,013.9.7	19,960.17.9
Other public works and immigration[5]	12,953.16.7	30,903.6.4	23,389.6.7	51,144.16.11	26,759.8.9	28,221.11.4
Other expenditure[6]	30,049.15.1	105,556.5.4	48,245.7.9	70,245.12.4	30,040.14.8	42,998.4.4
TOTAL EXPENDITURE	73,037.12.8	267,290.17.2	166,565.4.0	147,833.18.11	83,591.0.6	111,208.13.8

The surging revenue and expenditure of 1864 reflects the boom in commercial and public works activity that accompanied war in the Waikato and that preceded the crash of the latter half of the 1860s. The remarkably high expenditure for other public works in 1870 is on account of the Thames gold rush.

Notes for Auckland Province
1   Data compiled from relevant years of *Statistics of New Zealand*.
2   As this is for the calendar year, it includes the two months after the abolition of the provinces, when the former provincial authorities administered their 'provincial district' on behalf of the central government.
3   This category includes all executive and legislative expenses, including salaries of public officials, and judicial expenses, including magistrate's courts, police and prisons.
4   This category includes the 'roads and public works' category of 1862–64, later expanded into individual categories for roads, railways and telegraphs. Some harbour works and other expenses were also included in these figures in some years and I have been unable to separate these. This category encompasses both initial and recurrent expenditure.
5   This category includes hospitals, steam communication, most harbour expenditure, goldfields, lands and surveys, public buildings, and all other public works expenses.
6   This category includes education, registration of deeds, receipts in aid repaid, advances, deposits repaid and small sums for the purchase of Māori land.

Revenue and Expenditure for Taranaki Province[1]

Early revenue: £6,557.5.11 (1853); £4,718.11.10 (1856); £6,079.15.5 (1859).

	1862 (£)	1864 (£)	1867 (£)	1870 (£)	1873 (£)	1876 (£)[2]
REVENUE	15,179.16.6	52,346.15.2	12,317.4.9	7,477.4.10	4,465.14.10	34,897.15.11
Expenditure:						
Interest, sinking fund	0	246.16.7	600.0.0	0	0	0
Executive, legislative, judicial[3]	2,094.2.1	2,869.13.5	1,996.15.0	1,498.11.3	1,508.7.6	2,448.17.4
Roads and works[4]	1,905.5.11	10,435.7.0	2,837.10.0	535.15.2	2,166.17.10	18,854.16.5
Other public works and immigration[5]	5,020.8.7	10,745.19.10	1,730.11.3	1,890.11.6	1,366.14.8	8,631.15.5
Other expenditure[6]	3,568.11.9	28,732.13.9	5,147.3.8	2,212.19.9	1,171.18.3	5,477.2.0
TOTAL EXPENDITURE	12,588.8.4	53,030.10.7	12,311.19.11	6,137.17.8	6,213.18.3	35,412.11.2

A breakdown of other expenditure reveals just how dire the situation in Taranaki was during the 1860s: the educational component was a mere £7.4.3 in 1862 and nothing in 1867.

Notes for Taranaki Province
1   Data compiled from relevant years of *Statistics of New Zealand*.
2   As this is for the calendar year, it includes the two months after the abolition of the provinces, when the former provincial authorities administered their 'provincial district' on behalf of the central government.
3   This category includes all executive and legislative expenses, including salaries of public officials, and judicial expenses, including magistrate's courts, police and prisons.
4   This category includes the 'roads and public works' category of 1862–64, later expanded into individual categories for roads, railways and telegraphs. For Taranaki, however, its expenditure rarely extended beyond roads. Some harbour works and other expenses were also included in these figures in some years and I have been unable to separate these. This category encompasses both initial and recurrent expenditure.
5   This category includes hospitals, steam communication, most harbour expenditure, goldfields, lands and surveys, public buildings and all other public works expenses.
6   This category includes education, registration of deeds, receipts in aid repaid, advances and deposits repaid.

Revenue and Expenditure for Wellington Province[1]

	1857 (£)	1862 (£)	1864 (£)	1867 (£)	1870 (£)	1873 (£)	1876 (£)[2]
REVENUE	71,087.12.8	79,578.3.6	145,065.14.10	245,210.0.9	54,664.2.3	105,666.2.4	167,103.2.10
Expenditure:							
Interest, sinking fund	0	4,008.7.5	12,074.1.2	17,224.19.7	4,576.14.6	0	0
Executive, legislative, judicial[3]	9,088.12.6	9,055.1.5	10,537.0.7	13,166.17.5	7,114.7.3	11,197.11.5	18,350.15.1
Roads, railways, telegraphs[4]	73,415.17.0	40,725.11.11	43,275.15.0	47,212.3.6	4,735.19.3	41,744.16.5	29,397.12.6
Other public works and immigration[5]	95,747.19.6	8,475.7.7	10,494.2.3	35,654.2.1	12,248.13.7	18,331.18.3	71,244.3.7
Other expenditure[6]	4,845.5.0	31,002.2.2	62,208.0.5	131,951.18.2	9,755.19.11	29,084.10.1	48,558.7.8
TOTAL EXPNDTR	183,097.14.0	93,266.10.6	138,588.19.5	245,210.0.9	38,431.14.6	100,358.16.2	167,550.18.10

Revenue in 1853 was £35,772.1.7. The 1857 expenditure figures, which are the official estimates, reflect the bold, misplaced optimism of the early provincial years. The 1857 estimates of revenue amounted to only £57,605.18.6 without borrowing or £178,605.18.6 with anticipated loans – still not enough to cover the projected expenditure. Nonetheless, loans were raised and revenue actually exceeded the estimates.

Notes for Wellington Province

1   Data compiled from relevant years of *Statistics of New Zealand*, except expenditure for 1857, which is sourced from the *Acts and Proceedings of the Provincial Council of Wellington*.
2   As this is for the calendar year, it includes the two months after the abolition of the provinces, when the former provincial authorities administered their 'provincial district' on behalf of the central government.
3   This category includes all executive and legislative expenses, including salaries of public officials, and judicial expenses, including magistrate's courts, police and prisons.
4   This category includes the 'roads and public works' category of 1862–64, later expanded into individual categories for roads, railways and telegraphs. Some harbour works and other expenses were also included in these figures in some years and I have been unable to separate these. This category encompasses both initial and recurrent expenditure.
5   This category includes hospitals, steam communication, most harbour expenditure, goldfields, lands and surveys, public buildings and all other public works expenses. In 1864 and 1876 it includes harbour reclamation works.
6   This category includes education, registration of deeds, receipts in aid repaid, advances and deposits repaid. In 1864 it includes the purchase of the Manawatu.

Revenue and Expenditure for Hawke's Bay Province[1]

	1862 (£)	1864 (£)	1867 (£)	1870 (£)	1873 (£)	1876 (£)[2]
REVENUE	33,928.5.0	45,317.7.11	41,621.10.5	27,016.9.3	75,776.2.0	45,172.5.9
Expenditure:						
Interest, sinking fund	0	0	132.0.0	0	0	0
Executive, legislative, judicial[3]	3,158.2.5	4,310.0.9	5,098.0.0	3,290.17.3	4,046.10.1	5,421.2.11
Roads, railways, telegraphs[4]	13,153.1.1	19,027.7.6	12,538.11.7	5,395.5.6	13,153.16.4	20,987.17.11
Other public works and immigration[5]	2,583.13.8	6,148.2.1	7,843.8.2	3,021.19.5	3,839.3.2	8,168.17.8
Other expenditure[6]	11,843.14.8	10,943.12.3	19,009.10.8	8,659.1.3	10,522.18.8	12,085.1.1
TOTAL EXPENDITURE	30,738.11.10	40,429.2.7	44,621.10.5	20,367.3.5	31,562.8.3	46,662.19.7

Revenue in 1859, the first full calendar year of Hawke's Bay Province's existence, was £37,041.0.5.

Notes for Hawke's Bay Province
1   Data compiled from relevant years of *Statistics of New Zealand*.
2   As this is for the calendar year, it includes the two months after the abolition of the provinces, when the former provincial authorities administered their 'provincial district' on behalf of the central government.
3   This category includes all executive and legislative expenses, including salaries of public officials, and judicial expenses, including magistrate's courts, police and prisons.
4   This category includes the 'roads and public works' category of 1862–64, later expanded into individual categories for roads, railways and telegraphs. Some harbour works and other expenses were also included in these figures in some years and I have been unable to separate these. This category encompasses both initial and recurrent expenditure.
5   This category includes hospitals, steam communication, most harbour expenditure, goldfields, lands and surveys, public buildings and all other public works expenses.
6   This category includes education, registration of deeds, receipts in aid repaid, advances and deposits repaid.

Revenue and Expenditure for Nelson Province[1]

	1855 (£)[2]	1862 (£)	1864 (£)	1867 (£)	1870 (£)	1873 (£)	1876 (£)[3]
REVENUE	31,619.5.5	78,186.2.11	42,173.18.5	162,518.9.7	99,049.8.6	75,174.0.4	71,872.19.4
Expenditure:							
Interest, sinking fund	0	3,534.19.3	2,356.12.10	1,178.6.5	0	0	0
Executive, legislative, judicial[4]	5,206.4.10	4,373.1.7	6,846.0.10	7,090.3.4	7,173.4.1	11,398.4.9	8,744.18.0
Roads, railways, telegraphs[5]	21,280.17.0	20,805.4.1	15,068.10.5	74,382.12.0	26,145.12.7	16,784.12.2	12,350.10.8
Other public works and immigration[6]		8,021.18.10	8,580.11.1	37,430.19.1	33,286.5.7	27,484.17.1	22,793.0.8
Other expenditure[7]	1,420.1.8	6,568.6.1	12,223.1.3	58,594.6.1	18,604.15.0	17,038.11.4	27,984.10.0
TOTAL EXPENDITURE	27,907.3.6	43,303.9.10	45,074.16.5	178,676.6.11	85,209.17.3	72,706.5.4	71,872.19.4

Notes for Nelson Province

1   Data compiled from relevant years of *Statistics of New Zealand* except 1855, which is from *Statistics of the Province of Nelson, New Zealand for the Year 1855*.
2   This figure is for the financial year ending 30 September 1855. All other figures represent calendar years. It is not possible to separate public works expenditure for 1855 in a manner that conforms to the standard for subsequent years.
3   As this is for the calendar year, it includes the two months after the abolition of the provinces, when the former provincial authorities administered their 'provincial district' on behalf of the central government.
4   This category includes all executive and legislative expenses, including salaries of public officials, and judicial expenses, including magistrate's courts, police and prisons.
5   This category includes the 'roads and public works' category of 1862–64, later expanded into individual categories for roads, railways and telegraphs. Some harbour works and other expenses were also included in these figures in some years and I have been unable to separate these. This category encompasses both initial and recurrent expenditure.
6   This category includes hospitals, steam communication, most harbour expenditure, goldfields, lands and surveys, public buildings and all other public works expenses.
7   This category includes education, registration of deeds, receipts in aid repaid, advances and deposits repaid.

Revenue and Expenditure for Marlborough Province[1]

	1862 (£)	1864 (£)	1867 (£)	1870 (£)	1873 (£)	1876 (£)[2]
REVENUE	22,288.8.2	44,246.4.4	14,773.5.1	13,061.17.4	12,458.11.2	14,739.18.3
Expenditure:						
Interest, sinking fund	2,453.11.6	1,316.5.4	603.12.5	0	0	0
Executive, legislative, judicial[3]	1,457.4.6	9,355.17.4	2,995.11.5	2,954.17.11	2,558.7.2	2,175.5.0
Roads, railways, telegraphs[4]	19,086.14.8	30,165.11.11	4,969.12.7	2,191.14.0	1,233.16.8	3,753.1.9
Other public works and immigration[5]	3,826.9.5	4,014.7.7	3,378.17.3	2,821.8.2	2,777.13.3	2,400.13.8
Other expenditure[6]	3,036.10.6	14,067.8.5	2,816.11.5	1,357.13.7	3,700.1.6	6,410.17.10
TOTAL EXPENDITURE	29,860.10.7	58,919.10.7	14,764.5.1	9,325.13.8	10,269.18.7	14,739.18.3

Revenue in 1860, the first full calendar year of Marlborough Province's existence, was £20,721.12.1.

These figures capture how the early optimism of Marlborough, stoked by the minor Wakamarina gold rush, crashed by the late 1860s. The most embarrassing year was 1869, during which the paltry expenditure of £9,366 still exceeded revenue of £8,179.

Notes for Marlborough Province

1   Data compiled from relevant years of *Statistics of New Zealand*.
2   As this is for the calendar year, it includes the two months after the abolition of the provinces, when the former provincial authorities administered their 'provincial district' on behalf of the central government.
3   This category includes all executive and legislative expenses, including salaries of public officials, and judicial expenses, including magistrate's courts, police and prisons.
4   This category includes the 'roads and public works' category of 1862–64, later expanded into individual categories for roads, railways and telegraphs. Some harbour works and other expenses were also included in these figures in some years and I have been unable to separate these. This category encompasses both initial and recurrent expenditure.
5   This category includes hospitals, steam communication, most harbour expenditure, goldfields, lands and surveys, public buildings and all other public works expenses.
6   This category includes education, registration of deeds, receipts in aid repaid, advances and deposits repaid.

Revenue and Expenditure for Canterbury Province[1]

Early revenue: £9,176.3.1 (1853); £27,519.15.4 (1856); £92,825.8.3 (1859).

	1862 (£)	1864 (£)	1867 (£)	1870 (£)	1873 (£)	1876 (£)[2]
REVENUE	273,970.16.3	367,482.9.2	428,754.2.5	167,612.15.6	701,287.7.5	844,232.3.1
Expenditure:						
Interest, sinking fund	5,060.9.9	10,814.0.6	16,592.10.0	8,158.3.9	6,351.16.7	26,441.9.9
Executive, legislative, judicial[3]	13,629.8.11	22,801.1.5	50,115.2.6	16,301.15.9	22,150.10.5	40,294.0.0
Roads, railways, telegraphs[4]	134,488.6.10	227,603.18.11	208,356.13.7	80,262.17.11	219,852.16.0	495,356.16.0
Other public works and immigration[5]	52,077.10.11	76,715.16.5	102,456.9.5	35,505.10.2	93,305.17.0	59,299.7.8
Other expenditure[6]	21,150.2.3	35,914.1.4	51,223.6.11	23,422.1.1	54,787.19.2	338,947.18.4
TOTAL EXPENDITURE	226,405.18.8	373,848.18.7	428,754.2.5	163,650.8.8	396,448.19.2	960,339.11.9

Canterbury enjoyed flourishing revenue, with its land fund providing ample security for substantial loans. However, as these figures show, even Canterbury was affected by the nationwide economic stagnation at the end of the 1860s.

Notes for Canterbury Province
1   Data compiled from relevant years of *Statistics of New Zealand*.
2   As this is for the calendar year, it includes the two months after the abolition of the provinces, when the former provincial authorities administered their 'provincial district' on behalf of the central government.
3   This category includes all executive and legislative expenses, including salaries of public officials, and judicial expenses, including magistrate's courts, police and prisons.
4   This category includes the 'roads and public works' category of 1862–64, later expanded into individual categories for roads, railways and telegraphs. Some harbour works and other expenses were also included in these figures in some years and I have been unable to separate these. This category encompasses both initial and recurrent expenditure.
5   This category includes hospitals, steam communication, most harbour expenditure, goldfields, lands and surveys, public buildings and all other public works expenses.
6   This category includes education, registration of deeds, receipts in aid repaid, advances and deposits repaid.

Revenue and Expenditure for Westland County/Province[1]

	1870 (£)	1873 (£)	1876 (£)[2]
REVENUE	75,508.10.4	77,074.3.7	79,012.9.10
Expenditure:			
Interest, sinking fund	313.8.0	586.14.5	8,014.10.3
Executive, legislative, judicial[3]	15,550.11.4	10,529.18.10	10,650.17.1
Roads, railways, telegraphs[4]	18,311.4.8	10,071.17.4	25,541.1.11
Other public works and immigration[5]	16,142.9.9	12,791.9.8	15,408.2.1
Other expenditure[6]	9,896.15.5	38,505.14.9	19,251.4.5
TOTAL EXPENDITURE	60,214.9.2	72,485.15.0	78,865.15.9

Westland achieved autonomy as a county in 1868, with revenue of £104,631 and expenditure of £81,840 in its first year. The most fruitful years of the gold rush preceded separation from Canterbury, and Westland County/Province had to settle the region during the transition from rush euphoria to permanent occupation and large-scale industrial mining.

Notes for Westland County/Province
1   Data compiled from relevant years of *Statistics of New Zealand*.
2   As this is for the calendar year, it includes the two months after the abolition of the provinces, when the former provincial authorities administered their 'provincial district' on behalf of the central government.
3   This category includes all executive and legislative expenses, including salaries of public officials, and judicial expenses, including magistrate's courts, police and prisons.
4   This category includes the 'roads and public works' category of 1862–64, later expanded into individual categories for roads, railways and telegraphs. Some harbour works and other expenses were also included in these figures in some years and I have been unable to separate these. This category encompasses both initial and recurrent expenditure.
5   This category includes hospitals, steam communication, most harbour expenditure, goldfields, lands and surveys, public buildings and all other public works expenses.
6   This category includes education, registration of deeds, receipts in aid repaid, advances and deposits repaid.

Revenue and Expenditure for Otago Province[1]

	1854 (£)[2]	1862 (£)	1864 (£)	1867 (£)	1870 (£)	1873 (£)	1876 (£)[3]
REVENUE	4,495.14.5	284,671.11.9	595,039.14.9	400,570.15.6	377,141.12.1	505,516.15.3	793,606.6.7
Expenditure:							
Interest, sinking fund	0	3,196.2.9	20,955.12.0	37,955.14.10	38,371.3.3	35,834.5.4	28,776.12.9
Executive, legislative, judicial[4]	1,110.16.4	43,418.17.2	85,520.17.1	38,351.5.10	39,163.7.4	39,841.16.0	49,549.4.5
Roads, railways, telegraphs[5]	298.18.5	155,298.3.2	273,107.17.1	181,453.17.11	139,361.12.1	141,441.3.6	421,662.7.5
Other public works and immigration[6]	395.2.3	51,290.16.10	235,543.18.10	58,664.1.9	58,386.8.9	59,669.12.7	78,020.1.5
Other expenditure[7]	209.5.9	42,804.19.2	294,650.5.9	147,816.3.6	126,268.16.5	87,915.3.10	215,598.0.7
TOTAL EXPENDITURE	2,014.2.9	296,008.19.1	909,778.10.9	464,241.3.10	401,551.7.10	364,702.1.3	793,606.6.7

The figures for 1854 are provided to give context to the explosive growth of Otago after the gold rush; revenue steadily improved in the 1850s to £25,345.13.1½ in 1857 and £97,511.4.3 in 1860, the last year before the rush. Like Canterbury, Otago's revenue reflects the nationwide downturn at the end of the 1860s.

Notes for Otago Province
1   Data compiled from relevant years of *Statistics of New Zealand* except 1854, which is from the *Otago Provincial Government Gazette* (7 April 1855).
2   Unlike the other years, which represent calendar years, this represents the financial year ending 30 September 1854.
3   As this is for the calendar year, it includes the two months after the abolition of the provinces, when the former provincial authorities administered their 'provincial district' on behalf of the central government.
4   This category includes all executive and legislative expenses, including salaries of public officials, and judicial expenses, including magistrate's courts, police and prisons.
5   This category includes the 'roads and public works' category of 1862–64, later expanded into individual categories for roads, railways and telegraphs. Some harbour works and other expenses were also included in these figures in some years and I have been unable to separate these. This category encompasses both initial and recurrent expenditure.
6   This category includes hospitals, steam communication, most harbour expenditure, gold fields,

lands and surveys, public buildings and all other public works expenses. In 1864 this category includes £158,033.3.5 expended under the several Otago Loans Acts, some of which belongs in 'roads, railways, telegraphs' but cannot be separated from expenditure on other works such as public buildings and harbours.

7   This category includes education, registration of deeds, receipts in aid repaid, advances and deposits repaid.

Revenue and Expenditure for Southland Province[1]

	1862 (£)	1863 (£)	1864 (£)	1867 (£)
REVENUE	62,020.7.0	87,318.0.1	382,839.3.10[2]	39,148.0.2
Expenditure:				
Interest, sinking fund	1,890.0.0	642.10.0	13,705.0.0	0
Executive, legislative, judicial[3]	7,949.19.2	16,463.16.2	9,704.4.11	5,376.19.10
Roads, railways, telegraphs[4]	29,722.5.7	109,078.13.10	273,515.6.11	7,043.15.1
Other public works and immigration[5]	16,928.5.11	35,248.17.7	22,866.0.10	4,276.19.8
Other expenditure[6]	10,727.1.3	24,754.10.9	63,048.11.2	12,365.9.6
TOTAL EXPENDITURE	67,217.11.11	186,188.8.4	382,839.3.10	29,063.4.1

The figures for 1862–64 capture the wild optimism and excessive spending of early Southland, especially the wooden railway folly. The 1867 figures represent the subsequent years of gloom when revenue was meagre, loans could no longer be obtained and spending was heavily curtailed as a result. The 1870 figures are excluded as they are not particularly meaningful, with Southland's provincial machinery simply winding down ahead of reunion in October of that year.

Notes for Southland Province
1   Data compiled from relevant years of Statistics of New Zealand.
2   £332,071.17.6 of this revenue came from loans, meaning regular provincial revenue was only just over £50,000.
3   This category includes all executive and legislative expenses, including salaries of public officials, and judicial expenses, including magistrate's courts, police and prisons.
4   This category includes the 'roads and public works' category of 1862–64, later expanded into individual categories for roads, railways and telegraphs. Some harbour works and other expenses were also included in these figures in some years and I have been unable to separate these. This category encompasses both initial and recurrent expenditure.
5   This category includes hospitals, steam communication, most harbour expenditure, goldfields, lands and surveys, public buildings and all other public works expenses.
6   This category includes education, registration of deeds, receipts in aid repaid, advances, and deposits repaid.

APPENDIX D: Railways

Operational railways[1]	
YEAR	DISTANCE OPEN FOR TRAFFIC (km)[2]
1863	6
1864	19
1870	74
1873	233
1874	336
1875	872
1876	1156
1880	2073
1892	3008 (first year to exceed 3000)
1909	4304 (first year to exceed 4000)
1926	5050 (first year to exceed 5000)
1952	5696 (greatest extent)
2014	4128

The years after 1876 are presented to show the Great Public Works Policy's long-term consequences, and to place the construction of the 1870s into context. Over a fifth of total railways were constructed in the provincial period and over a third by the end of the works policy's first decade.

Notes

1   Data for 1870 onwards is from the *New Zealand Official Yearbook*, 1894 and G.T. Bloomfield, *New Zealand: A Handbook of Historical Statistics* (Boston: G.K. Hall and Co., 1984), 240, except for the 2014 figure, which is from the *CIA World Factbook*. The figure for 1863 indicates the length of the Christchurch to Ferrymead line at opening; the figure for 1864 adds the Invercargill to Makarewa wooden railway. The total for 1870 would be 87 km if the Makarewa line, then under reconstruction, were included.

2   The totals exclude the horse-drawn Dun Mountain Railway as well as all forms of urban, goldfields and bush tramways.

	Earnings[1]		
	1870 (£)	1873 (£)[2]	1876 (£)[3]
Central: total earnings	—	8,591.0.3	83,049.4.10
Central: profit on workings	—	7,049.3.1	10,975.6.4
Canterbury: total earnings	62,225.2.2	85,075.12.3	231,701.16.4
Canterbury: profit on workings	7,077.13.3	21,802.19.8	62,811.17.9
Otago/Southland: total earnings	400.0.0	20,969.17.3	146,708.7.10
Otago/Southland: profit on workings	27.5.9	—	53,810.3.5
National earnings	62,625.2.2	114,636.9.9	461,459.9.0
National profit on workings	7,104.19.0	—	127,597.7.6
National capital cost	—	1,115,304.12.8	1,639,014.7.9

Until abolition, the provincial governments operated Canterbury and Otago's railways, even though extensions and other capital works were undertaken by the central government from 1871. The first railways operated by the central government (Auckland to Onehunga, Wellington to Lower Hutt and the Foxton to Palmerston North tramway) opened during the 1873/74 financial year. Rapid expansion meant that by abolition the central government operated numerous railways throughout both islands.

Notes
1   All data calculated from relevant years of *Statistics of New Zealand* except central 1873 and capital cost 1876, which are from *AJHR* 1874 E-01, 23, 27–29 and *AJHR* 1876, E-01, 8. Except where noted, data are for the calendar year.
2   Central figures and capital cost are for the financial year ending 30 June 1874. Earnings for the Foxton line do not include June. The national earnings figure thus reflects two slightly different time periods and should accordingly be read with caution. Working expenses for Otago in 1873 are not given; thus a profit on working expenses cannot be calculated for Otago or nationally.
3   Capital cost is for the financial year ending 30 June 1876. This figure was chosen over the figure for 30 June 1877 since it encompasses the crucial 1875–76 election, and the 1876–77 financial year includes only the four final months of provincialism.

APPENDIX E: Voter Participation in 1853

The first table presents voter participation at the 1853 central and provincial election. It is based on D.G. Herron's figures, with minor modifications and editorial insertions where necessary.[1]

Electorate	Members of prov. councils	Voting % for prov. council	Members of the House of Reps	Voting % for House of Reps	Voting % for super-intendency
City of Auckland	6	≥68.6	3	≥61	
Suburbs of Auckland	4	≥67.7	2	N/A	
Southern Division	4	≥55.1	2	≥44	74
Northern Division	4	≥64.5	2	≥58	
Pensioner Settlements	4	≥70.1	2	≥60	
Bay of Islands	2	N/A	1	N/A	
Town of New Plymouth	2	≥62.8	1	N/A	
Grey and Bell	4	≥68.5	1	71	91.5
Omata	3	≥68.4	1	N/A	
City of Wellington	7	≥70.4	3	N/A	
Wellington Country	3	≥63.5	1	57.1	N/A
Wanganui & Rangitikei	2	N/A	1	N/A	
Wairarapa & Hawke's Bay	2	N/A	1	N/A	
Hutt	4	≥80.7	2	N/A	
Town of Nelson	5	≥78.1	2	N/A	
Suburban Districts	1	N/A			
Waimea East	2	N/A	2	>54.5 (as Waimea)	87.4
Waimea South	2	≥75.7			
Waimea West	1	N/A			
Wairau	2	N/A	1	N/A	
Motueka & Massacre Bay	2	≥57.5[2]	1	≥80.8	
Akaroa	2	N/A	1	80	
Town of Christchurch	3	≥75.9	1	72.1	73.9
Christchurch Country	4	≥68.6	2	≥70.4	
Town of Lyttelton	3	≥75.2	1	80	
Town of Dunedin	6	≥46	2	N/A	
Dunedin Country	3	≥62.5	1	N/A	N/A

In multi-member constituencies, where electors could cast as many votes as there were vacancies, it is only possible to estimate the lowest possible number of electors; estimates are marked with '≥'. Herron notes that in most cases, electors exercised all possible votes. N/A indicates that members were elected unopposed.

The second table presents voter turnout at the central and provincial elections in Canterbury in 1853. The figures are sourced from various editions of the *Lyttelton Times*.[3]

Electorate	Votes cast in General Assembly election	Votes cast in provincial council election	Votes cast for superintendency[4]
Town of Christchurch	95	≥98	181
Christchurch Country	≥159	≥156	
Lyttelton	90	≥94	94
Akaroa	44	≥46	43
TOTAL	388	394	318

In multi-member constituencies, where electors could cast as many votes as there were vacancies, it is only possible to estimate the lowest possible number of electors. All estimates are marked with '≥'.

Notes

1   D.G. Herron, 'The structure and course of New Zealand politics, 1853–1858' (PhD thesis, University of Otago, 1959), 115–16.

2   This figure is unreliable. One of the three candidates withdrew at midday on election day, by which point at least 54 votes had been cast. It is impossible to know how many more voters intended to vote and did not once there ceased to be a contest for the vacancies. (*NE*, 27 August 1853, 4.)

3   Statistics are sourced from the following 1853 editions of the *Lyttelton Times* (page numbers bracketed): 23 July (7), 20 August (6), 27 August (7), 3 September (6), 10 September (7), and 17 September (6).

4   Christchurch Country's polling booths were located in the towns of Christchurch and Lyttelton. Thus, Christchurch Country residents voted in those towns for the superintendency election and their totals are counted towards the totals for Town of Christchurch and Lyttelton. It appears that most, if not all, Christchurch Country voters cast their superintendency ballots in Christchurch rather than Lyttelton.

APPENDIX F: External Debt of New Zealand, 1867

These figures are taken from the *Appendices to the Journals of the House of Representatives*.[1] Most provinces had multiple loans; the total amount borrowed is shown.

PROVINCE	AMOUNT BORROWED	RATE OF INTEREST
Auckland	£500,000	6%
Taranaki	£75,000	7–8%
Hawke's Bay	£60,000	6%
Wellington	£155,000	8–10%
Nelson	£54,000	8–10%
Marlborough	N/A[2]	N/A
Canterbury	£830,000	6–8%
Otago	£685,000	6–10%
Southland	£380,000[3]	6%
TOTAL PROVINCIAL LOANS	£2,739,000[4]	
Colony of New Zealand	£3,650,000	4–6%
TOTAL LOANS	£6,389,000	

Notes
1   *AJHR* 1868 A-09, 6.
2   Although Marlborough was impoverished, overdrawn with the bank and indebted to the central government, it did not have any loans to service.
3   This is the sum guaranteed by the central government under the Southland Provincial Debt Act of 1865. Debtors were issued central debentures bearing interest at 6%, hence the interest rate does not reflect the original (higher) rate charged on the debentures when issued in 1863–64.
4   A total of £400,000 of debentures were not raised or issued, but as part of the Consolidated Loan Act and Public Debts Act, £400,000 was provided to take up these debentures.

Abbreviations

AE: *Auckland Examiner*

AJHR: *Appendices to the Journals of the House of Representatives*

ATL: Alexander Turnbull Library

BH: *Bruce Herald*

BPP: *British Parliamentary Papers: Colonies; New Zealand*

DN: *Daily News*

DNZB: *Dictionary of New Zealand Biography*: www.teara.govt.nz/en/biographies

DSC: *Daily Southern Cross*

EH: *Evening Herald*

EP: *Evening Post*

ES: *Evening Star*

GBPD: *Great Britain Parliamentary Debates*

GRA: *Grey River Argus*

HES: *Hokitika Evening Star*

IT: *Invercargill Times*

JHS: *Journal of Henry Sewell*

LT: *Lyttelton Times*

MP: *Marlborough Press*

NE: *Nelson Examiner*

NEM: *Nelson Evening Mail*

NOT: *North Otago Times*

NPA: New Provinces Act

NZ: *New Zealander*

NZH: *New Zealand Herald*

NZJH: *New Zealand Journal of History*

NZS: *New Zealand Spectator*

NZSA: New Zealand Settlements Act

OAP: Ordinances of the Auckland Province

OCP: Ordinances of the Canterbury Province

ODT: *Otago Daily Times*

OT: *Oamaru Times*

OW: *Otago Witness*

PD: *New Zealand Parliamentary Debates* (Hansard)

RAP: *Richmond Atkinson Papers*

SC: *Southern Cross*

SN: *Southland News*

ST: *Southland Times*

TA: *Thames Advertiser*

TarH: *Taranaki Herald*

TimH: *Timaru Herald*

WCT: *West Coast Times*

WI: *Wellington Independent*

Notes

Introduction

1   Philip A. Buckner, *The Transition to Responsible Government: British policy in British North America, 1815–1850* (Westport, CT: Greenwood Press, 1985), chapters 7–8; J.M.S. Careless, *The Union of the Canadas: The growth of Canadian institutions 1841–1857* (Toronto: McClelland and Stewart, 1967); Boyd Hilton, *A Mad, Bad, and Dangerous People? England, 1783–1846* (Oxford: Clarendon Press, 2006), 566–67; Benjamin T. Jones, *Republicanism and Responsible Government: The shaping of democracy in Australia and Canada* (Montréal: McGill-Queen's University Press, 2014), chapters 5–6.

2   W.G. McMinn, *A Constitutional History of Australia* (Oxford: Oxford University Press, 1979), chapter 3; Angela Woollacott, *Settler Society in the Australian Colonies: Self-government and imperial culture* (Oxford: Oxford University Press, 2015), chapter 4; Ann Curthoys and Jessie Mitchell, 'The advent of self-government, 1840s–90', in *The Cambridge History of Australia*, eds Alison Bashford and Stuart Macintyre (Cambridge: Cambridge University Press, 2013), 149–69.

3   H.T. Manning, 'Who ran the British Empire, 1830–1850?', *Journal of British Studies* 5(1), 1965, 89–90.

4   James Belich, *Replenishing the Earth: The settler revolution and the rise of the Anglo-world, 1783–1939* (Oxford: Oxford University Press, 2009), 185; Geoffrey B. Churchman and Tony Hurst, *The Railways of New Zealand: A journey through history* (Auckland: HarperCollins, 1990).

5   Belich, *Replenishing the Earth*, 185–92.

6   W. Rosenberg, 'Capital imports and growth: The case of New Zealand – foreign investment in New Zealand, 1840–1958', *Economic Journal* 71(281), 1961, 93–94.

7   W.P. Morrell, *The Provincial System in New Zealand, 1852–76* (Christchurch: Whitcombe and Tombs, 1964 [1932]).

8   Ibid., 221, 281.

9   I have expanded on this theme in 'A limited express or stopping all stations? Railways and nineteenth-century New Zealand', *Journal of New Zealand Studies* 16, 2013, 133–49 and 'Dreaming on a railway track: Public works and the demise of New Zealand's provinces', *Journal of Transport History*, 36(1), 2015, 1–20.

10   The leading study is Patrick Day, *The Making of the New Zealand Press: A study of the organizational and political concerns of New Zealand newspaper controllers, 1840–1880* (Wellington: Victoria University Press, 1990); also still important is Guy H. Scholefield's *Newspapers in New Zealand* (Wellington: A.H. and A.W. Reed, 1958). For more focused research, see Ross Harvey's wide-ranging scholarship.

11   Catherine Daley, 'Papers from the past, and problems from the present', *Turnbull Library Record* 43, 2010–11, 64–65.

12   D.G. Herron, 'The structure and course of New Zealand politics, 1853–1858' (PhD thesis, University of Otago, 1959).

13   The best study of a provincial government's goldfields policies is A.P.F. Browne, 'The Otago goldfields 1861–1863: Administration and public life' (MA thesis, University of Otago, 1974). For

more on education during the provincial period, see Alan Cumming and Ian Cumming, *History of State Education in New Zealand 1840–1975* (Wellington: Pitman Publishing, 1978), especially 26–85; John Mackey, *The Making of a State Education System: The passing of the New Zealand Education Act, 1877* (London: Geoffrey Chapman, 1967); and Maxine Stephenson, 'Thinking historically: Maori and settler education', in *Introduction to the History of New Zealand Education*, eds Elizabeth Rata and Ros Sullivan (North Shore: Pearson, 2009), 1–15.

14   e.g. J.B. Condliffe, *A Short History of New Zealand*, 8th edn (Christchurch: Whitcombe and Tombs, 1957 [1925]), 140; J.P. Cumming, 'The compact and financial settlement of 1856' (MA thesis, University of Auckland, 1963), 3; K.W. Robinson, 'Sixty years of federation in Australia', *Geographical Review* 51(1), 1961, 2.

15   A good illustration of how time and space has been gradually compressed – and how this has been a lengthy process – is in Eric Pawson, 'Time-space convergence in New Zealand, 1850s to 1990s', *New Zealand Journal of Geography* 94(1), 1992, 14–19.

16   For one of the most prominent recent expositions of the warfare-as-centralisation argument, see Tony Ballantyne, 'The state, politics and power, 1769–1893', in *The New Oxford History of New Zealand*, ed. Giselle Byrnes (Oxford: Oxford University Press, 2009), 112–17. For a brief argument for forestry's importance, see Keith Sinclair, *A History of New Zealand* (Auckland: Penguin, 1991 [1959]), 153.

17   Tom Brooking, *The History of New Zealand* (Westport, CT: Greenwood Press, 2004), 70; G.R. Hawke, *The Making of New Zealand: An economic history* (Cambridge: Cambridge University Press, 1985), 6–7; Muriel F. Lloyd Prichard, *An Economic History of New Zealand to 1939* (Auckland: Collins, 1970), 130–31.

18   Ron Palenski, *The Making of New Zealanders* (Auckland: Auckland University Press, 2012), 19–35.

19   The three leading studies, which have stimulated decades of debate, are Albert Fishlow, *American Railroads and the Transformation of the Antebellum Economy* (Cambridge: Harvard University Press, 1965); Robert William Fogel, *Railroads and American Economic Growth: Essays in econometric history* (Baltimore: Johns Hopkins Press, 1964); and Gary Hawke, *Railways and Economic Growth in England and Wales, 1840–1870* (Oxford: Clarendon Press, 1970).

20   Michael Freeman, *Railways and the Victorian Age* (New Haven and London: Yale University Press, 1999), 19. See also a concise summary of the argument against a narrow economic analysis in Derek Aldcroft, 'The railway age', *Refresh* 13, 1991, 5–8.

21   Two leading studies are John R. Kellett, *Railways and Victorian Cities* (London: Routledge, 1979 [1969]) and Jack Simmons, *The Railway in Town and Country, 1830–1914* (Newton Abbot: David and Charles, 1986).

22   Prominent recent examples include Richard J. Orsi, *Sunset Limited: The Southern Pacific Railroad and the development of the American West* (Berkeley: University of California Press, 2005), Claire Strom, *Profiting from the Plains: The Great Northern Railway and corporate development of the American West* (Seattle: University of Washington Press, 2003), William G. Thomas, *The Iron Way: Railroads, the Civil War, and the making of modern America* (New Haven and London: Yale University Press, 2011) and Richard White, *Railroaded: The Transcontinentals and the making of modern America* (New York: W.W. Norton, 2012). An interesting recent development of Fishlow's previously cited argument is Jeremy Atack, Fred Bateman, Michael Haines and Robert A. Margo, 'Did railroads induce or follow economic growth?: Urbanization and population in the American Midwest, 1850–1860', *Social Science History* 34(2), 2010, 171–97, which argues at least half of the increase in Midwest urbanisation in the late antebellum period may be attributable to railways.

23   Sarah H. Gordon, *Passage to Union: How the railroads transformed American life, 1829–1929* (Chicago: Ivan R. Dee, 1996), 347–48.

24   A.A. den Otter, *The Philosophy of Railways: The transcontinental railway idea in British North America* (Toronto: University of Toronto Press, 1997); John A. Eagle, *The Canadian Pacific Railway and the Development of Western Canada, 1896–1914* (Kingston: McGill–Queen's

University Press, 1989); Paul B. Goodwin Jr, 'The Central Argentine Railway and the economic development of Argentina, 1854–1881', *Hispanic American Historical Review* 57(4), 1977, 613–32; Raymond H. Pulley, 'The railroad and Argentine national development, 1852–1914', *The Americas* 23(1), 1966, 63–75.

25   Neill Atkinson, *Trainland: How railways made New Zealand* (Auckland: Random House, 2007), 20–38; James Watson, *Links: A history of transport and New Zealand society* (Wellington: GP Publications, 1996), 133–35.

26   W.A. Pierre, *Canterbury Provincial Railways: Genesis of the NZR system* (Wellington: New Zealand Railway and Locomotive Society, 1964); J.O.P. Watt, *Southland's Pioneer Railways 1864–1878* (Wellington: New Zealand Railway and Locomotive Society, 1965).

27   Philip Ross May, 'Preface', in *Miners and Militants: Politics in Westland, 1865–1918*, ed. Philip Ross May (Christchurch: Whitcoulls, 1975), x; Keith Sinclair, 'The significance of "the scarecrow ministry"', 1887–1891', in *Studies of a Small Democracy: Essays in honour of Willis Airey*, eds Robert Chapman and Keith Sinclair (Auckland: Blackwood and Janet Paul for the University of Auckland, 1963), 104. For another short allusion to this theme, see Raewyn Dalziel, 'The politics of settlement', in *The Oxford History of New Zealand*, eds W.H. Oliver and B.R. Williams (Wellington and Oxford: Oxford University Press, 1981), 103.

28   Norman Davies, *Vanished Kingdoms: The history of half-forgotten Europe* (London: Penguin, 2011), 732.

29   Bernard Attard, 'Making the colonial state: Development, debt, and warfare in New Zealand, 1853–76', *Australian Economic History Review* 52(2), 2012, 119–22.

30   P.J. Cain and A.G. Hopkins, *British Imperialism, 1688–2000* (Harlow: Longman, 2002 [1993]).

Chapter 1. A Divided Colony

1   The best work is Sonia Cheyne, 'Search for a constitution: People and politics in New Zealand's Crown colony years' (PhD thesis, University of Otago, 1975). See also A.H. McLintock, *Crown Colony Government in New Zealand* (Wellington: R.E. Owen, 1958); Diana Beaglehole, 'Political leadership in Wellington, 1839–1853', in *The Making of Wellington 1800–1914*, eds David Hamer and Roberta Nicholls (Wellington: Victoria University Press, 1990), 165–94; and chapter 2 of W.P. Morrell, *The Provincial System in New Zealand, 1852–76* (Christchurch: Whitcombe and Tombs, 1964 [1932]). Also useful are biographies of leading figures, most notably two of George Grey: J. Rutherford, *Sir George Grey K.C.B., 1812–1898: A study in colonial government* (London: Cassell, 1961) and Edmund Bohan, *To Be a Hero: Sir George Grey, 1812–1898* (Auckland: HarperCollins, 1998). Disappointingly, little is made of the 1846 constitution in Philip Temple, *A Sort of Conscience: The Wakefields* (Auckland: Auckland University Press, 2002).

2   For more on how shipping and New Zealand society shaped each other, see James Watson, *Links: A history of transport and New Zealand society* (Wellington: GP Publications, 1996), chapter 2, especially 54–56 for provincialism. Also valuable, especially for an overview of maritime technology developments, is Gavin McLean, *Captain's Log: New Zealand's maritime history* (Auckland: Hodder Moa Beckett, 2001); chapters 2–3 cover the provincial era. As McLean explains on 55–57, steamers visited infrequently from 1846; the first regular run did not begin until 1854 and a stable service was not provided until the late 1850s.

3   For more on the Hobson/Wellington dispute, the selection of Auckland as capital and the origin of Auckland/Wellington antagonism, see R.C.J. Stone, *From Tamaki-Makau-Rau to Auckland* (Auckland: Auckland University Press, 2001), chapter 10, especially 238–39.

4   J.C. Beaglehole, *Captain Hobson and the New Zealand Company: A study in colonial administration* (Northampton: Department of History of Smith College, 1928) remains a valuable, lively insight into the tensions between Hobson and the company, and the long-standing intrigues into which he was plunged in 1840.

5   David Eastwood, *Government and Community in the English Provinces, 1700–1870* (Houndmills: Macmillan, 1997); K.B. Smellie, *A History of Local Government* (London: George Allen and Unwin, 1968); Sidney Webb and Beatrice Webb, *English Local Government from the Revolution to the Municipal Corporations Act: The parish and the county* (London: Longmans, Green and Co., 1906); Webb and Webb, *English Local Government from the Revolution to the Municipal Corporations Act: The manor and the borough*, 2 vols (London: Longmans, Green and Co., 1908); and for a very brief introduction, B. Keith-Lucas, *English Local Government in the Nineteenth and Twentieth Century* (London: Historical Association, 1977).

6   Sidney Webb and Beatrice Webb, *English Local Government: Statutory authorities for special purposes* (London: Longmans, Green and Co., 1922).

7   Queensland, with a comparably small and scattered population, furnishes a useful comparative example: Pat Zalewski, 'The formation of municipal councils in early Queensland and their antecedents in England in the 19th century', *Queensland History Journal* 21(11), 2012, 763–74.

8   Proclamation of 3 May 1841, enclosure in Hobson to Secretary of State of Colonies, 26 May 1841, *BPP*.

9   Edward Jerningham Wakefield, *Adventure in New Zealand*, ed. Joan Stevens (Christchurch: Whitcombe & Tombs, 1955 [1845]), 197.

10 McLintock, *Crown Colony Government*, 265–67; Richard S. Hill, *Policing the Colonial Frontier: The theory and practice of coercive social and racial control in New Zealand, 1767–1867, Part One* (Wellington: V.R. Ward, 1986), 136–40.

11 *New Zealand Gazette*, 24 July 1841, 2.

12 Hill, *Policing the Colonial Frontier*, 158–77 passim.

13 *New Zealand Gazette*, 26 March 1842, 2.

14 *NE*, 29 October 1842, 2.

15 *NE*, 14 January 1843, 178.

16 Lord John Russell to Hobson, 9 December 1840, *BPP*.

17 John Miller, *Early Victorian New Zealand: A study of racial tension and social attitudes 1839–1852* (Oxford: Oxford University Press, 1958), 148–49.

18 Morrell, *Provincial System*, 30.

19 The only published work on FitzRoy's tenure is Paul Moon, *FitzRoy: Governor in crisis 1843–1845* (Auckland: David Ling, 2000). A superior account is Dean Cowie, '"To do all the good I can" – Robert FitzRoy: Governor of New Zealand 1843–45' (MA thesis, University of Auckland, 1994).

20 Hill, *Policing the Colonial Frontier*, 196.

21 *NE*, 27 April 1844, 30.

22 Robert FitzRoy, *Remarks on New Zealand in February 1846* (London: W. and H. White, 1846). The 'superintendent at Wellington' is mentioned once in passing, on page 64. For the reasons and political intrigues surrounding FitzRoy's recall, see Moon, *FitzRoy*, 233–36, or for a more detailed and largely complementary version, Cowie, 'Robert FitzRoy', 165–87.

23 This campaign is detailed in Patricia Burns, *Fatal Success: A history of the New Zealand Company*, ed. Henry Richardson (Auckland: Heinemann Reed, 1989), 263–65.

24 *GBPD* series 3, vol. 81, 17–19 June 1845, cc. 665–756, 761–846, 853–968.

25 These matters are major themes of such diverse publications as Burns, *Fatal Success*; McLintock, *Crown Colony Government*; Miller, *Early Victorian New Zealand*; and Paul Moon, *The Newest Country in the World: A history of New Zealand in the decade of the treaty* (Auckland: Penguin Books, 2007). See also chapters 4–6 of Alan Ward, *A Show of Justice: Racial 'amalgamation' in nineteenth century New Zealand* (Canberra: Australian National University Press, 1974).

26 *GBPD* series 3, vol. 81, 19 June 1845, c. 950, cc. 951–52.

27 Lord Stanley to George Grey, 27 June 1845, *BPP*.

28 John Darwin, *The Empire Project: The rise and fall of the British world system, 1830–1970* (Cambridge: Cambridge University Press, 2009), 59–60.

29   J.M. Ward, *Earl Grey and the Australian Colonies 1846–1857: A study of self-government and self-interest* (Melbourne: Melbourne University Press, 1958), 18–20.

30   Peter Burroughs, 'Imperial institutions and the government of empire', in *The Oxford History of the British Empire, Volume III: The nineteenth century*, ed. Andrew Porter (Oxford: Oxford University Press, 1999), 187.

31   J.M. Bumsted, 'The consolidation of British North America, 1783–1860', in *Canada and the British Empire*, ed. Phillip Bucknor (Oxford: Oxford University Press, 2008), 58–59.

32   Authoritative accounts of the 1846 constitution's genesis are McLintock, *Crown Colony Government*, 278–87 and W.P. Morrell, *British Colonial Policy in the Age of Peel and Russell* (London: Frank Cass and Co., 1966), 123–26, 313–16. Unfortunately, James Stephen's role in the constitution's genesis is not considered in Paul Knaplund, *James Stephen and the British Colonial System 1813–1847* (Madison: University of Wisconsin Press, 1953), though Knaplund's observations on Stephen's commitment to colonial self-rule shed light on the ideology that informed his work. Cheyne, 'Search for a constitution', chapter 5 is the best exploration of Stephen's role and makes a strong case for the constitution as his pet, not Grey's.

33   *GBPD* series 3, vol. 88, 14 August 1846, c. 737.

34   Ward, *Earl Grey*, 35–42 provides the best account of the connections between the New Zealand constitution and New South Wales proposals within the Colonial Office; New South Wales' derisive response is recounted vividly in Peter Cochrane, *Colonial Ambition: Foundations of Australian democracy* (Melbourne: Melbourne University Press, 2006), 158–66. See also W.G. McMinn, *A Constitutional History of Australia* (Oxford: Oxford University Press, 1979), 42–43.

35   *New Zealand Constitution Act 1846* (9 & 10 Victoria, c. 103).

36   For a summary of municipal corporations acting as electoral colleges, see Keith-Lucas, *English Local Government*, 9–10.

37   Earl Grey to George Grey, 23 December 1846, *BPP*. These instructions were drafted by Stephen and reflected his influence (Cheyne, 'Search for a constitution', 118).

38   Earl Grey to George Grey, 23 December 1846, *BPP*.

39   Cheyne, 'Search for a constitution', 114; McLintock, *Crown Colony Government*, 286; Ward, *Earl Grey*, 35–36.

40   Statistics New Zealand, 'A1.1 Total Population', *Long Term Data Series: A. Population*, available from www.stats.govt.nz/browse_for_stats/economic_indicators/NationalAccounts/long-term-data-series/population.aspx

41   G.M. Meiklejohn, *Early Conflicts of Press and Government: A story of the first* New Zealand Herald *and of the foundation of Auckland* (Auckland: Wilson and Horton, 1953) covers this in detail and remains one of the most exceptional historical works on New Zealand's press. The printing industry, if not the press, was seen as essential to colonial administration; for more on the fraught relationship between the press and government printing, see Rachel Salmond, *Government Printing in New Zealand, 1840 to 1843* (Wellington: Elibank Press, 1995).

42   Tensions between company, press and settlers are best explored by Patrick Day, *The Making of the New Zealand Press: A study of the organizational and political concerns of New Zealand newspaper controllers, 1840–1880* (Wellington: Victoria University Press, 1990), 24–33.

43   Ibid., 35.

44   *WI*, 3 February 1847, 2; *NZS*, 10 February 1847, 2.

45   *WI*, 12 June 1847, 2.

46   *NZS*, 12 June 1847, 2.

47   *NZS*, 10 February 1847, 2. Emphasis original.

48   *NE*, 13 February 1847, 198.

49   *NE*, 26 June 1847, 2.

50   Lishi Kwasitsu, *Printing and the Book Trade in Early Nelson* (Wellington: Elibank Press, 1996), 31.

51 *NZ*, 6 February 1847, 2. Meiklejohn, *Early Conflicts*, 115, has a useful graph of Auckland press activity.

52 *NZ*, 12 June 1847, 2.

53 *NZ*, 26 June 1847, 2.

54 R.C.J. Stone, *Young Logan Campbell* (Auckland: Auckland University Press, 1982), 114–15, 140.

55 *SC*, 10 July 1847, 2.

56 *NZ*, 26 June 1847, 2.

57 Earl Grey to George Grey, 23 December 1846, *BPP*.

58 Ibid.

59 *NZ*, 16 June 1847, 2. McLintock, *Crown Colony Government*, 289 speculates that *NZ* wrote with inside knowledge of Grey's intentions; no evidence is given for this assertion but it is probable.

60 *NZ*, 19 June 1847, 2.

61 *SC*, 10 July 1847, 2.

62 *NZS*, 16 June 1847, 2; *NZS*, 19 June 1847, 2; *WI*, 19 June 1847, 2.

63 *NZS*, 19 June 1847, 2.

64 For more on the Wairau Affray – senseless bloodshed provoked by impatient and ignorant settlers – see Miller, *Early Victorian New Zealand*, 70–81, and Hill, *Policing the Colonial Frontier*, 170–72.

65 *NE*, 3 July 1847, 67.

66 Ibid.

67 George Grey to Earl Grey, 3 May 1847, *BPP*.

68 George Grey to Earl Grey, 3 and 13 May 1847, *BPP*.

69 See text of proclamation in the *NZ*, 15 March 1848, 2.

70 Julie Evans, *Edward Eyre: Race and colonial governance* (Dunedin: University of Otago Press, 2005) is very rigorous but does not consider in depth the relationship between Grey and Eyre in terms of provincial or Pākehā governance – this is somewhat beyond Evans' scope anyway. McLintock, *Crown Colony Government*, covers the clash between the two, especially 213–21, but the best analysis is I.G. Lawson, 'An examination of the administration of Edward John Eyre as Lieutenant-Governor of the Province of New Munster, New Zealand 1848–1853' (MA thesis, University of New Zealand, 1954).

71 In two despatches (20 and 30 November 1847, *BPP*), Earl Grey advised Governor Grey that an act of parliament was required to suspend the constitution, that such an act would be sought and that, in the interim, it would be inexpedient for Governor Grey to take any further steps in implementing the constitution. This amounted to a de facto suspension.

72 *NZS*, 5 April 1848, 2; cf. similar sentiment in *NE*, 15 April 1848, 26; *WI*, 15 April 1848, 2.

73 *NZS*, 12 April 1848, 2.

74 *NE*, 15 April 1848, 26.

75 *WI*, 15 April 1848, 2; cf. *NE*, 22 April 1848, 34.

76 *SC*, 22 April 1848, 2.

77 Ibid.; *NZ*, 19 April 1848, 2.

78 *SC*, 29 April 1848, 2.

79 *NZ*, 29 April 1848, 2; cf. other issues such as 22 April and 10 May.

80 e.g. *SC*, 13 May 1848, 2.

Chapter 2. A Constitution for New Zealand

1 J. Rutherford, *Sir George Grey: A study in colonial government* (London: Cassell, 1961), chapter 17; Angus Ross, 'The New Zealand Constitution Act of 1852: Its authorship', *Historical and Political Studies* 1(1), 1969, 61–67. For the New Zealand Company's role, see Philip Temple, *A Sort of Conscience: The Wakefields* (Auckland: Auckland University Press, 2002), 470.

2 Rutherford, *Sir George Grey*, 235, 240.

3   James Milne, *The Romance of a Pro-consul* (London: Chatto and Windus, 1899), 116.

4   *NZH*, 3 December 1874, 3. Grey also credited Chief Justice William Martin as a valuable adviser.

5   *NE*, 30 December 1848, 175.

6   Felton Mathew, *The Founding of New Zealand: The journals of Felton Mathew, first surveyor-general of New Zealand, and his wife 1840–1847*, ed. J. Rutherford (Dunedin: A.H. and A.W. Reed, 1940), 222.

7   *NE*, 5 August 1848, 90.

8   William Fox, *The Six Colonies of New Zealand* (London: John W. Parker and Son, 1851), 139–40.

9   A.H. McLintock, *Crown Colony Government* (Wellington: R.E. Owens, 1958), 245.

10   Full account in the *NZS*, 23 December 1848, 3; 27 December 1848, 2; 30 December 1848, 3.

11   *NZS*, 27 December 1848, 2.

12   Ibid.

13   George Grey to Earl Grey, 29 November 1848, *BPP*. This was widely published the next year and formed the basis for public discussion, e.g. *NZS*, 21 July 1849.

14   Ibid.

15   Rutherford, *Sir George Grey*, 248–49.

16   30 August 1851, *BPP*.

17   *OW*, 20 December 1851, 2.

18   John McGlashan to Earl Grey, 24 January 1852, *BPP*.

19   Tom Brooking, *And Captain of Their Souls: An interpretative essay on the life and times of Captain William Cargill* (Dunedin: Otago Heritage Books, 1984), 47.

20   *NE*, 11 August 1849, 94.

21   James Barr ('An old identity'), *The Old Identities: Being sketches and reminiscences during the first decade of the Province of Otago, N.Z.* (Dunedin: Mills, Dick and Co., 1879), 113.

22   When the council's proceedings were closed, the *Spectator* retreated to a mere summary of (and meek agreement with) Grey's proposals for more representative government in future; 21 July 1849, 2; cf. its initial enthusiasm on 23 December 1848, 2.

23   The tension between Eyre and Grey (and Eyre's repeated attempts to circumvent Grey by communicating directly with the Colonial Office) is all that gives colour to otherwise tedious communication on petty matters in their despatches contained in New Munster Government (agency ACFP), series 8210 to 8213, Archives New Zealand.

24   *NE*, 25 August 1849, 102.

25   *NE*, 11 January 1851, 181.

26   Enclosure 2, George Grey to Earl Grey, 5 February 1851, *BPP*. (This petition had 161 signatories; 14 more were added in George Grey to Earl Grey, 10 March 1851.)

27   George Grey to Earl Grey, 12 February 1851, *BPP*, conveying a report of the meetings. See also Diana Beaglehole, 'Political leadership in Wellington, 1839–1853', in *The Making of Wellington 1800–1914*, eds David Hamer and Roberta Nicholls (Wellington: Victoria University Press, 1990), 189–90.

28   Fox, *Six Colonies*, 161.

29   *NZS*, 27 October 1849, 2.

30   *NZS*, 6 October 1852, 2; *WI*, 13 November 1852, 2, emphasis original.

31   C.E. Carrington, *John Robert Godley of Canterbury* (Cambridge: Cambridge University Press, 1950), 142–44.

32   See, for instance, the *SC*'s enthusiasm for constitutional news from a visiting brig – and disappointment that none eventuated – in the leader of 2 November 1852, 2. Even greater frustration is evident in the leader of 12 November 1852, 2, which derides postal arrangements for official correspondence between Britain and New Zealand.

33   *TarH*, 22 September 1852, 2.

34   Barr, *The Old Identities*, 165.

35 *OW*, 6 November 1852, 2.

36 *OW*, 13 November 1852, 2.

37 *LT*, 30 October 1852, 6.

38 George Grey to John Pakington, 23 February 1853, *BPP*.

39 The proclamation is attached to George Grey to John Pakington, 5 March 1853, *BPP*. Taranaki was originally called New Plymouth and renamed in 1858. For consistency, I refer to it exclusively as Taranaki.

40 *OW*, 22 January 1853, 2.

41 Grey remained bitter about this particular edit into his old age. Some four decades later, he lamented 'the dictation of a single man' that removed provisions for an upper house elected by the provincial councils; 1891 *Australasian Federation Convention Debates*, 617.

42 Ann Tyndale-Biscoe, 'The struggle for responsible government in the Province of Otago' (MA thesis, University of New Zealand, 1954).

43 *New Zealand Constitution Act* (15 and 16 Victoria 1852), clause 53.

44 John Pakington to George Grey, 16 July 1852, *BPP*.

45 Ibid.; W.P. Morrell, *The Provincial System in New Zealand, 1852–76* (Christchurch: Whitcombe and Tombs, 1964 [1932]), 53–54.

46 Kevin Heagney, 'Modelling tax policy development: Governor FitzRoy's tax reform 1844–45', Massey University Department of Economics and Finance Discussion Paper 09.08, August 2009.

47 Morrell, *Provincial System*, 68, 74, 92.

48 W.H. Scotter, 'Canterbury, 1857–68', in *A History of Canterbury, vol. II: General history, 1854–65 and cultural aspects, 1850–1950*, ed. W.J. Gardner (Christchurch: Whitcombe and Tombs, 1971), 132–33.

49 Paul Goldsmith, *We Won, You Lost, Eat That! A political history of tax in New Zealand since 1840* (Auckland: David Ling, 2008), 22–27. Goldsmith's National Party connections skew his analysis of more recent decades – he was elected as a National list MP in 2011 – but his overview of nineteenth-century colonial taxation is the most detailed to date and generally sound. For a focused analysis of the failed 1844 income tax, see Ogy Kabzamalov, 'New Zealand's forgotten income tax' *Te Mata Koi: Auckland University Law Review* 16, 2010, 26–53.

50 Jonathan Barrett and John Veal, 'Land taxation: A New Zealand perspective', *eJournal of Tax Research* 10(3), 2012, 573–88; Rob Vosslamber, 'Taxation for New Zealand's future: The introduction of New Zealand's progressive income tax in 1891', *Accounting History* 17(1), 2012, 105–22.

Chapter 3. The Dawn of Provincialism

1 The exclusion of women from the vote went almost without question; the first agitation for female enfranchisement in New Zealand came from 'Femina' (Mary Ann Müller) in Nelson in the second half of the 1860s. Her pioneering contributions were published in the *NE*. She was swiftly followed in the 1870s by Mary Taylor in Wellington and Mary 'Polly Plum' Colclough in Auckland. A selection of their writing is reproduced in *The Vote, the Pill and the Demon Drink: A history of feminist writing in New Zealand 1869–1993*, ed. Charlotte Macdonald (Wellington: Bridget Williams Books, 1993), 18–31. For more on the enfranchisement movement, see Patricia Grimshaw, *Women's Suffrage in New Zealand* (Auckland: Auckland University Press, 1972). Regarding Māori participation in the 1853 election, see Harry C. Evison, *Te Wai Pounamu: The Greenstone Island; A history of the Southern Maori during the European colonization of New Zealand* (Wellington and Christchurch: Aoraki Press, 1993), 356.

2 D.G. Herron, 'The structure and course of New Zealand politics, 1853–1858' (PhD thesis, University of Otago, 1959); 'Provincialism and centralism, 1853–1858', in *Studies of a Small Democracy: Essays in honour of Willis Airey*, eds Robert Chapman and Keith Sinclair (Auckland:

Blackwood and Janet Paul for the University of Auckland, 1963), 10–32; 'The circumstances and effects of Sir George Grey's delay in summoning the First New Zealand General Assembly', *Historical Studies Australia and New Zealand* 8(32), 1959, 364–82; 'Alsatia or utopia? New Zealand society and politics in the eighteen-fifties', *Landfall* 52, 1959, 324–41; 'The franchise and New Zealand politics, 1853–8', *Political Science* 12(28), 1960, 28–44. For Auckland, see H.J. Hanham, 'The political structure of Auckland, 1853–76' (MA thesis, University of New Zealand, 1950); R.D. McGarvey, 'Local politics in the Auckland Province, 1853–62' (MA thesis, University of New Zealand, 1954); R.C.J. Stone, 'Auckland party politics in the early years of the provincial system, 1853–58', *NZJH* 14(2), 1980, 153–78.

3   Herron, 'Provincialism and centralism', 20–25. This is especially plausible in light of Fitzherbert's centralist drift in the 1860s as colonial treasurer.

4   *PD* (1856–58), 18. Sewell also foreshadowed the need for new provinces in Hawke's Bay and Wanganui in his letter to Hugh Carleton, 4 October 1853 (Edward Stafford Papers, ATL MS-2046).

5   *LT*, 11 September 1858, 4.

6   Diana Beaglehole, 'The structure and course of politics in nineteenth-century Wellington' (MA thesis, Victoria University of Wellington, 1987), 110–49 passim. It is unlikely that a similar study for most other provinces would produce dramatically different results.

7   Jim McAloon, *No Idle Rich: The wealthy in Canterbury and Otago 1840–1914* (Dunedin: University of Otago Press, 2002), 105.

8   Thomas Gore Browne to Lord John Russell, 20 September 1855, *BPP*.

9   Godley's speech to the people of Christchurch, 18 December 1852, cited in C.E. Carrington, *John Robert Godley of Canterbury* (Cambridge: Cambridge University Press, 1950), 150.

10   *NE*, 13 August 1853, 3; a similar letter appears in 6 August 1853, 2. Nelson was not alone; James George recalled that Auckland's first elections featured 'disgracefull scenes of bribery and drunkeness and personation [*sic*], carried on by those who should know better'; *Reminiscences: A few odds and ends of remembrances* (Auckland: J. George, 1875–76), 503, MSS & Archives A-20, Special Collections, University of Auckland.

11   Herron, 'New Zealand politics, 1853–1858', 135.

12   John E. Martin, 'Political participation and electoral change in nineteenth-century New Zealand', *Political Science* 57(1), 2005, 41.

13   Neill Atkinson, *Adventures in Democracy: A history of the vote in New Zealand* (Dunedin: University of Otago Press, 2003), 35–36.

14   See Appendix E for data on voter participation.

15   Jim McAloon, *Nelson: A regional history* (Whatamango Bay: Cape Catley, 1997), 63–64.

16   Lowther Broad, *The Jubilee History of Nelson: From 1842 to 1892* (Nelson: Bond, Finney, and Co., 1892), 114–15.

17   Edmund Bohan, *Edward Stafford: New Zealand's first statesman* (Christchurch: Hazard Press, 1994), 64.

18   *NE*, 13 August 1853, 7.

19   *NE*, 20 August 1853, 5. Although 303 *votes* were recorded for the General Assembly, unlike the one-man-one-vote superintendency, this was a two-member constituency and each elector possessed two votes. If each elector (bar one) cast two votes, then only 152 electors participated.

20   Stone, 'Auckland party politics', 159.

21   *SC*, 24 June 1853, 2.

22   *SC*, 28 June 1853, 2.

23   One example is James George, chairman of the Progress Party in the mid-1850s, in his *Reminiscences*, 503.

24   Stone, 'Auckland party politics', 163–65.

25   *TarH*, 20 July 1853, 2.

26 B. Wells, *The History of Taranaki: A standard work on the history of the province* (New Plymouth: Edmondson and Avery, 1878), 151–52. Brown was one of Wells' informants.

27 Henry Sewell was particularly adamant on this point: see Sewell, 28 September 1853, *JHS*, vol. 1, 383, and Sewell to Hugh Carleton, 4 October 1853, Stafford Papers, ATL MS-2046.

28 Sewell, 28 September 1853, *JHS*, vol. 1, 387.

29 *WI*, 6 July 1853, 3.

30 *NZS*, 6 July 1853, 3, devoted just seven sentences to the election of Featherston, in a smaller font after the leader. Here it estimated an attendance of 'about one hundred persons'. The *Independent* on 9 July, 3, quickly retorted that attendance 'could not have been less than 250'.

31 *WI*, 9 July 1853, 3.

32 For E.G. Wakefield's role in Wellington's 1853 elections, the authoritative account is Peter Stuart, *Edward Gibbon Wakefield in New Zealand: His political career. 1853–4* (Wellington: Price Milburn, 1971), 59–70.

33 Patrick Day, *The Making of the New Zealand Press: A study of the organizational and political concerns of New Zealand newspaper controllers, 1840–1880* (Wellington: Victoria University Press, 1990), 96.

34 *WI*, 10 August 1853, 2.

35 *NZS*, 20 August 1853, 3.

36 Ibid. A total of 791 votes were cast. As an individual elector could cast up to four votes, the lowest possible number of electors was 198. The actual total was likely over 200; *WI*, 20 August 1853, 3.

37 Ibid. (for General Assembly figures) and *WI*, 13 August 1853, 2 (for provincial council figures).

38 Dorothy Ross, 'Government and the people: A study of public opinion in New Zealand from 1852–1876 in its relation to politics and government' (MA thesis, University of New Zealand, 1944), 16.

39 C.L. Innes ('Pilgrim'), *Canterbury Sketches: or, Life from the early days* (Christchurch: Lyttelton Times Office, 1879), 39.

40 Sewell, *JHS*, vol. 1, 347.

41 Ibid., 344. Tancred was described by contemporaries as possessing 'a great drawback in his voice … a peculiar nasal twang'; William Burke MSS, 39: http://christchurchcitylibraries.com/Heritage/Digitised/Burke/Burke39.asp

42 *LT*, 23 July 1853, 7.

43 Voting turnout is in Appendix E.

44 Herron, 'New Zealand politics, 1853–1858', 111.

45 Ibid., 137; Tom Brooking, *And Captain of Their Souls: An interpretative essay on the life and times of Captain William Cargill* (Dunedin: Otago Heritage Books, 1984), 97–98.

46 *OW*, 10 September 1853, 2.

47 Ibid.

48 *OW*, 1 October 1853, 2; 8 October 1853, 2.

49 *OW*, 24 September 1853, 2.

50 *OW*, 8 October 1853, 2.

51 Brooking, *Captain of Their Souls*, 98–99.

52 A healthy 62.4 per cent of registered electors voted; this figure was not surpassed until the first post-abolition election in 1879, when 73.7 per cent voted. Martin, 'Political participation', 44.

53 Atkinson, *Adventures in Democracy*, 23.

54 *NZS*, 20 July 1853, 2. Emphasis original. The superintendent was elected on 2 July, but writs for the provincial council and General Assembly elections were not issued until late July and held throughout August.

55 *NZS*, 20 July 1853, 2.

56 *NZS*, 13 August 1853, 2.

57 *WI*, 13 April 1853, 2.

58 William Gisborne, *New Zealand Rulers and Statesmen from 1840 to 1897*, rev. edn (London: Sampson Low, Marston & Company, 1897), 58.

59 William Pember Reeves, *The Long White Cloud*, 4th edn (Auckland: Golden Press, 1950 [1898]), 190.

60 D.G. Herron's treatment of this issue is authoritative: 'The circumstances and effects of Sir George Grey's delay in summoning the first New Zealand General Assembly', *Historical Studies Australia and New Zealand* 8(32), 1959, 364–82. For a complete picture it should be read in conjunction with Morrell, *Provincial System*, 74–79.

61 J. Rutherford, *Sir George Grey K.C.B., 1812-1898: A study in colonial government* (London: Cassell, 1961), 250–51; W.K. Jackson, *The New Zealand Legislative Council: A study of the establishment, failure and abolition of an upper house* (Dunedin: University of Otago Press, 1972), 10–20. Jackson argues this was a tool of expediency since suspension of the 1846 constitution was about to expire and framing an elective upper house acceptable to both the British parliament and New Zealand settlers was becoming too time-consuming. Philip Temple suggests the decision may also have been at E.G. Wakefield's instigation; *A Sort of Conscience: The Wakefields* (Auckland: Auckland University Press, 2002), 470–71.

62 Rutherford, *Sir George Grey*, 252.

63 Herron, 'Grey's delay', 380.

64 *TarH*, 26 April 1854, 2.

65 Ross, 'Government and the people', 16–17.

66 Pakington to Grey, 16 July 1852, *BPP*. The Colonial Office's dissatisfaction with Grey is detailed thoroughly by Herron.

67 Unfortunately, precise figures for prior experience exist only for Wellington: Beaglehole, 'Politics in nineteenth century Wellington', 46–51.

68 James Adam, *Twenty-Five Years of Emigrant Life in the South of New Zealand* (Edinburgh: Bell and Bradfute, 1874), 45.

69 Innes, *Canterbury Sketches*, 40–41.

70 *WI*, 26 November 1853, 2; William Swainson, *New Zealand and Its Colonization* (London: Smith, Elder and Co., 1859), 303.

71 *OW*, 14 January 1854, 3. Despite intentions, this did not prove to be a fully responsible executive; see Ann Tyndale-Biscoe, 'The struggle for responsible government in the Province of Otago, 1854–76' (MA thesis, University of New Zealand, 1954), 10–13.

72 *WI*, 5 November 1853, 3.

73 *New Zealand Parliamentary Record*, 2nd edn, ed. Guy H. Scholefield (Wellington: R.E. Owen, 1950 [1913]), 179, 187, 209, 229.

74 *WI*, 8 March 1854, 3. The missing MHR was Superintendent Featherston, who had already approved a provincial executive. It can be inferred that he too supported the motion.

75 *SC*, 26 May 1854, 2.

76 Whitaker later sat as an Auckland provincial councillor, October 1854–September 1855.

77 Swainson, *New Zealand*, 304.

78 *PD* (1854–55), 8.

79 Ibid.

80 *WI*, 17 June 1854, 3.

81 *TarH*, 7 June 1854, 2; cf. *LT*, 24 June 1854, 6.

82 Browne to William Molesworth, 14 February 1856, *BPP*.

83 *PD* (1854–55), 93.

84 *NE*, 13 May 1854, 2.

85 The most able and thorough account of this session, focusing on Wakefield's machinations within it, is Stuart, *Edward Gibbon Wakefield*, chapters 8–11. John E. Martin, *The House: New Zealand's House of Representatives 1854-2004* (Palmerston North: Dunmore Press, 2004), 20–22 gives a good brief account.

86 Martin, *The House*, 19.
87 J.M. Ward, *Colonial Self-Government: The British experience 1759–1856* (London: Macmillan, 1976), 315–16.
88 Ibid., 325–26.
89 Swainson, *New Zealand*, 306.
90 Ross, 'Government and the people', 24–25.
91 *SC*, 10 August 1855, 2.
92 *Melbourne Morning Herald* cited in *LT*, 14 January 1854, 8.
93 Morrell, *Provincial System*, 92.
94 *WI*, 6 December 1854, 2.
95 *PD* (1856–58), 1–2.
96 Browne to Molesworth, 14 February 1856, *BPP*.
97 11 May 1856, *JHS*, vol. 2, 233.
98 *PD* (1856–58), 17.
99 4 May 1856, *JHS*, vol. 2, 232.
100 25 May 1856, *JHS*, vol. 2, 244.
101 Bohan, *Stafford*, 95–103 provides a good account of the ministry's formation and first months.
102 The most detailed study of this stormy, complicated session and its financial resolutions is J.P. Cumming, 'The compact and financial settlement of 1856', MA thesis, University of Auckland, 1963.
103 Auckland's position is unambiguous in *Acts and Proceedings of the Auckland Provincial Council*, 1853–54, A-33.
104 The resolutions can be found in Appendix II, *JHS*, vol. 2, 338–41.
105 Statement of Stafford Ministry's views, C.W. Richmond to Gore Browne, 5 September 1856, *AJHR* 1858 B-05, 7.
106 *PD* (1856–58), 172.
107 Ibid., 206; *SC*, 24 June 1856, 2–3.
108 *TarH*, 19 July 1856, 2.
109 *SC*, 20 June 1856, 2.
110 29 June 1856, *JHS*, vol. 2, 253.
111 Cumming, 'The compact', 244.

Chapter 4. Provincial Ineptitude

1   Danny Keenan, '"Amalgamating Maori?": Maori, land tenure and "amalgamation" before 1860', in *Contested Ground/Te Whenua I Tohea: The Taranaki Wars 1860–1881*, ed. Kelvin Day (Wellington: Huia Publishers, 2010), 2–3.
2   C.W. Richmond to J. Chamberlain, 21 November 1854, *RAP*, vol. 1, 159.
3   Riemenschneider also had experience in Nelson and Otago. For more on Riemenschneider's life, the definitive biography is Peter Oettli, *God's Messenger: J.F. Riemenschneider and racial conflict in 19th century New Zealand* (Wellington: Huia Publishers, 2008).
4   J.F. Riemenschneider to William Martin, 30 September 1861, *AJHR* 1862 E-01, sec. 2, note on 24–25.
5   Georgina Bowen to Gertrude Markham, 5 April 1862, Bowen Family Papers, ATL MS-Papers-10473-2.
6   Damon Salesa, *Racial Crossings: Race, intermarriage, and the Victorian British Empire* (Oxford: Oxford University Press, 2011), 181–83.
7   Elizabeth Caldwell memoirs, ATL qMS-0361, 11, 24.
8   Thomas Hewetson, 30 September 1857, 'From the Slate River 1857', *Nelson Historical Society Journal* 3(5), 1979, 38.

9   *SC*, 15 March 1853, 2.

10 *OW*, 1 January 1853, 2.

11 For more on Akaroa's settlement and early history, see Peter Tremewan, *French Akaroa: An attempt to colonise southern New Zealand* (Christchurch: Canterbury University Press, 1990).

12 C.W. Adams, *A Spring in the Canterbury Settlement* (London: Longman, Brown, Green, and Longmans, 1853), 85.

13 Good descriptions of early Kaiapoi can be found in R.B. Paul, *Letters from Canterbury, New Zealand* (London: Rivingtons, 1857), 39–40 and Henry Sewell, 5–6 January 1854, *JHS*, vol. 1, 424, 428. For high country exploration, see David Relph, *From Tussocks to Tourists: The story of the central Canterbury high country* (Christchurch: Canterbury University Press, 2007), 73.

14 *LT*, 3 September 1853, 6; 29 October 1853, 5.

15 *LT*, 24 September 1853, 5.

16 *LT*, 22 October 1853, 8.

17 *LT*, 22 April 1854, 5.

18 9 April 1854, *JHS*, vol. 1, 488–90.

19 The Report of the Lyttelton and Christchurch Road Commission, 7 April 1854, is in the supplementary section of *LT*, 22 April 1854, 14.

20 A seven-part series by an anonymous ex-railway official, 'History of the Canterbury railways – how the early settlers solved a big transport problem', appeared in the *New Zealand Railways Magazine* 5(1–7), 1930. This paragraph draws on parts 2–3.

21 *LT*, 22 August 1857, 4.

22 See Henry W. Harper's vivid account of 25 December 1856 in *Letters From New Zealand, 1857–1911: Being some account of life and work in the Province of Canterbury, South Island* (London: Hugh Rees, 1914), 10.

23 Edward Brown Fitton, *New Zealand: Its present condition, prospects and resources* (London: Edward Stanford, 1856), 197.

24 *LT*, 13 January 1858, 5.

25 *LT*, 16 January 1858, 4.

26 Gordon Ogilvie, *Banks Peninsula: Cradle of Canterbury* (Wellington: GP Books, 1990), 37–38, 54.

27 *LT*, 9 January 1858, 4.

28 *WI*, 20 December 1854, 3.

29 *NZS*, 21 June 1854, 3.

30 *TarH*, 12 September 1857, 2.

31 *SC*, 24 April 1855, 2.

32 This session is studied in detail by R.D. McGarvey, 'Local politics in the Auckland province, 1853–62', (MA thesis, University of New Zealand, 1954), 134–49.

33 *SC*, 13 April 1855, 2. 17 April 1855, 2, reiterates the charges more vehemently, but with more partisan inclinations.

34 The best study of this election and wider political tactics is R.C.J. Stone, 'Auckland party politics in the early years of the provincial system, 1853–58', *NZJH* 14(2), 1980, 166–72.

35 D.G. Herron, 'The franchise and New Zealand politics, 1853–8', *Political Science* 12(28), 1960, 39.

36 *OW*, 7 January 1854, 2.

37 *OW*, 18 March 1854, 2.

38 *OW*, 29 April 1854, 2.

39 *OW*, 6 January 1855, 3; 20 January 1855, 3; 10 March 1855, 2.

40 *OW*, 24 March 1855, 3.

41 For more on Cargill and Cutten's falling-out, their 1857 reconciliation and its consequences for Otago political cliques, see Tom Brooking, *And Captain of Their Souls: An interpretative essay on the life and times of Captain William Cargill* (Dunedin: Otago Heritage Books, 1984), 106–09.

42   *OW*, 5 May 1855, 2.
43   *LT*, 2 June 1855, 7.
44   *OW*, 2 June 1855, 3.
45   *NE*, 5 September 1855, 2.
46   *OW*, 3 November 1855, 2.
47   *OW*, 20 October 1855, 2.
48   *LT*, 10 November 1855, 6.
49   *OW*, 13 October 1855, 2.
50   *NE*, 5 September 1855, 2.
51   The only substantial treatment is D.M. Tebay, 'The Hawke's Bay separation movement, 1856–58' (MA thesis, University of New Zealand, 1954). For brief overviews, see W.P. Morell, *The Provincial System in New Zealand, 1852–76* (Christchurch: Whitcombe and Tombs, 1964 [1932]), 107–08; Matthew Wright, *Hawke's Bay: The history of a province* (Palmerston North, Dunmore Press, 1994), 67–68.
52   Ray Fargher, *The Best Man Who Ever Served the Crown? A life of Donald McLean* (Wellington: Victoria University Press, 2007), 103.
53   Henry Brett, *White Wings*, vol. 2 (Auckland: Brett Printing, 1928), 96.
54   Frederick Wanklyn Williams, *Through Ninety Years, 1826–1916: Life and work among the Maoris in New Zealand* (Christchurch: Whitcombe and Tombs, 1939), 152.
55   Tebay, 'Hawke's Bay separation', 14–15.
56   *NZS*, 3 April 1850, 2.
57   Letter from 'Old Colonist' of Napier, *SC*, 23 December 1856, 3.
58   *NE*, 13 October 1855, 3.
59   Tebay, 'Hawke's Bay separation', 17.
60   *NE*, 28 November 1855, 2.
61   See the statements of roads made in *Acts and Proceedings of the Provincial Council of Wellington, 1855–57* (sessions 3–4).
62   Letter from 'Old Colonist', *SC*, 23 December 1856, 3.
63   *HBH*, 20 June 1868, 3.
64   *WI*, 29 December 1855, 3.
65   Tebay, 'Hawke's Bay separation', 28.
66   *HBH*, 21 November 1857, 2. 'Little Peddlington' was a common derisive nickname for a small town, especially one believed to possess ambitions beyond its station.
67   Tom L. Mills, 'Our early newspapers', *Typo* 3(27), 30 March 1889, 25.
68   David Hastings, *Extra! Extra! How the people made the news* (Auckland: Auckland University Press, 2013), 68.
69   *NZS*, 15 November 1856, 3.
70   Richard S. Hill, *Policing the Colonial Frontier: The theory and practice of coercive social and racial control in New Zealand, 1767–1867* (Wellington: V.R. Ward, 1986), 442.
71   *HBH*, 10 October 1857, 2.
72   Ibid., 5.
73   *HBH*, 17 October 1857, 2.
74   Tebay, 'Hawke's Bay separation', 69.
75   Ibid., 32–36.
76   *HBH*, 21 November 1857, 2. Emphasis original.
77   *HBH*, 7 November 1857, 3.
78   Tebay, 'Hawke's Bay separation', 74.
79   Petition of the Settlers of the District of Hawkes' Bay: Separation of the Hawkes' Bay District from the Province of Wellington, *AJHR* 1858 G-01, 1–4. The body of the petition punctuates the name as 'Hawke's Bay', but all titles incorrectly use 'Hawkes' Bay'.

80   Jim McAloon, *Nelson: A regional history* (Whatamango Bay: Cape Catley, 1997), 63–66.

81   *NE*, 18 October 1856, 2.

82   A good example of Elliott ridiculing Robinson's supporters – and defending himself from claims that he had deserted principles so strongly expressed in the 1853 campaign – is in *NE*, 22 October 1856, 2. Class prejudice is unashamedly invoked in *NE*, 29 October 1856, 2.

83   *NE*, 22 October 1856, 3. The letter is accompanied by Elliott's stern rebuke.

84   From the returning officer's account, the election of George Lee as Amuri provincial councillor, if not the superintendency ballot, was clearly illegal: Edward Jollie reminiscences, ATL MS-Papers-4207, 28. For Elliott's argument, see *NE* editions of 19, 26, and 29 November 1856.

85   *NE*, 17 December 1856, 2.

86   B.E. Dickinson, 'The ungentle shepherds', *Journal of the Nelson Historical Society* 3(4), 1978, 36.

87   *NE*, 25 April 1857, 4. For detailed treatment of Wairau policing, see Hill, *Policing the Colonial Frontier*, 504–08.

88   *NE*, 25 April 1857, 2.

89   *NE*, 30 May 1857, 2.

90   Ibid.

91   *NE*, 5 August 1857, 2.

92   *NE*, 15 August 1857, 3.

93   *Colonist*, 22 December 1857, 2.

94   *NE*, 21 October 1857, 3.

95   *NE*, 22 August 1857, 3.

96   *OW*, 2 February 1856, 3.

97   A.B. Ryan, 'The Southland secession movement' (MA thesis, University of New Zealand, 1947), 21; *PD* (1856–58), 200.

98   *OW*, 13 December 1856, 2.

99   *LT*, 24 June 1857, 7.

100 *LT*, 20 August 1856, 4.

101 See the entries of 15 November 1853 and 18 February 1854 in J.A.R. Menzies' diary, Hocken Collections, Uare Taoka o Hākena, Misc-MS-420.

102 *OW*, 18 April 1857, 6.

103 Ibid., 4.

104 J.T. Thomson survey report, in James Menzies Papers, ATL MS-Papers-0055-3.

105 *LT*, 6 June 1857, 6.

Chapter 5. 'Our Reactionary Policy'

1   *WI*, 3 June 1857, 2.

2   *SC*, 5 May 1857, 3.

3   Henry Labouchere to Thomas Gore Browne, 15 September 1857, *AJHR* 1858 B-05, 17–18.

4   The definitive account of this election and its aftermath, from which this paragraph draws, is Brad Patterson, 'Would King Isaac the First lose his head?: The power of personality in Wellington provincial politics, 1857–1861', *New Zealand Studies* 6(1), 1996, 3–16.

5   *NE*, 3 April 1858, 3.

6   *WI*, 20 March 1858, 2. See also *WI*, 1 September 1858, 5, for Clifford's defence of his colleagues' absences.

7   D.M. Tebay, 'The Hawke's Bay separation movement, 1856–58' (MA thesis, University of New Zealand, 1954), 100.

8   *SC*, 2 April 1858, 3. Ultimately, four of the five Nelson members who initially chose to stay home – Curtis, Domett, Monro and Weld – did attend, departing Nelson on 3 June (*NE*, 5 June 1858, 2), which they arrived in time to debate and support the New Provinces Act in August.

9   Domett, letter to his constituents, in *NE*, 20 March 1858, 2. His letter was accompanied by letters from the other non-travelling Nelson MPs; the only member who travelled for the start of the parliamentary session was Stafford.

10 *HBH*, 10 April 1858, 4.

11 Edward Stafford's memorandum on Acts of the General Assembly to Edward Bulwer-Lytton, 9 October 1858, *AJHR* 1860 A-04, 11.

12 *HBH*, 14 August 1858, 2.

13 *PD* (1858–60), 82.

14 Ibid., 97.

15 C.W. Richmond to T. Richmond, 23 August 1858, *RAP*, vol. 1, 418–19.

16 New Provinces Act (21 and 22 Victoria 1858, No. 70), clauses 9–10.

17 Ibid. This paragraph and the next summarise the first two clauses.

18 *WI*, 28 August 1858, 3.

19 *Canterbury Standard* cited in *WI*, 25 September 1858, 6.

20 Opening speech of the tenth session, 1 October 1858, *Journal of Proceedings of the Canterbury Provincial Council*, vol. 1, sessions 1–10, 282.

21 Doreen E. Kemp, 'William Sefton Moorhouse, 1825–1881' (MA thesis, University of New Zealand, 1950), 34.

22 Edward Stafford to C.W. Richmond, 19 June 1859, *RAP*, vol. 1, 466.

23 Domett to Richmond, 17 October 1859, *RAP*, vol. 1, 492. Emphasis original.

24 Domett to Richmond, 30 October 1859, *RAP*, vol. 1, 496.

25 Kemp, 'Hawke's Bay separation', 18–19.

26 Memorandum, Edward Stafford, 9 October 1858, *AJHR* 1860 A-04, 11.

27 Matthew Wright, *Hawke's Bay: The history of a province* (Palmerston North, Dunmore Press, 1994), 68.

28 *HBH*, 25 April 1859 (special edition), 1.

29 Alexander Alexander to Donald McLean, 7 January 1859, Donald McLean Papers, ATL MS-Papers-0032-0142.

30 For details about the divisions of Hawke's Bay's governing class in the late 1850s, see Wright, *Hawke's Bay*, 68–69.

31 *HBH*, 7 May 1859, 2.

32 Thomas Fitzgerald to Donald McLean, 27 April 1859, Donald McLean Papers, ATL MS-Papers-0032-0275.

33 *HBH*, 26 November 1859, 4.

34 *NZ*, 14 December 1859, 2. (The *NZ* was a vocal supporter of Hawke's Bay's secession and of Fitzgerald.)

35 *Press*, 18 July 1865, 2

36 Fitzgerald to McLean, 27 April 1859.

37 *HBH*, 31 March 1860, 4.

38 *HBH*, 21 July 1860, 6.

39 *HBH*, 18 August 1860, 6.

40 Two identical petitions were actually submitted, one with 31 signatures and the other with 25. *AJHR* 1860 G-05 and G-06.

41 Carnarvon to Browne, 6 May 1859, *AJHR* 1860 A-04, 25.

42 *PD* (1858–60), 657.

43 Ibid., 666–71.

44 Ibid., 683.

45 *PD* (1861–63), 249–57, 265–74, 325–28.

46 New Provinces Act Amendment Act (24 and 25 Victoria 1861, No. 26).

47 *NZ*, cited in *OW*, 24 November 1860, 9.

Chapter 6. Marlborough and Southland Implode

1   *NE*, 16 November 1859, 2.
2   *MP*, 20 January 1860, 3; 27 January 1860, 3; 14 April 1860, 3.
3   *MP*, 20 January 1860, 3.
4   *MP*, 6 January 1860, 3.
5   NE, 22 August 1857, 3; A.D. McIntosh, ed., *Marlborough: A provincial history* (Christchurch: Capper Press, 1977 [1940]), 208.
6   *MP*, 9 March 1860, 3.
7   McIntosh, *Marlborough*, 208, 225; *Statistics of New Zealand*, 1861.
8   *MP*, 25 May 1861, 2.
9   G.R. Hawke, *The Making of New Zealand: An economic history* (Cambridge: Cambridge University Press, 1985), 106.
10 *MP*, 8 June 1861, 2. See also McIntosh, *Marlborough*, 216–17.
11 *NEM*, 28 September 1866, 2.
12 *AJHR* 1861 G-03.
13 Fox to the superintendent of Marlborough, 5 September 1861, *AJHR* 1862 A-03, 8–9. Superintendent William Adams championed the railway proposal, but he had just resigned office and the new superintendent, W.D.H. Baillie, who took office on 28 August 1861, would have received the letter. Adams resigned to retain a more lucrative central government job that his Blenheim rivals were conspiring to strip from him for Eyes' benefit; McIntosh, *Marlborough*, 221.
14 Memorandum, William Fox, 28 September 1861, *AJHR* 1862 A-02, 3.
15 Duke of Newcastle to Fox, 20 January 1862, *AJHR* 1862 A-02, 6; John E. Martin, 'Refusal of assent – a hidden element of constitutional history in New Zealand', *Victoria University of Wellington Law Review* 41(1), 2010, 55.
16 McIntosh, *Marlborough*, 221.
17 Monro, address to Picton electors, 18 October 1861, *Colonist*, 1 November 1861, 3.
18 Communication between Thomas Carter and representatives of the central government, typically William Fox, 11 September 1863 to 26 August 1864, *AJHR* 1864 B-03, 11–23. The quotes are from 23.
19 Wrey's boosterism occupied letters, editorials, and ads in *NE*, 2, 9 and 16 July 1853.
20 *MP*, 27 May 1865, 2.
21 McIntosh, *Marlborough*, 254.
22 *LT*, 2 November 1859, 4.
23 Early Blenheim rejoiced in the name The Beaver. In the early 1860s, the name of both town and electorate were changed to Blenheim as it was less subject to mockery.
24 Council controversies not covered here are discussed in McIntosh, *Marlborough*, 207–72 passim.
25 *MP*, 30 June 1860, 2–3; 13 April 1861, 2.
26 This paragraph draws upon *WI*, 30 September 1862, 2.
27 This paragraph draws upon *NE*, 1 November 1862, 3.
28 Richard S. Hill, *Policing the Colonial Frontier: The theory and practice of coercive social and racial control in New Zealand, 1767–1867* (Wellington: Historical Publications Branch, Department of Internal Affairs, 1986), 753.
29 *MP*, 28 June 1865, 2.
30 McIntosh, *Marlborough*, 246.
31 *MP*, 1 July 1865, 2.
32 The rest of this paragraph and the next draw on *MP*, 8 July 1865, 2.
33 *Marlborough News*, cited in *NE*, 20 July 1865, 4.
34 *NE*, 6 July 1865, 2.
35 *Press*, 18 July 1865, 2.

36 *MP*, 5 July 1865, 2.
37 McIntosh, *Marlborough*, 250–51.
38 *WI*, 30 September 1862, 2.
39 Tom Brooking, *And Captain of Their Souls: An interpretative essay on the life and times of Captain William Cargill* (Dunedin: Otago Heritage Books, 1984), 116.
40 *AJHR* 1858 G-02, 2; *PD* (1858–60), 86.
41 A.H. McLintock, *The History of Otago: The origins and growth of a Wakefield class settlement* (Dunedin: Otago Centennial Historical Publications, 1949), 409.
42 *OW*, 16 July 1859, 3.
43 Helen A. Henderson ('Alpaca'), 'Historical account of Southland as a province, 1861–1870' (MA thesis, University of New Zealand, 1919), 12, and A.R. Dreaver, 'The Southland Province of New Zealand in the days of Dr J.A.R. Menzies (Superintendent 1861–1864)' (BA Honours thesis, University of New Zealand, 1929), 19. Although outdated narrative theses, valuable more for statistics and figures than arguments, these are the only theses on Southland politics in this period.
44 Macandrew to Browne, 21 February 1861, in *OW*, 2 March 1861, 5.
45 Francis Dillon Bell to James Menzies, 20 February 1861, Francis Dillon Bell Papers, ATL MS-Papers-0693-3.
46 Erik Olssen, 'Loyalty and localism – Southland's political odyssey', in *Murihiku: The Southland story*, ed. Paul Sorrell (Invercargill: Southland to 2006 Book Project Committee, 2006), 85; McLintock, *History of Otago*, 410–11.
47 Bell to Menzies, 20 April 1861, Bell Papers, ATL MS-Papers-0693-3.
48 Bell to Menzies, 9 January 1862, Bell Papers, ATL MS-Papers-0693-4.
49 *IT*, 25 November 1862.
50 J.O.P. Watt, *Southland's Pioneer Railways 1864–1878* (Wellington: New Zealand Railway and Locomotive Society, 1965), 14–15.
51 Opening speech of the second session, 17 January 1862, and opening speech of the third session, 23 October 1862, *Votes and Proceedings of the Southland Provincial Council, 1861–69*, 16, 32.
52 *IT*, 24 February 1863, 2. For detailed coverage of Southland's gold escort tribulations, see Hill, *Policing the Colonial Frontier*, 700–07.
53 *IT*, 6 March 1863, 2.
54 Bernard John Foster, 'Heale, Theophilus', *An Encyclopaedia of New Zealand 1966*: www.teara.govt.nz/en/1966/heale-theophilus. Unfortunately, Heale has not yet been included in the *DNZB*.
55 'Preliminary report regarding the Northern Railway', 31 July 1863, Menzies Papers, ATL MS-Papers-0055-03.
56 James Davies to James Menzies, 27 July 1863, *Appendix to the Votes and Proceedings of the Southland Provincial Council, 1861–69*, 198.
57 'Preliminary report regarding the Northern Railway'.
58 *IT*, 11 August 1863, 2.
59 Menzies to Domett, 6 March 1863, and Domett's reply, 10 April 1863, *AJHR* 1864 B-03, 33; Fox to Menzies, 20 February 1864, *AJHR* 1864 B-03, 43.
60 Domett to Menzies, 11 April 1863, *AJHR* 1863 B-05, 27 (see 23–24 for the allegedly sound reasoning referenced by Domett, expressed in Menzies' letter of 4 February 1863).
61 'Report on the Financial Condition of the Province of Southland', *AJHR* 1865 B-03A, 5.
62 *IT*, 25 November 1863, 2.
63 Menzies to Fox, 4 February 1864 (two letters), *AJHR* 1864 B-03, 39–40.
64 Fox to Menzies, 8 March 1864 and 27 April 1864, *AJHR* 1864 B-03, 41–42.
65 *DN*, 2 April 1864, 4–5.
66 *DN*, 9 April 1864, 4.
67 *DN*, 4 May 1864, 2.

68 *DN*, 17 May 1864, 3.
69 *ODT*, 12 May 1864, 4.
70 William Tarlton to the editor, *DN*, 16 April 1864, 3. Emphasis original.
71 Ibid., 2–3.
72 *DN*, 20 May 1864, 2.
73 *ST*, 2 June 1864, 2.
74 Erik Olssen, 'The peopling of Southland', in *Murihiku*, 73.
75 *Riverton Times*, 20 February 1864, 2.
76 *ST*, 18 August 1864, 2. Originally the central government only intended to advance money for three months.
77 The debate is reproduced in *ST*, 23 July 1864, 4. Tarlton elaborated further at an October meeting of electors, printed in *ST*, 8 October 1864, 3. See a lengthy exchange of letters between government officials and contractors in the *Appendix to the Votes and Proceedings of the Southland Provincial Council, 1861–69*, 200–15, especially Chalmers' letter to Menzies of 13 April 1864 admitting he authorised the use of inferior wood.
78 'Preliminary report regarding the Northern Railway'.
79 *ST*, 20 October 1864, 2.
80 *ST*, 25 October 1864, 2.
81 *ST*, 27 October 1864, 2.
82 *ST*, 5 December 1866, 2.
83 *ST*, 23 December 1864, 2.
84 *SN*, 1 April 1865, 2.
85 *ST*, 2 December 1864, 2.
86 Foster, 'Heale, Theophilus'.
87 Dreaver, 'Southland Province in the days of Menzies', 143–44.
88 'Report on the Financial Condition of Southland', *AJHR* 1865 B-03A, 3–5.
89 Ibid., 7.
90 *SN*, 30 March 1865, 2.

Chapter 7. The End of Secession

1 *Press*, 13 July 1861, 6.
2 *TimH*, 25 March 1865, 3.
3 *LT*, 27 July 1861, 2 and 4; 14 August 1861, 4.
4 *LT*, 21 August 1861, 4.
5 Alfred Cox, *Recollections: Australia, England, Ireland, Scotland, New Zealand* (Christchurch: Whitcombe & Tombs, 1884), 109. Cox went on to a career in provincial and national government. Ardent secessionists later accused him of flip-flopping – not a baseless charge, as Cox wanted local control of land revenue rather than a new province.
6 *LT*, 25 September 1861, 4.
7 *LT*, 5 February 1862, 4.
8 *TimH*, 11 June 1864, 4, and 7 January 1865, 4.
9 *TimH*, 25 March 1865, 3.
10 *TimH*, 14 June 1865, 3.
11 *NZH*, 3 March 1865, 6.
12 *DSC*, 3 March 1865, 4; 4 March 1865, 5; 18 March 1865, 5.
13 *NZS* 9 November 1864, 2; *WI*, 16 September 1865, 4; *EP*, 21 September 1865, 2. This is a rare example of Wellington's press finding common ground.
14 *WI*, 14 January 1865, 10.
15 *OT*, 25 February 1864, 4.

16 *LT*, 3 November 1864, 4.
17 *AJHR* 1865 G-08.
18 *LT*, 17 May 1862, 4.
19 *Colonist*, 16 August 1864, 4.
20 For example *DSC*, 26 August 1864, 4; *Press*, 20 January 1865, 3.
21 *Press*, 19 January 1865, 3.
22 W.P. Morrell, *The Provincial System in New Zealand, 1852–76* (Christchurch: Whitcombe and Tombs, 1964 [1932]), 162–63.
23 *LT*, 19 September 1865, 2. This editorial was either written by or reflects the views of Crosbie Ward, a leading Canterbury provincialist MP.
24 *ODT*, 3 August 1865, 5.
25 *TimH*, 2 September 1865, 4; 30 September 1865, 4.
26 *NE*, 24 August 1865, 3.
27 *HBH*, 2 September 1865, 2.
28 *LT*, 12 October 1865, 2.
29 New Provinces Act 1865, (29 Victoria 1865 No. 34).
30 *TimH*, 7 October 1865, 3.
31 *ODT*, 13 August 1867, 4.
32 Timaru and Gladstone Board of Works Act (31 Victoria 1867 No. 26).
33 Doreen E. Kemp, 'William Sefton Moorhouse, 1825–1881' (MA thesis, University of New Zealand, 1950), 128–31.
34 *TimH*, 3 July 1869, 2.
35 *DSC*, 26 August 1864, 4.
36 Rosamond Rolleston, *The Master: J.D. Ormond of Wallingford* (Wellington: A.H. and A.W. Reed, 1980), 98–100.
37 A.C. Wilson, *Wire and Wireless: A history of telecommunication in New Zealand, 1860–1987* (Palmerston North: Dunmore Press, 1994), 27–36 passim.
38 The first Telegraph Department annual report and papers on the Cook Strait cable are in *AJHR* 1865 D-01D and D-01E. Subsequent reports and papers are in *AJHR* 1866–69 section E.

Chapter 8. Life during Wartime

1 Bruce A. Hunter, 'The transfer of responsibility for native affairs from the imperial government to the General Assembly of the Colony of New Zealand' (MA thesis, University of New Zealand, 1949), 43–45.
2 For more see Ann Curthoys and Jessie Mitchell, 'The advent of self-government, 1840s–90', in *The Cambridge History of Australia*, eds Alison Bashford and Stuart Macintyre (Cambridge: Cambridge University Press, 2013), 156–59, 163; Julie Evans, Patricia Grimshaw, David Philips and Shurlee Swain, *Equal Subjects, Unequal Rights: Indigenous people in British settler colonies, 1830s–1910* (Manchester: Manchester University Press, 2003), 65–69.
3 C.E. Carrington, *John Robert Godley of Canterbury* (Cambridge: Cambridge University Press, 1950), 142.
4 Thomas Gore Browne to Edward Bulwer-Lytton, 14 October 1858, *BPP*.
5 Lord Carnarvon to Browne, 18 May 1859, *BPP*.
6 Alan Ward, *A Show of Justice: Racial 'amalgamation' in nineteenth century New Zealand* (Canberra: Australian National University Press, 1974), 93.
7 George Augustus Selwyn, memorandum of 8 May 1860, *AJHR* 1860 E-01, 23–24; see also John Stenhouse, 'Church and state in New Zealand, 1835–1870: Religion, politics, and race', in *Church and State in Old and New Words,* eds Hilary M. Carey and John Gascoigne (Leiden: Brill, 2011), 250.

8   *Press*, 27 July 1861, 1. Emphasis original.

9   Newcastle to George Grey, 5 June 1861 and 16 March 1862, *AJHR* 1861 E-01, section III, 4 and 8–9.

10 *PD* (1861–63), 438. Alan Ward concludes that '[m]ystery still surrounds the negotiations – or lack of negotiations arising from Newcastle's suggestion of March 1862 to constitute the Waikato as a Maori province', in his chapter 'A "savage war of peace"? Motives for government policies towards the Kīngitanga, 1857–1863', in *Raupatu: The confiscation of Māori land*, eds Richard Boast and Richard S. Hill (Wellington: Victoria University Press, 2009), 102.

11 *Colonist*, 18 May 1869, 3. For other examples see *DSC*, 2 June 1865, 4 (critical of a contemporary's proposal); *NZH*, 8 June 1865, 4 (deeply critical); *TarH*, 22 August 1868 (favourable).

12 *AJHR* 1858 B-05. New Zealand had no local bank until 1861 so loans had to be negotiated with representatives of Australian banks; see N.M. Chappell, *New Zealand Banker's Hundred: A history of the Bank of New Zealand 1861–1961* (Wellington: Bank of New Zealand, 1961), 14–16.

13 *NE*, 17 June 1857, 4.

14 *AJHR* 1863 B-07, 2.

15 W.P. Morrell, *The Provincial System in New Zealand, 1852–76* (Christchurch: Whitcombe and Tombs, 1964 [1932]), 118.

16 This is illustrated by the financial data in Appendix C.

17 C.W. Richmond to R. Chilman, 6 July 1856, *RAP*, vol. 1, 234.

18 *TarH*, 11 February 1860, 2.

19 *Statistics of New Zealand*, 1860.

20 J.C. Richmond to C.W. Richmond, 19 August 1859, *RAP*, vol. 1, 483.

21 B. Wells, *The History of Taranaki: A standard work on the history of the province* (New Plymouth: Edmondson and Avery, 1878), 186.

22 *TarH*, 22 February 1860, 2, and 10 March 1860, 2.

23 Natasha Andrea Elliot-Hogg, 'The Taranaki refugees 1860' (MA thesis, University of Waikato, 1999), 9–17.

24 Richard S. Hill, *Policing the Colonial Frontier: The theory and practice of coercive social and racial control in New Zealand, 1767–1867* (Wellington: Historical Publications Branch, Department of Internal Affairs,1986), 518–19.

25 Elliot-Hogg, 'Taranaki refugees', 21–22. Other provinces were less enthusiastic about accepting refugees. Elliot-Hogg, on 28–31, argues persuasively that Nelson was more amenable to accepting refugees since it could sympathise with Taranaki's plight because of the legacy of the Wairau Affray, and because additional labour was desirable in the wake of the effects of Marlborough's secession.

26 Wells, *History of Taranaki*, 228; William Swainson, *New Zealand and the War* (London: Elder, Smith and Co., 1862), 151. Sixty-eight civilians died in 1860. The normal death rate in the late 1850s was 12 or 13 per year.

27 Gail Lambert and Ron Lambert, *An Illustrated History of Taranaki* (Palmerston North: Dunmore Press, 1983), 42.

28 *TarH*, 17 November 1860, 3. By law, provincial councils had to meet at least once every 12 months, and some Taranaki councillors believed the law had been broken as it had been over a year since the start of the previous session (but less than a year since its end).

29 Elliot-Hogg, 'Taranaki refugees', 71–73.

30 *AJHR* 1861 B-05, 6, and *AJHR* 1862 B-01, 5.

31 *AJHR* 1862 A-11.

32 Ibid., 2.

33 W.B. Sutch, *Poverty and Progress in New Zealand* (Wellington: Modern Books, 1941), 59. Sutch's heavily rewritten later version, *Poverty and Progress: A re-assessment* (Wellington: A.H. and A.W.

Reed, 1969), does not deal in any greater detail with provincial government charitable aid to war victims or the destitute.

34 Peggy G. Koopman-Boyden and Claudia D. Scott, *The Family and Government Policy in New Zealand* (Sydney: Allen and Unwin, 1984), 99–100.

35 Margaret Tennant, *Paupers and Providers: Charitable aid in New Zealand* (Wellington: Allen and Unwin, 1989), 19–21.

36 Elliot-Hogg, 'Taranaki refugees', 74–77.

37 Hill, *Policing the Colonial Frontier*, 523.

38 B.J. Dalton, *War and Politics in New Zealand 1855–1870* (Sydney: Sydney University Press, 1967), 12.

39 Tony Ballantyne, 'The state, politics and power, 1769–1893', in *The New Oxford History of New Zealand*, ed. Giselle Byrnes (South Melbourne: Oxford University Press, 2009), 112, 117.

40 Bernard Attard, 'Making the colonial state: Development, debt, and warfare in New Zealand, 1853–76', *Australian Economic History Review* 52(2), 2012, 101–27, especially 101–03 and 115.

41 Damon Salesa, *Racial Crossings: Race, intermarriage, and the Victorian British Empire* (Oxford: Oxford University Press, 2011), 181.

42 J. Rutherford, *Sir George Grey K.C.B., 1812–1898: A study in colonial government* (London: Cassell, 1961), 464.

43 'Papers relative to imperial claims against the government of New Zealand', *AJHR* 1867 B-05A, 6.

44 'Finance accounts of the general government of New Zealand', *AJHR* 1864 B-01, 17.

45 G.S. Whitmore, Assistant Military Secretary, to George Grey's private secretary, 7 June 1862, *AJHR* 1862 A-06E, 8.

46 *WI*, 21 February 1862, 2.

47 'Memorandum on roads and military settlements in the Northern Island of New Zealand', *AJHR* 1863 A-08A, 1.

48 Michael Allen, 'An illusory power? Metropole, colony and land confiscation in New Zealand, 1863–1865', in *Raupatu*, eds Boast and Hill, 115.

49 E.A. Horsman, *The Diary of Alfred Domett, 1872–1885* (Oxford: Oxford University Press, 1953), 30–35.

50 R.C.J. Stone, 'Russell, Thomas', *DNZB*.

51 Rutherford, *Grey*, 496; Allen, 'An illusory power?', 120.

52 Malcolm McKinnon, *Treasury: The New Zealand Treasury, 1840–2000* (Auckland: Auckland University Press, 2003), 34–36.

53 Richard Boast, *Buying the Land, Selling the Land: Governments and Maori land in the North Island, 1865–1921* (Wellington: Victoria University Press, 2008), 50–55.

54 B.J. Lewis, 'Politics of the Auckland Province, 1862–1867' (MA thesis, University of Auckland, 1957), 92–93.

55 New Zealand Settlement Act 1863 (27 Victoria, No. 8), see especially clauses 2–5; New Zealand Loan Act 1863 (27 Victoria No. 11); Loan Appropriation Act 1863 (27 Victoria No. 12).

56 Bryan Gilling, 'Raupatu: The punitive confiscation of Māori land in the 1860s', in *Raupatu*, eds Boast and Hill, 17–18.

57 Loan Appropriation Act 1863, clause five.

58 Gilling, 'Raupatu', 19.

59 Hunter, 'Transfer of responsibility', 169; Henry Sewell, *The New Zealand Native Rebellion: Letter to Lord Lyttelton* (Auckland: Printed for the author, 1864).

60 Allen, 'An illusory power?', 131; Hunter, 'Transfer of responsibility', 170–83; Morrell, *Provincial System*, 146; Rutherford, *Grey*, 498–99 and 509–15.

61 Rutherford, *Grey*, 516–20.

62 J.E. Gorst, *The Maori King: Or, the story of our quarrel with the natives of New Zealand* (London: Macmillan, 1864), 398.

63   Ross B. Hamilton, 'Military vision and economic reality: The failure of the military settlement scheme in the Waikato, 1863–1880' (MA thesis, University of Auckland, 1968), 103. For the liberal terms of enlistment, see 22.

64   *DSC*, 2 March 1865, 5.

65   *ODT*, 15 March 1864, 4; *TarH*, 25 June 1864, 2.

66   *DSC*, 27 September 1864, 4; *Press*, 10 October 1864, 2.

67   See the telling account of J.H.A. St John, *Pakeha Ramblings Through Maori Lands* (Wellington: Robert Burrett, 1873), 76.

68   Jeanine Graham, *Frederick Weld* (Auckland: Auckland University Press, 1983), 84–87.

69   *AJHR* 1865 D-03, 11–15.

70   *AJHR* 1865 D-02 and D-02A; *AJHR* 1866 A-02, A-02A and A-02B.

71   *AJHR* 1867 A-08.

72   Morrell, *Provincial System*, 152.

73   *AJHR* 1864 B-02, 18–19, 29–30 and 33.

74   Ibid., 32 and 34.

75   Crown agents Julyan and Sargeant to Reader Wood, 23 July 1864, ibid., 34–35.

76   Chappell, *New Zealand Banker's Hundred*, 82–85.

77   *ODT*, 8 April 1864, 4.

78   For example *DN*, 13 April 1864, 4, and 16 April 1864, 4.

79   *Press*, 31 March 1864, 2.

Chapter 9. Separation: Provincialism's Apogee?

1   Claudia Orange, 'Busby, James', *Dictionary of New Zealand Biography*: www.teara.govt.nz/en/biographies/1b54/busby-james

2   *Acts and Proceedings of the Auckland Provincial Council, 1853–54*, A-11.

3   Dorothy Ross, 'Government and the people: A study of public opinion in New Zealand from 1852–1876 in its relation to politics and government' (MA thesis: University of New Zealand, 1944), 30–31.

4   All works by James Busby, published in Auckland. *A Picture of Misgovernment and Oppression in the British Colony of New Zealand* (n.p., 1853); *The First Settlers in New Zealand, and Their Treatment by the Government* (Williamson and Wilson, 1856); *Colonies and Colonization* (Philip Kunst, 1857); *A Letter to His Excellency Colonel Thomas Gore Browne, Governor-in-Chief of New Zealand, on 'Responsible Government' and the Governmental Institutions of New Zealand* (Philip Kunst, 1857); *The Federation of Colonies and the System Called 'Responsible Government'* (Richardson and Sansom, 1858); *The Pre-emption Land Question* (Richardson and Sansom, 1859); *Illustrations of the System Called Responsible Government, in a Letter to His Excellency Colonel Thomas Gore Browne* (W.G. Wilson, 1860); *The Right of a British Colonist to the Protection of the Queen and Parliament of England* (Philip Kunst, 1860). Busby continued to publish in the 1860s, rehashing previous arguments.

5   Busby's distrust of Auckland's major newspapers is apparent in *A Letter to His Excellency*. He viewed them as corrupt mouthpieces of political factions and complicit in the maintenance of 'federation'.

6   Busby, *Federation of Colonies*, 5.

7   Busby, *Letter to His Excellency*, 20. Emphasis original.

8   Busby, *Federation of Colonies*, 15.

9   Busby, *Letter to His Excellency*, 3, 7.

10 W.P. Morrell, *The Provincial System in New Zealand, 1852–76* (Christchurch: Whitcombe and Tombs, 1964 [1932]), 154.

11 *SC*, 7 November 1854, 2.

12 *SC*, 14 December 1860, 3. The *NZ* had previously declined to publish the communication in its 12 December 1860 edition. The publication that led to the libel charge was *Illustrations of the System*.

13 *AE*, 6 October 1858, 2.

14 *AE*, 16 October 1858, 2. The only time the *AE* addressed the New Provinces Act was in a correspondence section on 23 September 1858. In October, separatism was championed in leaders on the 6th, 16th, 20th, and 30th; it appeared twice more on 10 and 27 November.

15 *AE*, 25 July 1860, 2; The controversial leader, the lack of public acceptance of the *AE* and the wider press context is discussed within Kenton Storey, *Settler Anxiety at the Outposts of Empire: Colonial relations, humanitarian discourses, and the imperial press* (Vancouver: University of British Columbia Press, 2016), chapter 5.

16 *Colonist*, 11 January 1859, 3.

17 Busby, *Illustrations of the System*. Roughly three-quarters of this publication, claiming to address flaws and corruption endemic in the political order, is occupied by a verbose discussion of land policy. The remainder summarises, and in places self-plagiarises, *Federation of Colonies*.

18 The first petition received a response from London on 8 June 1854; see *SC*, 7 November 1854, 3. The Queen was not advised to take any action. Subsequent petitions received similar form letters. Guy H. Scholefield briefly details the *Aucklander*'s history in *Newspapers of New Zealand* (Wellington: A.H. & A.W. Reed, 1958), 82.

19 J.E. FitzGerald to John Robert Godley, 'FitzGerald's account of the first session of the General Assembly', Appendix I in *JHS*, vol. 2, 324.

20 *NE*, 17 January 1855, 2.

21 *WI*, 3 April 1866, 4.

22 *SC*, 29 October 1858, 3. It is unclear whether Atkin opposed all forms of separation, or just that advanced by Busby. His distaste for 'hand[ing] the Province over, bound hand and foot, to the tender mercies of the clerks in Downing-street' indicates that he did not advocate separation at any cost.

23 Busby, *Letter to His Excellency*, 6.

24 *OW*, 13 November 1858, 4.

25 The origins and early years of Otago separatism are discussed in M.C. Hercus, 'The separation movement in Otago: The origins and early history' (MA thesis, University of New Zealand, 1950) and Jocelyn M. Kerse, 'The rise and fall of Middle Island separation' (BA Honours thesis, University of Otago, 1973); Auckland separatism appears prominently in both H.J. Hanham, 'The political structure of Auckland, 1853–76' (MA thesis, University of New Zealand, 1950) and Lewis, 'Politics of the Auckland Province'; there is brief coverage of both in Morrell, *Provincial System*, especially 124–36, 157–59 and 168–74; Otago separatism is surveyed in some detail in A.H. McLintock, *The History of Otago: The origins and growth of a Wakefield class settlement* (Dunedin: Otago Centennial Historical Publications, 1949), 555–627 passim; and some political biographies locate individuals within the movement, e.g. Raewyn Dalziel, *Julius Vogel: Business politician* (Auckland: Auckland University Press, 1986), especially 43–45, 55–69.

26 Morrell, *Provincial System*, 125.

27 Dalziel, *Vogel*, 44; Hercus, 'Separation movement', 14; McLintock, *History of Otago*, 556.

28 *ODT*, 17 February 1862, 2.

29 Hercus, 'Separation movement', 5–11.

30 McLintock, *History of Otago*, 555.

31 Hercus, 'Separation movement', 30.

32 *ODT*, 16 November 1861, 2.

33 *ODT*, 11 January 1862, 2.

34 *ODT*, 24 March 1862, 4.

35 Ross, 'Government and the people', 44.

36 *ODT*, 26 April 1862, 4.

37 *ODT*, 2 June 1862, 4.

38 *ODT*, 12 May 1863, 4.

39 *ODT*, 24 March 1862, 4.

40 Representation Act 1862 (26 Victoria 1862, No. 11). Otago had seven members at the 1861 election for the third parliament of New Zealand, but on the creation of Southland the two Wallace members became Southland representatives, reducing Otago's representation to five.

41 Keith Sinclair, 'Richmond, Christopher William', *DNZB*: www.teara.govt.nz/en/biographies/1r9/richmond-christopher-william

42 'Fourth report of the Postal Service of New Zealand', 1862–63, *AJHR* 1863 D-02, 7–9.

43 McLintock, *History of Otago*, 558.

44 Dalziel, *Vogel*, 61.

45 *NE*, 12 October 1861, 6; 12 May 1862, 4.

46 *NE*, 7 June 1862, 2.

47 Jim McAloon, *Nelson: A regional history* (Whatamango Bay: Cape Catley, 1997), 90–93.

48 W.H. Scotter, 'Canterbury, 1857–68', in *A History of Canterbury, vol. II: General history, 1854–76 and cultural aspects, 1850–1950*, ed. W.J. Gardner (Christchurch: Whitcombe and Tombs, 1971), 145–46. See the *Press*, 14 March 1863, 1, for an example of Moorhouse's support for separation and the *Press* critiquing separatist arguments.

49 *IT*, 27 November 1863, 2; *DN*, 4 April 1864, 4.

50 *Lake Wakatip Mail*, 2 April 1864, 4.

51 *PD* (1861–63), 813.

52 Ibid., 814.

53 Ibid., 815–16.

54 *IT*, 27 November 1863, 2.

55 Dalziel, *Vogel*, 56.

56 I discuss relocation in relation to separation; for a more general overview, see John E. Martin, *The House: New Zealand's House of Representatives 1854–2004* (Palmerston North: Dunmore Press, 2004), 38–41.

57 *PD* (1861–63), 912, 918.

58 *AJHR* 1864 D-02, 1.

59 *DSC*, 27 November 1863, 3–5; 28 November 1863, 3.

60 *DSC*, 21 November 1863, 3.

61 *DSC*, 6 January 1864, 4.

62 'A Settler', *The Waikato and Ngaruawahia, the proposed new capital of New Zealand* (Auckland: Wilson and Burn, 1863).

63 *ODT*, 14 January 1864, 5.

64 *AJHR* 1864 D-02, 12–13.

65 Morrell, *Provincial System*, 137.

66 *NZH*, 30 November 1864, 3.

67 Ibid.

68 *DSC*, 24 February 1865, 4.

69 *ODT*, 21 February 1865, 5.

70 McLintock, *History of Otago*, 565–66.

71 Dalziel, *Vogel*, 67–69, 74–76.

72 Such depictions are common to New Zealand historiography; the direct quote comes from a discussion of the effects of Vogel's public works policy on Wellington in Alan Mulgan, *The City of the Strait: Wellington and its province – a centennial history* (Wellington: Wellington Provincial Centennial Council and A.H. and A.W. Reed, 1939), 177.

Chapter 10. 'Provincialism Will Soon Only Exist in History'

1   Stuart Macintyre and Sean Scalmer, 'Colonial states and civil society, 1860–90', in *The Cambridge History of Australia*, eds Alison Bashford and Stuart Macintyre (Cambridge: Cambridge University Press, 2013), 203.
2   Jim McAloon, *Nelson: A regional history* (Whatamango Bay: Cape Catley, 1997), 54.
3   Mike Johnston, *High Hopes: The history of the Nelson mineral belt and New Zealand's first railway* (Nelson: Nikau Press, 1987), 25–26, 31.
4   *Colonist*, 28 May 1858, 3.
5   W.P. Morrell, *The Provincial System in New Zealand 1852–76* (Christchurch: Whitcombe and Tombs, 1964 [1932]), 104.
6   *AJHR* 1860 A-05, 2.
7   Morrell, *Provincial System*, 104–05.
8   Dun Mountain Railway Act, 1861 (24 and 25 Victoria, No. 3 [local and personal]).
9   Johnston, *High Hopes*, 36–39.
10 *Colonist*, 4 February 1862, 2; *NE*, 5 February 1862, 2.
11 Johnston, *High Hopes*, 43, 46.
12 Dun Mountain Railway Act, clause 15.
13 Johnston, *High Hopes*, 49–51.
14 *NE*, 23 April 1862, 3; Lois Voller, *Rails to Nowhere: The story of the Nelson railway* (Nelson: Nikau Press, 1991), 12. Voller incorrectly identifies Fedor Kelling as member for Waimea *West* rather than Waimea *East*. His brother Carl later represented Waimea West.
15 *NE*, 24 May 1862, 3; H.F. Allan, *The Nelson Provincial Council* (Stoke: Nelson Historical Society, 1974), 26.
16 Nelson, Cobden, and Westport Railway Land Act, 1866 (30 Victoria, No. 33).
17 *NEM*, 22 December 1866, 2.
18 Alfred Saunders, *History of New Zealand*, vol. 2 (Christchurch: Smith, Anthony, Sellars and Co., 1899), 127.
19 'Report of the Select Committee on Mr Wrigg's Report on a Railway from Nelson to Cobden and Westport', *Votes and Proceedings of the Nelson Provincial Council* 1868, 31–35.
20 Barry O'Donnell, *When Nelson Had a Railway* (Wellington: Schematics, 2005), 4.
21 Allan, *Nelson Provincial Council*, 46. Allan's point that the central government paid less attention than provincial government to the development of Nelson's railway is sound, even though the reality was more complex. Central investment waxed and waned because of changes in government and unfavourable reports from engineers and surveyors, as examined by Voller in *Rails to Nowhere*.
22 A.H. McLintock, *The History of Otago: The origins and growth of a Wakefield class settlement* (Dunedin: Otago Centennial Historical Publications, 1949), 418–19.
23 Roderick John Bunce, 'James Macandrew of Otago: Slippery Jim or a leader staunch and true?' (PhD thesis, Victoria University of Wellington, 2013), 97–100.
24 *OW*, 14 April 1860, 5.
25 A.P.F. Browne, 'The Otago goldfields 1861–1863: Administration and public life' (MA thesis, University of Otago, 1974), 142–48.
26 *OW*, 25 September 1863, 4. The report is attached to the *Votes and Proceedings of the Otago Provincial Council*, 1863.
27 Otago correspondent of the *Press*, 25 September 1863, 2.
28 McLintock, *History of Otago*, 536.
29 *ODT*, 7 November 1866, 5.
30 *OW*, 25 May 1867, 11.
31 Erik Olssen, *A History of Otago* (Dunedin: John McIndoe, 1984), 71.

32   Ibid., 72–73. For more on Macandrew's campaign, see Bunce, 'James Macandrew', 116–19.

33   Erik Olssen, 'Loyalty and localism – Southland's political odyssey', in *Murihiku: The Southland story*, ed. Paul Sorrell (Invercargill: Southland to 2006 Book Project Committee, 2006), 86.

34   McLintock, *History of Otago*, 504.

35   W.H. Scotter, 'Canterbury, 1857–68', in *A History of Canterbury, vol. II: General history, 1854–76 and cultural aspects, 1850–1950*, ed. W.J. Gardner (Christchurch: Whitcombe and Tombs, 1971), 79–83.

36   Doreen E. Kemp, 'William Sefton Moorhouse, 1825–1881' (MA thesis, University of New Zealand, 1950), 42. Kemp's thesis is sometimes overly celebratory and skips past Moorhouse's difficulties. On this point, however, there is no reason to doubt her analysis of Moorhouse's commitment to the tunnel, his pet project.

37   Scotter, 'Canterbury, 1857–68', 85.

38   Opening speech of the tenth session, 1 October 1858, *Journal of Proceedings of the Canterbury Provincial Council*, vol. 1, sessions 1–10, 282.

39   W.A. Pierre, *Canterbury Provincial Railways: Genesis of the NZR system* (Wellington: New Zealand Railway and Locomotive Society, 1964), 19–20, and Scotter, 'Canterbury 1857–68', 86–87.

40   Moorhouse expected FitzGerald to support the tunnel plan and appointed him a member of the railway commission. FitzGerald, however, advocated more gradual development of public works, initially linking Christchurch and Lyttelton by means of a horse railway via Sumner and Evans Pass. Scotter, 'Canterbury, 1857–68', 85–86, and Kemp, 'Moorhouse', 46; Lyttelton and Christchurch Railway Ordinance, 1859 (Session 11, No. 13), OCP.

41   Loan Ordinance, 1859 (Session 11, No. 14), OCP.

42   *AJHR* 1860 A-05, 4.

43   Kemp, 'Moorhouse', 51–52; Scotter, 'Canterbury 1857–68', 89; *Lyttelton and Christchurch Railway Act, 1860* (24 Victoria No. 1 [local and personal]).

44   Lyttelton and Christchurch Railway Ordinance, 1860 (Session 13, No. 1), OCP.

45   Kemp, 'Moorhouse', 49.

46   Jean Garner, *By His Own Merits: Sir John Hall; pioneer, pastoralist and premier* (Hororata: Dryden Press, 1995), 130.

47   *LT*, 10 April 1861, 3.

48   Henry Grote Lewin, *The Railway Mania and its Aftermath, 1845–1852* (Newton Abbot: David and Charles, 1968 [1936]), 282–87.

49   *Press*, 25 May 1861, 2. Emphasis original.

50   Scotter, 'Canterbury, 1857–68', 94; R.B. O'Neill, *The Press, 1861–1961: The story of a newspaper* (Christchurch: Press Company, 1963), 23–25; Jenifer Roberts, *Fitz: The colonial adventures of James Edward FitzGerald* (Dunedin: Otago University Press, 2014), 193–99, 205.

51   *LT*, 20 July 1861, 4. The population figure is from the census returns in *Statistics of New Zealand*, 1861. The census was conducted in December 1861 and gave Canterbury's population as 16,040; the population in July would not have been much smaller.

52   The construction of Canterbury's railways within the context of the social and political upheavals of the period are treated in depth by Scotter, 'Canterbury, 1857–68', 95–129 and 151–55. Further details regarding the railway and its management can be found throughout Pierre, *Canterbury Provincial Railways*, especially finance on 36–39. This paragraph and the next summarise the most significant events.

53   Scotter, 'Canterbury, 1857–68', 89, 95–96.

54   Canterbury Loan Ordinance, 1862 (Session 19, No. 20), OCP; Kemp, 'Moorhouse', 65–68 for more on Moorhouse's attitude towards migration.

55   The enabling legislation was the Canterbury Great Northern Railway Act and the Canterbury Great Southern Railway Act (28 Victoria Nos. 1 and 2 [local and personal]). The southern route

was begun first because of disagreement over the northern alignment.

56 John Morrison to Edward Stafford, 26 February 1864 and 26 April 1864, Edward Stafford Papers, ATL MS-2047.

57 Bernard Attard, 'From free-trade imperialism to structural power: New Zealand and the capital market, 1856–68', *Journal of Imperial and Commonwealth History* 35(4), 2007, 512.

58 *LT*, 3 December 1863, 4. My description of the opening is written primarily with reference to this account, which is superior to that in the *Press*.

59 *Press*, 2 December 1863, 2.

60 *LT*, 3 December 1863, 4.

61 Pierre, *Canterbury Provincial Railways*, 17.

62 FitzGerald, not regarded for his business sense, had accumulated debt and relinquished control by the time he left Christchurch in April 1867, though only after protracted negotiations. O'Neill, *The Press*, 86–89.

63 *Press*, 25 May 1865, 2 (first quote); *LT*, 13 June 1865, 10 (second). The two accounts do not differ materially.

64 *Press*, 25 May 1865, 2. Quote altered to first person.

65 *Press*, 15 October 1866, 2.

66 Scotter, 'Canterbury, 1857–68', 152–53.

67 *Press*, 10 December 1867, 2.

68 Savings were £6,500 for wool exports, £9,000 for grain exports, and £9,000 for general merchandise imports. Scotter, 'Canterbury, 1857–68', 154.

69 W.H. Scotter, 'Canterbury, 1868–76', in *A History of Canterbury*, 267.

70 A.C. Wilson, *Wire and Wireless: A history of telecommunications in New Zealand, 1860–1987* (Palmerston North: Dunmore Press, 1994), 27.

71 Alan Mulgan, *The City of the Strait: Wellington and its province; a centennial history* (Wellington: Wellington Provincial Centennial Council and A.H. and A.W. Reed, 1939), 173.

72 *WI*, 25 April 1863, 3.

73 Summary of Wellington news in *NE*, 27 March 1863, 3.

74 James Coutts Crawford, *Remarks upon Railways, Suggesting the Opening of a Timber Trade in the Province of Wellington* (Wellington: Spectator Office, 1861).

75 *WI*, 11 June 1861, 5.

76 James Coutts Crawford, *Recollections of Travel in New Zealand and Australia* (London: Trubner and Company, 1880), 320.

77 See, for example, David Parsons, *Wellington's Railways: Colonial steam to Matangi* (Wellington: New Zealand Railway and Locomotive Society, 2010), 11–14.

78 *WI*, 25 April 1863, 3.

79 Ibid.

80 The Rimutaka Incline was one of the most dramatic railway lines in the world, representing the only complete long-term application of John Barraclough Fell's mountain railway system. (The Snaefell Mountain Railway on the Isle of Man, which is still operational, only uses the Fell third rail for braking, not traction.) The definitive history of the Rimutaka Incline is W.N. Campbell, *A Line of Railway: The railway conquest of the Rimutakas* (Wellington: New Zealand Railway and Locomotive Society, 1976).

81 *WI*, 2 May 1863, 3; 16 May 1863, 3.

82 *DSC*, 20 May 1863, 3.

83 *WI*, 2 May 1863, 3.

84 *WI*, 28 November 1863, 4.

85 *NZS*, 9 July 1864, 4.

86 *WI*, 19 June 1866, 4.

87 *WI*, 26 June 1866, 6; 3 July 1866, 6; 14 March 1868, 4. Testimony in court, as part of a private case

between J.R. Davies (the instigator of Southland's wooden railway) and Marchant over money the latter owed the former, revealed that Marchant sought a deal much to his advantage where, in the words of a letter he wrote to Davies, he would be 'getting paid for the railway before it is begun, and possessing it when it is finished'. It must be emphasised that this deal was offered in 1866, not 1863 as stated in Bernard John Foster, 'Stokes, Robert', *An Encyclopaedia of New Zealand 1966*: www.teara.govt.nz/en/1966/stokes-robert

88 *EH*, 20 November 1867, 2; *WI*, 21 November 1867, 5.

89 Mulgan, *City of the Strait*, 193–94.

90 D.G. Hoy, *Rails Out of the Capital* (Wellington: New Zealand Railway and Locomotive Society, 1970), 11.

91 Graham Bush, *From Survival to Revival: Auckland's public transport since 1860* (Wellington: Grantham House, 2014), 13–23.

92 S.R. Hill, 'Local politics in the Auckland Province, 1867–1871' (MA thesis, University of Auckland, 1958), 32.

93 *Albertland Gazette*, 4 November 1863, 2; *Coromandel Observer*, 7 July to 19 August 1867.

94 *SC*, 31 January 1862, 3.

95 *SC*, 7 January 1862, 5.

96 The earliest years of railways and tramways in Auckland Province have been essentially ignored. Although John Logan Campbell helped to promote the company responsible for the wooden tramway, only a single sentence acknowledges his association with the company in R.C.J. Stone, *The Father and His Gift: John Logan Campbell's later years* (Auckland: Auckland University Press, 1987), 30. Two short articles shed some light: Anne Stewart Ball, 'Beginning days of a railway: James Stewart and the Auckland to Drury railway': www.aucklandlibraries.govt.nz/EN/heritage/localhistory/countiesmanukau/transport/Pages/aucklandtodruryrailway.aspx; and Munroe Graham, 'The 150 year anniversary of the Drury tramway': www.bettertransport.org.nz/2012/04/the-150-year-anniversary-of-the-drury-tramway

97 There have been numerous studies of the role of railways in the American Civil War. A prominent recent example is William G. Thomas, *The Iron Way: Railroads, the Civil War, and the making of modern America* (New Haven and London: Yale University Press, 2011).

98 For example *SC*, 12 July 1861, 4; *DSC*, 23 August 1862, 5; 25 December 1862, 2; 6 November 1863, 5.

99 *DSC*, 14 February 1863, 3; Auckland Loan Act, 1863 (Session 15, No. 8), OAP; Auckland and Drury Railway Act, 1863 (27 Victoria, No. 2).

100 *Journals of the Auckland Provincial Council*, 1864, A-03; cf. 1865, A-02, 16–18.

101 For example *DSC*, 30 July 1864, 6; *NZH*, 15 July 1864, 3.

102 F.E. Gee, 'The North Island Main Trunk Railway, New Zealand: A study in the politics of railway construction' (MA thesis, University of New Zealand, 1949), 7–8; *DSC*, 16 February 1865, 4. Although not directly connected to the initiation of the Drury railway, see also the trunk railway proposals in 'A Settler', *The Waikato and Ngaruawahia, The Proposed New Capital of New Zealand* (Auckland: Wilson and Burn, 1863).

103 *DSC*, 17 February 1865, 5; 31 May 1865, 5.

104 R.C.J. Stone, *Makers of Fortune: A colonial business community and its fall* (Auckland: Auckland University Press, 1973), 10.

105 *DSC*, 17 August 1867, 3–4.

106 *TarH*, 23 July 1864, 3.

107 Ibid.

108 *TarH*, 30 July 1864, 2; see also *NZS*, 6 August 1864, 3.

109 *Wanganui Chronicle*, 3 August 1864, cited in *Press*, 13 August 1864, 3.

110 *OW*, 12 August 1864, 5.

111 See, for instance, a lengthy treatment of the subject by the *Wanganui Times* reproduced in *TarH*,

21 October 1865, 5.

112 *Wanganui Chronicle*, 3 August 1864, cited in *Press*, 13 August 1864, 3.

113 Detailed treatments of the gauge question sometimes focused on matters of cost and speed rather than the problem of breaks-of-gauge at provincial borders, e.g. *NE*, 17 April 1866, 2. However, fears of breaks-of-gauge were also treated, e.g. *Press*, 13 December 1866, 2.

114 *NE*, 24 September 1867, 4.

115 *AJHR* 1867 F-04, 3.

116 I have given this interprovincial dispute lengthier treatment in André Brett, 'Scars in the country: The centralisation of New Zealand statehood' (BA Honours thesis, University of Melbourne, 2009), 20–21 and 'The great Kiwi (dis)connect: The New Provinces Act of 1858 and its consequences', *Melbourne Historical Journal* 40, 144–45.

117 Wilson, *Wire and Wireless*, 35.

118 Ron Palenski, *The Making of New Zealanders* (Auckland: Auckland University Press, 2012), 19–35; Eric Pawson, 'Local times and standard time in New Zealand', *Journal of Historical Geography* 18(3), 1992, 278–87.

Chapter 11. The Watershed of 1867 and the Westland Experiment

1   Although I concur with much of what Bernard Attard has argued recently regarding New Zealand's centralisation and the relationship between warfare and the dynamics of colonial development, some of his arguments are based on P.J. Cain and A.G. Hopkins' 'gentlemanly capitalism' thesis that understates the agency of colonial actors. Attard, 'From free-trade imperialism to structural power: New Zealand and the capital market, 1856–68', *Journal of Imperial and Commonwealth History* 35(4), 2007, 505–27; Attard, 'Making the colonial state: Development, debt and warfare in New Zealand, 1853–76', *Australian Economic History Review* 52(2), 2012, 101–27; P.J. Cain and A.G. Hopkins, *British Imperialism, 1688–2000* (Harlow: Longman, 2002 [1993]).

2   Breakdown of debt by province can be found in Appendix F.

3   *New Zealand Times*, 16 September 1867, reprinted in *NE*, 5 October 1867, 3.

4   Calculated from Wray Vamplew, ed., *Australians: Historical statistics* (Sydney: Fairfax, Syme and Weldon Associates, 1987). Population figures for every year in every colony were not available, hence the choice of 1870–71 to allow a relatively even comparison. No marked spikes in borrowing occurred in the previous three to four years; thus the comparison with New Zealand is valid.

5   *AJHR* 1866 B-06, 7.

6   Edmund Bohan, *Edward Stafford: New Zealand's first statesman* (Christchurch: Hazard Press, 1994), 225–30; W.P. Morrell, *The Provincial System in New Zealand 1852–76* (Christchurch: Whitcombe and Tombs, 1964 [1932]), 178–79.

7   Bohan, *Stafford*, 230–32.

8   *PD* (1866), 894.

9   Attard, 'Making the colonial state', 119.

10 See table in J. Rutherford, *Sir George Grey K.C.B., 1812–1898: A study in colonial government* (London: Cassell, 1961), 565.

11 Attard, 'Making the colonial state', 117–18.

12 David Hamer, 'Fitzherbert, William', *Dictionary of New Zealand Biography*: www.teara.govt.nz/en/biographies/1f11/fitzherbert-william

13 Morrell, *Provincial System*, 187–88 expands on these previous unsuccessful ideas.

14 *AJHR* 1867 B-01A, 6.

15 Ibid., 7–8.

16 For extended analysis of the consolidated loan proposals and debate, see Morrell, *Provincial*

System, 184–89.

17 Bohan, *Stafford*, 250–51.

18 Malcolm McKinnon, *Treasury: The New Zealand Treasury, 1840–2000* (Auckland: Auckland University Press, 2003), 35.

19 Southland Provincial Debt Act (29 Victoria, No. 68), clause 19.

20 Morrell, *Provincial System*, 187.

21 A selection is collected among petitions on other topics in *AJHR* 1867 G-01.

22 Municipal Council Ordinance 1860 (Session 14, No. 2), OCP. Although the provincial council passed it in 1860, it did not receive the governor's assent until 1861.

23 *NE*, 6 November 1861. Apprehension appeared on both sides of the Canterbury press, e.g. *LT*, 15 June 1861, 4; *Press*, 17 August 1861, 1.

24 Christchurch City Council Ordinance 1862 (Session 19, No. 21), OCP; Lyttelton Municipal Council Ordinance 1863 (Session 20, No. 22), OCP; first schedule of the Municipal Corporations Act 1867 (31 Victoria No. 24); although Hokitika was formed under the Municipal Council Ordinance, doubts about the validity of its first elections required the passage of the Hokitika Municipal Ordinance 1866 (Session 26, No. 4), OCP, before it became operational.

25 W.H. Scotter, 'Canterbury, 1857–68', in *A History of Canterbury, vol. II: General history, 1854–76 and cultural aspects, 1850–1950*, ed. W.J. Gardner (Christchurch: Whitcombe and Tombs, 1971), 132–33. No other form of direct taxation then existed, compounding the distaste for any possibility that the road boards might introduce rates. For legislation establishing the boards, see the Roads Districts Ordinance 1863 (Session 20, No. 19), OCP.

26 Morrell, *Provincial System*, 192, 298.

27 *AJHR* 1862 A-04A, and the first schedule of the *Municipal Corporations Act 1867* (31 Victoria No. 24).

28 *PD* 1 (1867), 235–39.

29 Bohan, *Stafford*, 241.

30 This paragraph draws on A.H. McLintock, *The History of Otago: The origins and growth of a Wakefield class settlement* (Dunedin: Otago Centennial Historical Publications, 1949), 571–73 and Ann Tyndale-Biscoe, 'The struggle for responsible government in the Province of Otago, 1854–76' (MA thesis, University of New Zealand, 1954), 108–18.

31 *ODT*, 10 June 1867, 4.

32 *NZH*, 7 August 1867, 4. Interestingly, the *DSC* featured a moderately favourable editorial on 8 August 1867, 2, as it believed the bill would curb centralising tendencies of the *provinces* and benefit outlying districts in the true spirit of provincialism – though at the same time the paper would not 'shed many tears' were it withdrawn. However, its Wellington correspondents readily condemned the bill as 'utterly unconstitutional' and 'destructive' to provincial interests (13 August 1867, 4).

33 *WI*, 17 August 1867, 4.

34 *ODT*, 7 August 1867, 4.

35 *Press*, 14 September 1867, 2.

36 *DSC*, 13 August 1867, 4.

37 *EH*, 15 August 1867, 2.

38 The vote broke down along the following provincial lines, with the numbers given as for/against: Auckland 3/11, Taranaki 3/0, Hawke's Bay 2/0; Wellington 2/5; Nelson 4/2; Marlborough 1/1 (unsurprisingly, Adams of Picton voted for the measure and Eyes of Blenheim against); Canterbury 7/4 (reflecting the unrest of hinterlands combined with inner MPs being members of the government); Otago 3/11; Southland 2/2. Seven of the parliament's 70 members did not vote, with Featherston and Fitzherbert paired.

39 Scotter, 'Canterbury 1857–68', 162.

40   *WI*, 10 August 1867, 3 (cf. *NZH*, 13 August 1867, 4); *WI*, 17 August 1867, 4.

41   W.J. Gardner, 'Hall, John', *Dictionary of New Zealand Biography*: www.teara.govt.nz/en/biographies/1h5/hall-john

42   *PD* 1 (1867), 302.

43   *WI*, 13 August 1867, 3.

44   *Wanganui Times*, 8 June 1867, reprinted in the *Hawke's Bay Weekly Times*, 17 June 1867, 139.

45   *NZH*, 13 August 1867, 4; *WI*, 6 August 1867, 3.

46   Municipal Corporations Act 1867, clauses 22, 191.

47   *NZH*, 26 August 1867, 3.

48   Municipal Corporations Act 1867, part 16 (clauses 239–65).

49   Arthur Dudley Dobson, *Reminiscences of Arthur Dudley Dobson, Engineer, 1841–1930*, 2nd edn (Christchurch: Whitcombe and Tombs, 1930), 37–39.

50   Scotter, 'Canterbury 1857–68', 138.

51   *LT*, 30 July 1864, 4.

52   Philip Ross May, *Hokitika: Goldfields capital* (Christchurch: Pegasus Press, 1964), 17–18.

53   Ibid., 18.

54   All population figures from A.J. Harrop, *The Romance of Westland: The story of New Zealand's golden coast* (Christchurch: Whitcombe and Tombs, 1923), 59. Some sources suggest Hokitika itself was home to 50,000 people, but J. Halket Millar refutes this in *Westland's Golden 'Sixties* (Wellington: A.H. and A.W. Reed, 1959), 171.

55   Harrop, *Romance of Westland*, 61, 74.

56   Philip Ross May, *The West Coast Gold Rushes*, rev. edn (Christchurch: Pegasus Press, 1967 [1962]); May, *Gold Town: Ross, Westland* (Christchurch: Pegasus, 1970), and May and Bernard Conradson's chapters in *Miners and Militants: Politics in Westland, 1865–1918*, ed. May (Christchurch: Whitcoulls, 1975). The first edition of May's *West Coast Gold Rushes* (1962) remains necessary for scholars as May removed his extensive documentation from the second edition. Although May and Conradson are the leading authorities, other sources are also significant. Harrop's *Romance of Westland* is largely a narrative that strings together quotes but has some useful information. Millar's *Westland's Golden 'Sixties* is a colourful, imaginative account of the goldfields' personalities and tribulations. J.H.M. Salmon, *A History of Gold-mining in New Zealand* (Wellington: Government Printer, 1963), 124–76, provides a handy if sometimes hastily prepared overview of the West Coast experience with much Nelson context – often overlooked by writers focusing on Westland.

57   May, 'Politics and gold: The separation of Westland, 1865–7', in *Miners and Militants*, 1. This chapter is the definitive account of Westland's secession.

58   *Press*, 1 May 1863, 1.

59   Ibid.

60   Moorhouse even served as Westland's MHR, elected unopposed for 1866–68, amid howls of criticism from Timaru. Timaru's secessionists sympathised with Westland's cause and believed Moorhouse sought Canterbury's territorial integrity regardless of whether it conformed to Westland's interests. Doreen E. Kemp, 'William Sefton Moorhouse, 1825–1881' (MA thesis, University of New Zealand, 1950), 133.

61   *WCT*, 23 September 1865, 2.

62   *WCT*, 12 September 1865, 2; 2 September 1865, 2.

63   *HES*, 7 January 1867, 2; 11 January, 2; 20 February, 2; 6 March, 2.

64   Charles Wentworth Dilke, *Greater Britain: A record of travel in English-speaking countries during 1866 and 1867*, vol. 1 (London: Macmillan, 1868), 335; Millar, *Westland's Golden 'Sixties*, 132.

65   May, 'Politics and gold', 13–16.

66   Ibid., 18.

67   John Hall's extensive private communications are contained in ATL MS-Group-0033; particularly

significant for Westland are the inwards letters in MS-Copy-Micro-0694-11.

68 John Hall to Thomas Bright, *WCT*, 23 September 1867, 2. This letter (or a similar one to Edmund Barff) was also published in the *HES*, 23 September 1867, 2.

69 Memorandum by John Hall, *AJHR* 1868 A-01, 61.

70 E.g. H.C. Field to John Hall, 1, 21 and 22 August 1868 and John Bryce to John Hall, 3 September 1868, MS-Copy-Micro-0694-14. Wanganui's desire for a county, however, saw no result.

71 *WI*, 26 September 1867, 3.

72 May, 'Politics and gold', 21.

73 *HES*, 15 February 1867, 2; *WCT*, 5 October 1867, 2; *GRA*, 8 October 1867, 2.

74 *WCT*, 28 September 1867, 2; 1 October, 3. *HES*, 6 November 1867, 2.

75 *GRA*, 12 October 1867, 2 and 24 October, 2. See 1 October, 2, for its desire to join Nelson. This was motivated by Nelson's successful management of its goldfields; see May, 'Politics and gold', 22–24 for more.

76 Emilie Monson Malcolm, *My Own Story: An episode in the life of a New Zealand settler of 50 years back* (Auckland: Brett Printing and Publishing, 1904).

77 Erik Olssen, 'Loyalty and localism – Southland's political odyssey', in *Murihiku: The Southland story*, ed. Paul Sorrell (Invercargill: Southland to 2006 Book Project Committee, 2006), 86.

78 *AJHR* 1864 A-01, 14

79 Basil Howard, *Rakiura: A history of Stewart Island, New Zealand* (Wellington: A.H. and A.W. Reed, 1974 [1940]), 180. See also John Hall-Jones' admirable social history of exploration and settlement, *Stewart Island Explored* (Invercargill: Craig Printing, 1994).

80 Useful letters during Hall's tenure can be found in MS-Copy-Micro-0694-13 and -14, as well as telegrams in MSY-1096.

81 J.L.C. Richardson, *Our Constitutional History* (Timaru: Herald Office, 1868), 48.

82 *EH*, 15 August 1867, 2.

Chapter 12. The Great Public Works Policy

1 For more, see W.K. Jackson, *The New Zealand Legislative Council: A study of the establishment, failure and abolition of an upper house* (Dunedin: University of Otago Press, 1972).

2 Ray Fargher, *The Best Man Who Ever Served the Crown?: A life of Donald McLean* (Wellington: Victoria University Press, 2007), 296–300; Raewyn Dalziel, *Julius Vogel: Business politician* (Auckland: Auckland University Press, 1986), 97–98.

3 Stevan Eldred-Grigg, *Diggers, Hatters and Whores: The story of the New Zealand gold rushes* (Auckland: Random House, 2011), 151–57.

4 *Colonist*, 19 January 1869, 2; Jim McAloon, *Nelson: A regional history* (Whatamango Bay: Cape Catley, 1997), 78.

5 W.P. Morrell, *The Provincial System in New Zealand 1852–76* (Christchurch: Whitcombe and Tombs, 1964 [1932]), 204, 209–10; A.D. McIntosh, ed., *Marlborough: A provincial history* (Christchurch: Capper Press, 1977 [1940]), 257–58.

6 *AJHR* 1869 B-02, 9.

7 The centrality of railways to the reunion debate is explored by R.S. Innes, 'Railways and the reunion of Otago and Southland, 1867–1870' (PGDipArts thesis, University of Otago, 1976).

8 Erik Olssen, 'Loyalty and localism – Southland's political odyssey', *Murihiku: The Southland story*, ed. Paul Sorrell (Invercargill: Southland to 2006 Book Project Committee, 2006), 86.

9 Innes, 'Railways and the reunion', 63.

10 *AJHR* 1870 A-15; Otago and Southland Union Act (33–34 Victoria, No. 93).

11 *ST*, 23 September 1870, 2; 27 September 1870, 2.

12 *PD* 7 (1870), 344.

13 For example *NZH*, 7 April 1868, 2, contained financial proposals to invoke Southern ire.

14 *PD* 6 (1869), 540–01.

15 *TimH*, 23 April 1870, 2. Stafford, having lost the confidence of his Nelson electors after the fall of his ministry, resigned there and became the member for Timaru.

16 *Star*, 13 November 1869, 2. Because the first two years of Rolleston's term, 1868–70, were marked by economy in response to extravagances in Moorhouse's final term, he had to place less emphasis on public works in his statements than he would have wished. W.H. Scotter, 'Canterbury, 1868–76', in *A History of Canterbury, vol. II: General history, 1854–76 and cultural aspects, 1850–1950* (Christchurch: Whitcombe and Tombs, 1971), 252.

17 E.g. *OW*, 12 June 1869, 1.

18 Philip Ross May, *The West Coast Gold Rushes* (Christchurch: Pegasus Press, 1967 [1962]), 359–63.

19 A particularly striking example is in Philip Ross May, *Gold Town: Ross, Westland* (Christchurch: Pegasus Press, 1970), 39, especially when viewed with the town map on 100–01.

20 *BH*, 24 June 1868, 6. Richardson implied but did not say explicitly that the neutered provincial councils would manage immigration.

21 *TimH*, 30 April 1870, 2.

22 *WI*, 20 July 1869, 2.

23 *Wairarapa Mercury*, 15 January 1869, 2.

24 *AJHR* 1869 B-02, 14–15.

25 Dalziel, *Vogel*, 103–04.

26 Ibid., 88–89, though Vogel was still an Otago MHR for the Goldfields; in January 1871 he became member for Auckland City East.

27 *AJHR* 1870 B-02, 3.

28 Edmund Bohan, *Edward Stafford: New Zealand's first statesman* (Christchurch: Hazard Press, 1994), 290.

29 Quotes and details about the Great Public Works Policy are from *PD* 7 (1870), 102–08, except where indicated. An almost identical version appears in *AJHR* 1870 B-02, 12–20.

30 This text is a composite of *PD* 7 (1870), 108, and the official press summary provided by the government in *EP*, 29 June 1870, 2. The final sentence does not appear in *PD* (the sentiment is expressed less clearly), while the press summary has mistakes in the network description, e.g. 'Milton' for 'Winton'.

31 Some scholarly writers have made this error, e.g. Leslie Lipson, *The Politics of Equality: New Zealand's adventures in democracy* (Chicago: University of Chicago Press, 1948), 146, and Rosslyn J. Noonan, *By Design: A brief history of the Public Works Department Ministry of Works 1870–1970* (Wellington: Government Printer, 1975), 8.

32 *EP*, 29 June 1870, 2.

33 *ODT*, 4 July 1870, 3; cf. *HBH*, 1 July 1870, 2; *Press*, 30 June 1870, 2; *WCT*, 30 June 1870, 2.

34 *EP*, 29 June 1870, 2.

35 Ibid.

36 F.E. Gee 'The North Island Main Trunk Railway, New Zealand: A study in the politics of railway construction' (MA thesis, University of New Zealand, 1949), 13.

37 *EH*, 29 June 1870, 2.

38 *BH*, 29 June 1870, 5.

39 *EP*, 29 June 1870, 2; also 30 June 1870, 2.

40 *NE*, 29 June 1870, 2. The *NEM* shared these sentiments: 1 July 1870, 2. The *Colonist* was alone among the Nelson press in praising the scheme: 8 July 1870, 2. Oddly, the *NE* had previously supported Vogelesque plans, as highlighted by a Wellington correspondent on 29 June 1870, 3.

41 *TimH*, 2 July 1870, 2.

42 *OW*, 23 July 1870, 2. A public meeting in Dunedin seeking support for the works policy broke down with no resolutions. At least one attendee felt that the resolutions in favour were lost as a result of many supporters leaving early because the venue – the Post Office Hall rather than the

Princes Theatre – was uncomfortable, poorly ventilated and had such poor acoustics that speeches were inaudible (*ODT*, 16 July 1870, 3). Vogel's *DSC* felt the meeting was dominated by 'two local demagogues' (25 July 1870, 3).

43 *WCT* of 7, 9, 12 and 13 July 1870. Greymouth did offer similar objections but with less fervour and mainly to bolster its campaign for annexation by Nelson, e.g. *GRA*, 16 July 1870, 2.

44 *DSC*, 6 July 1870, 4; 7 July 1870, 3.

45 *ODT*, 30 June 1870, 4; cf. support from restive North Otago in *OT*, 1 July 1870, 2, and 12 July 1870, 2.

46 *WI*, 5 July 1870, 2 (see also 2 July 1870, 2). It echoed this theme on 15 September 1870, 2, accusing centralists of 'insidious attacks on the constitution' in an attempt to achieve colonial unity while provincialism sought unity through 'that spirit of colonisation which led to the very foundation of the colony'.

47 *NE*, 6 July 1870, 3. Allegedly just six people voted for the original motion (*OW*, 9 July 1870, 13); unsurprisingly the *Examiner* neither reported this nor that the amendment passed amid prolonged applause.

48 *Press*, 7 July 1870, 3.

49 Doreen E. Kemp, 'William Sefton Moorhouse, 1825–1881' (MA thesis, University of New Zealand, 1950), 150.

50 *HBH*, 22 July 1870, 3. Both meetings were controversial; the speakers at the second meeting condemned the first, but a *Press* correspondent was quick to slur the second for 'prevailing rowdyism' (21 July 1870, 2).

51 *TarH*, 9 July 1870, 2.

52 *HBH*, 1 July 1870, 2; also 5 July 1870, 2.

53 *OT*, 12 July 1870, 2.

54 George Bowen to Earl Granville, 3 July 1870, *AJHR* 1871 A-01, 16; Vogel made little of this aspect at the time but emphasised it later in life (Vogel Family Papers, ATL MS-Papers-0178-013). Unfortunately, no Māori newspapers, let alone any with English translations, exist in the Māori Niupepa Collection (www.nzdl.org/niupepa and since 2015 also available on Papers Past) for June or July 1870, so I have been unable to gauge the Māori press' reaction.

55 W.R. Armstrong, 'The politics of development: A study of the structure of politics from 1870 to 1890' (MA thesis, Victoria University of Wellington, 1960), 79–85; some contemporary politicians alluded to this, cf. E.C.J. Stevens to Edward Stafford, 2 August 1871, Edward Stafford Papers, ATL MS-2050.

56 William Downie Stewart, *William Rolleston: A New Zealand statesman* (Christchurch: Whitcombe and Tombs, 1940), 88–89.

57 Bohan, *Stafford*, 301.

58 *WI*, 21 July 1870, 3.

59 William Gisborne, *New Zealand Rulers and Statesmen from 1840 to 1897*, rev. edn (London: Sampson, Marston and Company, 1897), 192; Vogel Family Papers, ATL MS-Papers-0178-013.

60 G.G. Harvey, 'The place of the railways in the transport problem of the North Island 1870–1936' (MA thesis, University of New Zealand, 1937), 47–48. Jim McAloon notes this view was not universal and some Canterbury elite supported Vogel's plans; *No Idle Rich: The wealthy in Canterbury and Otago 1840–1914* (Dunedin: University of Otago Press, 2002), 101.

61 Immigration and Public Works Act, Railway Act, Railways Act, Canterbury Gauge Act, and the Immigration and Public Works Loan Act (33 and 34 Victoria, Nos 77–80).

62 *AJHR* 1870 D-30.

63 Ibid., 3.

64 Noonan, *By Design*, 9.

65 *EP*, 13 September 1870, 2.

66 *Press*, 14 September 1870, 2; cf. *WI*, 15 September 1870, 2.

67 *ODT*, 14 September 1870, 2.
68 Pollen to McLean, 2 September 1870, Donald McLean Papers, ATL MS-Papers-0032-0507.

Chapter 13. Suffocation of the Provinces

1   Raewyn Dalziel, *Julius Vogel: Business politician* (Auckland: Auckland University Press, 1986), 111–13.
2   Dorothy Ross, 'Government and the people: A study of public opinion in New Zealand from 1852–1876 in its relation to politics and government' (MA thesis: University of New Zealand, 1944), 57; W.H. Scotter, 'Canterbury, 1868–76', in *A History of Canterbury, vol. II: General history, 1854–76 and cultural aspects, 1850–1950* (Christchurch: Whitcombe and Tombs, 1971), 267–68.
3   See the *Lake Wakatip Mail* for January and February 1871, especially 9 February 1871, 2.
4   Alfred Murray Leslie, 'The general election of 1871 and its importance in the history of New Zealand' (MA thesis, University of New Zealand, 1956), 94–96.
5   A.H. McLintock, *The History of Otago: The origins and growth of a Wakefield class settlement* (Dunedin: Otago Centennial Historical Publications, 1949), 526–35.
6   *ODT*, 24 November 1870, 2; 26 November 1870, 3
7   McLintock, *History of Otago*, 532.
8   Dalziel, *Vogel*, 124.
9   *AJHR* 1871 B-02A, 3–6.
10 *AJHR* 1871 B-02, 9–11 details the financial reforms.
11 For more on this plan and its debate, see Dalziel, *Vogel*, 128; W.P. Morrell, *The Provincial System in New Zealand 1852–76* (Christchurch: Whitcombe and Tombs, 1964 [1932]), 227–28.
12 Railways Act 1871, schedules 1–3 (35 Victoria, No. 76). Morrell, *Provincial System*, 228, incorrectly implies no railways were authorised in Westland. He is correct that no *main* lines were authorised, but the Greymouth to Brunner coalfields railway was in Westland.
13 Morrell, *Provincial System*, 231–32; Ross, 'Government and the people', 47.
14 *PD* 11 (1871), 985.
15 Superintendents of Marlborough Election Act, 1872 (36 Victoria, No. 69); Superintendent of Taranaki Empowering Act, 1873 (37 Victoria, No. 13); Superintendents of Hawke's Bay Election Act, 1873 (37 Victoria, No. 14)
16 *BH*, 10 July 1872, 8; *EH*, 2 May 1872, 2; *NZH*, 29 July 1872, 2; *TarH*, 4 May 1872, 2; *TarH*, 19 June 1872, 2; *Tuapeka Times*, 18 January 1872, 6.
17 E.g. *WI*, 16 March 1872, 2.
18 *DSC*, 1 January 1872, 2.
19 John Ormond to Donald McLean, 3 January 1872, Donald McLean Papers, ATL MS-Papers-0032-0485.
20 *AJHR* 1872 D-01A, 3, and D-07C; *OW*, 27 January 1872, 1.
21 Raewyn Dalziel, *The Origins of New Zealand Diplomacy: The agent-general in London, 1870–1905* (Wellington: Victoria University Press, 1975), 35–37.
22 *AJHR* B-02A, 12, 16.
23 *NZH*, 13 April 1872, 2.
24 *ODT*, 26 July 1872, 2.
25 Edmund Bohan, *Edward Stafford: New Zealand's first statesman* (Christchurch: Hazard Press, 1994), 316.
26 *AJHR* 1872 B-02C, 9.
27 W.R. Armstrong, 'The politics of development: A study of the structure of politics from 1870 to 1890' (MA thesis, Victoria University of Wellington, 1960), 103.
28 Fuller accounts of the 1872 session and its personalities are in Bohan, *Stafford*, 315–27, and Dalziel, *Vogel*, 148–52.

29 William Gisborne, *New Zealand Rulers and Statesmen from 1840 to 1897*, rev. edn (London: Sampson Low, Marston & Company, 1897), 195; cf. Henry Sewell to Edward Stafford, 8 October 1872, Stafford Papers, for harsher contemporary sentiment.

30 Morrell, *Provincial System*, 237; Dalziel, *Vogel*, 153.

31 Rolleston to Featherston, May 1873, in William Downie Stewart, *William Rolleston: A New Zealand statesman* (Christchurch: Whitcombe and Tombs, 1940), 110.

32 Bohan, *Stafford*, 338; Dalziel, *Vogel*, 159–60.

33 *AJHR* 1873 B-02, 10.

34 This policy is outlined in *AJHR* 1873 B-02, 10–17.

35 *EH*, 21 August 1873, 2.

36 *Press*, 9 August 1873, 2; cf. *ODT*, 5 August 1873, 4.

37 *ODT*, 14 August 1873, 3.

38 Dalziel, *Vogel*, 163.

39 *WI*, 16 September 1873, 2.

40 *Star*, 18 September 1873, 3.

41 *ES*, 27 September 1873, 2.

42 *Tuapeka Times*, 22 May 1873, 4, and 26 June 1873, 4; *ST*, 8 July 1873, 2.

43 *DSC*, 14 March 1873, 3; *ES*, 3 July 1873, 2; *NZH*, 18 January 1873, 3, and 18 April 1873, 2.

44 *Waikato Times*, 3 July 1873, 2. Interestingly, this candidate, Hugh Lusk, was brought over to Grey's anti-abolition, pro-Auckland side in late 1875.

45 County of Westland Act, 1868 (32 Victoria, No. 60).

46 Bernard Conradson, 'Politics and penury: County and province, 1868–76', in *Miners and Militants: Politics in Westland, 1865–1918*, ed. Philip Ross May (Christchurch: Canterbury University Press, 1975), 33.

47 J.A. Bonar to John Hall, 18 May 1868, ATL MSY-1096.

48 Conradson, 'Politics and penury', 38–39.

49 *WCT*, 29 October 1872, 2.

50 *GRA*, 12 August 1871, 2.

51 *AJHR* 1870 F-03.

52 Compare *WCT*, 10 July 1872, 2, with 2 October 1872, 2. Also note the *WCT*'s opposition to annexation was coupled with support for expanding Westland's boundaries to the north. Securing the customs revenue of Westport was a temptation to Hokitika.

53 *Colonist*, 13 August 1872, 4.

54 Conradson, 'Politics and penury', 42.

55 Province of Westland Act, 1873 (37 Victoria, No. 35). For public support, cf. *GRA*, 21 August 1873, 2 (supportive) and *WCT*, 25 August 1873, 2 (ambivalent).

56 Morrell, *Provincial System*, 243.

57 *Colonist*, 2 July 1874, 3.

58 *AJHR* 1874 D-04.

59 *AJHR* 1874 D-06. New Zealand's population at March 1874 was 344,984; G.T. Bloomfield, *New Zealand: A handbook of historical statistics* (Boston: G.K. Hall and Co., 1984), 41. Most of the 15,102 arrived by this date; assuming they all had, they comprised 4.38 per cent of the population.

60 'Financial Statement', 22 June 1875, *Votes and Proceedings of the Provincial Council of Hawke's Bay*, 1875.

61 See Appendix D for mileage and financial details.

62 *AJHR* 1874 E-03, 8.

63 Paul Mahoney, *The Era of the Bush Tram in New Zealand* (Wellington: Transpress, 2004), 83–84, 171. This boom began in the early 1870s and, although it fluctuated in accordance with the wider

economy, endured into the early twentieth century; cf. Rollo Arnold, 'The virgin forest harvest and the development of colonial New Zealand', *New Zealand Geographer* 32, 1976, 105–26.

64 *DSC*, 4 July 1874, 2; cf. *NZH*, 3 July 1874, 2; *New Zealand Tablet*, 4 July 1874, 5; *TarH*, 4 July 1874, 2; *TimH*, 3 July 1874, 3.

65 The leading examples are Tom Brooking and Eric Pawson, *Seeds of Empire: The environmental transformation of New Zealand* (London: I.B. Tauris, 2011) and Tom Brooking and Eric Pawson, eds, *Environmental Histories of New Zealand* (Melbourne: Oxford University Press, 2002). These give little time to the events of 1874, a particularly surprising omission in the case of the latter.

66 A detailed examination of provincial regulations and attitudes is M.M. Roche, *Forest Policy in New Zealand: An historical geography, 1840–1919* (Palmerston North: Dunmore Press, 1987), 22–41.

67 *ODT*, 29 October 1868, 2.

68 Stephen Utick, *Captain Charles, Engineer of Charity: The remarkable life of Charles Gordon O'Neill* (Crow's Nest: Allen and Unwin, 2008), 93–94, 105–06.

69 Dalziel, *Vogel*, 171.

70 Graeme Wynn, 'Conservation and society in late nineteenth-century New Zealand', *NZJH* 11(2), 1977, 130.

71 *Wanganui Chronicle*, 5 August 1874, 2.

72 *Press*, 24 July 1874, 2.

73 *EH*, 7 August 1874, 2; *GRA*, 8 August 1874, 2; *ODT*, 13 August 1874, 3; *Press*, 8 August 1874, 2; *TarH*, 8 August 1874, 2.

74 John Halkett, *The Native Forests of New Zealand* (Wellington: GP Publications, 1991), 90; Keith Sinclair, *A History of New Zealand*, 4th edn (Auckland: Penguin Books, 1991 [1959]), 153.

75 Dalziel, *Vogel*, 173.

76 *DSC*, 11 June 1874, 2.

77 *Press*, 13 August 1874, 2.

78 *ST*, 8 July 1873, 2.

79 Dalziel, *Vogel*, 174.

80 *Press*, 8 August 1874, 2.

81 *TarH*, 12 August 1874, 2.

82 A.D. McIntosh, ed., *Marlborough: A provincial history* (Christchurch: Capper Press, 1977 [1940]), 272.

83 P.A. Muirhead, 'Public opinion in Canterbury on the abolition of the provinces, 1873–6' (MA thesis, University of New Zealand, 1936), 49–58.

84 cf. *EH*, 7 August 1874, 2; *GRA*, 8 August 1874, 2; *Lake Wakatip Mail*, 11 August 1874, 2; *Mount Ida Chronicle*, 21 August 1874, 2; *ST*, 7 August 1874, 2; *Waikato Times*, 6 August 1874, 2, and 8 August 1874, 2; *WCT*, 8 August 1874, 2.

85 *Thames Advertiser*, 7 August 1874, 2, and 8 August 1874, 2.

86 *WCT*, 19 August 1874, 2; *GRA*, 21 August 1874, 2.

87 *WCT*, 10 August 1874, 2.

88 *EP*, 6 August 1874, 2.

89 *Marlborough Express*, 8 August 1874, 5.

90 *Star*, 13 August 1874, 3.

91 *ODT*, 13 August 1874, 3.

92 Olive Trotter, *John Larkins Cheese Richardson: 'The gentlest, bravest and most just of men'* (Dunedin: Otago University Press, 2010), 147–48.

93 *BH*, 7 August 1874, 5.

Chapter 14. Provincialism's Fortress is Burning

1   Raewyn Dalziel, *Julius Vogel: Business politician* (Auckland: Auckland University Press, 1986), 175.

2   W.R. Armstrong, 'The politics of development: A study of the structure of politics from 1870 to 1890' (MA thesis, Victoria University of Wellington, 1960), 123.

3   *NZH*, 21 August 1874, 3.

4   *NZH*, 16 September 1874, 2.

5   J.A. Dowie, 'The course and character of capital formation in New Zealand, 1871–1900', *New Zealand Economic Papers* 1(1), 1966, 45–46.

6   Lionel Frost, 'The economy', in *The Cambridge History of Australia*, eds Alison Bashford and Stuart Macintyre (Cambridge: Cambridge University Press, 2013), 321. For figures of new railway capital formation, see N.G. Butlin, *Investment in Australian Economic Development 1861–1900* (Canberra: Department of Economic History, Australian National University, 1976 [1964]), 322.

7   G.T. Bloomfield, *New Zealand: A handbook of historical statistics* (Boston: G.K. Hall and Co., 1984), 329, 343.

8   £4m was borrowed under the Immigration and Public Works Loan Act, 1874 (38 Victoria, No. 25). GDP from Statistics New Zealand, 'E1.1 Nominal Gross Domestic Product', *Long-Term Data Series: E. National Income*: www.stats.govt.nz/browse_for_stats/economic_indicators/NationalAccounts/long-term-data-series/national-income.aspx

9   J. Rutherford, *Sir George Grey, K.C.B., 1812–1898: A study in colonial government* (London: Cassell, 1961), 589.

10 *NZH*, 8 September 1874, 2.

11 *AJHR* 1875 A-05, 1–4.

12 Ibid., 4–5.

13 Grey's petitions are more fully explored in R.H. Ellis, 'Sir George Grey's petitions to the Colonial Office over the abolition of the provinces' (MA thesis, University of Otago, 1968).

14 *AJHR* 1875 A-11.

15 *ODT*, 22 October 1874, 2.

16 A.H. McLintock, *The History of Otago: The origins and growth of a Wakefield class settlement* (Dunedin: Otago Centennial Historical Publications, 1949), 591.

17 *Star*, 5 January 1875, 2.

18 Judith Bassett, *Sir Harry Atkinson, 1831–1892* (Auckland: Auckland University Press, 1975), chapter 4.

19 Charles Brown to Harry Atkinson, 7 August 1875, *RAP*, vol. 2, 399.

20 *PD* 17 (1875), 220.

21 Ibid.

22 *AJHR* 1875 A-05, 3.

23 *AJHR* 1875 A-08.

24 *AJHR* 1875 A-02, 25.

25 *PD* 17 (1875), 522.

26 W.P. Morrell, *The Provincial System in New Zealand 1852–76* (Christchurch: Whitcombe and Tombs, 1964 [1932]), 256.

27 *Clutha Leader*, 23 September 1875, 5, is an especially clear statement of why provincialists demanded an election.

28 *ODT*, 17 August 1875, 2 (first quote), *EP*, 31 August 1875, 2 (second quote); cf. *Marlborough Express*, 4 September 1875, 4; *New Zealand Tablet*, 13 August 1875, 10.

29 Abolition of Provinces Act (39 Victoria, No. 21), clause 25.

30 *PD* 17 (1875), 642.

31 *PD* 18 (1875), 94, 147–48.

32 Ibid., 147, 390.

33 Ibid., 390–91.

34 Hori Kerei is the Māori version of George Grey. Parata is best remembered for his 1877 case against the bishop of Wellington in which the Treaty of Waitangi was referred to in Chief Justice James Prendergast's judgement as 'a simple nullity'.

35 I have consulted *Te Waka Maori o Niu Tirani*, 8 June 1875 to 13 February 1877 and *Te Wananga*, 14 June 1875 to 10 February 1877.

36 *Te Wananga*, 16 October 1875, 287.

37 These are J.L. Hunt's figures from his definitive study 'The election of 1875–6 and the abolition of the provinces' (MA thesis, University of Auckland, 1961), 323. Pro-abolition did not always mean pro-government; the government could only rely on approximately 43 members.

38 E.g. John Young, 'The political conflict of 1875', *Political Science* 13(56), 1961, 77.

39 *EP*, 24 December 1875, 2.

40 *EP*, 4 December 1875, 2.

41 Morrell, *Provincial System*, 261; Rutherford, *Grey*, 594.

42 *Bay of Plenty Times*, 27 November 1875, 2; *Waikato Times*, 2 December 1875, 2.

43 Young, 'Political conflict' explores this, though he sometimes exaggerates the extent to which businessmen formed an oligarchy while downplaying the Works Policy's revolutionary role in the lives of working people.

44 Hunt, 'Election of 1875–6', 360–65 provides more detail.

45 *TA*, 24 November 1875, 2; cf. Thames *Evening Star*, 24 November 1875, 2; 1 December 1875, 2.

46 *TA*, 13 November 1875, 2; 29 December 1875, 2.

47 *NZH*, 10 January 1876, 3.

48 *NZH*, 20 January 1876, 2.

49 James George, *Reminiscences: A few odds and ends of remembrances* (Auckland: J. George, 1875–76), 581, MSS & Archives A-20, University of Auckland.

50 Hunt, 'Election of 1875–6', 270–72.

51 E.g. Morrell, *Provincial System*, 301. He may qualify the 'essence of provincialism' as 'local administration of local revenues', but it is drawing a long bow to connect these desires in Southland and Oamaru with opposition to abolition.

52 Linda M. Cowan, 'Immediate reactions in Otago to the movement for the abolition of provincial government, 1874–76' (PGDipArts thesis, University of Otago, 1972), chapter three.

53 Hunt, 'Election of 1875–6', 159–61.

54 *NOT*, 12 January 1876, 2.

55 *Westport Times*, 17 October 1876, 2.

56 *ST*, 12 January 1876, 2.

57 Erik Olssen, 'Loyalty and localism – Southland's political odyssey', in *Murihiku: The Southland story*, ed. Paul Sorrell (Invercargill: Southland to 2006 Book Project Committee, 2006), 87.

58 J. Denise Marshall, 'Southland's attitudes to the abolition of the provinces, 1874–1877' (BA Honours thesis, University of Otago, 1975), 89–91.

59 *Tuapeka Times*, 5 January 1876, 3.

60 *TimH*, 29 December 1875, 4; *Star*, 22 December 1875, 2.

61 *Otago Guardian*, in *EH*, 13 January 1876, 2.

62 *Clutha Leader*, 13 January 1876, 3.

63 Hunt, 'Election of 1875–6', 324.

64 *Clutha Leader*, 17 February 1876, 4.

65 *Press*, 22 January 1876, 2.

66 John Cookson, 'How British? Local government in New Zealand to c. 1930', *NZJH* 41(2), 2007, 147.

67 *TarH*, 12 January 1876, 6.

68   Cookson, 'How British?', 147.

69   *ST*, 2 November 1876, 2; *NOT*, 2 November 1876, 2.

70   *TA*, 1 November 1876, 2.

71   *Akaroa Mail*, 5 January 1877, 2.

72   *GRA*, 2 November 1876, 2; *DSC*, 2 November 1876, 2; also 1 November 1876, 2 (editorial mislabelled 31 October).

73   Ebenezer Fox to Julius Vogel, 6 November 1876, Julius Vogel Papers, ATL MS-Papers-2072-30.

74   *Colonist*, 2 November 1876, 2.

75   *Evening Mail*, 3 November 1876, 2.

76   *ST*, 7 November 1876, 2.

77   *AJHR* 1876 A-01B contains most communications; Carnarvon's reply is A-07B.

78   *Wellington Argus*, gleefully reprinted by Oamaru's abolitionist *Evening Mail*, 7 November 1876, 2.

79   *AJHR* 1876 A-04, 3–23 contains a lengthy exchange between Macandrew and Vogel on this topic.

80   Morrell, *Provincial System*, 267–69.

81   *AJHR* 1877 A-02A, 1.

82   *Marlborough Express*, 4 November 1876, 6; 18 November 1876, 6.

83   W.J. Gardner, 'The effect of the abolition of the provinces on political parties in the New Zealand House of Representatives, 1876–7' (MA thesis, University of New Zealand, 1936), 163–66, 201–05.

84   T.G. Wilson, *The Grey Government, 1877–9: An episode in the rise of liberalism in New Zealand* (Auckland: Auckland University Bulletin No. 45, History Series No. 5, 1954), 11.

85   Gardner, 'Political parties', 184–89.

86   John E. Martin, *The House: New Zealand's House of Representatives 1854–2004* (Palmerston North: Dunmore Press, 2004), 76.

87   E.C.J. Stevens to Edward Stafford, 3 December 1878, Edward Stafford Papers, ATL MS-2050.

88   Roy Shuker, *The One Best System?: A revisionist history of state schooling in New Zealand* (Palmerston North: Dunmore Press, 1987), 45.

89   John Mackey, *The Making of a State Education System: The passing of the New Zealand Education Act, 1877* (London: Geoffrey Chapman, 1967), 151–52.

90   W.B. Sutch, 'Local government – a history of defeat', in *Local Government in New Zealand*, ed. R.J. Polaschek (Wellington: New Zealand Institute of Public Administration, 1956), 22.

91   Pinky L. Green, 'The Province of Wellington and the abolition of the provincial form of government in New Zealand, 1874–6' (MA thesis, University of New Zealand, 1954), 110.

92   James Ng, *Windows on a Chinese Past: How the Cantonese goldseekers and their heirs settled in New Zealand*, vol. 1 (Dunedin: Otago Heritage Books, 1993), 227–33.

93   For more see Graham Bush, *Local Government and Politics in New Zealand* (Auckland: Auckland University Press, 1995), especially chapter one; or Sutch, 'Local government' for a particularly pessimistic interpretation.

94   A.H. Cook, '"The slowly dying cause": A study of Otago provincialism after the abolition of the provinces, 1875 to 1884' (MA thesis, University of Otago, 1969), 312; cf. Cookson, 'How British?', 143–60.

95   Wilson, *Grey Government*, 53.

96   Cook, 'Slowly dying cause', 319.

Conclusion

1   A useful case study with instructive maps, largely of the post-provincial era, is J.B. Gerrard, 'The significance of the railways in the Auckland Province: Their influence on development and settlement and their role as a means of passenger transport' (MA thesis, University of New Zealand, 1949).

2   See, for instance, the failure to connect Nelson's isolated and now closed railway line to the national network, the fact Taupo never had a railway, and the missing link of the North Island's East Coast Main Trunk between Gisborne and the Bay of Plenty. At the time of writing, the Napier–Gisborne railway has recently been mothballed and its future existence is doubtful; should shortsighted politicians fail to restore the railway to an operational condition, it will turn the East Coast's lamentable missing link into a gaping chasm.

3   For Earl Grey's Australian proposals, see J.M. Ward, *Earl Grey and the Australian Colonies, 1846-1857: A study of self-government and self-interest* (Melbourne: Melbourne University Press, 1958).

4   Thomas D'Arcy McGee, *Notes on Federal Governments, Past and Present* (Montreal: Dawson Brothers, 1865), 45–50.

5   William Ross in *Canada's Founding Debates*, eds Janet Ajzenstat, Paul Romney, Ian Gentles and William D. Gairdner (Toronto: University of Toronto Press, 1999), 268–89.

6   W.L. Morton, *The Critical Years: The union of British North America, 1857-1873* (Toronto: McClelland and Stewart, 1964), especially chapters 11–12.

7   Tony Ballantyne, 'On place, space and mobility in nineteenth-century New Zealand', *NZJH* 45(1), 2011, 55. Note also Philippa Mein Smith, 'New Zealand federation commissioners in Australia: One past, two historiographies', *Australian Historical Studies* 34(122), 2003, 305–25.

8   For the 'twelve hundred impediments' quote, see John Hall in the *Australasian Federation Convention Debates* (1890), 64. Hall and other New Zealand delegates discussed the other reasons in various speeches at the 1890 and 1891 conventions.

9   Keith Sinclair, 'Why New Zealanders Are Not Australians: New Zealand and the Australian federal movement, 1881-1901', in *Tasman Relations: New Zealand and Australia, 1788-1988*, ed. Keith Sinclair (Auckland: Auckland University Press, 1987), 90–103; C.M.H. Clark, *A History of Australia, vol. 5: The people make laws, 1888-1915* (Melbourne: Melbourne University Press, 1981), 35–36.

10   *Australasian Federation Convention Debates* (1891), 327–28.

11   Ged Martin, *Australia, New Zealand, and Federation, 1883-1901* (London: Menzies Centre for Australian Studies, 2001), 102.

12   A similar argument has been made by Joanne Smith, 'Twelve hundred reasons why there is no Australasia: How colonisation influenced federation', *Australian Cultural History* 27(1), 2009, 43.

13   Norman Davies, *Vanished Kingdoms: The history of half-forgotten Europe* (London: Penguin, 2011), 732.

14   Graham Bush had the field to himself for many years, producing the seminal work *Local Government and Politics in New Zealand* (Auckland: Auckland University Press, 1995); see also the special local government issue of *Political Science* 50(2), 1999. A popular entry-level text for political students has a solitary chapter on local government: Christine Cheyne, 'Strengthening local government', in *New Zealand Government and Politics*, 5th edn, ed. Raymond Miller (Oxford: Oxford University Press, 2010), 269–83.

15   Geoffrey Sawer, *Australian Federalism in the Courts* (Melbourne: Melbourne University Press, 1967), 208. A.J. Brown notes that Australia's inability to create new states or redraw the boundaries of existing ones is a leading example of a disconnect between constitutional framework and political reality; see Brown, 'Federalism, regionalism and the reshaping of Australian governance', in *Federalism and Regionalism in Australia: New approaches, new institutions?*, eds J.A. Bellamy and A.J. Brown (Canberra: Australian National University ePress, 2006), 20–21.

16   Mike Reid, 'The central–local government relationship: The need for a framework?', *Political Science* 50(2), 1999, 165–66.

17   See the Local Government Commission's reports: 'Draft Proposal for Reorganisation of Local Government in Northland', November 2013: www.lgc.govt.nz/assets/Uploads/Draft-Proposal-for-

Reorganisation-in-Northland-2013.pdf; 'Hawke's Bay Local Government Reorganisation: Final
Proposal', June 2015: www.lgc.govt.nz/assets/Hawkes-Bay-June-2015/Hawkes-Bay-Proposal-
June-2015.pdf; and 'Draft Proposal for Reorganisation of Local Government in Wellington',
December 2014, 2 vols: www.lgc.govt.nz/assets/Wellington-Reorganisation/Wellington-
reorg-Draft-Proposal-Wellington-Volume-1.pdf and www.lgc.govt.nz/assets/Wellington-
Reorganisation/Draft-Proposal-Volume-2-Main-Report-for-website-v2-3-2015-02-12-MLG.pdf.
A range of potential amalgamations are discussed by Christine Cheyne in 'The Auckland effect:
What next for other councils?' in *Along a Fault-line: New Zealand's changing local government
landscape*, eds Jean Drage, Jeff McNeill and Christine Cheyne (Wellington: Dunmore Publishing,
2011), 41–58..
18 See the Department of Internal Affairs' official site on the Better Local Government reforms:
www.dia.govt.nz/better-local-government
19 Peter Fowler, 'Hawke's Bay Says "No" to Amalgamating Councils', Radio New Zealand News,
15 September 2015: www.radionz.co.nz/news/regional/284256/hawke's-bay-says-'no'-to-
amalgamating-councils
20 Local Government Commission, 'Results of Polls on Proposal to Unite Nelson City and Tasman
District': www.lgc.govt.nz/assets/Uploads/NelsonTasmanPollResults.pdf

Bibliography

PRIMARY

Archival and manuscripts

Alexander Turnbull Library
Bell, Francis Dillon Papers, MS-Papers-0693.
Bowen Family Papers, MS-Papers-10473.
Caldwell, Elizabeth memoirs, qMS-0361.
Hall, John Papers, MS-Group-0033.
Jollie, Edward reminiscences, MS-Papers-4207.
McLean, Donald Papers, MS-Group-1551.
Menzies, James Papers, MS-Papers-0055.
Stafford, Edward Papers, MS-2045-2050.
Vogel Family Papers, MS-Papers-0178.
Vogel, Julius Papers, MS-Papers-2072.

Others
Burke, William MSS. Christchurch City Libraries: http://christchurchcitylibraries.com/Heritage/
    Digitised/Burke/Burke39.asp
George, James. *Reminiscences: A few odds and ends of remembrances.* Auckland: J. George, 1875–76.
    MSS & Archives A-20, Special Collections, University of Auckland.
Menzies, James. Diary, 1853–57. Misc-MS-420, Hocken Collections, Uare Toaka o Hākena,
    Dunedin.

Official
Acts and Proceedings of the Auckland Provincial Council. (Later *Votes and Proceedings*, then *Journals
    of.*)
Acts and Proceedings of the Provincial Council of Wellington.
Appendices to the Journals of the House of Representatives.
Appendix to the Votes and Proceedings of the Southland Provincial Council, 1861–69.
Australasian Federation Convention Debates, 1891.
British Parliamentary Papers: Colonies; New Zealand. Shannon: Irish University Press, 1969. Also
    available from the University of Waikato: http://digital.liby.waikato.ac.nz/bppnz
Canada's Founding Debates. Edited by Janet Ajzenstat, Paul Romney, Ian Gentles and William D.
    Gairdner. Toronto: University of Toronto Press, 1999.
Department of Internal Affairs. 'Better Local Government': www.dia.govt.nz/better-local-
    government
Great Britain Parliamentary Debates.
Journal of Proceedings of the Canterbury Provincial Council.
Local Government Commission 'Draft Proposal for Reorganisation of Local Government in
    Wellington', December 2014, 2 vols: www.lgc.govt.nz/assets/Wellington-Reorganisation/

Wellington-reorg-Draft-Proposal-Wellington-Volume-1.pdf and www.lgc.govt.nz/assets/
Wellington-Reorganisation/Draft-Proposal-Volume-2-Main-Report-for-website-v2-3-2015-02-
12-MLG.pdf

——— 'Draft Proposal for Reorganisation of Local Government in Northland', November 2013:
www.lgc.govt.nz/assets/Uploads/Draft-Proposal-for-Reorganisation-in-Northland-2013.pdf

——— 'Hawke's Bay Local Government Reorganisation: Final Proposal', June 2015: www.lgc.govt.
nz/assets/Hawkes-Bay-June-2015/Hawkes-Bay-Proposal-June-2015.pdf

——— 'Results of Polls on Proposal to Unite Nelson City and Tasman District': www.lgc.govt.nz/
assets/Uploads/NelsonTasmanPollResults.pdf

New Munster Government (agency ACFP). Despatches from the Colonial Office to the Lieutenant-
Governor. Series 8210, NM1. Archives New Zealand.

New Munster Government (agency ACFP). Despatches from the Governor-in-Chief to the
Lieutenant-Governor. Series 8211, NM2. Archives New Zealand.

New Munster Government (agency ACFP). Despatches from the Lieutenant-Governor to the
Colonial Office. Series 8212, NM3. Archives New Zealand.

New Munster Government (agency ACFP). Despatches from the Lieutenant-Governor to the
Governor-in-Chief. Series 8213, NM4. Archives New Zealand.

New Zealand Official Yearbook, 1894.

New Zealand Parliamentary Debates.

New Zealand Parliamentary Record, 2nd edition. Edited by Guy H. Scholefield. Wellington:
Government Printer, 1950 (1913).

Ordinances of the Auckland Province.

Ordinances of the Canterbury Province.

Otago Provincial Government Gazette.

Statistics of New Zealand 1853–77.

Statistics New Zealand. *Long Term Data Series*: www.stats.govt.nz/browse_for_stats/economic_
indicators/NationalAccounts/long-term-data-series.aspx

Statistics of the Province of Nelson, New Zealand for the Year 1855.

Votes and Proceedings of the Provincial Council of Hawke's Bay.

Votes and Proceedings of the Nelson Provincial Council.

Votes and Proceedings of the Otago Provincial Council.

Votes and Proceedings of the Southland Provincial Council, 1861–69.

Newspapers

Akaroa Mail, 1877.

Albertland Gazette, 1862–64.

Auckland Examiner, 1858–60.

Bay of Plenty Times, 1875–76.

Bruce Herald, 1868–76.

Clutha Leader, 1875–76.

Colonist (Nelson), 1857–76.

Coromandel Observer, 1867.

Daily News (Invercargill), 1864. (See also *Southland News*; it was the *Daily News* only for part of
1864.)

Daily Southern Cross, 1862–76. (See also *Southern Cross*; it was the *Southern Cross* until 1862.)

Evening Herald (Wanganui), 1867–76. (Later the *Wanganui Herald*.)

Evening Mail (Oamaru), 1876. (Later the *Oamaru Mail*.)

Evening Post (Wellington), 1865–76.

Evening Star (Auckland), 1873. (Later the *Auckland Star*.)

Evening Star (Thames), 1875–76. (Later the *Thames Star.*)

Grey River Argus (Greymouth), 1867–76.

Hawke's Bay Herald (Napier), 1857–76.

Hawke's Bay Weekly Times, 1867.

Hokitika Evening Star, 1867.

Invercargill Times, 1862–64. (It became the *Southland Times* in 1864.)

Lake Wakatip Mail, 1864–74.

Lyttelton Times, 1852–65. (Published in Christchurch from 1863.)

Marlborough Express, 1874–76.

Marlborough Press, 1860–65. (First published in Blenheim, then Picton from 1861.)

Mount Ida Chronicle, 1874–76.

Nelson Evening Mail, 1866–70.

Nelson Examiner, 1842–74.

New Zealand Gazette, 1841–42.

New Zealand Herald (Auckland), 1863–76.

New Zealand Spectator (Wellington), 1847–64.

New Zealand Tablet, 1874–76.

New Zealander (Auckland), 1847–59.

North Otago Times, 1872–76. (It was the *Oamaru Times* until 1872.)

Oamaru Times, 1864–72. (It became the *North Otago Times* in 1872.)

Otago Daily Times (Dunedin), 1861–76.

Otago Witness (Dunedin), 1851–72.

Press (Christchurch), 1861–76.

Riverton Times, 1864.

Southern Cross (Auckland), 1847–62. (It became the *Daily Southern Cross* in 1862.)

Southland News, 1865. (See also *Daily News.*)

Southland Times, 1864–76. (It was the *Invercargill Times* until 1864.)

Star (Christchurch), 1869–76. (The evening paper of the *Lyttelton Times.*)

Taranaki Herald (New Plymouth), 1852–76.

Te Waka Maori o Niu Tirani, 1875–77.

Te Wananga, 1875–77.

Thames Advertiser, 1874–76.

Timaru Herald, 1864–76.

Tuapeka Times, 1872–76.

Waikato Times, 1873–76.

Wairarapa Mercury, 1869.

Wanganui Chronicle, 1874–76.

Wellington Independent, 1847–74.

West Coast Times (Hokitika), 1865–76.

Westport Times, 1876.

Other publications

Adam, James. *Twenty-Five Years of Emigrant Life in the South of New Zealand.* Edinburgh: Bell and Bradfute, 1874.

Adams, C.W. *A Spring in the Canterbury Settlement.* London: Longman, Brown, Green, and Longmans, 1853.

Adderley, C.B. *Self-Government in New Zealand.* London: Savill and Edwards, 1852.

Barr, James ('An Old Identity'). *The Old Identities: Being sketches and reminiscences during the first decade of the Province of Otago, N.Z.* Dunedin: Mills, Dick and Co., 1879.

Busby, James. *Colonies and Colonization*. Auckland: Philip Kunst, 1857.

———. *The Federation of Colonies and the System Called 'Responsible Government'*. Auckland: Richardson and Sansom, 1858.

———. *The First Settlers in New Zealand, and Their Treatment by the Government*. Auckland: Williamson and Wilson, 1856.

———. *Illustrations of the System Called Responsible Government, in a Letter to His Excellency Colonel Thomas Gore Browne*. Auckland: W.G. Wilson, 1860.

———. *A Letter to His Excellency Colonel Thomas Gore Browne, Governor-in-Chief of New Zealand, on 'Responsible Government' and the Governmental Institutions of New Zealand*. Auckland: Philip Kunst, 1857.

———. *A Picture of Misgovernment and Oppression in the British Colony of New Zealand*. Auckland: n.p., 1853.

———. *The Pre-emption Land Question*. Auckland: Richardson and Sansom, 1859.

———. *The Right of a British Colonist to the Protection of the Queen and Parliament of England*. Auckland: Philip Kunst, 1860.

Cox, Alfred. *Recollections: Australia, England, Ireland, Scotland, New Zealand*. Christchurch: Whitcombe and Tombs, 1884.

Crawford, James Coutts. *Recollections of Travel in New Zealand and Australia*. London: Trubner and Company, 1880.

———. *Remarks upon Railways, Suggesting the Opening of a Timber Trade in the Province of Wellington*. Wellington: Spectator Office, 1861.

Dilke, Charles Wentworth. *Greater Britain: A record of travel in English-speaking countries during 1866 and 1867*, 2 volumes. London: Macmillan, 1868.

Dobson, Arthur Dudley. *Reminiscences of Arthur Dudley Dobson, Engineer, 1841–1930*, 2nd edn. Christchurch: Whitcombe and Tombs, 1930.

Earl Grey. *The Colonial Policy of Lord John Russell's Administration*, 2 volumes. London: Richard Bentley, 1853.

Fitton, Edward Brown. *New Zealand: Its present condition, prospects and resources*. London: Edward Stanford, 1856.

Fowler, Peter. 'Hawke's Bay Says "No" to Amalgamating Councils'. Radio New Zealand News, 15 September 2015: www.radionz.co.nz/news/regional/284256/hawke's-bay-says-'no'-to-amalgamating-councils

Gorst, J.E. *The Maori King: Or, the story of our quarrel with the natives of New Zealand*. London: Macmillan, 1864.

Harper, Henry W. *Letters From New Zealand, 1857–1911: Being some account of life and work in the Province of Canterbury, South Island*. London: Hugh Rees, 1914.

Hewetson, Thomas. 'From the Slate River 1857'. *Nelson Historical Society Journal* 3(5), 1979 [written 30 September 1857], 37–39.

Innes, C.L. ('Pilgrim'). *Canterbury Sketches: or, Life from the early days*. Christchurch: Lyttelton Times Office, 1879.

FitzRoy, Robert. *Remarks on New Zealand in February 1846*. London: W. and H. White, 1846.

Fox, William. *The Six Colonies of New Zealand*. London: John W. Parker and Son, 1851.

Malcolm, Emilie Monson. *My Own Story: An episode in the life of a New Zealand settler of 50 years back*. Auckland: Brett Printing and Publishing, 1904.

Mathew, Felton. *The Founding of New Zealand: The journals of Felton Mathew, first surveyor-general of New Zealand, and his wife 1840–1847*. Edited by J. Rutherford. Dunedin: A.H. and A.W. Reed, 1940.

McGee, Thomas D'Arcy. *Notes on Federal Governments, Past and Present*. Montreal: Dawson Brothers, 1865.

Paul, R.B. *Letters from Canterbury, New Zealand*. London: Rivingtons, 1857.

Richardson, J.L.C. *Our Constitutional History*. Timaru: Herald Office, 1868.

Scholefield, Guy H., ed. *The Richmond Atkinson Papers*. 2 volumes. Wellington: R.E. Owen, 1960.

'A Settler'. *The Waikato and Ngaruawahia, The Proposed New Capital of New Zealand*. Auckland: Wilson and Burn, 1863.

Sewell, Henry. *The Journal of Henry Sewell, 1853–7*. 2 volumes. Edited by W. David McIntyre. Christchurch: Whitcoulls Publishers, 1980.

———. *The New Zealand Native Rebellion: Letter to Lord Lyttelton*. Auckland: Printed for the author, 1864.

St John, J.H.A. *Pakeha Ramblings Through Maori Lands*. Wellington: Robert Burrett, 1873.

Swainson, William. *New Zealand and Its Colonization*. London: Elder, Smith and Co., 1859.

———. *New Zealand and the War*. London: Elder, Smith and Co., 1862.

Wakefield, Edward Jerningham. *Adventure in New Zealand*. Edited by Joan Stevens. Christchurch: Whitcombe and Tombs, 1955 (1845).

Williams, Frederick Wanklyn. *Through Ninety Years, 1826–1916: Life and work among the Maoris in New Zealand*. Christchurch: Whitcombe and Tombs, 1939.

SECONDARY

Books

Allan, H.F. *The Nelson Provincial Council*. Stoke: Nelson Historical Society, 1974.

Arnold, Rollo. *New Zealand's Burning: The settlers' world in the mid 1880s*. Wellington: Victoria University Press, 1994.

Atkinson, Neill. *Adventures in Democracy: A history of the vote in New Zealand*. Dunedin: University of Otago Press, 2003.

———. *Trainland: How railways made New Zealand*. Auckland: Random House, 2007.

Barrington, John. *Separate but Equal?: Māori schools and the Crown 1867–1969*. Wellington: Victoria University Press, 2008.

Bashford, Alison and Stuart Macintyre, eds. *The Cambridge History of Australia*. Cambridge: Cambridge University Press, 2013.

Bassett, Judith. *Sir Harry Atkinson, 1831–1892*. Auckland: Auckland University Press, 1975.

Beaglehole, J.C. *Captain Hobson and the New Zealand Company: A study in colonial administration*. Northampton: Department of History of Smith College, 1928.

———. *New Zealand: A short history*. London: George Allen and Unwin, 1936.

Belich, James. *Making Peoples: A history of the New Zealanders from Polynesian settlement to the end of the nineteenth century*. Auckland: Penguin Books, 1996.

———. *Replenishing the Earth: The settler revolution and the rise of the Anglo-world, 1783–1939*. Oxford: Oxford University Press, 2009.

Bloomfield, G.T. *New Zealand: A handbook of historical statistics*. Boston: G.K. Hall and Co., 1984.

Boast, Richard. *Buying the Land, Selling the Land: Governments and Māori land in the North Island, 1865–1921*. Wellington: Victoria University Press, 2008.

——— and Richard S. Hill, eds. *Raupatu: The confiscation of Māori land*. Wellington: Victoria University Press, 2009.

Bohan, Edmund. *Edward Stafford: New Zealand's first statesman*. Christchurch: Hazard Press, 1994.

———. *To Be a Hero: Sir George Grey, 1812–1898*. Auckland: HarperCollins, 1998.

Brett, Henry. *White Wings*, 2 volumes. Auckland: Brett Printing, 1928.

Broad, Lowther. *The Jubilee History of Nelson: From 1842 to 1892*. Nelson: Bond, Finney, and Co., 1892.

Brooking, Tom. *And Captain of Their Souls: An interpretative essay on the life and times of Captain William Cargill*. Dunedin: Otago Heritage Books, 1984.

——. *The History of New Zealand*. Westport, CT: Greenwood Press, 2004.

——, and Eric Pawson, eds. *Environmental Histories of New Zealand*. Melbourne: Oxford University Press, 2002.

——, and Eric Pawson. *Seeds of Empire: The environmental transformation of New Zealand*. London: I.B. Tauris, 2011.

Buckner, Philip A. *The Transition to Responsible Government: British policy in British North America, 1815–1850*. Westport, CT: Greenwood Press, 1985.

Burdon, Randal. *The Life and Times of Julius Vogel*. Christchurch: Caxton Press, 1948.

Burns, Patricia. *Fatal Success: A history of the New Zealand Company*. Edited by Henry Richardson. Auckland: Heinemann Reed, 1989.

Bush, Graham. *Local Government and Politics in New Zealand*. Auckland: Auckland University Press, 1995.

——. *From Survival to Revival: Auckland's public transport since 1860*. Wellington: Grantham House, 2014.

Butlin, N.G. *Investment in Australian Economic Development 1861–1900*. Canberra: Department of Economic History, Australian National University, 1976 (1964).

Byrnes, Giselle, ed. *The New Oxford History of New Zealand*. South Melbourne: Oxford University Press, 2009.

Cain, P.J., and A.G. Hopkins. *British Imperialism, 1688–2000*. Harlow: Longman, 2002 (1993).

Campbell, W.N. *A Line of Railway: The railway conquest of the Rimutakas*. Wellington: New Zealand Railway and Locomotive Society, 1976.

Careless, J.M.S. *The Union of the Canadas: The growth of Canadian institutions 1841–1857*. Toronto: McClelland and Stewart, 1967.

Carrington, C.E. *John Robert Godley of Canterbury*. Cambridge: Cambridge University Press, 1950.

Chappell, N.M. *New Zealand Banker's Hundred: A history of the Bank of New Zealand 1861–1961*. Wellington: Bank of New Zealand, 1961.

Churchman, Geoffrey B., and Tony Hurst. *The Railways of New Zealand: A journey through history*. Auckland: HarperCollins, 1990.

Clark, C.M.H. *A History of Australia, vol. 5: The people make laws, 1888–1915*. Melbourne: Melbourne University Press, 1981.

Cochrane, Peter. *Colonial Ambition: Foundations of Australian democracy*. Melbourne: Melbourne University Press, 2006.

Condliffe, J.B. *New Zealand in the Making: A survey of economic and social development*. London: George Allen and Unwin, 1930.

——— *A Short History of New Zealand*, 8th edn. Christchurch: Whitcombe and Tombs, 1957 (1925).

Cumming, Alan, and Ian Cumming. *History of State Education in New Zealand 1840–1975*. Wellington: Pitman Publishing, 1978.

Dalton, B.J. *War and Politics in New Zealand 1855–1870*. Sydney: Sydney University Press, 1967.

Dalziel, Raewyn. *Julius Vogel: Business politician*. Auckland: Auckland University Press, 1986.

——. *The Origins of New Zealand Diplomacy: The agent-general in London, 1870–1905*. Wellington: Victoria University Press, 1975.

Darwin, John. *The Empire Project: The rise and fall of the British world system, 1830–1970*. Cambridge: Cambridge University Press, 2009.

Davies, Norman. *Vanished Kingdoms: The history of half-forgotten Europe*. London: Penguin, 2011.

Day, Patrick. *The Making of the New Zealand Press: A study of the organizational and political concerns of New Zealand newspaper controllers, 1840–1880*. Wellington: Victoria University Press, 1990.

den Otter, A.A. *The Philosophy of Railways: The transcontinental railway idea in British North America.* Toronto: University of Toronto Press, 1997.

Eagle, John A. *The Canadian Pacific Railway and the Development of Western Canada, 1896–1914.* Kingston: McGill–Queens University Press, 1989.

Eastwood, David. *Government and Community in the English Provinces, 1700–1870.* Houndmills: Macmillan, 1997.

Eldred-Grigg, Stevan. *Diggers, Hatters and Whores: The story of the New Zealand gold rushes.* Auckland: Random House, 2011.

Evans, Julie. *Edward Eyre: Race and colonial governance.* Dunedin: University of Otago Press, 2005.

——, Patricia Grimshaw, David Philips, and Shurlee Swain, *Equal Subjects, Unequal Rights: Indigenous people in British Settler colonies, 1830s–1910.* Manchester: Manchester University Press, 2003.

Evison, Harry C. *Te Wai Pounamu: The Greenstone Island; A history of the southern Maori during the European colonization of New Zealand.* Wellington and Christchurch: Aoraki Press, 1993.

Fairburn, Miles. *The Ideal Society and its Enemies: The foundations of modern New Zealand society, 1850–1900.* Auckland: Auckland University Press, 1989.

Fargher, Ray. *The Best Man Who Ever Served the Crown? A life of Donald McLean.* Wellington: Victoria University Press, 2007.

Fishlow, Albert. *American Railroads and the Transformation of the Antebellum Economy.* Cambridge: Harvard University Press, 1965.

Fogel, Robert William. *Railroads and American Economic Growth: Essays in econometric history.* Baltimore: Johns Hopkins Press, 1964.

Fraser, Lyndon. *Castles of Gold: A history of New Zealand's West Coast Irish.* Dunedin: Otago University Press, 2007.

Freeman, Michael. *Railways and the Victorian Age.* New Haven and London: Yale University Press, 1999.

Gardner, W.J., ed. *A History of Canterbury, vol. II: General history, 1854–76 and cultural aspects, 1850–1950.* Christchurch: Whitcombe and Tombs, 1971.

Garner, Jean. *By His Own Merits: Sir John Hall; Pioneer, pastoralist and premier.* Hororata: Dryden Press, 1995.

Gisborne, William. *New Zealand Rulers and Statesmen from 1840 to 1897*, revised edition. London: Sampson Low, Marston & Company, 1897.

Goldsmith, Paul. *We Won, You Lost, Eat That! A political history of tax in New Zealand since 1840.* Auckland: David Ling, 2008.

Gordon, Sarah H. *Passage to Union: How the railroads transformed American life, 1829–1929.* Chicago: Ivan R. Dee, 1996.

Graham, Jeanine. *Frederick Weld.* Auckland: Auckland University Press, 1983.

Grey, Alan. *Aotearoa and New Zealand: A historical geography.* Christchurch: Canterbury University Press, 1994.

Grimshaw, Patricia. *Women's Suffrage in New Zealand.* Auckland: Auckland University Press, 1972.

Halkett, John. *The Native Forests of New Zealand.* Wellington: GP Publications, 1991.

Hall, D.O.W., and W.P. Morrell. *A History of New Zealand Life.* Christchurch: Whitcombe and Tombs, 1957.

Hall-Jones, John. *Stewart Island Explored.* Invercargill: Craig Printing, 1994.

Harrop, A.J. *The Romance of Westland: The story of New Zealand's golden coast.* Christchurch: Whitcombe and Tombs, 1923.

Hawke, G.R. *The Making of New Zealand: An economic history.* Cambridge: Cambridge University Press, 1985.

——. *Railways and Economic Growth in England and Wales, 1840–1870.* Oxford: Clarendon Press, 1970.

Hight, J., and H.D. Bamford. *The Constitutional History and Law of New Zealand*. Christchurch: Whitcombe and Tombs, 1914.

Hill, Richard S. *Policing the Colonial Frontier: The theory and practice of coercive social and racial control in New Zealand, 1767–1867*. Wellington: Historical Publications Branch, Department of Internal Affairs, 1986.

Hilliard, Chris. *The Bookmen's Dominion: Cultural life in New Zealand 1920–1950*. Auckland: Auckland University Press, 2006.

Hilton, Boyd. *A Mad, Bad, and Dangerous People? England, 1783–1846*. Oxford: Clarendon Press, 2006.

Horsman, E.A. *The Diary of Alfred Domett, 1872–1885*. Oxford: Oxford University Press, 1953.

Howard, Basil. *Rakiura: A history of Stewart Island, New Zealand*. Wellington: A.H. and A.W. Reed, 1974 (1940).

Hoy, D.G. *Rails Out of the Capital*. Wellington: New Zealand Railway and Locomotive Society, 1970.

Jackson, W.K. *The New Zealand Legislative Council: A study of the establishment, failure and abolition of an upper house*. Dunedin: University of Otago Press, 1972.

Johnston, Mike. *High Hopes: The history of the Nelson mineral belt and New Zealand's first railway*. Nelson: Nikau Press, 1987.

Jones, Benjamin T. *Republicanism and Responsible Government: The shaping of democracy in Australia and Canada*. Montréal: McGill-Queen's University Press, 2014.

Keith-Lucas, B. *English Local Government in the Nineteenth and Twentieth Century*. London: Historical Association, 1977.

Kellett, John R. *Railways and Victorian Cities*. London: Routledge, 1979 (1969).

King, Michael. *The Penguin History of New Zealand*. Auckland: Penguin Books, 2003.

Knaplund, Paul. *James Stephen and the British Colonial System 1813–1847*. Madison: University of Wisconsin Press, 1953.

Koopman-Boyden, Peggy G., and Claudia D. Scott. *The Family and Government Policy in New Zealand*. Sydney: Allen and Unwin, 1984.

Kwasitsu, Lishi. *Printing and the Book Trade in Early Nelson*. Wellington: Elibank Press, 1996.

Lambert, Gail and Ron Lambert. *An Illustrated History of Taranaki*. Palmerston North: Dunmore Press, 1983.

Lewin, Henry Grote. *The Railway Mania and its Aftermath, 1845–1852*. Newton Abbot: David and Charles, 1968 (1936).

Lipson, Leslie. *The Politics of Equality: New Zealand's adventures in democracy*. Chicago: University of Chicago Press, 1948.

Lloyd Prichard, Muriel F. *An Economic History of New Zealand to 1939*. Auckland: Collins, 1970.

Mackey, John. *The Making of a State Education System: The passing of the New Zealand Education Act, 1877*. London: Geoffrey Chapman, 1967.

Mahoney, Paul. *The Era of the Bush Tram in New Zealand*. Wellington: Transpress, 2004.

Martin, Ged. *Australia, New Zealand, and Federation, 1883–1901*. London: Menzies Centre for Australian Studies, 2001.

Martin, John E. *The House: New Zealand's House of Representatives 1854–2004*. Palmerston North: Dunmore Press, 2004.

May, Philip Ross. *Gold Town: Ross, Westland*. Christchurch: Pegasus, 1970.

———. *Hokitika: Goldfields capital*. Christchurch: Pegasus Press, 1964.

———, ed. *Miners and Militants: Politics in Westland, 1865–1918*. Christchurch: University of Canterbury, 1975.

———. *The West Coast Gold Rushes*. Christchurch: Pegasus Press, 1962.

———. *The West Coast Gold Rushes*, 2nd edn. Christchurch: Pegasus Press, 1967 (1962).

McAloon, Jim. *Nelson: A regional history*. Whatamango Bay: Cape Catley, 1997.

———. *No Idle Rich: The wealthy in Canterbury and Otago 1840–1914*. Dunedin: University of Otago Press, 2002.

Macdonald, Charlotte, ed. *The Vote, the Pill and the Demon Drink: A history of feminist writing in New Zealand 1869–1993*. Wellington: Bridget Williams Books, 1993.

McIntosh, A.D., ed. *Marlborough: A provincial history*. Christchurch: Capper Press, 1977 (1940).

McKinnon, Malcolm. *Treasury: The New Zealand Treasury, 1840–2000*. Auckland: Auckland University Press, 2003.

McLean, Gavin. *Captain's Log: New Zealand's maritime history*. Auckland: Hodder Moa Beckett, 2001.

McLintock, A.H. *Crown Colony Government in New Zealand*. Wellington: R.E. Owen, 1958.

———. *The History of Otago: The origins and growth of a Wakefield class settlement*. Dunedin: Otago Centennial Historical Publications, 1949.

McMinn, W.G. *A Constitutional History of Australia*. Oxford: Oxford University Press, 1979.

Meiklejohn, G.M. *Early Conflicts of Press and Government: A story of the first* New Zealand Herald *and of the foundation of Auckland*. Auckland: Wilson and Horton, 1953.

Mein Smith, Philippa. *A Concise History of New Zealand*. Cambridge: Cambridge University Press, 2005.

Millar, J. Halket. *Westland's Golden 'Sixties*. Wellington: A.H. and A.W. Reed, 1959.

Miller, John. *Early Victorian New Zealand: A study of racial tension and social attitudes 1839–1852*. Oxford: Oxford University Press, 1958.

Milne, James. *The Romance of a Pro-consul*. London: Chatto and Windus, 1899.

Moon, Paul. *FitzRoy: Governor in crisis 1843–1845*. Auckland: David Ling Publishing, 2000.

———. *The Newest Country in the World: A history of New Zealand in the decade of the treaty*. Auckland: Penguin Books, 2007.

Morrell, W.P. *British Colonial Policy in the Age of Peel and Russell*. London: Frank Cass and Co., 1966.

———. *The Provincial System in New Zealand, 1852–76*. Christchurch: Whitcombe and Tombs, 1964 (1932).

Morton, W.L. *The Critical Years: The union of British North America, 1857–1873*. Toronto: McClelland and Stewart, 1964.

Mulgan, Alan. *The City of the Strait: Wellington and Its Province; A centennial history*. Wellington: Wellington Provincial Centennial Council, 1939.

Ng, James. *Windows on a Chinese Past: How the Cantonese goldseekers and their heirs settled in New Zealand*, 4 volumes. Dunedin: Otago Heritage Books, 1993.

Noonan, Rosslyn J. *By Design: A brief history of the Public Works Department Ministry of Works 1870–1970*. Wellington: Government Printer, 1975.

O'Donnell, Barry. *When Nelson Had a Railway*. Wellington: Schematics, 2005.

Oettli, Peter. *God's Messenger: J.F. Riemenschneider and racial conflict in 19th century New Zealand*. Wellington: Huia Publishers, 2008.

Ogilvie, Gordon. *Banks Peninsula: Cradle of Canterbury*. Wellington: GP Books, 1990.

Oliver, W.H. *The Story of New Zealand*. London: Faber and Faber, 1960.

———, and B.R. Williams, eds. *The Oxford History of New Zealand*. Wellington and Oxford: Oxford University Press, 1981.

Olssen, Erik. *A History of Otago*. Dunedin: John McIndoe, 1984.

O'Neill, R.B. *The Press, 1861–1961: The story of a newspaper*. Christchurch: Press Company, 1963.

Orsi, Richard J. *Sunset Limited: The Southern Pacific Railroad and the development of the American West*. Berkeley: University of California Press, 2005.

Palenski, Ron. *The Making of New Zealanders*. Auckland: Auckland University Press, 2012.

Parsons, David. *Wellington's Railways: Colonial steam to Matangi*. Wellington: New Zealand Railway and Locomotive Society, 2010.

Pierre, W.A. *Canterbury Provincial Railways: Genesis of the NZR system*. Wellington: New Zealand Railway and Locomotive Society, 1964.

Reeves, William Pember. *The Long White Cloud*, 4th edn. Auckland: Golden Press, 1950 (1898).

Relph, David. *From Tussocks to Tourists: The story of the Central Canterbury high country*. Christchurch: Canterbury University Press, 2007.

Roberts, Jenifer. *Fitz: The colonial adventures of James Edward FitzGerald*. Dunedin: Otago University Press, 2014.

Roche, M.M. *Forest Policy in New Zealand: An historical geography, 1840–1919*. Palmerston North: Dunmore Press, 1987.

Rolleston, Rosamond. *The Master: J.D. Ormond of Wallingford*. Wellington: A.H. and A.W. Reed, 1980.

Rusden, George W. *History of New Zealand*, 3 volumes, 2nd edn. Melbourne: Melville, Mullen and Slade, 1895 (1883).

Rutherford, J. *Sir George Grey K.C.B., 1812–1898: A study in colonial government*. London: Cassell, 1961.

Salesa, Damon. *Racial Crossings: Race, intermarriage, and the Victorian British Empire*. Oxford: Oxford University Press, 2011.

Salmon, J.H.M. *A History of Gold-mining in New Zealand*. Wellington: Government Printer, 1963.

Salmond, Rachel. *Government Printing in New Zealand, 1840 to 1843*. Wellington: Elibank Press, 1995.

Saunders, Alfred. *History of New Zealand*, 2 volumes. Christchurch: Smith, Anthony, Sellars, and Co., 1899.

Sawer, Geoffrey. *Australian Federalism in the Courts*. Melbourne: Melbourne University Press, 1967.

Scholefield, Guy H. *Newspapers in New Zealand*. Wellington: A.H. and A.W. Reed, 1958.

Scott, K.J. *The New Zealand Constitution*. Oxford: Oxford University Press, 1962.

Shuker, Roy. *The One Best System?: A revisionist history of state schooling in New Zealand*. Palmerston North: Dunmore Press, 1987.

Sinclair, Keith. *A History of New Zealand*. Auckland: Penguin Books, 1991 (1959).

Simmons, Jack. *The Railway in Town and Country, 1830–1914*. Newton Abbot: David and Charles, 1986.

Smellie, K.B. *A History of Local Government*. London: George Allen and Unwin, 1968.

Stewart, William Downie. *William Rolleston: A New Zealand statesman*. Christchurch: Whitcombe and Tombs, 1940.

Stone, R.C.J. *The Father and His Gift: John Logan Campbell's later years*. Auckland: Auckland University Press, 1987.

———. *From Tamaki-Makau-Rau to Auckland*. Auckland: Auckland University Press, 2001.

———. *Makers of Fortune: A colonial business community and its fall*. Auckland: Auckland University Press, 1973.

———. *Young Logan Campbell*. Auckland: Auckland University Press, 1982.

Storey, Kenton. *Settler Anxiety at the Outposts of Empire: Colonial relations, humanitarian discourses, and the imperial press*. Vancouver: University of British Columbia Press, 2016.

Strom, Claire. *Profiting from the Plains: The Great Northern Railway and corporate development of the American West*. Seattle: University of Washington Press, 2003.

Stuart, Peter. *Edward Gibbon Wakefield in New Zealand: His political career. 1853–4*. Wellington: Price Milburn, 1971.

Sutch, W.B. *Poverty and Progress in New Zealand*. Wellington: Modern Books, 1941.

———. *Poverty and Progress: A re-assessment*. Wellington: A.H. and A.W. Reed, 1969.

Temple, Philip. *A Sort of Conscience: The Wakefields*. Auckland: Auckland University Press, 2002.

Tennant, Margaret. *Paupers and Providers: Charitable aid in New Zealand*. Wellington: Allen and Unwin, 1989.

Thomas, William G. *The Iron Way: Railroads, the Civil War, and the making of modern America*. New Haven and London: Yale University Press, 2011.

Tremewan, Peter. *French Akaroa: An attempt to colonise southern New Zealand*. Christchurch: Canterbury University Press, 1990.

Trotter, Olive. *John Larkins Cheese Richardson: 'The gentlest, bravest and most just of men'*. Dunedin: Otago University Press, 2010.

Utick, Stephen. *Captain Charles, Engineer of Charity: The remarkable life of Charles Gordon O'Neill*. Crow's Nest: Allen and Unwin, 2008.

Vaggioli, Felice. *History of New Zealand and Its Inhabitants*. Translated by John Crockett. Dunedin: University of Otago Press, 2000 (1896).

Vamplew, Wray, ed. *Australians: Historical statistics*. Sydney: Fairfax, Syme and Weldon Associates, 1987.

Voller, Lois. *Rails to Nowhere: The story of the Nelson railway*. Nelson: Nikau Press, 1991.

Ward, Alan. *A Show of Justice: Racial 'amalgamation' in nineteenth century New Zealand*. Canberra: Australian National University Press, 1974.

Ward, J.M. *Colonial Self-Government: The British experience 1759–1856*. London: Macmillan, 1976.

——. *Earl Grey and the Australian Colonies 1846–1857: A study of self-government and self-interest*. Melbourne: Melbourne University Press, 1958.

Watson, James. *Links: A history of transport and New Zealand society*. Wellington: GP Publications, 1996.

Watt, J.O.P. *Southland's Pioneer Railways 1864–1878*. Wellington: New Zealand Railway and Locomotive Society, 1965.

Webb, Sidney and Beatrice Webb. *English Local Government from the Revolution to the Municipal Corporations Act: The parish and the county*. London: Longmans, Green and Co., 1906.

——. *English Local Government from the Revolution to the Municipal Corporations Act: The manor and the borough*. Two volumes. London: Longmans, Green and Co., 1908.

——. *English Local Government: Statutory authorities for special purposes*. London: Longmans, Green and Co., 1922.

Wells, B. *The History of Taranaki: A standard work on the history of the province*. New Plymouth: Edmondson and Avery, 1878.

White, Richard. *Railroaded: The transcontinentals and the making of modern America*. New York: W.W. Norton and Co., 2012.

Wilkinson, Doug. *Wellington's First Railway: A centennial history of the Wellington–Lower Hutt line*. Wellington and Dunedin: Southern Press, 1974.

Wilson, A.C. *Wire and Wireless: A history of telecommunication in New Zealand, 1860–1987*. Palmerston North: Dunmore Press, 1994.

Woollacott, Angela. *Settler Society in the Australian Colonies: Self-government and imperial culture*. Oxford: Oxford University Press, 2015.

Wright, Matthew. *Hawke's Bay: The history of a province*. Palmerston North: Dunmore Press, 1994.

Articles and book chapters

Aldcroft, Derek. 'The railway age'. *Refresh* 13, 1991, 5–8.

Allen, Michael. 'An illusory power? Metropole, colony and land confiscation in New Zealand, 1863–1865'. In Boast and Hill, *Raupatu*, 110–42.

Anonymous. 'History of the Canterbury railways – how the early settlers solved a big transport problem', seven parts. In the *New Zealand Railways Magazine* 5(1–7), 1930.

Arnold, Rollo. 'The virgin forest harvest and the development of colonial New Zealand'. *New Zealand Geographer* 32, 1976, 105–26.

Atack, Jeremy, Fred Bateman, Michael Haines, and Robert A. Margo. 'Did railroads induce or follow economic growth?: Urbanization and population in the American Midwest, 1850–1860'. *Social Science History* 34(2), 2010, 171–97.

Attard, Bernard. 'From free-trade imperialism to structural power: New Zealand and the capital market, 1856–68'. *Journal of Imperial and Commonwealth History* 35(4), 2007, 505–27.

——. 'Making the colonial state: Development, debt, and warfare in New Zealand, 1853–76'. *Australian Economic History Review* 52(2), 2012, 101–27.

Ball, Anne Stewart. 'Beginning days of a railway: James Stewart and the Auckland to Drury railway': www.aucklandlibraries.govt.nz/EN/heritage/localhistory/countiesmanukau/transport/Pages/aucklandtodruryrailway.aspx

Ballantyne, Tony. 'On place, space and mobility in nineteenth-century New Zealand'. *New Zealand Journal of History* 45(1), 2011, 50–70.

——. 'Reading the newspaper in colonial Otago'. *Journal of New Zealand Studies* 12, 2011, 47–63.

——. 'The state, politics and power, 1769–1893'. In Byrnes, *The New Oxford History of New Zealand*, 99–124.

Barrett, Jonathan, and John Veal. 'Land taxation: A New Zealand perspective'. *eJournal of Tax Research* 10(3), 2012, 573–88.

Beaglehole, Diana. 'Political leadership in Wellington, 1839–1853'. In *The Making of Wellington 1800–1914*, edited by David Hamer and Roberta Nicholls, 165–94. Wellington: Victoria University Press, 1990.

Blackley, Roger. 'Cruising the colonial: Newspapers and shop windows'. *Journal of New Zealand Studies* 12, 2011, 65–76.

Brett, André. 'Dreaming on a railway track: Public works and the demise of New Zealand's provinces'. *Journal of Transport History* 36(1), 2015, 1–20

——. 'The great Kiwi (dis)connect: The New Provinces Act of 1858 and its consequences'. *Melbourne Historical Journal* 40, 2012, 129–48.

——. 'A limited express or stopping all stations? Railways and nineteenth-century New Zealand'. *Journal of New Zealand Studies* 16, 2013, 133–49.

Brown, A.J. 'Federalism, regionalism and the reshaping of Australian governance'. In *Federalism and Regionalism in Australia: New approaches, new institutions?*, edited by J.A. Bellamy and A.J. Brown, 11–32. Canberra: Australian National University ePress, 2006.

Bumsted, J.M. 'The consolidation of British North America, 1783–1860'. In *Canada and the British Empire*, edited by Phillip Bucknor, 43–65. Oxford: Oxford University Press, 2008.

Burroughs, Peter. 'Imperial institutions and the government of empire'. In *The Oxford History of the British Empire, Volume III: The nineteenth century*, edited by Andrew Porter, 170–97. Oxford: Oxford University Press, 1999.

Cheyne, Christine. 'The Auckland effect: What next for other councils?' In *Along a Fault-line: New Zealand's changing local government landscape*, edited by Jean Drage, Jeff McNeill and Christine Cheyne, 41–58. Wellington: Dunmore Publishing, 2011.

——. 'Strengthening local government'. In *New Zealand Government and Politics*, 5th edn, edited by Raymond Miller, 269–83. Oxford: Oxford University Press, 2010.

Coleridge, Kathleen. 'Booktrade advertisements in Wellington newspapers 1840–1859'. *Bibliographical Society of Australia and New Zealand Bulletin* 18(4), 1994, 199–213.

——. 'Printing and publishing in Wellington, New Zealand in the 1840s and 1850s'. *Bibliographical Society of Australia and New Zealand Bulletin* 10(2–3), 1986, 61–81.

——. 'Thriving on impressions: The pioneer years of Wellington printing'. In *The Making of Wellington*, edited by David Hamer and Roberta Nicholls, 89–105. Wellington: Victoria University Press, 1990.

Conradson, Bernard. 'Politics and penury: County and province, 1868–76'. In May, *Miners and Militants*, 25–47.

Cookson, John. 'How British? Local government in New Zealand to c. 1930'. *New Zealand Journal of History* 41(2), 2007, 143–60.

Curthoys, Ann and Jessie Mitchell. 'The advent of self-government, 1840s–90'. In Bashford and Macintyre, *The Cambridge History of Australia*, 149–69.

Daley, Catherine. 'Papers from the past, and problems from the present'. *Turnbull Library Record* 43, 2010–11, 64–72.

Dalziel, Raewyn. 'The politics of settlement'. In Oliver and Williams, *The Oxford History of New Zealand*, 87–111.

Dickinson, B.E. 'The ungentle shepherds'. *Journal of the Nelson Historical Society* 3(4), 1978, 35–40.

Dowie, J.A. 'The course and character of capital formation in New Zealand, 1871–1900'. *New Zealand Economic Papers* 1(1), 1966, 38–58.

Foster, Bernard John. 'Heale, Theophilus'. *An Encyclopaedia of New Zealand 1966*: www.teara.govt. nz/en/1966/heale-theophilus

———. 'Stokes, Robert'. *An Encyclopaedia of New Zealand 1966*: www.teara.govt.nz/en/1966/stokes-robert

Frost, Lionel. 'The economy'. In Bashford and Macintyre, *The Cambridge History of Australia*, 315–41.

Gardner, W.J. 'Hall, John'. *Dictionary of New Zealand Biography*: www.teara.govt.nz/en/ biographies/1h5/hall-john

Gibbons, Peter. 'The far side of the search for identity: Reconsidering New Zealand history'. *New Zealand Journal of History* 37(1), 2003, 38–49.

Gilling, Bryan. 'Raupatu: The punitive confiscation of Māori land in the 1860s'. In Boast and Hill, *Raupatu*, 13–30.

Goodwin, Paul B. Jr. 'The Central Argentine Railway and the economic development of Argentina, 1854–1881'. *The Hispanic American Historical Review* 57(4), 1977, 613–32.

Graham, Munroe. 'The 150 year anniversary of the Drury Tramway': www.bettertransport.org. nz/2012/04/the-150-year-anniversary-of-the-drury-tramway

Hamer, David. 'Fitzherbert, William', *Dictionary of New Zealand Biography*: www.teara.govt.nz/en/ biographies/1f11/fitzherbert-william

Harvey, Ross. 'The bibliography of nineteenth-century newspapers in New Zealand'. *Australian and New Zealand Journal of Serials Librarianship* 2(2), 1991, 19–33.

———. 'Circulation figures of some nineteenth century newspapers'. *Archifacts* 1988/4–1989/1, December 1988–March 1989, 20–29.

———. 'Economic aspects of nineteenth century New Zealand newspapers'. *Bibliographical Society of Australia and New Zealand Bulletin* 17(2), 1993, 55–78.

———. 'The power of the press in colonial New Zealand: More imagined than real?' *Bibliographical Society of Australia and New Zealand Bulletin* 20(2), 1996, 130–45.

———. 'Towards a bibliography of New Zealand newspapers'. *Bibliographical Society of Australia and New Zealand Bulletin* 11(2), 1987, 41–49.

Herron, D.G. 'Alsatia or utopia? New Zealand society and politics in the eighteen-fifties'. *Landfall* 52, 1959, 324–41.

———. 'The circumstances and effects of Sir George Grey's delay in summoning the first New Zealand General Assembly'. *Historical Studies Australia and New Zealand* 8(32), 1959, 364–82.

———. 'The franchise and New Zealand politics, 1853–8', *Political Science* 12(28), 1960, 28–44.

———. 'Provincialism and centralism, 1853–1858'. In *Studies of a Small Democracy: Essays in honour of Willis Airey*, edited by Robert Chapman and Keith Sinclair, 10–32. Auckland: Blackwood and Janet Paul for the University of Auckland, 1963.

Heagney, Kevin. 'Modelling tax policy development: Governor FitzRoy's tax reform 1844–45'. Massey University Department of Economics and Finance Discussion Paper 09.08, August 2009.

Kabzamalov, Ogy. 'New Zealand's forgotten income tax'. *Te Mata Koi: Auckland University Law Review* 16, 2010

Keenan, Danny. '"Amalgamating Māori?"': Māori, land tenure and "amalgamation" before 1860'. In *Contested Ground/Te Whenua I Tohea: The Taranaki Wars 1860–1881*, edited by Kelvin Day, 1–17. Wellington: Huia Publishers, 2010.

Kirkpatrick, Rod. 'Scissors and paste: Recreating the history of newspapers in ten country towns'. *Bibliographical Society of Australian and New Zealand Bulletin* 22(4), 1998, 232–46.

Macintyre, Stuart, and Sean Scalmer. 'Colonial states and civil society, 1860–90'. In Bashford and Macintyre, *The Cambridge History of Australia*, 189–217.

Manning, H.T. 'Who ran the British Empire, 1830–1850?' *Journal of British Studies* 5(1), 1965, 88–121.

Martin, John E. 'Political participation and electoral change in nineteenth-century New Zealand'. *Political Science* 57(1), 2005, 39–58.

———. 'Refusal of assent – a hidden element of constitutional history in New Zealand'. *Victoria University of Wellington Law Review* 41(1), 2010, 51–84.

May, Philip Ross. 'Politics and gold: The separation of Westland, 1865–7', in May, *Miners and Militants*, 1–24.

McKenzie, J.D.S. 'Education articles in the *Wellington Independent* June–July 1849: A question of authorship'. *New Zealand Journal of History* 1(2), 1967, 199–203.

Mein Smith, Philippa. 'New Zealand federation commissioners in Australia: One past, two historiographies'. *Australian Historical Studies* 34(122), 2003, 305–25.

Mills, Tom L. 'Our early newspapers'. *Typo* 3(27), 30 March 1889, 25.

Olssen, Erik. 'Loyalty and localism – Southland's political odyssey'. In *Murihiku: The Southland story*, edited by Paul Sorrell, 84–107. Invercargill: Southland to 2006 Book Project Committee, 2006.

———. 'The Peopling of Southland'. In *Murihiku: The Southland story*, edited by Paul Sorrell, 71–83. Invercargill: Southland to 2006 Book Project Committee, 2006.

Orange, Claudia. 'Busby, James'. *Dictionary of New Zealand Biography*: www.teara.govt.nz/en/biographies/1b54/busby-james

Pawson, Eric. 'Local times and standard time in New Zealand'. *Journal of Historical Geography* 18(3), 1992, 278–87.

———. 'Time–space convergence in New Zealand, 1850s to 1990s'. *New Zealand Journal of Geography* 94(1), 1992, 14–19.

Patterson, Brad. 'Would King Isaac the First lose his head?: The power of personality in Wellington provincial politics, 1857–1861'. *New Zealand Studies* 6(1), 1996, 3–16.

Pulley, Raymond H. 'The railroad and Argentine national development, 1852–1914'. *The Americas* 23(1), 1966, 63–75.

Reid, Mike. 'The central–local government relationship: The need for a framework?' *Political Science* 50(2), 1999, 165–81.

Robinson, K.W. 'Sixty years of federation in Australia'. *Geographical Review* 51(1), 1961, 1–20.

Rosanowski, John. 'The West Coast railways and New Zealand politics, 1878–1888'. *New Zealand Journal of History* 4(1), 1970.

Rosenberg, W. 'Capital imports and growth: The case of New Zealand – foreign investment in New Zealand, 1840–1958'. *Economic Journal* 71(281), 1961, 93–113.

Ross, Angus. 'The New Zealand Constitution Act of 1852: Its authorship'. *Historical and Political Studies* 1(1), 1969, 61–67.

Scotter, W.H. 'Canterbury, 1857–68'. In Gardner, *A History of Canterbury*, 75–246.

———. 'Canterbury, 1868–76'. In Gardner, *A History of Canterbury*, 247–365.

Sinclair, Keith. 'Richmond, Christopher William'. *Dictionary of New Zealand Biography*: www.teara.govt.nz/en/biographies/1r9/richmond-christopher-william

———. 'The significance of 'the Scarecrow Ministry', 1887–1891'. In *Studies of a Small Democracy: Essays in honour of Willis Airey*, edited by Robert Chapman and Keith Sinclair. Auckland: Blackwood and Janet Paul for the University of Auckland, 1963.

———. 'Why New Zealanders are not Australians: New Zealand and the Australian federal movement, 1881–1901'. In *Tasman Relations: New Zealand and Australia, 1788–1988*, edited by Keith Sinclair, 90–103. Auckland: Auckland University Press, 1987.

Smith, Joanne. 'Twelve hundred reasons why there is no Australasia: How colonisation influenced federation'. *Australian Cultural History* 27(1), 2009, 35–45.

Stenhouse, John. 'Church and state in New Zealand, 1835–1870: Religion, politics, and race'. In *Church and State in Old and New Words*, edited by Hilary M. Carey and John Gascoigne, 233–60. Leiden: Brill, 2011.

Stephenson, Maxine. 'Thinking historically: Māori and settler education'. In *Introduction to the History of New Zealand Education*, edited by Elizabeth Rata and Ros Sullivan, 1–15. North Shore: Pearson, 2009.

Stone, R.C.J. 'Auckland party politics in the early years of the provincial system, 1853–58'. *New Zealand Journal of History* 14(2), 1980, 153–78.

———. 'Auckland's political opposition in the Crown colony period, 1841–53'. In *Provincial Perspectives: Essays in honour of W.J. Gardner*, edited by Len Richardson and W. David McIntyre, 15–35. Christchurch: Whitcoulls Limited for the University of Canterbury, 1980.

———. 'Russell, Thomas'. *Dictionary of New Zealand Biography*: www.teara.govt.nz/en/biographies/1r20/russell-thomas

Sutch, W.B. 'Local government – a history of defeat'. In *Local Government in New Zealand*, edited by R.J. Polaschek, 12–43. Wellington: New Zealand Institute of Public Administration, 1956.

Vosslamber, Rob. 'Taxation for New Zealand's future: The introduction of New Zealand's progressive income tax in 1891'. *Accounting History* 17(1), 2012, 105–22.

Ward, Alan. 'A "savage war of peace"? Motives for government policies towards the Kingitanga, 1857–1863'. In Boast and Hill, *Raupatu*, 62–109.

Wynn, Graeme. 'Conservation and society in late nineteenth-century New Zealand'. *New Zealand Journal of History* 11(2), 1977, 124–36.

Young, John. 'The political conflict of 1875'. *Political Science* 13(56), 1961, 56–78.

Zalewski, Pat. 'The formation of municipal councils in early Queensland and their antecedents in England in the 19th century'. *Queensland History Journal* 21(11), 2012, 763–74.

Unpublished theses

Armstrong, W.R. 'The politics of development: A study of the structure of politics from 1870 to 1890'. MA thesis, Victoria University of Wellington, 1960.

Beaglehole, Diana. 'The structure and course of politics in nineteenth-century Wellington'. MA thesis, Victoria University of Wellington, 1987.

Brett, André. 'Scars in the country: Infrastructure and the centralisation of New Zealand statehood'. BA Honours thesis, University of Melbourne, 2009.

Browne, A.P.F. 'The Otago goldfields 1861–1863: Administration and public life'. MA thesis, University of Otago, 1974.

Bunce, Roderick John. 'James Macandrew of Otago: Slippery Jim or a leader staunch and true?' PhD thesis, Victoria University of Wellington, 2013.

Cheyne, Sonia. 'Search for a constitution: People and politics in New Zealand's Crown colony years'. PhD thesis, University of Otago, 1975.

Cook, A.H. '"The slowly dying cause": A study of Otago provincialism after the abolition of the provinces'. MA thesis, University of Otago, 1969.

Cowan, Linda M. 'Immediate reactions in Otago to the movement for the abolition of provincial government, 1874–76'. PGDipArts thesis, University of Otago, 1972.

Cowie, Dean. '"To do all the good I can" – Robert FitzRoy: Governor of New Zealand 1843–45'. MA thesis, University of Auckland, 1994.

Cumming, J.P. 'The compact and financial settlement of 1856'. MA thesis, University of Auckland, 1963.

Dreaver, A.R. 'The Southland Province of New Zealand in the days of Dr J.A.R. Menzies (superintendent 1861–1864)'. BA Honours thesis, University of New Zealand, 1929.

Elliot-Hogg, Natasha Andrea. 'The Taranaki refugees 1860'. MA thesis, University of Waikato, 1999.

Ellis, R.H. 'Sir George Grey's petitions to the Colonial Office over the abolition of the provinces'. MA thesis, University of Otago, 1968.

Gardner, W.J. 'The effect of the abolition of the provinces on political parties in the New Zealand House of Representatives, 1876–7'. MA thesis, University of New Zealand, 1936.

Gee, F.E. 'The North Island Main Trunk Railway, New Zealand: A study in the politics of railway construction'. MA thesis, University of New Zealand, 1949.

Gerrard, J.B. 'The significance of the railways in the Auckland province: Their influence on development and settlement and their role as a means of passenger transport'. MA thesis, University of New Zealand, 1949.

Green, Pinky L. 'The Province of Wellington and the abolition of the provincial form of government in New Zealand, 1874–6'. MA thesis, University of New Zealand, 1954.

Hamilton, Ross B. 'Military vision and economic reality: The failure of the military settlement scheme in the Waikato, 1863–1880'. MA thesis, University of Auckland, 1968.

Hanham, H.J. 'The political structure of Auckland, 1853–76'. MA thesis, University of New Zealand, 1950.

Harvey, G.G. 'The place of the railways in the transport problem of the North Island 1870–1936'. MA thesis, University of New Zealand, 1937.

Henderson, Helen A. ('Alpaca'). 'Historical account of Southland as a province, 1861–1870'. MA thesis, University of New Zealand, 1919.

Hercus, M.C. 'The separation movement in Otago: The origins and early history'. MA thesis, University of New Zealand, 1950.

Herron, D.G. 'The structure and course of New Zealand politics, 1853–1858'. PhD thesis, University of Otago, 1959.

Hill, S.R. 'Local politics in the Auckland province, 1867–1871'. MA thesis, University of Auckland, 1958.

Hilliard, Chris. 'Island stories: The writing of New Zealand history 1920–1940'. MA thesis, University of Auckland, 1997.

Hunt, J.L. 'The election of 1875–6 and the abolition of the provinces'. MA thesis, University of Auckland, 1961.

Hunter, Bruce A. 'The transfer of responsibility for native affairs from the imperial government to the General Assembly of the colony of New Zealand'. MA thesis, University of New Zealand, 1949.

Innes, R.S. 'Railways and the reunion of Otago and Southland, 1867–1870'. PGDipArts thesis, University of Otago, 1976.

Kemp, Doreen E. 'William Sefton Moorhouse, 1825–1881'. MA thesis, University of New Zealand, 1950.

Kerse, Jocelyn M. 'The rise and fall of Middle Island separation'. BA Honours thesis, University of Otago, 1973.

Lawson, I.G. 'An examination of the administration of Edward John Eyre as Lieutenant-Governor of the Province of New Munster, New Zealand 1848–1853'. MA thesis, University of New Zealand, 1954.

Leslie, Alfred Murray. 'The general election of 1871 and its importance in the history of New Zealand'. MA thesis, University of New Zealand, 1956.

Lewis, B.J. 'Politics of the Auckland province, 1862–1867'. MA thesis, University of New Zealand, 1957.

Marshall, J. Denise. 'Southland's attitudes to the abolition of the provinces, 1874–1877'. BA Honours thesis, University of Otago, 1975.

McGarvey, R.D. 'Local politics in the Auckland province, 1853–62'. MA thesis, University of New Zealand, 1954.

Muirhead, P.A. 'Public opinion in Canterbury on the abolition of the provinces, 1873–6'. MA thesis, University of New Zealand, 1936.

Rees-Jones, Margaret. 'The pioneering press of Poverty Bay 1872–1914'. PhD thesis, RMIT University, 2004.

Ross, Dorothy. 'Government and the people: A study of public opinion in New Zealand from 1852–1876 in its relation to politics and government'. MA thesis, University of New Zealand, 1944.

Ryan, A.B. 'The Southland secession movement'. MA thesis, University of New Zealand, 1947.

Standish, M.W. 'Government administration in New Zealand 1848–1852'. MA thesis, University of New Zealand, 1948.

Tebay, D.M. 'The Hawke's Bay separation movement, 1856–58'. MA thesis, University of New Zealand, 1956.

Tyndale-Biscoe, Ann. 'The struggle for responsible government in the Province of Otago, 1854–76'. MA thesis, University of New Zealand, 1954.

Ward, J.A. 'Politicians-in-waiting?: The case for a "popular" involvement in agitation for representative and responsible government in the Province of Wellington 1840–1853'. MA thesis, Massey University, 2005.

Wood, G.A. 'The political structure of New Zealand, 1858–61'. PhD thesis, University of Otago, 1965.

Young, John. 'The politics of the Auckland province: 1872–1876'. MA thesis, University of New Zealand, 1960.

Index

Bold page numbers indicate illustrations and information in captions.
Numbers in the form 306n38 refer to endnotes.